THE IDEA
OF WOMEN
IN
FUNDAMENTALIST
ISLAM

Lamia Rustum Shehadeh

University Press of Florida

Gainesville · Tallahassee · Tampa · Boca Raton
Pensacola · Orlando · Miami · Jacksonville · Ft. Myers

08 07 06 05 04 03   6 5 4 3 2 1

Library of Congress Cataloging-in-Publication Data
Shehadeh, Lamia Rustum, 1940-
The idea of women in fundamentalist Islam / Lamia Rustum Shehadeh.
p. cm.
Includes bibliographical references and index.
ISBN 0-8130-2606-7 (cloth : alk. paper)
1. Women in Islam. 2. Women—Islamic countries—Social conditions.
3. Women—Religious aspects—Islam. 4. Feminism—Religious aspects—
Islam. 5. Islamic fundamentalism. I. Title.

BP173.4.S48 2003
297'.082—dc21   2003040243

The University Press of Florida is the scholarly publishing agency
for the State University System of Florida, comprising Florida A&M
University, Florida Atlantic University, Florida Gulf Coast University,
Florida International University, Florida State University, University
of Central Florida, University of Florida, University of North Florida,
University of South Florida, and University of West Florida.

University Press of Florida
15 Northwest 15th Street
Gainesville, FL 32611–2079
http://www.upf.com

The Idea of Women in Fundamentalist Islam

Florida A&M University, Tallahassee
Florida Atlantic University, Boca Raton
Florida Gulf Coast University, Ft. Myers
Florida International University, Miami
Florida State University, Tallahassee
University of Central Florida, Orlando
University of Florida, Gainesville
University of North Florida, Jacksonville
University of South Florida, Tampa
University of West Florida, Pensacola

Dedicated to the loving memory of my parents,
who made me what I am today

I have always sensed that the writings of the freedom-loving fighters
do not go in vain, mainly because they [writings] awaken the sleepy,
inflame the senses of the half-hearted, and lay the ground for a
mass-oriented trend following a specific goal. . . . Something
must be happening under the influence of writing.

Sayyid Qutb, *Dirasat Islamiyyah* [Islamic studies]

Contents

Preface

There are many women who are greater than men. There are many men who are baser than women. What is manhood? It is generosity, intelligence, and piety. Whoever possesses these three things is surely a man.

Ahmadi, *Iskandar-nama*

Islam is a complete lifestyle and world order with a clear and distinct view of the universe. Its adherents are endowed with a unique Muslim personality steeped in the values and ideals of Islam and charged with the propagation of the message of Islam toward the development of an ideal Muslim community in an ideal Muslim world. The institutions of marriage and the family have a central position in this scheme.

Seeking to forge a modern indigenous identity, Muslims tend to fall into two groups: the liberal reformers or modernists, who believe in combining Islamic traditions with Western liberalism to generate a solid defensive shield against the West and its civilization, and conservatives, who cling to tradition in the belief that any deviation would subvert all Islamic social structures and efface all barriers facing incipient Western domination. The two groups share a view of women as being at the center of the movements of reforming or preserving tradition, the key to the survival of the human race, its culture, and its continuity. The surge of religious fundamentalism since the 1970s, in locations as diverse as the United States, Algeria, Iran, Israel, and India, has raised concern and stimulated the interest of scholars and laypeople alike, becoming an entrenched symbol of the twentieth century. The 1970s witnessed a mushrooming of Islamic movements and ideas dubbed as "fundamentalist," "revivalist," and "Islamist" among others, climaxing in the Iranian Revolution and the ousting of the Pahlavi monarchy to be replaced by the Islamic Republic.

The subject of Islamic fundamentalism is as relevant today as ever before. With the twentieth century behind us and a new millennium dawning, it is opportune to take stock of some of the forces that shaped the twentieth century on the political, social, economic, religious, and cultural levels, and study them analytically.

As a living religion and the faith of nearly one-fifth of the world population, Islam has become an important force on the national and international scene. It believes in God's revelation, prophets, ethical responsibility and accountability, and the Day of Judgment.

While some may argue that the political rhetoric of fundamentalists is of small consequence, being mere discourse, I differ and would argue that Islamic political rhetoric is part and parcel of political strategies that influence the perceptions and actions of the ruling elite and their opponents alike. Certain forms of this rhetoric facilitate fundamentalist efforts to create political openings and power, being based on utilitarian pragmatism. One such rhetoric is gender discourse.

Perusing religious bookstores, street vendors' stalls, book fairs, publishers' outlets, and even drugstores in the Middle East today, one gains the impression that books on women in Islam are more abundant than any other subject. They range from biographies of the wives of the Prophet to guides on women's behavior, and from rhetorical discussions of the role of women in society to women's dress and cosmetics. Despite the plethora of such publications and the bountiful literature on Islamic fundamentalism and ideology, little can be found on fundamentalist gender ideology, although sporadic articles on a few ideologues' views on women may be found in some periodicals and multiauthored volumes. The impact of fundamentalism on women's political and socioeconomic roles has attracted scholars who argue either its negative impact on women in these areas, or the positive aspect of politicizing women and promoting their issues. However, both groups remain essentialists in their approach and do not construct a gender theory or offer any analysis of it.

It is certainly not enough to consider the factual status of women in any one region, accounts of which abound in contemporary literature. This study, therefore, attempts to outline the discourse of some prominent fundamentalists relating to women and their role in society, and the manner in which this role has been utilized in constructing an Islamic society. It will also examine the curious and paradoxical popularity of fundamentalism among women, especially because its teachings actually promote their suppression and isolation.

The book, then, will try to reach an understanding of the strong bond between fundamentalist ideology and gender, and between its gender theory and conservative Islam, and elucidate apparent complexities and paradoxes that plague fundamentalist discourse. Selected prominent fundamentalists whose religio-political writings and political practices played a crucial role in the resurgence of twentieth-century Islam will be introduced and their lives and works analyzed. A gender theory will be offered, the marginalization of gender issues within the mainstream Islamic fundamentalist studies challenged, and some of the misconceptions of the role and placement of women exposed and analyzed.

I wish to thank the Department of Near Eastern Languages and Civilizations at Harvard University, in the person of Professor William Graham, for appointing me a visiting scholar for the spring semester of 1999–2000, thereby enabling me to pursue and complete my research on this highly complex subject. I also wish to thank the Civilization Sequence Program and the Faculty of Arts and Sciences at the American University of Beirut, in the persons of Director Peter Shebay'a and Dean Khalil Bitar, for making it possible for me to take my sabbatical. My thanks and appreciation also go to friends and relatives who encouraged me to pursue this project, particularly my son Halim, who silently put up with a disrupted routine and willingly served as a sounding board to my ideas. And, finally, words fail to describe my appreciation for my husband, Isam Shehadeh, who agreed to an extended separation and whose constant encouragement, reading, rereading of the manuscript, suggestions, patience, and understanding of my moodiness and seclusion allowed this book to see the light of day.

Chapter 1

Introduction

> Santayana's famous dictum that one compares only when one is unable to get to the heart of the matter seems to me . . . the precise reverse of the truth. It is through comparison, and of comparables, that whatever heart we can actually get to is to be reached.
>
> Clifford Geertz, *Local Knowledge*

In the immediate aftermath of the Second World War, in the era of emerging independent nations, many newly independent Muslim nations, inspired by the West and its culture, pursued paths of modernism and development. Their Westernization ranged from the adoption of "modern" Western dress to outright emulation of Western states, institutions, and societies. While the impact of the West on the development of such concepts as nationalism, socialism, and secularism advanced smoothly and enthusiastically, the issue of gender relations proved more enigmatic and complex.

In more recent years, however, "modernity," erroneously identified with Westernization or "Westoxification,"came under attack through the assertion of Islamic alternatives.[1] The reassertion of Islam into everyday life is a complex and multifaceted phenomenon that has pervaded the Muslim world from the Sudan to Sumatra, producing a wide spectrum of leadership and organizations that have influenced the private and public lives of Muslims and given birth to a variety of Islamic movements, organizations, and institutions. Governments have turned to Islam to enhance their legitimacy and mobilize popular support, with Islam slowly coming to be regarded as the panacea for all social, political, and economic ills of the Muslim world. With the 1979 Islamic revolution in Iran and the ousting of the Pahlavi regime, political Islam, as a comprehensive sociopolitical ideology, stunned and perplexed the world. This was followed in the eighties by the genesis of Islamist movements in most countries of the region. Islamic governments have been instituted in Sudan and Afghanistan since 1991–92, and the "paradox of democracy" in Algeria brought about by the electoral victory of the Islamic Salvation Front in December 1991 confounded the world. In Egypt, Morocco, Lebanon, Syria, Pakistan, Tunisia, Iraq, Jordan, Kuwait, the Occupied Territories, Indonesia, Burma, India, Sri Lanka, and the Philippines, Islamic fundamentalism is a force to be reckoned with. Even Turkey does not seem to have made the transition to secularism unscathed. These movements have advocated the reconstruction of the Islamic moral order, which, according to them, had been corrupted and adulterated. As a result, there has followed a reinstitution of the veil and segregation of the sexes, with women from North Africa to Southeast Asia flocking to don the Islamic dress and redefine their identity to accommodate their concept of modernity within the new religious and cultural framework. Resultant changes are also to be seen in such personal matters as prayer, fasting, and family values.

R. H. Dekmejian describes the environment that spawned fundamentalism as being different from earlier periods of crisis, with four distinctive features: pervasiveness throughout the whole Muslim world; comprehensiveness throughout all economic, social, political, cultural, psychological, and spiritual dimensions; cumulativeness of the failure of existent governments in nation building, socioeconomic development, and military proficiency; and xenophobia, the fear that Islam and the Islamic way of life and culture are in danger of extinction. Fundamentalism thus emerges as a reformist and puritanical movement, with Islam as its ideology and complete way of life and its objective being the establishment of an ideal Islamic state around the edifice of the *Shari'ah*.[2] John Esposito, explaining the objectives of fundamentalists, states, "They do not seek to reproduce the past, but to reconstruct society through a process of Islamic reform in which the principles of Islam are applied to contemporary needs. Each speaks of a comprehensive reformation or revolution, the creation of an Islamic order and state, since they regard Islam as comprehensive in scope and a faith-informed way of life."[3]

The dilemma of Muslims, however, is easily understood once it becomes clear that Islam is seen as the highest and final form of religion, transcending all others. It is supposed to regulate man's relations with God and the rest of humankind, providing, thereby, an ideal society and civilization. There is, thus, an "organic holistic" view of life in which religion is closely intertwined with politics, law, and society. In the political domain, the Sunni traditional perspective emphasizes realism based on Islamic norms and the obedience to those in authority, while the Shi'ite perspective emphasizes the final authority of the Twelfth Imam, in whose absence no form of government can be perfect. The traditional Shi'ite image of sociopolitical revival is that of the "renewer" *(mujaddid)* from within, and not by external force. Traditional Islam accepts the traditional commentaries on the Qur'an, and views the Qur'an as the word of God in both content and form. The traditional school accepts the six orthodox collections of Hadith of Sunni Islam, in addition to the "Four Books" of Shi'ite Islam. The Shari'ah is accepted as the Divine Law, as understood and interpreted by the classical schools of jurisprudence during the second and third centuries after Islam.[4]

The founding jurists themselves, however, were more interested in the immediate needs of their societies in their own historical contexts than in establishing an immutable, permanent, eternal law. In the tenth century, only four schools of Sunni jurisprudence were recognized as orthodox: the Maliki, the Hanbali, the Hanafi, and the Shafi'i. Their law books became standard textbooks, and any attempt to depart from them was considered *bid'ah* [innovation—heresy]. As a result, *ijtihad* [interpretation of the Qur'an] was gradually abandoned in favor of *taqlid* [imitation] or submission to the four schools. Although there were individual protests during succeeding generations, Muslims became habituated to *taqlid*, especially during the periods of decline. Consequently, jurists gave undue importance to legal details, thereby shifting the emphasis from principles to particulars of the law, leading to rigidity in the application of obscure details and violation of the spirit of legal principles.[5]

The Shi'ites date back to the defeat of the first Imam, Ali Ibn Abi Talib, and the controversy over his succession. They make up about 10 percent of the Muslim world and are concentrated mainly in Persia or modern Iran, and South Asia. The word Shi'a means "one who loves and follows Ali and his descendants." Loyalty to *'ahl al-bayt* [house of the Prophet, Ali, and his descendants] is at the core of their belief. Their tradition focuses on death, martyrdom, and sacrifice. A sense of injustice pervades their weltanschauung, beginning with Ali and his assassination, followed by the martyrdom of his two sons, Hasan and al-Hussayn.[6] They believe in the existence of twelve divinely guided imams, the last of whom disappeared in the tenth century to return at some future date as the messianic deliverer, the Mahdi. The Mahdi would then establish an Islamic government that would bring communal suffering to an end and ensure justice and equity. Pending his return at the end of time, Shi'ites acknowledge the leadership of their religious scholars in both mundane and spiritual affairs. While there is no substantial difference between the Sunnis and Shi'ites in core theological beliefs, Shi'ite Islam carries within itself the seeds of renewal and revolution.[7] Although both radical Sunnis and Shi'ites believe that revolution is justified, it is easier for the Shi'ites to justify it since, according to their traditional teachings, any state not ruled by the descendants of Ali is ipso facto illegitimate.

Shi'ite fundamentalism in Iran and Lebanon differs from comparable Sunni movements in the prominent role the clergy plays in all facets of life and in the Shi'ite belief in charismatic religious leaders and saviors. These peculiarities relate to the separation of politics and clerical rule and the monopolization of sacred knowledge by clerics in Iran, starting in the sixteenth century and becoming solidly established in the nineteenth century. With the proclamation of Twelver Shi'ism as the religion of the Safavid state and the subsequent conversion of the majority of Iranians to Shi'ism, a great deal of importance was attached to the state and the role of the sovereign. The shah, by assuming the role of the agent of the hidden Imam, acquired a religiously based authority. By the eighteenth century, an independent group of Shi'ite ulema emerged, whose independent interpretations were accepted by the majority of the population. They were known as *mujtahid*, independent of any state organization or patronage, who slowly became a major religious force challenging the shah's religious establishment, until the time of the last Safavid shah, when great *mujtahid* like Muhammad Baqir Majlisi came to dominate the whole political system. The stage was now set for the modern duality of monarch and *mujtahid*, either in cooperation or in conflict.[8]

In the nineteenth century, a hierarchy of ulema developed, a rare occurrence in Islamic tradition. Above the rank and file of mullahs (ulema) come the *mujtahid* [authorities on matters of jurisprudence], and above these, the *marji' taqlid* [model of imitation—prominent figure of authority]. Theoretically, one of the latter's rank, in each generation, was to be recognized as *marji' a'la* [highest authority]. This is the same "virtuous jurist" *(faqih)* that Khomeini preaches about. Traditionally, God is the leader of the Shi'ite community, followed in authority by the Prophet Muhammad and, third, by the infallible Imams. Khomeini, however, extended that leadership to the *faqih* in charge of spiritual and temporal authority until the hidden Imam appears "at the end of time."[9]

Within the past two decades, Islam has become a popular field of study and the focus of wide-ranging research. Few issues, however, have attracted more attention and interest than those involving the status of women. The subject of gender relations in Islam is highly charged at both the popular and scholarly levels. Thus, while some blame Islam for the abject condition of Muslim women, others see in it the solution of all their ills.

Ever since the Islamic resurgence of the 1970s, fundamentalists have stressed the importance of Islamization or re-Islamization of society, rather than its modernization or Westernization. The latter, according to them, could destroy Islamic culture and identity and, thereby, Islam and the Muslim *ummah* [community] far more effectively than any form of political aberration. Since women and the family unit are considered pivotal in the formation and development of society, they have come to be regarded as the "primary culture bearers" and, therefore, the last bastion in the defense against foreign infiltration. Consequently, the *hijab* [veil] has become not only a sign of modesty and religious faith but also a symbol of the defense of Islam, the preservation of the family, and, therefore, the identity of Muslim society.

Fundamentalism, as a powerful contemporary and, possibly, future political and social movement, is not limited to any one country or region. It is on the rise all over the world, projecting religion as a major player in domestic, regional, and international affairs. Studies on Islamic fundamentalism in the last decade have viewed it either as a monolith or as diverse as the regions it sprang from. It has been described as representing two trends, one radical and the other moderate. What is surprising, however, is the dearth of theoretical studies on the role of women in Islamic fundamentalist discourse, despite the large number of Muslim women involved (450 million) and the importance assigned to women in Muslim society.

This pioneering study is basically textual, attempting a systematic exposition of the normative fundamentalist gender theory implicit within the discourses studied. It then proceeds to determine whether the diversity in the political, social, and economic domains within the discourse of the different ideologues, be they male or female, Sunni or Shi'ite, radical or moderate, applies to gender relations as well, and whether their discourse is distinctive or remains within the classical or traditional mold of Islam. The value and originality of this work lie in the collection and presentation of gender ideologies of the most prominent ideologues, indeed, the architects of twentieth-century Islamic fundamentalist movements, ensuring its universal representation across confessional, sexual, and orientational (radical or moderate) lines. They also lie in the normative theory deduced and its critique, leading to a possible understanding and motivation, be it conscious or subconscious, of this universal stand.

It is probably fair to say at this point that terms like "fundamentalist," "Islamist," "revivalist," "resurgent," and "neotraditionalist," in common use today to describe contemporary Islam, are not easy to live with, especially since the Arabic language itself does not provide a comparative all-inclusive term. The commonly used term, *usuliyyah*, being a translation of the English term, is not subscribed to by the "fundamentalists" themselves. The two Arabic terms most often used to describe "fundamentalism" are *salafiyyah* [that which pertains to ancestry], first devised by Muhammad Abduh, referring to the first generation of Muslims who supported and fought alongside the Prophet during the seventh century; and *Islamiyyah*, which, like *usuliyyah*, is a new term of uncertain origin, used to identify those who wish to reestablish the ideal Islamic society of the seventh century. But, just as we cannot live very easily with these terms, we cannot do without them, either. They have often proved to be obstacles in their lack of clear definition, describing widely diverse phenomena and often harboring an implicit bias or value judgment. This is particularly apparent in relation to the term "fundamentalist." Yet, we cannot do without some sort of label or definition in studying or discussing such a vast field as Islam and the Muslim world, unless we group its manifold phenomena into distinctive categories and assign them suitable designations. Islamic thinker Hasan Hanafi claims, "[I]t is difficult to find a more appropriate term than the one recently used in the West, 'fundamentalism,' to cover the meaning of what we name Islamic awakening or Islamic revival."[10] While *al-usuliyyah al-Islamiyyah* is the most appropriate Arabic term, connoting a search for and a return to the fundamentals of Islamic faith, the foundations of the Islamic *ummah* [community], and the basis of legitimate authority *(shar'iyyat al-hukm)*, such terms as *tajdid*, referring to periodic renewal of the faith, and *islah*, referring to reform, are more frequently used by Muslims.

Some Western scholars, like Olivier Roy, however, have argued for the use of the term "Islamist" instead of "fundamentalist," while others, like Emmanuel Sivan, have opted for "Islamic radicalism" or "revolutionary Islam," and still others for the terms "revivalist" and "resurgent" Islam. I personally prefer the term "fundamentalism" because of the wide usage in the West by such scholars as Rubin, Dekmejian, Voll, Marty, and Appleby, as well as the media, of the term "Islamic fundamentalism." Also, Roy and Sivan, who have used other conceptualizations, have frequently referred to the movement as "fundamentalist." Further, it is more useful to use one term to designate the complex cluster of movements, events, and people involved in the reaffirmation of Islamic faith during the twentieth century. It needs to be made clear, however, that these fundamentalists are not trying to lead their lives in emulation of the seventh century; rather, they are inspired by that era and believe the principles that guided its community then can still serve them today, albeit in a modern framework.

Fundamentalism and, particularly, the issue of gender relations in fundamentalist discourse is a difficult and complex topic. Hence, a high degree of objectivity and caution is required in examining relevant material to elucidate the theoretical and, I believe, the political foundational framework of Islamic fundamentalist discourse on gender. Moreover, this discourse cannot be adequately understood without gauging the extent to which Muslim women themselves have participated in it and the manner in which they have viewed their status in the ideal Islamic state. Hence, Zaynab al-Ghazali, the most prominent female Islamic fundamentalist and activist, has been included alongside the major male ideologues studied. No other female Sunni fundamentalist of comparable stature and influence is available for inclusion, while those who have appeared in the Shi'ite sect have written exclusively in Persian and have not been translated yet, such as Marzieh Hadidchi (Ms. Dabbagh).[11]

Despite the plethora of publications on Islamic fundamentalism and women in Islam, there is still a dearth of material on Islamic gender theory in general and Islamic fundamentalism in particular. Extensive studies have been published on issues of the Islamic state, revolution, ideology, and fundamentalism, and many others on the role of women and their status in Islam and the Qur'an. Also, a number of studies on the status of women in the discourse of the ideologues studied here have been undertaken to date, however, those articles that have appeared are sporadic and discuss, in cursory fashion, the discourse of one or two of the major ideologues. This may be due to an assumption that gender theory is a shallow phenomenon or that its ideology is not worthy of an in-depth study. Moreover, while social, economic, cultural, and religious factors may account for the central position the gender issue carves for itself in fundamentalist discourse, a more serious theoretical analysis is needed to further our understanding of this phenomenon that commands a vital position in all Islamic fundamentalist discourses of the twentieth century. Although its features may occasionally be colored by local factors, it still possesses such regional and universal dimensions as to make a universal gender theory possible. However, despite growing academic interest in the contemporary political history of the region and, in particular, Islamic fundamentalism, gender issues have featured only marginally in scholarly works. The mainstream of Islamic fundamentalist studies, though overabundant, has chosen to follow a gender-blind methodology. Hence, the importance and relevance of this study. As will be shown, the study of the discourses of fundamentalist ideologues demonstrates that gender relations and women's affairs reside at their core. Therefore, to marginalize women's issues in fundamentalist discourse is to drastically misunderstand the political history involved and its impact on one half of the Muslim population, estimated at about half a billion women. Such marginalization also results in available data being uneven in quality and mass, thus hindering further integrated research and analysis.

As will become evident, the importance relegated to gender issues by fundamentalist ideologues is not purely patriarchal. Inasmuch as patriarchy plays an important role, it is manipulated for purely political purposes, as made evident by the political and historical developments of the last century, just as women's issues are. This study, therefore, follows the thread of the fundamentalist control of women into the center of the gender maze of contemporary fundamentalism. To that end, it is important to avoid the extensive value-laden literature on women and seek primary sources to place available data in its proper perspective, critically evaluate them from within the fundamentalist framework, and identify possible alternatives.

While the argument herein may seem to have feminist or Islamic feminist overtones, it is neither. It relies totally on a deconstruction of fundamentalist gender discourse to arrive at a universal theory capable of explaining all idiosyncrasies and contradictions inherent in the individual discourses, and setting a solid foundation for a new perspective and insight into the twentieth-century concept of political Islam. This will also lead to a better understanding of the Muslim woman's status throughout history, not from a religious perspective but from a purely political one. It certainly is not the first instance, nor will it be the last, in which religion and women are manipulated for political objectives.

It will be demonstrated that, while each author has his or her own style and peculiar circumstances, those reviewed here all share a similar philosophical outlook. Their consistent emphasis on the status of women in society and their relationship to men, and their overwhelming similarities in general guidelines, act as a vehicle for the attainment of political power. Thus, fundamentalists revive patriarchy and its restrictive control of women to assure overwhelming male support and to divert attention from the real problems of society and their failure to deal with them. Also, the pragmatic need to maintain social control necessitates the use of women, the weakest and most visible social link and, therefore, the easiest to subjugate, to demonstrate to society and the world at large an illusion of control. The control of women thus emerges as an efficient vehicle for social control. Authoritarian measures seem to acquire legitimacy and acceptability when presented as a return to a full implementation of the Shari'ah. This is best demonstrated by a critique of these legal concepts and the methods of their manipulation to legitimate or discredit behavior for social and political control. Such manipulation is made possible by the vagueness or universality and all-encompassing nature of Qur'anic verses that refer to gender issues and relations. They offer only general guidance and are, therefore, open to various interpretations, more so since, according to fundamentalist ideology, man's understanding is finite and incapable of fathoming eternal truths. The Hadith, furthermore, by the ideologues' own admission, allow a wide margin of interpretation in view of the number of available texts and their religious and historical validity. Also, by the ideologues' own admission, the Shari'ah has been infiltrated by local customs and conventions over the centuries and conditioned by the human understanding of Islam and the principle of *ijtihad*, which had remained active in Sunni Islam until the twelfth century. Thus, fundamentalism emphasizes its version of modernism and distances itself from traditional ulema and their conservatism, while Muslim scholars like Fazlur Rahman argue for the accompaniment of Qur'anic edicts by a *ratio legis*, "When the situation so changes that the law fails to reflect the *ratio*, the law must change."[12] When it comes to its vision of gender, though, fundamentalism occupies the same position that traditional Islam has maintained over the centuries, namely, that women's anatomy and biology, as perceived by male ideologues, ordain their destiny.

The ideologues selected for this study have been chosen not only because they represent the two radical and moderate trends, the two sexes, and the two Islamic sects, providing thereby a wide spectrum from which to develop a universal gender theory, but also for the formative role they have all played in the development of the three geocultural trends that have emerged. They may, indeed, be described as the masters of twentieth-century fundamentalism. Thus, although Hasan al-Banna has written only one essay on the subject of women, he has been selected for having been responsible for the establishment of the first Islamic fundamentalist movement in the Arab world, in 1928, under the name of the Muslim Brotherhood. It quickly spread throughout the Muslim world and became the prototype of all such subsequent movements. Al-Banna strove to relate all economic, political, social, philosophical, and moral issues to Islam. Due to his importance in initiating the fundamentalist movement in the twentieth century, the establishment of the Muslim Brotherhood, and the dearth of material on women, his political philosophy and the development of the Brotherhood are discussed at length.

Abu al-'A'la al-Mawdudi was the most renowned Pakistani fundamentalist and the founder of the Pakistani Sunni fundamentalist association, Jama'at-i Islami. He had a tremendous impact on Muslims throughout the world. His conception of Islam as a system and method, together with his doctrines of *jahiliyyah* and *hakimiyyah*, became the central issues of modern Islamic fundamentalism. He wrote two books on women in Islam and published a number of articles.

Sayyid Qutb was the Egyptian ideologue who developed the ideological basis of Islamic activism, which materialized later in the appearance of radical and violent fundamentalist groups, one of which was al-Takfir wal Hijra; and it was he who called for a total revolution against all human systems. Qutb further developed the doctrines of *jahiliyyah* and *hakimiyyah* and viewed societies as being responsible for the paganism of their rulers. Qutb was not interested in women per se and did not write any independent treatises on their status. However, the subject pervades all his writings. Thus Qutb and Mawdudi best represent the radical trend.

Zaynab al-Ghazali, also an Egyptian, is the most prominent woman associated with the Muslim Brotherhood and is a prolific writer. Due to her experience, position, connections with the Brotherhood, activism, and ideological views, al-Ghazali may be looked upon as an ideologue and an archetype for the young Islamist woman. She founded the Muslim Women's Association. Although she pledged full cooperation with the Muslim Brothers, she conceived the association from the outset as being equal to and equivalent with, yet deliberately separate from, them. Yet, she took an oath pledging her personal efforts to the cause advanced by Hasan al-Banna. Her inclusion in this study is imperative to illuminate the extent to which Muslim women themselves have participated in the fundamentalist movement and the manner in which they perceive their status in the ideal

Islamic state. The limitation of the selection to only one Sunni female ideologue is dictated by the dearth of comparable women and the scarcity of texts among both the Sunni and Shi'ite sects.

In 1979, Ayatollah Ruhollah Khomeini achieved a Persian Shi'ite revolution in Iran, resulting in the formation of an Islamic state, the Islamic Republic of Iran, the first of its kind. He based the legitimacy of the government on the guardianship of the jurist, known as *wilayat al-faqih*, and called for almost total adherence to himself, the Imam's representative. His views on women are to be gleaned from the plethora of his writings.

Mortaza Mutahhari was an Iranian religious scholar and writer and one of the closest associates of Ayatollah Ruhollah Khomeini. Although the Iranian Revolution gave Mutahhari visibility as a political figure, it is his writings, supported vehemently by the revolutionary authorities, that constitute his chief legacy, which contributed greatly to the creation of the intellectual climate of the Iranian Revolution of 1979. Both Khomeini and Mutahhari represent the Shi'ite radical trend. Mutahhari published two books on the subject of women and numerous articles on their status.

By all accounts, Hasan al-Turabi is the mastermind of the coup that brought theocracy to Sudan in 1989. He created the Sunni National Islamic Front in Sudan and became known for his conciliatory tone, which has come to epitomize the new and more flexible leadership in the region's Islamist movements. Al-Turabi is also the founder of the Popular Islamic and Arab Conference. One of his most committed supporters is Rashid al-Ghannoushi. Although al-Turabi discussed the status of women in his many writings and interviews, he wrote only one book on the subject.

Rashid al-Ghannoushi, the founder of the Sunni Tunisian Islamic Tendency Movement and the leader of the al-Nahda Party, presents a democratic outlook in his view of the Islamic state and speaks of reform and pluralism. He and Turabi represent the moderate trend. Al-Ghannoushi, like those who preceded him, was mesmerized by the gender argument, and in addition to several references in his works, he devoted two of his books and a number of articles to the subject.

Sheikh Muhammad Hussein Fadlallah of Lebanon recognized Khomeini publicly in 1981, in return for which the latter named him *marji' al-taqlid* [source of tradition/imitation]. He served as president of the Lebanese Council of Hizbullah and the vice president of the Central Council of the International Hizbullah in Tehran. He has attempted to keep the concept of *wilayat al-faqih* within the framework of the encompassing *marji'iyyah*, which, by definition, signifies pluralism. However, despite his association with Hizbullah, he is regarded as a Shiʿite moderate. He has given numerous talks and written several books on the subject.

It is thus evident that the ideologues selected for study in this work, albeit lopsidedly Sunni, are the masterminds and architects of the fundamentalist movement in the twentieth century and at the beginning of the twenty-first. And, although some have already passed away, the impact and imprint they have had on the inception and development of fundamentalism are still conspicuously visible in the younger fundamentalist movements. Their writings have been translated into many languages and distributed throughout the Muslim world. To varying degrees, and among different Islamic countries, they have acquired tremendous eminence and grandeur, their portraits displayed in houses, offices, government buildings, public squares, and streets. Their impact on Islamic revivalism is best demonstrated by the contemporary resurgence of Islam, reflecting and incorporating many of their ideas and programs.

To conclude, it is important to emphasize that this study is only an attempt at presenting an overview of the ideologues' views on the role of women in Islamic society, their deconstruction, highlighting thereby the paradoxes within the discourse itself and between the theoretical discourse and the reality of its application. This, then, permits the formulation of a universal gender theory. While the impact of this discourse on the actual lives of Muslim women in fundamentalist societies is admittedly important, it is not the focus of this study, although references to such an impact are widely quoted throughout. It may, however, provide the basis of an important sequel.

I hope to have established a clear presentation of the Islamic fundamentalist gender ideology as portrayed by their most prominent ideologues and thinkers, stressing the significance allocated it in their discourse. I also hope to have provided a database to help readers work out their own theories and interpretations, while simultaneously providing a unified theory in explanation of fundamentalist rationale regarding gender relations.

Chapter 2

✖

Hasan al-Banna

Hasan al-Banna has been described as the twentieth-century Sunni revivalist incarnate: "He was the unique embodiment of the Sufi spiritualist, Islamic scholar and activist leader, who possessed a rare ability to evoke mass support by translating doctrinal complexities into social action . . . Banna's movement . . . succeeded in galvanizing and organizing a mass following as no other Islamic movement had done in recent centuries. Banna was singularly unconcerned with ideological intricacies since he was committed to revival of the Islamic community without regard to its internal, sectarian, or other divisions."[1]

Born to a modest family in October 1906 in the small town of Mahmudiyyah, northeast of Cairo, al-Banna grew up in a devout Islamic environment, his father having studied at the al-Azhar University. Al-Banna attended a Qur'anic school, supplemented by private sessions at home. In 1923, he was admitted to Dar al-'Ulum seminary (a teachers college), an extension of al-Azhar, graduating in 1927 at the age of twenty-one. He was given a teaching position at the elementary school of Isma'iliyyah, where he taught Arabic to schoolchildren by day and instructed laborers, small merchants, and civil servants of Isma'iliyyah in Islam by night. He also held discussion groups in coffeehouses and other popular meeting places. In 1927, he endorsed the foundation of the Young Men's Muslim Association, and in 1928, at the age of twenty-two, founded his own Society of Muslim Brothers. Its mission was Islamic activism and aiding the poor. This marked the beginning of an ominous Islamic movement that was to mushroom in Egypt and abroad. As soon as it was consolidated, he and his followers, committed to Islamic renewal, toured the countryside spreading the message of Islam in mosques, homes, workplaces, clubs, and coffeehouses.[2]

Al-Banna managed to establish an effective organizational and propagandist machine and slowly started to inch toward a political career and organize his paramilitary units. In 1940, a supreme council of *jawwalah* [graduate scouts] was initiated and headed by al-Banna himself. During the Second World War, he came into conflict with the Egyptian government and the British authorities and in 1941 started to be repeatedly arrested. By 1948, he had established al-Tanzim al-Sirri or al-Khass [secret or special apparatus], a clandestine organization, to terrorize opponents: homes were raided, cinemas bombed, hotels set on fire, and unveiled women were harassed. This policy of terror was soon to be adopted by other upcoming, militant fundamentalist movements in the rest of the Arab world.[3] His Society of Muslim Brothers had grown into a formidable enemy of the Egyptian monarchy, which had it dissolved in December 1948 despite his incessant efforts to negotiate with Nuqrashi Pasha's government. On December 28, 1948, the assassination of the prime minister by a Muslim Brother unleashed an unprecedented campaign of persecution against the Brotherhood, culminating on February 12, 1949, in the assassination of Hasan al-Banna himself, presumably by government agents.[4]

During his lifetime, al-Banna was the decision maker of the Brotherhood and its pacesetter vis-à-vis the changing political, social, economic, and religious climates. Thus, when he died having left only two significant works, his autobiography and a collection of his personal letters, his followers came into ideological turmoil and indecision, especially during the persecutions of 1954. It was not until Sayyid Qutb's prolific writings began to appear between 1954 and 1966 that the ideological vacuum created by the death of al-Banna was filled.[5]

It was during his stay in Cairo and Isma'iliyyah to finish his studies that al-Banna was first exposed to a Western political presence in the form of the British occupation of the Suez Canal Zone. He was shocked by the religious and cultural challenge this presented to traditional Egyptian society. Faced with the growing ills of Egyptian society and lack of religious piety, which he attributed to Western secularism and materialism, he called for a return to Islam as the panacea for Muslim decadence and impotence. He saw Islam as self-sufficient and the only perfect and comprehensive system that could wake Egyptian society from its slumber. He emphasized the necessity of a return to the normative period of the Prophet and the first caliphs for the reestablishment of the Islamic government. The only sources to be used for such an endeavor were to be the Qur'an and the six canonical treatises of the Hadith.[6]

During his stay in Cairo, al-Banna came in contact with Rashid Rida and his teachings through *al-Manar*, the journal published by Rida himself. In addition to Rashid Rida and the Salafiyyah movement, other factors, such as his father's instruction, nationalism, and Sufism, helped develop al-Banna's pluralistic intellectual basis for the formation of his Islamic movement. Thus, in the 1940s, the Muslim Brothers stood out as a powerful nationalist force in the struggle against the British occupation of Egypt and the spread of Zionism in Palestine. Al-Banna stated that his movement was "a *Salafiyyah* message, a Sunni way, a Sufi truth, a political organization, an athletic group, a scientific and cultural union, an economic enterprise and a social idea."[7]

According to his own account, six unknown young men appeared at his door one evening in March 1928, declared, "You are our master and our guide," and urged him to lead them in a campaign against the enemies of God. Following a lengthy discussion, al-Banna replied, "We are all brothers in the service of Islam. We are, therefore, the Muslim Brotherhood." The six thereupon bestowed upon him the title of sheikh, and Banna's Islamic movement came into being. By the 1930s, the Brotherhood had developed strong links with the media, published its own Islamic newspapers and a weekly entitled *al-Ikhwan al-muslimin* [The Brotherhood] and launched several branches in various Egyptian cities, as well as in Syria, Lebanon, and Iraq, among others. By the beginning of World War II, the Brotherhood had grown into a sizable, well-structured political movement, with more than 100,000 active members totally devoted to their Supreme Guide and his teachings.[8]

During its first stages, the Brotherhood was mainly interested in educating the youth in proper Islamic ethics and the virtues and goals of the Muhammadan prophecy, in addition to the universal virtues of truthfulness, chastity, and good social relations. Al-Banna emphasized the duties every Brother was obligated to espouse: brotherhood, cordiality, responsibility, sacrifice, attendance, and perseverance. He also named the "ten evils" the Brothers should avoid: colonialism; political, personal, and sectarian differences and divisions; interest taking; emulation of foreign corporations and the West; secular laws; atheism and intellectual chaos; desires and lewdness; immorality and weak leadership; and lack of pragmatism in discourse and analysis.[9] But, as the Brotherhood became more political, the "Special Apparatus" (the underground resistance) was established and carried out clandestine operations against the British and Jews. The Brotherhood further created cells within the army and police force.[10]

Al-Banna's chief contribution to the modern Islamic movement, distinguishing it from previous movements in Islamic history, lay in an activist ideology and organizational skills and structure, charismatic leadership, mass following, and pragmatic orientation. Al-Banna envisaged the development of his society in stages: the first emphasized the propagation of the message through lectures, public speech, and publications; the second involved the formation of the *jawwalah*, who developed their physical and martial skills while continuing and refining their training in religious discipline; and the third and final stage was to be the establishment of the Islamic order. At one point, al-Banna threatened the Egyptian government to resort to force, seize power, and establish the Islamic state unless it heeded the demands of the Brotherhood to alleviate the burdens suffocating the Egyptian people. However, he never defined the conditions that would precipitate such a revolution but asked his followers to be patient until the whole nation had been Islamized and psychologically prepared to accept such a regime. Al-Banna described his movement as "a new spirit making its way into the heart of this nation."[11]

The wisdom of this gradualist approach, weakened by the persecution of the Brothers after his death, was rejected by the younger Islamist generation of the 1970s and 1980s, who were infused by the radical ideology of Sayyid Qutb, and many radical groups were formed dedicated to revolution and resistance to the state. Among those was the Society of Muslims, better known as al-Takfir wal-Hijrah [Apostasy and Emigration], led by Shukri Mustafa. This group came into the limelight when it kidnapped and killed the minister of religious foundations in 1977. Al-Jihad [Holy War], another such group, came to prominence after the assassination of President Anwar Sadat in 1981.[12]

Like other fundamentalists who were to follow, al-Banna believed that the root cause of Egypt's problems, be they social, economic, or political, lay in the deviation of Egyptians from true Islamic guidelines. Therefore, the objective of his movement was to lead Egyptians back to a true understanding of Islam and the fulfillment of Islamic principles. This entailed leading a life based on the Qur'an and Sunna and ensuring a government that enforced the Shari'ah and its stipulations. The corruption that had pervaded Egypt for centuries, due to the passivity of the ulema and the self-centered policies of the rulers, had lulled Egyptian society away from the true teachings of Islam. This had led, in turn, to its decline, rendering it vulnerable to the encroaching Western imperialism and its deleterious effect on Egyptian culture and religion.[13]

One should remember that al-Banna was never an original thinker, but, due to his commitment to Islam, his compassion for the ordinary Egyptian, his charisma, and his genius and talent for organization, he was able to put into effect the ideas of such reformers as Muhammad Abduh, Jamal al-Din al-Afghani, and Rashid Rida by building a grassroots organization. Thus, he transformed "an elite intellectual fashion" into a mass movement that would change the milestones of Arab-Islamic history of the twentieth century.[14]

Another of al-Banna's contributions was a succinct evaluation of the impact of history at large on Islam, and of Islamic history in particular. These, according to him, have no normative standing in themselves, their only significance residing in the principle of their utility for Islam and Muslim society, thus favoring *"maslahah"* [utility or greatest good] and *ijtihad* [interpretation of Qur'anic text] as the best means to help Islam face the problems of the modern world.[15]

Al-Banna believed that Islam, in addition to providing the ideal framework for life, including the educational, political, social, and economic dimensions, "uplifts the human soul and sanctifies universal Brotherhood."[16] The regulations of life as sanctioned by Islam manage to curb any form of extreme behavior and help the believer to achieve a balanced fulfillment. This becomes even more important when one remembers that a Muslim does not live in isolation but as a member of a community. Only in such a society would such Muslim virtues as economic well-being, political unity, justice, and freedom, as well as social equality, come to fruition. Islam, according to al-Banna, is based on four major principles: a pure creed to bring people closer to God, a life of worship and good deeds to give meaning to one's life, unity of all sects and divisions, and a just legislation based on "good laws derived from the *Qur'an* and the Sunna."[17] Thus, Ishak Musa Husaini describes al-Banna's Islamic state as a three-legged table based on Islamic principles, a united nation, and an Islamic government; the removal of any of these would bring the table down.[18] The Islamic state, having gradually become the focal point of the Islamic order envisaged by the Brothers, is best manifested by the Brothers' slogan still alive to this day: "God is our objective; the Qur'an is our constitution; the Prophet is our leader; struggle is our way; and death for the sake of God is the highest of our aspirations."[19] Al-Banna considered noninvolvement in political life an "Islamic crime." According to him, "Every piece of earth on which the banner of Islam is raised, is a home for every Muslim to protect, work, fight for . . . [for] Islam is a homeland and a nationality."[20]

The message of the Muslim Brothers proved to be very attractive to

men, but not so to women. Although women participated in certain activities as wives or relatives of the Brothers, the active membership of
the female sector of the Brotherhood, the Society of Muslim Sisters, was
rather small, never exceeding the peak number of 5,000 that it achieved in
1948–49. This is despite al-Banna's urging women to join, emphasizing the
important role they would play in the Islamic reformation, and establishing the Institution for Mothers in 1933. But the Brothers were soon to
realize they had failed to attract the educated female, despite promises of
"true" emancipation, for fear of a return to the institution of the harem
among others. However, the Muslim Brothers rejected what they called
the Western model for Muslim women. They taught that women and female sexuality were exploited in the West as commodities in such fields as
advertisement, secretarial work, modeling, and sales, to enhance profits.

However, while the Brothers encouraged women to seek education and
forbade them no field of study as long as they were modest in their behavior and dress, they admitted that education or professionalism should not
be the most desirable objective of women; their real mission was that of
mothers and wives attending to their homes and families. Thus, Hasan
Ismail al-Hudaybi, the successor of al-Banna as Supreme Guide, encapsulated the Brotherhood's position on women in his declaration that "the
woman's natural place is the home, but if she finds that after doing her
duty in the home she has time, she can use part of it in the service of
society, on condition that it is done within the legal limits which preserve
her dignity and morality."[21] A woman is, furthermore, more of an asset to
her community when she acknowledges her primary position in the family unit and gives precedence to her marital and motherly duties over her
own career or any goals she might aspire to outside her own family, even if
it is to serve the movement, unless, of course, she has her husband's approval. The Muslim Brotherhood admits the importance of having female
nurses, obstetricians, secretaries, and teachers in an Islamic state, but the
family unit should always come first on the ladder of a woman's priorities.

Since the family is the nucleus of society, any factor that might disrupt
it, such as sexual temptation or illicit extramarital relations, should be immediately curbed through the imposition of the veil, the segregation of the
sexes, peer pressure, and self-control. Thus, married life within Islamic pa-
rameters is conducive to a virtuous existence. The Brotherhood's sexual
ideology emphasizes the natural biological differences between the sexes
and presents a corollary of distinct psychological traits peculiar to each
sex as immutable scientific facts. Men are characterized by their physical

strength, rational and logical capabilities, and independence, in contradistinction to the physical weakness, emotional and nurturing qualities, and the vulnerability and dependency that characterize women. Such preordained qualities naturally imply the confinement of women to the home and limitation of their role to the bearing and rearing of children, and the acknowledgement of man's superiority and dominance as expressed in sura 4:34:

> Men are in charge of women, because Allah hath made the one of them to excel the other, and because they spend of their property [for the support of women]. So good women are the obedient, guarding in secret that which Allah hath guarded. As for those from whom ye fear rebellion, admonish them and banish them to beds apart, and scourge them. Then if they obey you, seek not a way against them.

However, the Brothers are careful to admit the broader needs of society for women in times when there is need for their political participation for propaganda purposes or when male members are in exile, imprisoned, or fighting. Women are thus considered to be as responsible as men for the welfare of the state and society as a whole and must, therefore, be included in the political process and consulted as citizens by the government and as wives by their husbands. The productive functions of women should, therefore, be controlled, but never terminated. Finally, following in the footsteps of Rashid Rida, the Brothers maintained that women were to be treated equally with men, except in heading the household, leading prayers, or holding the office of a caliph or supreme imam.[22]

Just as Hasan al-Banna carved his own path in political Islam in contradistinction to previous reformers, he broke new ground by including social and economic issues in his Islamic program: the state would take an active part in instilling respect for public morality and imposing penalties on public infractions. Thus, prostitution, alcohol, and gambling would be prohibited, dance halls closed, and adultery punished by flogging; schools would be segregated and new curricula devised for girls that would be different from that of boys; and, finally, songs, lectures, movies, plays, and books would be censored. This was in addition to controlling the correct observance of religious practices.[23]

Although Hasan al-Banna's ideas regarding the role of women in a Muslim society were generally traditional, he couched his traditionalism in modern and scientific terminology. He stressed the important role women play in society, for they account for half the population and constitute the most effective sector in determining the role society as a whole will play, since women represent the first school that shapes the new generation and develops its character and personality. Thus, the destiny of a whole people rests in the hands of the mother who sculpts the path the child will follow in perceiving his society and fitting into it and the *ummah* as a whole, and fashions his personality as a youth and even as a man later on in life. Islam has, accordingly, assigned gender roles an important part in the Qur'anic text and the Shari'ah as a whole. Al-Banna explains that Islam has elevated women to full partnership with men in rights and duties and called them "the sisters of men"; in fact, they "derive from each other," for Islam has accorded women their full personal, civil, political, and human rights. However, despite this basic equality, and due to biological and natural differences, different gender roles have been assigned for the benefit of women and their protection. Such God-given natural roles are those of wife, mother, and housekeeper. Their natural place in society as such would be the home. Such roles necessitate the raising of women according to strict moral standards; their guardians will be rewarded by God for adhering to them and punished if they stray. The same responsibility is required from all those in positions of responsibility and guardianship. Thus, the imam is in charge of his congregation, men of their families, women of their homes, and servants for the wealth of their masters. Women should further be educated in the arts of reading, writing, arithmetic, religion, early Islamic history, hygiene, child rearing, and home economics, but not in such superfluous fields as law, foreign languages, or the sciences.

Another principle governing women's behavior stems from a common Muslim belief that the major feature controlling gender relations is sexual attraction. This basic instinct in both sexes necessitates their segregation in the interest of safeguarding morality and preventing adultery and the consequent breakup of marriage and destruction of the family unit. Women should, therefore, be prevented from being in the company of strangers unchaperoned and should be confined to their homes, except on occasions such as religious festivities. When they do go out, they should avoid adornments, cover up their bodies, refrain from any eye contact with men, stand behind them in mosques, and use separate entrances and exits. This is to protect men from the seduction of women and women from the attraction of men. With all this in mind, it is obvious, according to al-Banna, that women should not participate in public life, even though there is no such clear admonishment in the Scripture. However, if she is forced to do so by extenuating circumstances, she is to apply all the relevant Islamic regulations in dress, adornment, and avoidance of seduction.[24]

Al-Banna, as is evident from the preceding exposé of his life and ideology, did not give much attention to the problem that commanded a pivotal position in the fundamentalist discourse of later ideologues: the status of women. In fact, as he himself remarks, even the short essay he wrote on the subject was solicited by some colleagues. This apparent lack of interest may be attributed to several factors. Although Huda Sha'rawi (see chapter 7) had removed her veil in 1923 and led the Egyptian feminist movement until her death in 1947, and Qasim Amin had called for the liberation of women at the turn of the century, the feminist movement in the West was at low ebb and a reactionary movement had already set in and was in ascendance, which meant that feminism in Egypt, as well as the rest of the Middle East, was in decline as well. A second and more important factor is his immersion in the spreading of the Islamic message and the foundation and organization of his Muslim Brothers without the benefit of a current or preexisting role model. This was coupled with his involvement in Egyptian politics in the 1930s and 1940s, leaving him no time to concentrate on a subject he thought was clear and straightforward and, therefore, needed no further effort. The third factor contributing to the limited attention he affords this matter is his traditionalism. Thus, he declared in the introduction to the paper he wrote on women that this was solicited by one of his friends, and, although he recognized the importance of the subject in view of the significant role women play in society, the viewpoint of Islam is quite clear and straightforward and, therefore, needs no elaboration or edification. If there seems to be a problem, it is because Muslims no longer understand the teachings of Islam, and those who do, do not want to implement them, yielding thereby to the wave of Westernization that has invaded the country and blinded them. Any attempt, therefore, to abuse the flexibility of Islam and reinterpret its tenets in this matter to meet their personal desires and needs would be a diversion from its true message. This essay, according to al-Banna, is, therefore, only a reminder to Muslims of the traditional Islamic position on the subject of women and their role in society.

This traditional view is evident from the aforementioned exposition of the Brotherhood's and his own views on the subject: Women's role is confined to the family and the home; they are not to leave their homes, except in extenuating circumstances and after securing the permission of their husbands. When they leave the house, they should be clad in Islamic garb and avoid the presence of strange men and eye contact. Since women make up half the population and raise the other half, it is important to educate them in matters conducive to the correct upbringing of children, anything else being superfluous and wasteful. This is also enjoined by their natural difference from men in biology and intellect.

It is fascinating that, at a time when traditionalism and adherence to the Qur'anic text and the Shari'ah are the hallmarks of the ideologues' teachings regarding women's roles in society, they have no compunction in contradicting their stand when it is to their advantage to do so. Hence, al-Banna himself, who had stressed the domestic role of women, urged and encouraged them to join the Brotherhood and participate in its activities, momentarily setting aside the importance of their maternal roles, their natural differences, and intellectual inferiority. He also advocated omission of the payment of the *mahr* [dower], explicitly stipulated in the Qur'an, to facilitate marriages of the Brothers in times of economic crises.[25] At such times, he would have women leave the "sanctity" of their homes and their "natural" roles to help support the family, a duty used by the Brothers to show the superiority and rightful dominance of men at home.

Furthermore, although al-Banna resorts to the practice of *maslahah* for the interpretation of Qur'anic precepts for political and economic purposes, he refuses to resort to this method to emancipate women, or at least loosen the chains imposed upon them by tradition. Instead, he increases the strictures and reinforces old ones to isolate women further from the public sphere. Thus, while language and poetry have always been the domains of women even in the most conservative of societies, women, according to al-Banna and the Brotherhood, are barred from studying foreign languages, in an effort to protect them from any pernicious influence of Western literature. The implication here is that women, like children, are incapable of differentiating between good and evil and, like the latter, are in need of guidance to avoid being corrupted.

Chapter 3

✳

Abu al-'A'la al-Mawdudi

Abu al-'A'la al-Mawdudi has been described as "a systematic thinker and a prolific writer, a dynamic orator, a seasoned politician, an astute and indefatigable organization builder, a charismatic leader, who almost single-handedly shaped modern Muslim discourse on the social, economic and political teachings of Islam." Political scientist Mumtaz Ahmad has credited him with having imported "a new language—a political language—to Islamic discourse."[1] Mawdudi's analysis of the Qur'an and Hadith laid the foundation for a new Islamic system dealing with Islamic law, political theory, economics, social relations, and Islamic philosophy and culture, to serve as an Islamic alternative to both Western liberalism and Soviet Marxism. Thus, no account of the contemporary fundamentalist movement would be complete without attention to his preeminent role.

Until his resignation in 1972 as *amir* of the Jama'at-i Islami, the organization he had established in 1941, he was the single best-known and most controversial religious figure of Pakistan. Translations of his prolific writings propelled his fame beyond the subcontinent of India and Pakistan to all Muslim countries, where he was revered as the foremost modern interpreter of Islam. His writings in Urdu are still considered the strongest expression of the themes basic to modern fundamentalism. His books have been translated into Arabic, English, Turkish, Persian, Hindi, French, German, Swahili, Tamil, and Bengali, among other languages. The extent of his intellectual and political influence makes the study of his life, ideology, revolutionary Islamic vision, and views on women imperative to the understanding of the spread of political Islam in the twentieth century. In fact, his influence has been so pervasive that one encounters the terms first coined by him quoted in all the social, political, and economic domains of contemporary Islamist discourse. His views have influenced such thinkers as Sayyid Qutb of Egypt and shaped events that took place in countries ranging from Morocco to Malaysia, including the Iranian Revolution of 1978–79.[2]

It is important, at this point, to provide a short sketch of Mawdudi's life and a summary of his ideology to place his views on women in perspective. He was born on September 25, 1903, in the present-day Andhra Pradesh of India in the state of Hyderabad, to a respected, religious family whose paternal ancestry extends back to the Prophet Muhammad; a number of his ancestors were prominent Sufi leaders of the Chishti order. He took up journalism as a profession and assumed the editorship of the newspaper *Muslim* (1921–23), and later of *al-Jam'iyyat* (1925–28), both being the journals of Jam'iyyat-i 'Ulami'-i Hind, an organization of Muslim religious scholars. During this period, he produced his first major book, *al-Jihad fi al-Islam* [Holy war in Islam], expounding the principles of the Islamic law of war and peace. In 1928, dissatisfied with his profession and the increasingly nationalistic orientation of al-Jam'iyyat, he resigned his post as editor and moved from Delhi back to Hyderabad, where he devoted himself to research and writing, having received his certificate in religious training in 1926, and became one of the ulema. It was here that he was "reconverted" to Islam, grew a beard, adopted Indo-Muslim clothing, and assumed a new outlook of political imperatives couched in religious regalia. His "conversion" to Islam, Mawdudi explained, meant discovering a new significance and meaning in Islam that had previously eluded him. This led him to take up editorship of the monthly *Tarjuman al-Qur'an* in 1933, which became the platform for his ideas.

In the mid-1930s, he began writing on cultural and political issues facing Indian Muslims. He feared an imminent "gigantic flood" that could overwhelm Muslim society—namely, Western ideas and customs already pervading the country and distancing the youth from their religious roots. To stem this flood, he set out to instruct young Muslims in Islam and its superiority over any other system through his writings. In the meantime, he received an invitation from the philosopher and poet Muhammad Iqbal to join him in the eastern part of Punjab, in the district of Pathankot, where they established an academic and research center, Dar al-Islam, to train competent scholars in Islam, produce outstanding works on Islam, and reconstruct Islamic law.

Slowly, al-Mawdudi came to realize that the best method to transform any society would be to prepare a small, highly disciplined and dedicated, well-informed group to assume leadership in social and political matters. In August 1941, in response to the Muslim League's declaration of the Lahore Resolution to establish a Muslim state in Pakistan, al-Mawdudi, with a small group of supporters, established the new organization of Jamaʿat-i Islami. He was elected as its head and remained so until his health failed in 1972. His goal, contrary to that of the Muslim League, was to restructure Indian society in an Islamic pattern through the creation of a small devout group to act as leaven for society as a whole. When Pakistan was created in 1947, Mawdudi and his Jamaʿat started clamoring for a true Islamic society. He was arrested on a number of occasions and sentenced to death in May 1953. His sentence was commuted to life imprisonment under intense public pressure, and he was released shortly afterward. Following the ban of the Jamaʿat and other political parties in 1958, al-Mawdudi lived quietly in Lahore under strict surveillance. In July 1962, the ban was lifted, and in January 1964 al-Mawdudi and forty-three leaders of Jamaʿat were again arrested and charged with disturbing public order. His first act, following their release in October of the same year, was to support Fatimah Jinnah as a candidate for the presidency of Pakistan against Ayyub Khan. He continued to work through the Jamaʿat-i Islami until his death in 1979.[3]

The adherents of Abu al-ʾAʿla al-Mawdudi viewed him as a religious scholar, a politician, a thinker, and most important as a *mujaddid* [renewer]. His authority has been invoked whenever a reinterpretation of Islam was attempted. Al-Mawdudi himself bestowed upon all *mujaddid* interpretive powers and explained:

> Though a *mujaddid* is not a prophet, yet in spirit he comes very close to prophethood. He is characterized by a clear mind, penetrating vision, unbiased straight thinking, special ability to see the Right Path (*al-sirat al-mustaqim*) clear of all extremes, always balanced, the power to think independently of contemporary, as well as centuries old, social and other prejudices, courage to fight against the evils of the time, inherent ability to lead and guide, and an unusual competency to undertake *ijtihad*, and the work of reconstruction.[4]

The only difference, then, between prophethood and *tajdid* [renewal] would be the divine message, since both prophet and *mujaddid* have the same work/objective, not a mere transmission of the message but total education. The "ideal *mujaddid* can be a true successor to prophethood." Although al-Mawdudi based his authority on erudition in traditional religious sources, he stressed his proficiency in modern subjects as well, bringing to mind the qualities of the awaited Mahdi. He defined his authority as superior to all others: "I recognize no king or ruler above me; nor do I bow before any government; nor do I view any law as binding on me . . . nor do I accept any tradition or custom." Al-Mawdudi's acceptance of modernity and his rejection of the authority of the ulema thus constituted his new approach to Islam and cast him in the role of the *mujaddid*.[5]

Al-Mawdudi's teachings required a bold reinterpretation of the Qur'an and Sunna, shedding the burden of the traditional interpretations of the past. He is quoted as having declared his relief at not having received his education at a *madrasah* [school], thus enabling him to keep his mind free of the shackles of traditional thought. Although he respected many of the theologians and *mujaddidin* of the past, he did not consider their decisions as final since their work could still be revised and improved upon by modern research. Al-Mawdudi asserted the right to exercise one's reason or personal interpretation even of God's clear commands, albeit from within the spirit of such commands. Personal judgment thus releases al-Mawdudi from both a literal understanding of the Qur'an and a slavish attachment to traditional jurisprudence and provides the means through which Islam's eternal truths could be adapted to changing circumstances. *ijtihad* to al-Mawdudi is then the vehicle of motion within the Islamic system, and the means of creativity and action to ensure a dynamic Muslim life.[6]

Al-Mawdudi maintained:

> The conservative approach, represented by Orthodox ulema, is unrealistic. It fails to take note of the fact that life is ever-changing . . . New situations arising, new relationships being formed and new problems emerging . . . The approach fails to grapple with the problems of the day [and] is bound to fail. And when estrangement is effected between religion and life, then even the private life cannot remain religion's preserve . . . Furthermore, the conservative elements had not the full understanding of the constitutional, political, economic and cultural problems of the day. The result was that they could not talk the language of today and failed to impress the intelligentsia and the masses alike.[7]

Already in 1926 the young al-Mawdudi had declared that "Islam is a revolutionary ideology and a revolutionary practice which aims at destroying the social order of the world totally and rebuilding it from scratch . . . and jihad [holy war] denotes the revolutionary struggle."[8] Islam, al-

Mawdudi argues, cannot be one of many political parties, but the only valid one. Its objectives are permanent and draw upon the capabilities of all prominent individuals at any given time in history for an Islamic revolution, their duty being the establishment of an Islamic state. Such a revolution would require providing Muslims with a set of beliefs, a new philosophy of life, a new set of values and moral commitment, and, most importantly, a complete transformation of personality and goals. This internal change would ultimately lead to a cataclysmic transformation of the community itself and the establishment of a new society and state, in effect, a new Islamic order.[9] Al-Mawdudi, thus, viewed Islam as a holistic ideology not dissimilar to Western ideologies of capitalism and communism. Not only were these two ideologies alien to the Muslim weltanschauung, al-Mawdudi argued, but they were also incapable of addressing Muslim concerns and problems. However, while intent on resisting Western ideologies and demonstrating the viability of Islam as an ideology, al-Mawdudi borrowed such Western terminology as "Islamic revolution," "Islamic state," and "Islamic ideology."[10] Al-Mawdudi thus claims that Islam is not only a personal religion but extends as well to the social, economic, and political domains of society. It is no longer merely a set of rituals but encompasses all aspects of one's life, and proceeds "from the sanctuary of man's heart to the arena of socio-political relations; from the mosque to the parliament; from the home to the school and the economy; from art, architecture and science to law, state and international relations."[11]

Al-Mawdudi's teachings focused on the purification of Islam, the crystallization of its ethos, actualization of its precepts, and its modernization without the accretions of Western civilization. Such an Islamic order could serve as a common denominator for all Muslims, promoting their unity and resurrecting Islamic faith. Islam would then "emerge as the World-Religion to cure man of all his maladies." To accomplish this, Mawdudi advocated two principles: first, that the word of God is the ultimate measure of man's behavior, and second, that only one possible contemporary interpretation of that word may exist.[12]

Al-Mawdudi had a dialectic vision of contemporary Islam and the historical progression of Muslim society. He saw it as a struggle between the traditional Muslim culture of India and the West, a struggle that would eventually culminate in an Islamic revolution and an Islamic state that would implement extensive social, economic, and political reforms and ultimately establish a utopian Islamic order. The reassertion of Islam would, thus, bring about a rejection of the West and its culture and any identity change Western imperialism might try to impose upon Muslims. He viewed the evils of Western imperialism in its propagation of women's liberation, secularism, and nationalism, all of which run contrary to the teachings of Islam. What concerned him most was the preservation of dress, language, and customs he considered essential for the preservation of Muslim culture and the creation of a new Muslim identity. These changes would not be possible, al-Mawdudi realized, without recasting Muslim life and thought in a modernizing mold (*tajdid*). Such an impetus of modernization was not to be limited to the use of modern technology but must adopt modern values, ideas, and institutions as well.[13] He wrote,

> We aspire for an Islamic renaissance on the basis of the Qur'an. To us, the Qur'anic spirit and Islamic tenets are immutable; but the application of this spirit in the realm of practical life must always vary with the change of conditions and increase of knowledge . . . Our way is quite different both from the Muslim scholar of the recent past and modern Europeanized stock. On the one hand, we have to imbibe exactly the Qur'anic spirit and identify our outlook with the Islamic tenets, while, on the other, we have to assess thoroughly the developments in the field of knowledge and changes in conditions of life that have been brought about during the last eight hundred years; and third, we have to arrange these ideas and laws of life on genuine Islamic lines, so that Islam should once again become a dynamic force, the leader of the world, rather than its follower.[14]

Thus, the new Muslim, to al-Mawdudi, must be more than a merely devout individual. He must also be modern with a modern mode of life, political aspirations, and cultural outlook. Traditional Islam only fettered Muslims to an anachronistic existence in the contemporary world. Failure to adopt modern science and social thought and organization would keep Muslims weak and unable to effect any change in the balance of power between themselves and the West. Amelioration of their position in the power structure was, therefore, to be achieved through the revitalization of Muslim life by the assimilation of modern ideas.[15]

Al-Mawdudi's major contribution to modern Islamic thought is his presentation of Islam as a comprehensive system of life, as well as his offering "a set of clear, well-argued definitions of key Islamic concepts within a coherently conceived framework." A person cannot, therefore, be a true Muslim unless he fulfills his personal as well as political, economic, and social obligations. To achieve that, al-Mawdudi built a systematic theory of the Islamic state on the basis of the new concepts he had introduced. The main purpose of the Islamic state would be "to enjoin what is good and forbid what is evil" (3:110). Such a state would not merely apply law and order and collect taxes; rather, it would have the moral mission of regulating and supervising the lives of its citizens. In this state, sovereignty (al-hakimiyya) would be God's alone to be exercised, on His behalf, by a just ruler well versed in jurisprudence and a firm believer in such an ideological state. This principle, al-Mawdudi contended, "negates [altogether] the concept of the legal and political sovereignty of human beings, individually or collectively . . . God alone is the Sovereign and His Commandments are the law of Islam."[16] "In such a state," declared al-Mawdudi, "no one can regard any field of his affairs as personal and private."[17]

This Islamic state, al-Mawdudi explained, would share some aspects of a Western state, such as a legislature, an independent judiciary, and a constitution, among others. It would, thus, be a "theo-democracy" where all citizens participate in the formation of its basic policy. The ideal society in such a state is segregated "to preserve the moral life of the nation and to safeguard the evolution of society on healthy lines, free mingling of both sexes has been prohibited. Islam effects a functional distribution between the sexes and sets different spheres of activity for [each]. Women should, in the main, devote themselves to the household duties in their homes, and men should attend to their jobs in the socio-economnic spheres." Cinema, theater, and the fine arts, al-Mawdudi contends, lead to moral corruption. "Islam does not approve of such pastimes, entertainment and recreations, as they tend to stimulate sensual passions and vitiate the canons of morality."[18] In such a virtuous society, the human faculties of reason and choice should be dissolved in the divinely ordained Islamic order.

It was, therefore, crucial for al-Mawdudi that society be Islamized before the Islamic state was established to gain legitimacy in the eyes of the citizens, without which the Islamic state could not hope to succeed. Education assumes an important role in this society for the gradual preparation of the population for the coming Islamic revolution. If the Islamic state were to be imposed on a non-Islamic population or society, it would have to be autocratic, thus, dooming any possibility of sociopolitical transformation. Democracy is pivotal for al-Mawdudi's Islamic state because it would not allow divisive sociopolitical issues, the Muslim population having already been "programmed" to abide by the Shariʿah. Accordingly, the government, instead of enforcing an Islamic state, would simply be implementing the will of the people. Thus, the form of the Islamic state would hinge equally on the character of the people and the mode of its application. As society changes, there would be no need for a violent seizure of power, since a peaceful, gradual takeover of the centers of political power would have brought about large-scale reforms from the top down.[19]

Al-Mawdudi's view of the economic system in Islam rests on the belief that God created earth and all it contains for the benefit of man. It is, therefore, every individual's birthright to attempt to secure a portion of this earth for his livelihood. As all individuals share this right equally, none can be deprived of it, nor can one have precedence over another in fulfilling it. The Shariʿah, thus, does not discriminate against any individual, class, or race in employing any means at their disposal to provide for their livelihood or in preventing them from training in or practicing any profession. Nor does it discriminate against any class or race by creating a monopoly of one form or another for a particular class or race. It is, therefore, the equal right of all to endeavor to locate the share allotted them by God for their livelihood and to have an equal opportunity to do so.[20]

Throughout his years of political activity, al-Mawdudi never stopped writing. By the time of his death in 1979, he had published more than seventy books and numerous articles. Concepts like "the Islamic system of life," "Islamic movement," "Islamic ideology," "Islamic politics," "Islamic constitution," "political system of Islam," "hakimiyyah" [God's sovereignty], "jahiliyyah" [un-Islamic society], and "tawhid" [unicity], first introduced by al-Mawdudi, soon became common parlance among later Islamists all over. Al-Mawdudi, in his lucid Urdu style, authored works in Islamic exegesis and Hadith and wrote on Islamic law, economics and social relations, Islamic philosophy and culture, and political theory, and, most importantly, he wrote on Islam as an ideological alternative to Western liberalism and Soviet Marxism. The simplicity of his style and short intellectual discussions made it possible for the greater majority of people to understand him in preference to the intellectual elite. The rationale of this approach was to popularize Islam and facilitate the participation of the masses and secular intellectuals in all religious activities. Thus, some of al-Mawdudi's significance lay in creating an intellectual medium where mundane and sociopolitical themes could be addressed in an Islamic context. Al-Mawdudi distanced himself from the traditional ulema and described himself as belonging "to that school of Islamic Jurisprudents" who claim any duly lettered person should have "his own direct access to the

Holy Qurʾan and the Sunna to seek commandments and exemplification."[21]

When queried about the particular incident that set him on his Islamist path, al-Mawdudi answered:

I am not the kind of person whose life can be drastically changed by any one incident. It is only after a great deal of thought and consideration that I establish my goals, and then I work gradually to achieve them. But, there was one incident that had a considerable impact upon me. In 1973, after staying in Hyderabad for nine years, I went back to Delhi where I witnessed a great change among the Muslims; they were rapidly moving away from Islam. In Delhi, the situation was completely different . . . I saw Muslim *shurafa* [honorable] women walking the streets without *purdah* [veil], an unthinkable proposition only a few years ago. This change shocked me so greatly that I could not sleep at night, wandering what had brought this sudden change among Muslims.[22]

Moreover, during his visits to several Arab countries, al-Mawdudi confirmed news media reports of the alarming disregard of Shariʿah guidelines of dress by Arab women in emulation of the West.

The most critical problem confronting modern civilization, al-Mawdudi proclaimed, is its basic pillar of gender relations, which, if askew, would adversely influence its future. Thus, to build a pure society, the sexual instinct must be legislated and limited to the marital bed for procreation and the swelling of social volume. The West achieved gender equality by sharing all responsibilities, thereby debasing sex to a pleasurable instinct and robbing it of its social significance. Islamic social order, on the other hand, separates the spheres of men and women and restricts their mingling through rigid moral regulations in contradistinction to the West, which throws the two sexes together without barriers, resulting in sexual anarchy. The Western concept of gender equality would have women share the workplace with men, attain economic independence, and mingle freely with the other sex, thereby promoting immorality, promiscuity, perversion, and declining birthrates. This would subvert their natural duties and create a social imbalance that would bring about a breakdown of the family unit, the pillar of society. The only remaining link between men and women in such a situation is animal lust, ignoring thereby the golden mean of women that resides in providing them with the opportunity to grow and enhance their potential in discharging their part in the advancement of civilization through fulfilling their role as mothers. This demonstrates what al-Mawdudi calls the human natural limitation in its inability to view life in all its dimensions. Human beings tend to be fascinated by one aspect of life to the disregard of other related issues, as demonstrated by their social behavior, particularly in its sexual dimension. Thus, ascetics view sex as the work of the devil, and women the cause of man's degradation, while the West adulates the body and its pleasures. Only Islam is capable of providing for every aspect of human nature while avoiding both excess and deficiency. It is the only system to come up with the perfect balance between human nature and the laws of nature.[23]

God, al-Mawdudi argues, created all creatures in pairs, male and female, instinctively attracted to each other for procreation and survival of the race. However, whereas animals employ sex solely for procreational purposes, humans have no control over their sex urge: their glands function continuously to maintain various bodily functions and stimulate sexual desire and prowess. This is further propagated by the instincts of survival and self-interest (pleasure), both of which necessitate attraction and attachment to the opposite sex. However, human sexual prowess was not intended merely to provide pleasure but also to contribute to the makeup of society and civilization and strengthen the bonds between men and women through the bearing and rearing of children. In so doing, sex transforms individualism into social coherence for the advancement of civilization. This, then, makes it clear that gender relations constitute the focal point of the initiation of social life and order and, therefore, the determining factor of the success or failure of civilization as a whole.[24]

To build a pure, progressive society, therefore, sex must be channeled, not as an end in itself but as a means of social progress and advancement. Unbridled sex leads to social disorder and anarchy. Its suppression, on the other hand, leads to a deterioration of intellectual and physical prowess and health. Hence, for best results, it has to be adjusted to a golden mean to build family units along correct guidelines governing the relationship between husband and wife. Sexual activity is to be harnessed to the home, creating a lasting bond between the partners and forming an all-important family, the nucleus of society and civilization. This is achieved through marriage, the duty of all Muslims, which legalizes sex and confines it to marital relations. Extramarital sex is banned, since it would result in a breakdown of the family unit, cause serious communicable diseases and moral disintegration, and lead to lower birthrates and proliferation of prostitution and illegitimate children who stand to inherit the animal traits responsible for their conception. Accordingly, illegal sex and adultery are prohibited and severely punished as crimes against society. To prevent them, an ideal relationship between men and women should be defined and their respective rights and privileges within the family sphere delineated unequivocally.[25]

In an Islamic society, marriage is a simple ceremony that does not require the services of judges, priests, or clerics. It can be performed anywhere in the presence of two witnesses to the offer of marriage by the male and its acceptance by the female. Islamic marriage laws, admits al-Mawdudi, favor men since men direct and provide for the family, maintain order, and administer discipline in the home. The husband is the "man of the family, on whose shoulders rests the religious responsibility of the family. He must uphold the tenets of faith, and his authority symbolizes that of God in the world."[26] Such a position is clearly reflected in the duties and prerogatives of the husband: the *mahr* [dower], whose amount is determined by the husband's material means, is paid by him in exchange for his wife's marital duties and favors: "Lawful unto you are all beyond those mentioned [captives], so that ye seek them with your wealth in honest wedlock, not debauchery. And those of whom ye seek content [by marrying them], give unto them their portions as a duty" (4:24). If the *mahr*'s amount exceeds the man's means, it will constitute a barrier to divorce. The wife may choose to give it up partially or totally. However, should the husband renege, the wife may abstain sexually.[27]

The husband has to provide for the family, while his wife runs the household (4:34). The extent of the provision should be within the husband's means and may be withheld if the wife is intransigent in any way. On the other hand, the wife may resort to the courts should her husband fail to provide for her. Should he continue to do so, the judge may divorce him from his wife. If his failure is due to an inability to provide, the wife is advised to seek financial help from her family; otherwise, divorce is decreed.[28]

The husband is enjoined to treat his wife well: He should not abstain sexually, unless for a valid cause. Even there, if abstinence exceeds four months, he is obliged to divorce her. He should not harm his wife physically, or punish her excessively, as in refusing to divorce her even when their relationship is over. In case of multiple marriages, the husband must treat all wives equally in kindness, material provisions, and sex but not necessarily in love, since this is often involuntary. If the husband mistreats his wife, she may go to court or seek divorce, although marital disputes are best dealt with through the intercession of both families.[29]

In return, al-Mawdudi continues, the wife is directed to be faithful to her husband and obey him in all things, except when his demands are contrary to God's laws, for example, if he orders her not to pray or fast, or if he directs her to drink alcoholic beverages, discard her veil in public, or commit sexual misdeeds. Should the wife "step out of her house against the will of her husband, she is cursed by every angel in the heavens, or by everything other than men and *jinn*, by which she passes, till she returns."[30]

In case of recalcitrance, al-Mawdudi asserts, the husband may rebuke his wife. If this is ineffective, he may escalate to sexual deprivation, to be followed by a physical beating, controlled to avoid physical harm or disfigurement. If this proves too excessive, the wife may appeal to the courts. Another measure of man's authority over his wife is his power of divorce. However, this is an extreme measure to be applied only as a last resort.

There are three forms of separation, according to al- Mawdudi: The first is initiated only by the husband and should be pronounced after each menstrual cycle for three months, to allow time for possible reconciliation while both partners continue to cohabit. Divorce may not take place during menstruation, since women are not in a normal state then and may have involuntary offensive reactions. Moreover, irrevocable divorce pronounced (pronounced thrice simultaneously) is contrary to Islamic teaching and Hadith. Once it becomes final, following three separate divorces, the husband may not remarry his wife until she marries another and is later divorced or widowed. This is specifically designed, al-Mawdudi declares, to discourage final or irrevocable divorce.[31]

Divorce may be initiated by the wife by returning part or all of her *mahr* as payment for divorce (*khul'*), but only if the husband agrees. If he does not, she may go to court; she may remarry him later if she chooses to. For *khul'* to be accepted, however, the husband must be impotent or sterile, a leper, or insane. In certain cases, a one-year waiting period is allowed for therapy and if this fails, *khul'* is initiated. Impotence and sterility, however, are considered valid only if the wife was unaware of their existence at the time of marriage, or if they develop after marriage.

In all this, al-Mawdudi explains, the courts have to be Islamic, with a Muslim judge, for judgments to be valid. Islamic jurisprudence has been set by Azhar scholars as reference in these matters, taking into account religious, social, moral, and economic factors, as well as the particular circumstances of each individual case.[32]

Annulment of marriage, al-Mawdudi elaborates, may be allowed if either of the partners has a defect that prevents their union, albeit if it was unknown prior to marriage. Such defects include sterility of the husband, which is cause for immediate annulment, and impotence of the husband, which is effective after one year of unsuccessful therapy. Madness is to be treated for one year, after which, if unsuccessful, annulment takes place. Al-Mawdudi, however, advocates annulment in all of the above cases, since the wife may be too young at the time of marriage to appreciate the problem, and continuance of such a marriage would be deleterious to family life. A fourth factor conducive to annulment is disappearance of the husband. While consensus here is for the wife to wait for four years before remarrying, al-Mawdudi finds exception if the husband left his wife without any financial support, in which case the court either divorces her immediately or grants her the right to divorce herself. Another exception would be if the wife is young and could be tempted into adultery if she remains lonely for too long. The court would then ask her to observe a waiting period of six to twelve months, at the end of which she is divorced. However, if the wife is virtuous but not too young, she is to wait four years if her husband is lost in a Muslim country where he may be traced, at the end of which she would be divorced. If he is lost in battle, she is to wait for one year only, but if he is lost during a civil war and remains missing after cessation of fighting, she is to observe the ʿiddah [waiting period] of death. However, if he is lost in a backward or uninhabited region where he cannot be traced, the wife cannot be divorced at all. However, in all these cases, final judgment should take into account the wife's age and circumstances, as well as the waiting period already completed. If the lost husband should return after the waiting period and the wife has remarried, ʿUmar, the second caliph, dictated that he would have no rights over her, while Ali, the fourth caliph, believed the wife should return to her first husband, and ʿUthman, the third caliph, ruled the first husband would have to choose between reclaiming his wife or asking for the return of the mahr. Al-Mawdudi himself tends to agree with ʿUmar.[33]

Furthermore, if one of the partners renounces Islam, the marriage is automatically void. If the marriage of an immature girl, who cannot give her consent, is arranged by her father or grandfather, she is bound by it. If other parties arrange it, she may contest upon reaching the first sign of maturity or lose all hope of contesting it thereafter. This applies to virgins only; nonvirgins may sue for annulment at any time, unless they acqui-esce after maturation.[34]

To accuse his wife of adultery, all the husband has to do, according to al-Mawdudi, is to swear to this four times and swear to it a fifth time, damn-ing himself if lying. The wife is not judged if she, in turn, swears four times that his accusations are false, and on a fifth time calls on the wrath of God if she is lying (24:6–9). This should take place in the presence of a judge, where each partner is given the right to confess his or her wrongdoing or where the li'an [swearing] takes place. Afterward, the judge rules for sepa-ration, which is then permanent and irrevocable. The mahr, however, can-not be retrieved. If the li'an is refused by the husband, the wife may sue him for libel, and if she refuses the same, she loses her mahr.[35]

Al-Mawdudi formulated a master plan to ensure an ideal gender rela-tionship: Men and women are born equal and have equal rights and duties toward the advancement of society. As such, they should enjoy equal civic and economic rights and share the same sphere of work. This does not mean, however, that women necessarily participate in the same fields of work as men, unless they are proved to possess the same instincts, bodily functions, abilities, and psychological traits. Actually, Mawdudi asserts, the reverse has been shown to be true. As soon as sexual traits are established in the embryo, physical makeup proceeds in different directions in males and females. Thus, the female skeleton and bodily functions are prepared for bearing children, actually dictating her future duties. Furthermore, upon reaching puberty and commencing menstruation, all her physical and mental functions change: there is a loss of body heat, a fall in blood pressure and pulse rate, a reduction in protein, fat, and gas metabolism, and in the elimination of phosphates and chloride, as well as a depression of breathing, a slurring of speech, impairment of concentration and intellec-tual prowess, lethargy, and, more significantly, a drastic change in endo-crine gland function, tonsils, and lymph nodes, causing reduced immunity. These changes reduce women to a disease-like state, causing them to lose control of brain and nervous system functions, leading to involuntary ac-tions that incapacitate them and render them unfit to work, often hysteri-cal and, occasionally, suicidal.[36]

The condition of women deteriorates even further during pregnancy, when their nervous systems and mental acuities remain unbalanced for several months, and experts advise that during the final month of gesta-tion women should be barred from any physical or mental effort. Further, in the postdelivery period, women remain susceptible to a variety of diseases and mental aberrations, such that, all in all, they remain essentially incapacitated for one year from the onset of pregnancy. And when they do recover, they regain half of their previous potential at best. Following all that is a period of child nursing when women live not for themselves but for their children, their very essence being transformed into the necessary nourishment. And when this is over, they are totally immersed in the care and raising of their children for protracted periods of time.[37]

From the foregoing it becomes clear, al-Mawdudi argues, that even if men and women are equal in physical and mental prowess, women's innate instincts and traits dictate different duties. Men, unlike women, are not tied to home and children. Women are predetermined for this: they are homebound during the three to seventeen days of monthly menstruation, and the more pronounced incapacitation of pregnancy, breast-feeding, and child care. It would, therefore, be unfair to burden them with the same duties as men, who do not suffer these hardships. Consequently, they are not to be equal earners or equally immersed in politics, jurisprudence, commerce, industry, agriculture, law enforcement, or defense. Inferentially, then, Mawdudi goes on, those who advocate that women share the same duties as men are actually seeking the destruction of all feminine traits and the impairment of their competence and aptitude in all facets of endeavor. To prepare women for male functions is contrary to the needs of humanity and those of women themselves. Since women are preordained for love, mercy, kindness, tenderness, and emotionality, they are rendered submissive and weak and, therefore, unfit to participate in public life, which demands aggression, a cool temperament, and judgment. The discrepancy is further underlined by man's position during sexual intercourse as initiator-aggressor, in contrast to the woman's docile recipient role.[38]

It is clear, al-Mawdudi affirms, that woman's advancement cannot and should not be achieved at the expense of her innate nature. She excels over men in certain fields and they in others. Thus, one will never find a female genius of the caliber of Aristotle, while there will never be a male mother. Civilization needs both traits: strength and fortitude, as well as softness and kindness, necessitating a just division of labor based on natural traits and attributes; a fact demonstrated by all the natural sciences. Any other arrangement is doomed to failure and social disintegration.[39] Natural division of labor, then, provides that men lead and command the home, in view of women's biologic limitations. They are also responsible for the care, protection, and provision of the family. Women, on the other hand, are assigned the bearing of and caring for children, the discharging of home duties and functions, and the provision of a happy, relaxing atmosphere at home. Finally, society is charged with overseeing these duties and assuring their perpetuation to avert social disorder.[40]

However, this has not been accomplished yet, because humans are naturally weak and inadequate and tend to follow the easiest course available. Thus, al-Mawdudi continues, some groups, as in monastic orders and Hinduism, adopt very strict moral codes suppressing sexual desires and instincts. However, disturbing proper male-female relations is bound to have negative repercussions on society and drive women to immoral actions. Others emphasize physical needs and pleasures. These, however, enhance and nurture base animalistic behavior, detrimental to society and destructive of family relations and birthrates. Some transform family life into virtual prisons through rigid rules and regulations, while still others allow women complete freedom and equality with men, resulting in the virtual destruction of family relations and structure. Faced with such excessive or deficient systems, Islam emerges, al-Mawdudi affirms, as the only complete social system that offers the exact degree of justice and balance, based on a respect of all aspects of human nature. In fact, Islam is so perfect that no human could have devised it. Only God could have stipulated such marriage guidelines designating man, the aggressor, in charge, and his wife submissive, obeying his will.[41] Islam, thus, legislated human sexual relations to create social order and prevent sexual anarchy: sexual activity is prohibited with those who cohabit (mothers, sons, sisters, etc.), with other men's wives, and outside the home. To ensure the satisfaction and release of men's sex drive, God has directed wives not to feign protracted fasting or prayer to avoid sexual intercourse, at the risk of being considered sinners.[42]

Women, as human beings, have the same rights as men, but the latter enjoy qualitative privileges as directors and protectors. Thus, women are excused from all outside duties like Friday prayers, jihad, and funerals, but they cannot travel, except in the company of a *mahram* [unmarriageable male], or leave home except for necessary activities and with the permission of the husband. They are allowed to choose a husband, but only after having obtained the approval of their fathers, grandfathers, brothers, or other responsible male relatives. Men, on the other hand, can travel freely and marry any Muslim, Jewish, or Christian woman, and may have sexual relations with their concubines and maids. Men are not to be tyrannical or abusive at home and should allow their wives to advance and grow within Islamic regulations and their feminine nature.[43]

No social order but Islam has allowed women proper economic rights. The West, asserts al-Mawdudi, tried to rectify this by allowing women total freedom to work, giving rise to serious social problems. Islam chose a middle road: women are given generous inheritance rights, in addition to dowries from their husbands, to dispose of at will or to invest, keeping all accruing proceeds. Furthermore, their husbands are obligated to provide all necessary financial support and security. Women are also protected by a set of civil rights whereby they are allowed to choose their husbands, unless they are socially inferior; they are permitted to abandon or divorce oppressive, cruel, or miserly husbands; they have absolute equality with men in civil and criminal laws; their husbands are directed to treat them fairly and well; and widows and divorcées are allowed to remarry at will, without the need of male permission or approval. Women are also urged to seek education, as are men, but in subjects that prepare them for marriage and home life.[44]

To conserve this social order, al-Mawdudi goes on, Islam has set down several protective measures:

1. Proper civic training to obey social directives. This is implemented through faith, which assures voluntary total obedience to God's teachings. Adherence to them promotes shyness and prohibits adultery and the seduction of exposed beauty, adornments, sound, voice, and smell.[45]

2. Prohibitive punishments to prevent all crimes against society, especially adultery, defined as illegal, extramarital sex, which inexorably leads to family and social breakdown: it is banned and severely punished by Islam. Likewise, slander, which promotes moral laxity, ruins reputations, breaks marital and family ties, and renders parenthood suspect, is banned and severely punished as well.[46]

3. Preventive measures to purify society from sexual anarchy: Islam forbids nudity and exhibitionism for both men and women. Men are to cover the area between navel and knees. Women, however, should cover all their bodies, except the hands and face, in the presence of all except husbands, from puberty until they are too old to attract or seduce, at which time they are exempted from such rituals, but only at home. Men are not to enter their homes unannounced, to avoid surprising their wives in improper dress or positions, and strangers are not to enter a house without permission. Men are forbidden to be alone with women other than their wives and should not touch them.

In mixing with men, Islam has dictated that women use the veil, not merely as a means of isolation as behind a curtain, but as symbolic of a number of protective measures and attitudes. Thus, men and women should avoid staring at or touching each other, except in the case of physicians in the course of physical examination or judges investigating problems or allegations, and in situations where a woman is being rescued from fire or drowning. Women are to cover the face as well, in the spirit of the Qur'an, although this is not explicitly specified in the text. The face may be covered by drawing part of the outer garment over it, by an actual veil, or some other means.[47]

Women, al-Mawdudi states, are not to exhibit adornments and jewelry, except to husbands and *mahram*. They are excused from attending prayers in mosques with men. If they do attend the mosque, they are limited to night prayers, without adornments and without raising their voices, and are to stand behind the men.[48] The hajj, on the other hand, is mandatory for all, but women may only perform it accompanied by their husbands or *mahram*, and should avoid mingling with men as much as possible. They may participate in Friday festivities and religious feasts, but only at night, and may not go to funerals or mix with men in schools, offices, factories, parks, and theaters. In wartime, they are allowed to assist in nursing the wounded and providing food and drink for the men.[49]

Modern man, according to al-Mawdudi, has been afflicted by "white jaundice"—Western civilization—a "disease" that interferes with objective thinking and analysis, leading to misinterpreting some Qur'anic passages or quoting them out of context to appear vacuous and ridiculous. Differences among societies, al-Mawdudi continues, stem from differences in their concept of humanity and the universe. Islam holds that the universe was created and controlled by God alone. Hence, humans can progress and prosper only by worshipping and obeying Him, according to the dictates of the Qur'an and the Prophet. Humans are responsible for their actions and accountable to God in the hereafter. Therefore, they should always strive to please Him to win eternal life. Islam tries to assist them to do this through a set of moral guidelines or a sociopolitical system designed to train them to differentiate between good and evil and to familiarize them with all facets of life.[50]

Islam believes all people to be of common origin, irrespective of color or race, any differences being generated by their way of thinking, moral values, or goals. Islam therefore creates a moral, intellectual society in which all mankind can unite in equality to prosper in righteousness and fear of God, built around the family unit, which provides the necessary offspring and training. To this end, sexual intercourse is a necessity; Islam disapproves of chastity and considers monasticism an ugly, unnatural phenomenon. It also urges all relatives by blood or marriage, as well as neighbors, to remain united and to cooperate for the collective good.[51]

Finally, al-Mawdudi claims that, based on sura 4:34, "Men are in charge of women," and al-Bukhari's hadith, "No group led by a woman can succeed," women have no place in government or state councils, and their only sphere of action is the home.[52]

What seems to be at stake for al-Mawdudi is not the role of women as such but the validity of the Islamic vision, where no differentiation between sacred and secular is permitted. The role of women as prescribed by the Qurʾan and Hadith is part of God's general plan for man's happiness in this world and the next, and can, therefore, neither be changed nor altered. The only permissible change is that which would remove all remaining vestiges of Western customs in an effort to purify society and bring it back to the path of God. Thus, at the heart of the debate is the limitation of a woman's role to that of wife and mother. This is not merely her role but her sole identity, for marriage in Islam is seen as a central institution around which society and civilization are built.

Al-Mawdudi advocated a bold reinterpretation of the Qurʾan, Sunna, and Hadith and was gratified not to have been educated at a *madrasah*, thus keeping his mind unfettered by traditional thought. He considered himself a *mujaddid*, "close in spirit to prophethood," characterized by a "clear mind, penetrating vision, unbiased straight thinking . . . clear of all extremes . . . [and with the] power to think independently of contemporary and centuries-old social and other prejudices . . . and an unusual competency to undertake *ijtihad* and the work of reconstruction."[53] *Ijtihad* is to be applied not only to ambiguous (*mutashabihat*) Qurʾanic verses but also to unambiguous commands (*muhkamat*) of God.[54] Al-Mawdudi even questions the ability of a Muslim to differentiate between the prophetic actions of the Prophet, which require obedience, and his fallible human actions. He draws upon examples to emphasize the derivative nature of the Prophet's authority and the "nonbinding character of his personal behavior." God alone, al-Mawdudi asserts, possesses absolute authority, thus freeing man from "bondage" to any other authority. The Prophet is, thus, to be obeyed only as the representative of God's authority and not by virtue of his human position. Hence, his followers are to obey his divine commands but are free to decide for themselves whether he is acting in his personal capacity or not, at any given time. Al-Mawdudi goes even further in describing any imitation of the Prophet's dress or personal habits as an "extreme innovation." When the Prophet acted in his capacity as a human being, he was indicating to Muslims the importance of free thought. He "taught them the true principles of democracy, and instructed them on how to exercise freedom of opinion, and taught them of their right to oppose any human, even a perfect one."[55] Such fallibility prepares the ground for al-Mawdudi to practice *ijtihad* and reinterpret the Qur'anic precepts and the Sunna of the Prophet. He maintains that "even the noble Companions were overcome by human weakness, one attacking another."[56] He even labeled Abu Hurayra a liar, quoted Aisha as having criticized Anas for transmitting traditions he was too young to remember, and quoted Hassan bin Ali accusing both Abu Hurayra and Ibn al-Zubayr of lying.[57]

Thus, we find that al-Mawdudi stretched rationalism and human independence and freedom to their limits. Yet, this is blatantly contradicted by his stance on women's nature, their role in society, and total obedience to their husbands. Not only does he not digress, even slightly, from traditional interpretations, but he goes on to draw extensively on Hadith and Sunna, which he had just denuded of all authenticity, to shackle women with ever heavier, tighter chains. Thus, although he admits that covering the face and hands is not stipulated in the Qur'an, he would require it of all Muslim women. Moreover, although he arrogates to himself the post of *mujaddid* and describes himself as superior to all others ("I recognize no king or ruler above me; nor do I bow before any government; nor do I view any law as binding on me . . . nor do I accept any tradition or custom")[58] and goes so far as to permit the interpretation of unambiguous (*muhkamat*) verses, he nevertheless refuses to interpret any verse or hadith in favor of women and continues to suppress them. Moreover, al-Mawdudi misinterprets or embellishes Qur'anic verses with passages beneficial to his arguments and ignores others that elevate women to an equal position with men. Thus, he claims that the veil, in all its manifestations (facial cover, segregation) is sanctioned by the Qur'an. But, despite the absence of any such directive in the Qur'an or in the behavior of the Prophet's wives, he insists on imposing these strictures on all "virtuous" Muslim women. The *hijab*, according to him, functions as a safeguard of the Islamic state, the implication being that greater rights for women and increased sociopolitical interaction of the sexes would lead to immorality and anarchy. Hence, the *hijab*, as such, contrary to his other logical and rational arguments, has no redeeming features for women but is simply a means of preventing the downfall of the state. Again, what is implicit here is the insidious role he attributes to women whose harmful activities should be regulated and controlled to ensure peace and tranquility. Yet, he argues elsewhere that women who are too old to be attractive do not have to observe the same strictures. However, he does not mention whether this argument extends to the young, but ugly and unattractive, nor does he confront the matter of older wives who may or may not continue to be attractive to their husbands, and, most importantly, he does not specify who is to determine the measure of these women's beauty and attractiveness, man or God.

In contradistinction to the Qur'an and Hadith, al-Mawdudi devises a number of arguments to keep women confined to their homes, such as their alleged mental deficiencies, which, if indeed present, should not only dictate their confinement but also render them completely unsuited for any function, even the "divinely" ordained care of home and children. Their feminine nature and innate delicacy and tenderness would also deter their ability to face the harsh, aggressive, external world. Furthermore, their confinement to the home to discharge their domestic duties, shielding them from any other experience, can only serve to incapacitate them even further by making them limited in ability and scope. Al-Mawdudi also allows women to leave the home only for "necessities," but don't men leave home for "necessities" as well? And do these "necessities" have limits, or do they differ with time, place, and circumstance? In the past, women participated in wars, alongside the Prophet, without being limited by their "nature." Shouldn't they now be recruited in the struggle against "imperialism and the West"? Women, at the time of the Prophet, participated in politics, paid homage to the Prophet, and helped create the first Islamic state. Has their nature changed so much since then to warrant their confinement and segregation? Further, the Prophet asked Muslims to learn their religion from his wife, Aisha, who was allowed to answer questions on religious matters and give binding opinions. Imam Muhammad bin Jarir al-Tabari appointed women judges in emulation of Aisha. Shouldn't women, now, after so much advancement and progress, be allowed the same rights and privileges in entering into politics and jurisprudence?

It would seem that al-Mawdudi misinterpreted the verse "Remain at home without adornment," which is really directed at the Prophet's wives, and not at all women. Were his interpretation correct, how could he account for all the privileges and activities of women at the time, which would have been impossible had they been segregated and confined to the home. Moreover, he seems oblivious to the preceding five verses which state that the Prophet's wives were unlike other women and were, therefore, destined to suffer more and be doubly rewarded for their good deeds and total submission to God and His Prophet. It was in this context that they were directed to stay at home.[59] He also seems oblivious to the context that necessitated the segregation of the Prophet's wives and the stipulation that strange men announce themselves before entering the Prophet's home. Moreover, al-Mawdudi imposes this last injunction even on husbands lest they surprise their wives improperly dressed. This is surprising, since not only are there no Qur'anic strictures in this matter, but the Qur'an actually specifies that women may show their "adornments" and bare themselves only to their husbands. Al-Mawdudi also misinterprets the verse "Men are in charge of women," which, in fact, allows men a higher position in the family sphere only as providers and not for any other superior quality they may have. Such a superior role of men within the family, and for a specific reason, does not cancel any other role women might wish to undertake.

Another digression from the Qur'an lies in forbidding women to attend public prayers in mosques. Again, nowhere in the Qur'an is there any restriction of women's daytime movements, including public prayers, nor is there any directive to blacken windowpanes to prevent women from looking out or being seen by outsiders. Moreover, even though the verse on polygamy is highly controversial and in need of a new interpretation, al-Mawdudi opted to adopt the interpretation unanimously agreed upon by the ulema (whom he professes to despise) over the past thirteen centuries. This is all the more curious in light of his comment on the ulema's interpretations: "I would like to state unequivocally that these are not 'interpretations,' but 'distortions of meaning,' which cannot be given place within the limits of the term 'interpretation' of the Qur'an ... To try, thus, to clothe a verse with a false meaning is sheer hypocrisy and dishonesty."[60]

Contradictions abound within al-Mawdudi's own arguments: In his discourse on modernity and modernization, he stated,

We aspire for Islamic renaissance on the basis of the Qur'an. To us, the Qur'anic spirit and Islamic tenets are immutable; but the application of this spirit in the realm of practical life must always vary with the change of conditions and increase of knowledge . . . Our way is quite different, both from the Muslim scholar of the recent past and modern Europeanized stock. On the one hand, we have to imbibe the Qurʾanic spirit exactly and identify our outlook with the Islamic tenets, while, on the other, we have to thoroughly assess developments in the field of knowledge and changes in the conditions of life that have been brought during the last eight hundred years; . . . and we have to arrange these ideas and laws of life on genuine Islamic lines, so that Islam should, once again, become a dynamic force; the leader of the world rather than its follower.[61]

Al-Mawdudi, thus, redefined the attributes of a Muslim when he emphasized the role of modernity in the realms of politics, sociology, and culture. He considered traditional Islam as confining Muslims to an anachronistic life in the modern world. Revivalism was to be the vehicle through which Muslims would adopt modern social thought and organization and assimilate modern ideas into the fabric of Islamic thought. Studying this liberal, motivational approach, one would logically assume that, since women constitute "half of society" and "rear the other half," and since they were created of "the same soul" as men, they should benefit from some of these liberal aspirations, at the very least. Instead, al-Mawdudi not only strayed from the "Qurʾanic spirit" in the matter of women's rights and status, but he went on to subdue women further, almost eliminating them altogether from the public scene.

His insistence on the Islamic dress code for women not only negated his modernistic outlook but left no room for interpreting relevant Qurʾanic verses. Thus, we are not clear on the nature of "adornments," since we remain unsure of the habits of Arab women at the time. What is clear is that they wore a long, free-flowing veil from head to foot, the underlying dress being slightly transparent, prompting the Prophet to ask one of his wives to draw her veil, which was a part of her traditional dress, around her bosom, and to cover her ornaments or "adornments." These could have been worn anywhere on the body, the bosom, navel, or belly, in addition to arms, legs, and feet. In short, the verse is not clear and simply addressed the traditional dress of the time. Moreover, it is interesting that al-Mawdudi, in addition to isolating women from the onslaught of modernity, seemed to forget that he once described the emulation of the Prophet's clothing and personal habits as an innovation (*bidʿah*). What is most surprising (or is it?) is that he rejected the ruling of the Family Law Commission that women be given the right to divorce, but allowed them to claim this right in the marriage contract. If this is proper, surely it cannot be contrary to Islamic regulations, and al-Mawdudi, here, could have proven himself the liberal he claimed to be by concurring with the commission. Instead, he went even further in rejecting the proposition of compulsory registration of divorce, an action that merely protects the rights of women without diminishing the authority of the husband. Also, despite his claims of modernity, he refused to set a minimum age of marriage for women. He even rejected a proposal to set clear criteria to determine whether the consent of a bride had been obtained (a Qur'anic injunction), and preferred to delay any investigation into this matter until *after* the wedding, at which time the bride might present actual proof of such lack of consent. In case the bride had not reached puberty yet, she would have to present her claim on the same day of reaching puberty or forfeit her right to object forever.[62] This fact in itself demonstrates the prejudice al-Mawdudi harbored against women and the obstacles he willfully placed in their path to keep them subordinated and isolated.

Moreover, al-Mawdudi not only liberated Muslims from tradition but also instructed them in their rights of freedom, equality, and independence in thought and interpretation, and he warned them against emulating anyone, even the Prophet, and to obey only God, the only sovereign. The acceptance of any other sovereign becomes a "sin against divine majesty equivalent to the worst offence known to Muslim vocabulary—idolatry or associating partners with God (*shirk*) in His exclusive prerogatives."[63] Yet, he enjoins women to obey their husbands and be submissive to them since they are symbolic of God's sovereignty on earth! He foregoes his "interpretive" clarification of Qur'anic verses to concur in the right of a husband to beat his wife albeit without inducing physical harm, and goes on to curse any woman who leaves her home without her husband's approval. And, when he enjoins husbands to beat their wives, he seems to have forgotten that he has described women as being delicate, tender, weak, merciful, and loving, and men as physically strong and aggressive. How, then, can he rationalize the abuse of such weak women by their much stronger husbands? Moreover, the weakness he attributes to women is difficult to reconcile with the hard labor of housework and the arduous agricultural work women perform in rural areas side by side with men.

Al-Mawdudi also incapacitates women emotionally, mentally, and intellectually, to the point of describing them as occasionally suicidal. He entrusts them with the care of children, their upbringing and education, and with providing a serene and tranquil home atmosphere for the benefit of their husbands. Al-Mawdudi does not seem to realize that the performance of such tasks requires qualities he has already stripped women of. He emphasizes the role of education in shaping the character of the people in a viable Islamic state, but prevents 50 percent of the population, the fraction responsible for the upbringing of future generations, from being properly educated.

He maintains that it is the natural right of every individual to secure his share of the produce of the earth, no one having the right to deprive another of this nor of establishing precedence or superiority over another. Nor does Islamic law set any limitations on any individual, class, or race, or deter them from utilizing all their talents and prowess to survive or enter into any endeavor or profession. "It is the equal right of all human beings to struggle and seek their portion out of the means of sustenance provided by God on earth, which was created by Him, and the opportunities of this struggle should be kept equally open to every one of them."[64] However, al-Mawdudi, in complete contradiction, relegates women to a totally confined existence, a virtual limbo, since, in his eyes, they do not seem to fit the mold of an "individual," "class," or "race" to be entitled to the privilege of equality in his Islamic economic system.

While al-Mawdudi vehemently advocated the seclusion of women on the basis of their physical weakness and mental incompetence, which precluded their holding public office or acting as heads of state, he went on to make a volte-face by supporting the candidacy of Fatimah al-Jinnah for presidency against Ayyub Khan in the elections of 1964–65, citing the adage that the end justifies the means. This would have been palatable had al-Mawdudi's stance been limited to a simple seclusion of women, but he had stripped them of all criteria that would have qualified them for any role other than household chores, let alone the presidency. The *fatwa* [legal opinion] employed was that prevalent conditions permitted the candidacy of a woman for the presidency. What is also worthy of attention here is the position adopted by Ayyub Khan, a professed liberal who had initiated the Family Law Commission. Supported by the ulema, he decried the candidacy of Fatimah al-Jinnah as being contrary to religious regulations! Once again, we find women's issues being used by politicians for their personal gains and motives.

Finally, we find that the revolution propagated by al-Mawdudi against traditionalism and Western culture represents a form of *ijtihad*. However, it is noted that *ijtihad* is permissible only to himself and those who share his own interpretation of the Qur'an, the Sunna, and Hadith. His brave struggle for modernization and reinterpretation of Islamic sources is wielded to support his right to such *ijtihad* and to realize his vision of an Islamic state, not for the proclaimed universal benefit of Muslims. Thus, while he professes to espouse and preach liberalism, he actually sets the pace for a new form of *taqlid* [tradition].

Chapter 4

✳

Sayyid Qutb

The 1967 Israeli defeat of the Arabs had a shattering impact on Egypt in particular. Soul-searching to explain such a humiliating defeat echoed throughout the country: the socialists attributed it to a lethargic bureaucracy, elitism, and social inequalities; technocrats related it to Israel's scientific and technological superiority; and religious leaders called it a defeat of the disbelievers. The socialists recommended an authentic policy of socialism, the technocrats pushed for modernization, and the religious leaders sought a fundamentalist return to Islam. To aid Egyptians in dealing with their new problems and reorganizing their lives, Islamist ideologues prescribed a total redefinition of national goals and prioritized them relative to family, community, and God. The most articulate and radical of these ideologues was Sayyid Qutb.[1]

Elie Kedourie describes Sayyid Qutb as "a talented and persuasive writer, endowed with a sharp analytical mind, which enabled him to establish clear and well-defined distinctions between the organizing ideas of Islam and those of Western civilization."[2] His full name is Sayyid Qutb Ibrahim Husayn Shadhili. He is Egypt's most renowned activist of the twentieth century, surpassing even Hasan al-Banna. He was a literary critic, a novelist, and a poet, in addition to being the foremost Egyptian Islamic thinker. He is to be compared with Pakistan's Abu al-ʾAʿla al-Mawdudi and Iran's Ayatollah Ruhollah Khomeini. He was born in 1906 in Musha, a village in the district of Asyut in Upper Egypt, hailing from a family of farmers in economic decline at the time, though still prestigious because of the father's educated status. He was frail as a child and was sent to the *kuttab* school of the village where he studied the Qurʾan and other traditional disciplines. By age ten, he had already memorized the Qurʾan to fulfill his mother's wish that he study at the al-Azhar University to become a religious scholar.[3]

A number of factors determined the path Qutb was to follow and modulated his intellect and writings. The first factor was his interest in the aesthetics of the Qur'an, which led him to an in-depth study of the sacred text. His book *al-Taswir al-fanni fi al-Qur'an* [Artistic imagery of the Qur'an], which was published in 1944–45, demonstrates his admiration of the Qur'anic style and documents his "conversion" to Islam. "My young and naïve imagination," declares Qutb, "magnified the images expressed by the Qur'an. Although it was a naïve imagery, it stirred me and regaled my sensitivities. I would always treasure these images, especially while in states of rapture and animation."[4] The second factor came about during his visit to the United States (1948–51) during which he obtained his master's degree in education and made his final commitment to Islam. Despite his admiration for the West and his desire to emulate its literature and educational system, he was shocked by the prevailing "materialism," "racism," and "pro-Zionist" sentiments, forging thereby the first phase of his alienation from Western culture and a return to his Islamic roots. He denounced what he called American decadence reminiscent of the last days of Rome. Qutb traced the origin of this decadence to the Renaissance, reaching its peak with the advent of such "pseudoscientists" as Darwin, who traced man's ancestors to the apes, and Freud, who taught that the essence of man is his sexuality.

The third factor was the devastating Arab defeat by the Israelis and the failure of Arab socialism and nationalism to absorb the loss. The fourth was embodied in the social and economic demise of the Egyptians and the recurrent failure of socialism, nationalism, and secularism to rectify matters. The fifth and most important factor, however, that tipped Qutb irrevocably into radicalism was his experience in Liman Tura Prison (1954–64) in the wake of his conviction for an attempt on Nasser's life. Thus, while his priorities had so far been to modernize Islam and present it as the panacea for all socioeconomic and political ills, his own torture, the savagery of the prison guards, and their inhumanity in neglecting the wounded to death prompted him to alter his priorities and radicalize his ideology. This was brought to a peak by an episode in 1957 that resulted in the death of more than twenty imprisoned Brothers and the injury of an even larger number, compounded by his feelings of isolation and alienation from a passive world complacent to the crimes committed against him and his Brothers.[5]

Sayyid Qutb was a prolific writer, publishing more than twenty-four books and several articles and poems. His work reflects a deep concern and emotional involvement in and commitment to the human condition and the problems of the Egyptians, in particular, at the political, social, economic, and religious levels. Moreover, it shows a gradual move from observer and interpreter of social ills to revolutionary radical who envisioned a new Islamic order. Thus, his work can be categorized into poetry and literature; Qur'anic aesthetics; philosophy of social justice; sociology of religion; Qur'anic exegesis; and Islam and the West. Some of his works have been translated into English, German, French, Turkish, Persian, and Urdu, among other languages.[6]

He began his writing career as a secular author and journalist. The first phase of his work was liberal and mostly literary, including poetry, stories, and articles, as well as literary criticism.[7] During this period, he was greatly influenced by such modernists as Taha Husayn, Abbas al-Aqqad, and Ahmad al-Zayyat. Reading the works of this period, one is impressed by the number of references to Western literary figures and by his individualism, liberalism, and romanticism. Like his contemporaries, he was greatly influenced by the West as a model to be emulated. He is purported to have later described himself during this period as a *mulhid* [atheist].[8]

The second phase of his published works is to be regarded as a "dialectical response" to secularism and Westernization and an emphasis on a more dynamic understanding of Islam, be it on the popular or intellectual levels. This Islamic phase was to reach its peak during his stay in prison with the publication of his "gospels of radicalism," namely *Fi zilal al-Qur'an* [In the shade of the Qur'an], *Ma'alim fi al-tariq* [Signposts on the road], *Hadha al-din* [This religion], and *al-Mustaqbal fi hadha al-din* [The future in this religion]. Thus, Gilles Kepel described *Signposts on the Road* as the "royal road to the ideology of the Islamist movement of the seventies."[9] Qutb could not resolve the resentment he had of those who were free outside the prison walls and did nothing to defend those whom he considered unjustly imprisoned and tortured. He perceived them as accomplices in these crimes and, therefore, declared them to be infidels, living in the age of ignorance *(al-jahiliyyah)*. While his book *al-'Adalah al-ijtima'iyyah* [Social justice] does not belong to this period, it has taken its place alongside those published in this period as a radical interpretation of Islam. In this last phase, Qutb rejects all forms of government that do not subscribe to his understanding of the Islamic order. Thus, reform is no longer enough, and a radical transformation with a totally new beginning is necessary for the establishment and extension of God's Islamic system. Only then can the

"Kingdom of God on earth" be realized and the Muslims recapture their past glory.[10]

His metamorphosis is best explained by Qutb himself, speaking to the Indian scholar Abu al-Hasan al-Nadawi, who visited him in February 1951.

> There is no doubt that I am a disciple of al-Aqqad, both in literature and in literary style. It is to him that I owe my ability to think clearly; he stopped me from imitating al-Manfaluti and al-Rafi'i. What has made me take this direction, however, which is more than mere literature or literary criticism or poetic symbols, is that I never ceased to seek information regarding the spirit and what it may contain. When I was young, I was enamored of reading about the virtuous ones and their noble deeds, this inclination is still growing within me as time goes on. Al-Aqqad is a man of pure intellect; he will only examine a problem through reason and intellect, so I proceeded to quench my thirst at other springs nearer the spirit. I then took the trouble to study the poetry of Orientals, such as Tagore. I used to believe, moreover, that someone like al-Aqqad, with his great wisdom and personality, would not submit to such necessities and confusions as the government and the authorities, but he reconciled himself to them. His advanced age may have been the reason: a man may, in old age, put up with things he could not bear as a young man.[11]

Leonard Binder maintains that "Qutb, throughout his intellectual life, was deeply influenced by an emotional rather than legalistic conception of the Islamic faith, and that he has contributed to the construction of a new fundamentalist orientation which has the potential to unleash great social energy in the form of a popular movement that is neither vulnerable to state control, nor subservient to traditional and parochial elite."[12] Upon reading Qutb's work, one is thus struck by the simplicity, clarity, and repetitiveness of his style, his honesty and commitment to his ideals, his passion and belief in scientific objectivity, and his fertile imagination.

Sayyid Qutb is now considered to be the most renowned Islamist of the second half of the twentieth century. He has imbued Hasan al-Banna's activism with an intellectual aura and given his message a clear, succinct philosophy and logic. His writings, in their simplicity and clarity, have appealed to both the traditionalist population and the Western-educated elite. His fame, however, may also be attributed to his theory of political violence, which has been adopted in toto by the younger Islamist generations, for example, al-Jihad al-Islami [Islamic Holy War], al-Takfir wal-Hijrah [Apostasy and Emigration], Tanzim al-Fanniyyah al-'Askariyyah [the Technical Military Academy Group], Jund Allah [the Soldiers of God], and al-Jama'ah al-Islamiyyah [the Islamic Association]. Other groups outside Egypt that followed suit are the Islamic Salvation Front of Algeria, the Tunisian Islamic Tendency Movement, Hamas in the West Bank and the Gaza Strip, and the Muslim Brotherhood in Syria, Sudan, and Jordan, among others. His intellectual followers include Mustafa al-Khudayri, Abd al-Majid al-Shadhly, and Muhammad Jawad Yasin. In fact, it has been suggested that Qutb's role in inspiring Islamic movements has even superceded that of Khomeini.[13] His name has been adopted by his followers, who came to be known as the Qutbists (al-Qutbiyyun). Assaf Husain, a contemporary fundamentalist, has called him "the ideologue of the *Ikhwan*"; Abbas Muhammad Abd Allah characterized him as "one of the greatest thinkers of Islamic contemporary thought"; Mahdi Fadlallah referred to him as "the most famous personality in the Muslim world in the second half of the twentieth century"; Muhammad Qutb regarded him as "the revolutionary of contemporary Islamic thought"; and Olivier Carré described him as *"le grand inspirateur de ce nouveau souffle."*[14] Kenneth Cragg, finally, says, "He was no crude *muqallid* [imitator], a pundit incapable of relating to modernity . . . he was a thinker who expressly rejected a West he had come to know." Cragg even compared him to the Prophet Muhammad in his "active political agitation and resistance" and the belief that if persuasion and preaching failed, the only recourse left would be violence.[15]

His trip to the United States played a central role in his departure from the literary and educational career he had pursued so far and his adoption of Islam as his religion and political order. He became disenchanted with the West and looked elsewhere for the sense of identity and moral purpose that he and others in the Arab Muslim world lacked. He was shocked by the sexual permissiveness of the West, the equality of men and women, separation of state and church, absolute freedom of expression, and the pursuit of worldly pleasures, and he became convinced that Islam was the only road available for a new vision and the recapture of lost values.[16]

Sayyid Qutb came to personify opposition to the West and those Muslim leaders who were leading Muslims astray. He accused such Muslims and their followers of living in a state of *jahiliyyah* [ignorance of revelation's truth]. Qutb drew extensively on the writings of such critics of Western culture as Arnold Toynbee and Alexis Carrel, author of *Man the*

Unknown (New York, 1939), to validate his attack against Western individualism and "moral depravity." His writings portray unyielding commitment to the Qur'an and Sunna. If the Qur'an is an eternal message, which it is, then it should be implemented by all. Islam to Qutb became a *'aqidah* [creed] and living doctrine that could transform an inert and uncommitted human being into one who is dynamic and goal oriented. Thus, he says, "Only religious belief *('aqidah)* can enable man to communicate with the all-powerful God, and that belief endows the feeble individual with such strength and support that even the forces of wealth and oppression are unable to shake him."[17] The inviolate truths that Qutb was committed to were the unity of God *(tawhid)*, the finality of the Qur'an, which is self-existent, the supremacy of Muhammad, Islam as a perfected religion with a divine law that sets the norms for human society, the obligations of the Five Pillars and their fulfillment, and the establishment of the Islamic state. Islam is thus a comprehensive system that details a particular way of life that, if followed meticulously, will be the panacea for the ills of the Muslim world and the human condition.

Qutb characterizes the universal Islamic concept by:

1. The oneness of God *(tawhid)*, which is simultaneously the essential comprehensive characteristic of the Islamic doctrine and one of its components. *Tawhid* means "There is no ruler save God, no legislator, no organizer of human life and of human relationships to the world, to living things or human beings save God. From Him alone is received all guidance and legislation, all systems of life, norms governing relationships and the measure of values."[18]

2. Divinity *(uluhiyyah)*, which is eternal, though its understanding is subject to the conditions of the interpreter and his interpretive skills. Thus, while the text is solid, human learning and knowledge are ever changing and the text can, therefore, be read, interpreted, and understood differently by different generations and individuals. The text cannot be contradicted by a past or contemporary discourse, only by other textual evidence. This is due to the permanence of the Scripture and the imperfection of human thought, its lack of permanence, its incapacity of transcendence, and its victimization by paganism. Furthermore, the human mind is highly influenced by its environment and easily led by emotions, needs, and desires.[19]

3. Constancy *(thabat)*, which refers to the Qur'an and its divine truths. Thus, human interrelations, their position in the universe, their destiny, and their relationship with the universe and with God are con-

stant and unchanging, providing them with stability and happiness. Qutb argues that, since man's condition is fixed, revelation, which is fixed inasmuch as it deals with this condition, replaces reason.[20]

4. Comprehensiveness (shumuliyyah). According to Qutb, religion should dominate all aspects of life, since it lends meaning to human life through its discourse on the human and the divine, the social and the individual, the public and the private. Due to man's temporal and spatial finitude and his limitations in knowledge, experience, and understanding, together with his natural weakness, inclinations, lusts, and desires, he can never attain God's comprehensive vision or replace it.[21]

5. Balance/equilibrium (al-tawazun), which prevents the formation of rash and exaggerated behavior by balancing the known with the unknown and the revealed, which humans can comprehend, with the hidden, which man has to accept on faith.[22]

6. Positiveness (al-'iyjabiyyah), which pertains to man's interactions with God, the universe, and life in general, for Islam necessitates activism as part of man's affirmation of his faith.[23]

7. Realism (waqi'iyyah), which requires Muslims to deal with the world pragmatically and not as a mere abstraction, thereby making the practice of Islam feasible and within human reach. Yet, this view is simultaneously idealistic, since it aims at establishing the most perfect order within the reach of man. Qutb affirms that man is perceived in Islam as someone "who eats, marries, procreates, loves, hates, hopes, and fears." Islam keeps in mind his "nature, capacities, virtues, evils, strengths, and weaknesses." Islam nowhere portrays man as an inferior being or underestimates his role on earth, just as it does not portray him as an angel or elevate him to the rank of divinity.[24] The Islamic system, according to Qutb, "is not restricted solely to a replica of the first Islamic society, but is every social form governed by the total Islamic view of life . . . The Islamic system has room for scores of models which are compatible with the natural growth of a society and the new needs of the contemporary age, as long as the total Islamic idea dominates these models in its expansive external perimeter."[25] Islam is not only the sustenance of man; it is the ultimate arbiter that provides a framework for all aspects of life and a measure by which people are to be judged. "The mission of Islam is always to propel life to renewal, development, and progress, and to press human potentialities to build, to go forth, and to elevate."[26]

God, according to Qutb, has created a unified universe requiring both material and spiritual care. Thus, contrary to Christianity, Islam commands a "unity of life," where Divine Law needs to be implemented by a state. The state is necessary to facilitate the performance of Muslims and to "protect" Islam. Therefore, "Where Islam is dispossessed of power, the greater part of its teachings remains as mere ink on paper."[27] However, to make the Islamic alternative possible, a clear break from the existing social order is imperative. Thus, the profession of faith, according to him, and the belief in the Five Pillars are no longer enough as a mark of Islamism. The believing Muslim must, in addition, reject the new *jahiliyyah* represented by all man-made laws, governments, and systems and adopt the Shari'ah as the common denominator of all Muslims.[28] Qutb thus introduces a new concept of God's sovereignty *(hakimiyyah)* in a rejectionist reaction to the prevalent secular state. Though Qutb borrowed the term of *hakimiyyah* from al-Mawdudi, he imbued it with a Qutbian flare in his totalitarian ideology in response to Nasser's secular state. The means of achieving this utopia lies in emulating the Kharijite example of the first century of Islam in migrating, in the footsteps of the Prophet, and resorting to revolutionary warfare to quench the prevalent society of ignorance.[29] *Hakimiyyah* must be adopted to "revolt fully against human rulership in all its shapes and forms . . . destroy the Kingdom of man to establish the Kingdom of God on earth . . . and cancel human laws to establish the supremacy of Divine Law alone." [30]

The implementation of such a vision necessitates the formation of a vanguard group *(tali'ah)*, whose raison d'être would be jihad and which acts as the mainspring of the revolution, together with its principles of *tawhid* and justice, and the ultimate vehicle for the assumption of power. Qutb maintained,

> If this vanguard is to find its way, it needs signposts to point toward the commencement of its long road, to tell it what role it will have to play to attain its goal, to inform it of its real function . . . These signposts will, likewise, tell it what position must be taken towards the *jahiliyyah* that reigns over the earth. How should the vanguard define itself relative to that of *jahiliyyah*? When should it mix with people and when should it separate from them? How and in what terms should it speak the language of Islam to them? . . . It is for this long-awaited vanguard that I have written *Signposts.*[31]

Teaching and preaching will have to be coupled with jihad in order to establish the Kingdom of God on earth. Revolution to Qutb acquires new

meanings: in addition to the methods to be employed in crushing the enemies of Islam, revolution comes to acquire new theological, metaphysical,
and political connotations. Islam came to be seen as an upheaval against the
status quo of the state of ignorance *(jahiliyyah)* pervading society at all
levels, not as an act of vengeance but to implement social justice and harmony. In so doing, Islam becomes a matter of moral responsibility based
on the principles of *tawhid* and *wahdah* [unity].[32]

The "spirit of Islam," according to Qutb, is that "entertained by those
who follow up the nature of this religion as well as its history and is felt
behind its legislations and directions. . . . This spirit is difficult to express
in a few words, but is revealed in the direction and goal [of Islam], in
events, incidents, and in behavior and rituals." It is what "draws the high
horizon which Islam asks its believers to look up to and try to attain, not
only by performing the duties and obligations, but also by personally
volunteering [to perform] what is more than duties and obligations."[33]
Qutb attributed major events of the past to this spirit, which helped transform Islam from an abstraction into actuality through such individuals
as Muhammad and Ibn Hanbal. Thus, the study of Islamic history is not
confined to events but includes the understanding of the dialectic between the "spirit of Islam" and the heroes of Islam, who had received this
"universal emanation." "Only those individuals, who really have understood and accepted Islam, have been able to perform their duties, obligations, and much more as a sign of comprehending Islam in its fullest meaning."[34] "The nature of the Islamic method," asserts Qutb, "is the insistence
on the establishing of the Kingdom of God on earth and the bringing of
all humanity from the worship of created things to the worship of God
alone."[35]

Qutb insisted that Islam was not embodied in its history. History is
only a manifestation and cannot be viewed as a normative expression of
right and wrong. Indeed, Muslims could create a contemporary history
based on their immediate needs and current conditions or issues. Thus,
Qutb veers away from traditional religious scholars who sanctified history
and relied upon the interpretations of earlier scholars like Abu Hanifa, al-
Shafi'i, Ibn Hanbal, and Ibn Malik as their guides in jurisprudence, and
followed al-Ghazali, al-Ash'ari, and al-Baqillani in matters of theology.
Qutb rejects all old or traditional historically oriented interpretations,
which might have been suitable at an earlier time and place but are of no
intrinsic value at present. In fact, their only significance would be to im-
press upon the Muslims the flexibility of Islam and the existence of multiple interpretations, whose importance relies mainly on their relevance to

the present. Qutb thus transforms history into an instrument of change and renewal.

The Islamic state is to be founded on the Qur'an as its constitution; on *shura* [consultation] as the method of governing; and on a ruler who is bound by the teachings of Islam and the will of the people. Such a state would have a just and efficient government, consistent with the traditions of society, and would, therefore, be able to ensure its people's welfare.[36] The freedom of the individual in such a state, Qutb maintains, should be modulated to assure him social happiness and contentment. Any deviation is to be ascribed to the custodians of the law and not Islam. Social justice, Qutb argues, cannot always be at the expense of the individual, whose desires and aspirations should be ensured as a reward for his diligence and efficiency.

Social justice, Qutb maintains, has three pillars: the individual's absolute freedom from burdens and limitations; equality of all, males and females, provided physical differences, social customs, and varying responsibilities permit; and mutual responsibility, which dictates that an individual's freedom not encroach on that of others for the good of the community. Social justice in Islam is achieved by rewarding certain actions and prohibiting others and by implementing Divine Law. This should result in a harmonious and balanced existence of individuals as a cohesive group and a mutual responsibility between the group and the individual. The authority invested in man by God should be reflected in his obedience to Divine Law and the practice of social, economic, and political justice. Justice is administered when the conscience is liberated from fear, equality pervades society, and mutual social responsibility is practiced. Qutb asks the individual to put his trust in God and to fear nothing in this world, yet he realizes that the individual, in addition to his spiritual life, requires the physical means of survival, such as shelter and food, ensured only through the provision of solid material foundations and the prevention of the exploitation of the majority by minority groups. Qutb realizes, however, the difficulty of attaining such social justice amid capitalists, journalists, "dark skinned Britishers," politicians, and a number of unfaithful ulema, who constitute the internal and foreign enemies, comprising imperialists, crusaders, and missionaries.[37]

He goes on to denounce several so-called scientists who sought to demean men and women. Thus, Darwin claimed animal origins for mankind, while Freud stressed its filthy sexual nature and Marx its insignificance compared to economic and material factors. They would have contributed to the destruction of all moral values, even civilization itself, had their authors and their concepts not failed.[38]

While Islam, Qutb continues, acknowledges the equality of all humankind and, therefore, the importance of justice in society, it nonetheless admits differences between individuals based on capability, piety, strength, and natural endowment. Hence, when Islam speaks of equality, it is not equality of wealth, which depends largely on the individual's natural endowments, but the provision of equal opportunity for all. The right of private property reconciles efforts and reward in keeping with human nature and community needs and generates self-respect, autonomy, dignity, and fortification of personality "so that they are suited to be trustworthy agents for this religion standing against wrongdoing, calling the ruler to account, and admonishing him without the fear of having their livelihood cut off if it is in his hands."[39] Humans, Qutb argues, are created with a passion for good things in life and a desire to bequeath to their posterity the fruits of their labor in the form of "wealth." If they are not permitted to do this, they will feel exploited and be robbed of their incentive to work and produce for the benefit of society. Moreover, to establish real equality, soul and conscience should be cleansed of inequality and injustice before these can be eliminated from established social and political institutions.[40]

The human factor in the deterioration of society into *jahiliyyah*, Qutb argues, like al-Mawdudi before him, is gender relations. This takes place when free sexual relations and the resultant illegitimate children become the foundations of society; when passion and violence rule gender relations instead of duty and specific gender roles within the family; when woman's only role becomes that of seduction and ornamentation; and when she leaves her domestic duties for outside employment and spends her energies on material production rather than the "manufacture of humanity." However, a society that regulates its gender relations will flourish, since the appropriate roles of both sexes are equally important. Thus, any society that attempts to dispense with women's services will inevitably engineer its own demise. Islam has set the framework of the ideal gender relationship and ordained for each of the sexes a special role to be fulfilled before any other task is attempted, to enhance and enrich the quality of life, which supercedes material possessions, and its goals transcend mere food and drink.

The main role of a woman is the guardianship of morality and the upbringing of children. Her role in the family is greatly emphasized by Qutb, who sees the relationship between man and woman as pure, noble, and elevated. God uses it to extend life and improve it and to develop civilization. The family is viewed as the "nursery of the future," with women as its guardians. Islam has, thus, revolutionized the condition of women far beyond anything Western civilization has ever achieved and given them all the rights they could ever need. The virtuous woman, therefore, has nothing to fear from Islam, for she has the right to own property, earn her livelihood, marry whom she chooses, and move about freely, as long as she is properly and decently dressed.[41] Islam has also granted women the right to education. Thus, the Qur'an states, "The seeking of knowledge is an obligation for every Muslim, man and woman" (96:1-4). Furthermore, the Qur'an obliges every Muslim to pay *zakat* [alms]. "Surely those, the men and the women, who make free will offerings and have lent to God a good loan, it shall be multiplied for them" (57:18).

In Islam, Qutb maintains, all humans are absolutely equal, having arisen from the same source. Thus, sura 7:189 says, "It is He who created you out of one living soul, and made of it its spouse, that it might rest in her." Men and women are equal in the religious and spiritual spheres, as well as in economic and property matters, but they differ in matters relating to experience and responsibility. Here, Islam relies on the natural attributes and instincts that distinguish men from women in determining each gender's duties and privileges, to avoid wasteful competition.[42] Attempts to highlight Islamic male superiority based on sura 4:34 represent a lack of understanding of Islamic jurisprudence. Thus, the fact that men are stipulated to be responsible for women is a natural corollary of men being in the midst of the social firmament, which provides for the necessary physical experience and mental preparation for leadership. This is further abetted by men's divinely assigned duty of shouldering the burden of financial support for the home. All this qualifies them to rule and direct. Women's nature, on the other hand, restricts them to the home and the care of children, which in itself is a preparation for the future and occupies most of their time, especially during pregnancy and nursing. Consequently, women are best isolated from society and its affairs. Moreover, these responsibilities stimulate sentimental and emotional attributes to the detriment of reason and planning. Thus, to require of women the role of guardianship assigned to men would be an act of "oppression," since they are not prepared for it. Whenever natural law is violated, human life is threatened and chaos could ensue. Hence, children raised under the guardianship of their mothers, due to the father's weakness or absence, are usually perverted in one form or another.[43]

Furthermore, the matter of two female witnesses being necessary in sura 2:282, where one male suffices, Qutb explains, is due to the female's natural emotional handicap that renders her more volatile and labile, qualities necessary to meet the needs of children. This is in contrast to men's stability and objectivity, qualities needed for their role. Thus, while testifying in court, if she is emotionally influenced, the other witness would correct and stabilize her. Also, since she is confined to the home, she is not familiar with business jargon and might be confused if called on to testify. The issue, then, has nothing to do with the superiority of men over women or lack of equality but is a matter of practicality.[44] As for the fact that men inherit double the share of women, Qutb believes it to be fair, since it is men who are charged with the responsibility of financial support of women and children, while women's wealth remains intact. Thus, a married woman's livelihood is ensured by her husband, while widows are cared for by their inheritance and single women by their male relatives.[45]

Divine wisdom has assigned biologically based functions within the family and society at large. While women are completely protected and cared for by men, they are exempt from jihad, a duty required of men alone, since women's physical constitution allows them to procreate and prepare males for both jihad and life. Qutb points out that the Qur'an does not specify the exact role women are to play during the jihad, for they are neither commanded nor forbidden to perform this religious duty; and although there were women warriors in Islam, they were the exception, and as such, it is concluded that God did not prescribe jihad for them. Furthermore, wars decimate men but spare women, who are then needed more than ever to bear more males to fill the void, especially since fewer men are needed for impregnation—one man for every four women, whereas a thousand men cannot make one woman conceive more than she would from a single man.[46]

Women, argues Qutb, supercede men in representing half of humanity, being the source of the human race and the keepers of the home, the nest of childhood. Moreover, in the conception process, while both mother and father contribute equally in forming the nucleus of the ovum, the mother goes on to contribute the cytoplasm surrounding the nucleus and, as such, plays a much more extensive role in the formation of the embryo. The reproductive role of men is brief, while that of women extends to nine months, during which the embryo feeds on materials derived from the mother's blood through the placenta. This is a crucial function of women, Qutb claims, for women who do bear children attain full growth and potential after one or two pregnancies, while those who bear no children are not as fully balanced or neurologically stable.[47] To support his stance, Qutb quotes the French surgeon Alexis Carrel (1873–1944), biologist and Nobel laureate, who states,

> The differences between men and women do not stem from the physical differences in their genitalia, but from more basic aspects: the ovarian hormones, which differentiate all women's cells and tissues from the males', as well as their physical make-up, and most importantly their central nervous system. These are naturally subject to variation and change, and have to be nurtured to maintain these differences and not emulate males, for women's role in the building of civilization is more important than that of men. As such, women should not sway from their natural functions.[48]

Islam, maintains Qutb, gave women more rights fourteen centuries ago than France does today (1960). Thus, a woman's name and civil identity are safeguarded by allowing her to retain her maiden name upon marriage. She also has the right to contract, enter into business ventures, make a will, own property, and amass wealth. In the West, women are obliged to work because men stopped supporting them, resulting in their being cheapened, demeaned, and exploited, without receiving pay equal to that of men. They then fought for the right to vote in order to be elected to Parliament and have a decisive voice in shaping their future, but failed. Thus, France, Qutb goes on, does not allow women to dispense with their wealth at will without the consent of their next of kin, while Islam does. However, it does permit prostitution, while Islam does not. Further, when women are preferentially employed in certain venues, such as stores, embassies, and news media, it is solely to exploit their femininity and sexuality for financial gain.[49] In Communism, Qutb argues, men and women are equal in work opportunities. This, however, is only materialistic equality, freeing men from the responsibility of supporting women, thereby freeing both for sin and immorality.[50] The so-called women's liberation in the West is false and has resulted in social breakdown, destruction of family values, and preponderance of immorality and sexual anarchy.[51]

Qutb emphasizes the important role of family in society and, therefore, in the Islamic system he envisions. In contradistinction to traditional Islam, which regards the marriage contract as being like any other civil contract, he conceives of marriage as a holy bond of pure love between a man and a woman entered into voluntarily by both parties. However, each of the two partners must adhere to their biologically determined roles and discharge their related duties. To emphasize the important role of the family in society, Qutb enumerates the numerous verses dealing with the subject in the Qur'an, attesting to the pivotal role of the family in the Islamic social system. The Islamic system itself, argues Qutb, is an extended family system set up in such a way as to accommodate man's instincts, needs, and requirements. It is a part of the divine order where all living creatures and organisms are created in couples. Thus, the exact nature of society can be determined by an examination of the family structure, based on a division of labor, controlled sexual relations, and the discipline and education of children. Hence, all other social institutions will fail or succeed in their functions to the extent that they adhere to the rules and regulations governing the family unit.[52]

Qutb, like al-Mawdudi, extols the virtues of marriage and calls on all Muslims to marry, preferably within their faith, since marriage can exist harmoniously only if the partners share common beliefs, and a Christian or a Jewish wife would imprint her home with her own character and bring up the children far removed from their religion. Keeping in mind the important role a wife and mother play in a family, the new vanguard of Muslims must pay grave attention to the upbringing of the virtuous Muslim female, which will ensure, in turn, a speedy construction of the Islamic community.[53]

Also, like al-Mawdudi, Qutb argues that Islam stipulates that no woman may be married against her will, that marriage rites are conducted publicly in front of witnesses, and that marriage should be permanent, to ensure a stable family. Islam has further legislated family relations and dictates the duties and privileges of both partners. God assigned women the task of bearing children, nursing, and caring for them. This is a major task that women perform without prior training or preparation, and it occupies all their time. Women have also been endowed with tenderness, love, and speedy responsiveness to cope with any and all needs of their children instinctively, without hesitation, in the face of all obstacles and at any cost. Accordingly, God decreed that men protect and provide for them, to allow them to fulfill this sacred task, which would be impossible if they had to work and fend for themselves.[54]

In contradistinction, God endowed men with physical strength, firmness, less reactivity, but more thoughtfulness and planning, the traits of the hunter-warrior needed to protect and feed the family. This renders them more fit for leadership, hence, they are assigned as head of the family and their women. Women actually demand such leadership to safeguard their happiness and contentment. It is well known that, whenever the husband is weak and the wife dominates, their children suffer and develop delinquencies, breakdowns, and aberrations. Further, whenever these natural and divine considerations have been ignored, upheavals and calamities have befallen mankind.[55]

A virtuous, faithful wife, Qutb argues, is wholeheartedly obedient, since marital duties are dictated by God. Intransigence of the wife is not tolerated by Islam, since it rocks the foundations of the family. It is, therefore, punishable in escalating steps: she is initially warned and admonished; followed by sexual abstinence of the husband, which deprives the wife of her most effective influence over her husband, but should not exceed four months; and, finally, by a punitive beating designed not to harm but to bring the wife to her senses, especially in that women are impressed and satisfied by a demonstration of male prowess. If all this is unsuccessful, family mediation is sought, to be followed by divorce as a last resort.[56] On the other hand, if a wife is neglected by a husband who does not wish to divorce her, she may entice and mollify him by giving up part or all of her dowry or other material belongings, to "buy" her freedom.[57]

Islam, maintains Qutb, like Mawdudi before him, recognizes men's natural instincts and legislates their release, especially since the desire for sex and children is a very powerful instinct. However, it should be properly controlled. Sex plays a pivotal role in the home, which is a building block of society, but its excess impedes mental acuity. Therefore, to reach its full potential, the mind requires active sex glands with some measure of control of the sex urge. Sex, however, is not merely a vehicle for pleasure but has transcendental aims dictated by God and, as such, represents a form of worship through marriage and is to be limited to the marital bed. As such, Islam dictates marriage as a duty. Furthermore, to discourage temptation, seduction, and extramarital sex, men and women are instructed not to stare at each other or expose their private parts. Women should not display their ornaments, except on properly exposed areas—face and hands—and should cover their heads, necks, and bosoms to avoid exciting men. They should also refrain from body movements suggestive of hidden ornaments. Older women, no longer interested in or physically able to have sex, are exempt from these conditions, since they can no longer excite men.[58]

In agreement with Mawdudi, Qutb argues that men are usually oversexed, which may lead to sexual anarchy with deleterious effects on marriage and family. This must be satisfied but properly controlled. Polygamy, here, becomes a safety valve, especially in cases where the wife is sterile, chronically ill, or frigid. It is also useful and necessary in situations where a surfeit of women exists, as in wars that decimate men, to provide them with homes and support. Men may marry up to four women at a time, preferably Muslim, and if not possible, women of the Book. In this manner, their sexual urge is satisfied, and, in the process, a solid family status is ensured as a cornerstone of a pure Islamic society.[59] Here, Qutb continues, again in agreement with Mawdudi, God stipulates that all wives be treated equally and justly. This stipulation, however, applies to material and sexual aspects, since emotional justice and equality is humanly impossible. However, any emotional favoritism should be masked. If justice is not possible, then men should limit themselves to one wife.[60]

Qutb asserts that divorce is the abomination of permissible acts in the family unit and is to be used only as a last resort. However, it is the safety valve of marriage if love ceases and all attempts at mediating differences fail, since continued cohabitation under these circumstances will reflect badly on the whole family, especially the children.[61] Upon divorce, Qutb goes on, there is a three-month waiting period (*'iddah*) to ensure non-pregnancy or to establish paternity. It also serves as a cooling-off period that may save the marriage. The wife remains in her marital home for the duration of the *'iddah* and is then free to leave if the husband does not recant. If pregnant, however, she remains at home until she delivers, and the husband will pay for the child's nursing and care. If the wife is to remarry the same husband after an irrevocable divorce (divorced three times), she has to marry another and get divorced or be widowed before she may return to her first husband.[62]

If divorce takes place before consummation of the marriage, Qutb explains, the wife will retain half her dower (*mahr*), and if she has none, she should be properly compensated. Under such circumstances, the *'iddah* becomes unnecessary.[63] Divorce, however, cannot take place during the wife's menstruation. The husband has to wait until it is over, then divorce his wife without having sexual contact with her.[64] Upon divorce, the husband cannot claim any expenses incurred during the marriage, unless the wife decides to "buy" her divorce. The husband is to treat his divorcée well and kindly, since she has become his sister.[65] A divorced woman, Qutb maintains, has a divine duty toward her children to nurse and care for them for two years, unless both parents agree to forego this for the good of the children. The husband then will continue to provide for his wife during this period.[66] A widow undergoes a waiting period as well, but for a period of four months and ten days before she remarries, if she is not pregnant. If she is pregnant, she cannot remarry until after delivery. If she so desires, she may remain in her marital home and be cared for for one year, provided she neither sees other men nor remarries.[67]

Islam, Qutb maintains, strives for a pure society and, therefore, bans adultery and sodomy and punishes them severely: adulterous men and women are flogged and stoned. The Qur'an stipulates that unwed adulterers receive one hundred lashes, and the Sunna dictates stoning for married ones, their punishment being more severe because they are experienced in correct sexual behavior. Lashing may be followed by stoning or banishment, the severity of the sentence being at the discretion of the judge.[68] However, due to the severity of the punishment, the crime has to be attested to by four male witnesses before any conviction is determined.[69] If the accusation proves to be false, the accuser receives eighty lashes and is pronounced corrupt, not to be trusted or believed until fully repentant. If the accuser is the husband, no witnesses are needed, since no one can possibly accuse his wife falsely; he merely swears four times that he is truthful and, on the fifth time, calls on God's wrath if he is lying. The punishment would be for the wife to return her *mahr*, be divorced, and then stoned to death. However, if the accused wife swears four times that her husband is lying and on the fifth time calls for God's wrath if she is not truthful, she is pronounced innocent and her husband is declared a liar. If she is pregnant, the child would be named after her and not after the husband.[70] Finally, the faithful may not have sexual relations with adulterers until they have repented; homosexuals are cursed, berated, and beaten with shoes but are to be forgiven upon repentance. This punishment was later changed to death of both parties to purify society.[71]

Reading Qutb's works, one is struck by his idealism, commitment, piety, passion, romanticism, and humaneness. His early novels reflect his romanticism and his sensitivity to the condition of Egyptians—men and women—and social justice. In his novel *Tifl min al-qaryah* [A child from the village] (1946), he reveals himself as compassionate and sensitive to the economic ills and social conditions of his village. He views women with compassion; he is sensitive to their plight and confinement in the home while their husbands have the freedom to enjoy natural beauty and work productively—no matter how limited that productivity is—in the hope of transcending their human condition. Women, on the other hand, are not only confined to the home and, therefore, incapable of such transcendence, they are forbidden to wear colorful clothes and adorn themselves. Yet, in the second phase of his life, we find Qutb confining women to the home and forbidding them outside employment because it would expose them to licentiousness and sexual freedom and lead to the disruption of the family unit and the ultimate destruction of society. In fact, he describes working women as the third sex. He forbids them to adorn themselves and requires them to wear the veil. In his novel *Ashwak* [Thorns] (1947), he describes marriage as a permanent bond between two partners based on love and trust. Yet, a little later, we encounter a different Qutb, someone who still regards marriage as more noble than a mere civil contract but imposes the strictest constraints on the female partner and subordinates her to the absolute authority of her husband. The principles of love and trust that were to constitute marriage were replaced by duty and obedience. At this point, one wonders why he remained single all his life—whether it was from a preference for celibacy, or disillusionment with love and women—when he viewed marriage as a religious obligation and enjoined all Muslims, males and females, to marry.

While, later on in life, Qutb describes women as emotional, temperamental, and spontaneous, in *Tifl min al-qaryah* he describes an emotional scene with the father, who had just bade farewell to his son, in which the father breaks down in tears while his wife, the boy's mother, controlled and tranquil, calms him down and reassures him of better days to come. It is only after she enters her room and is alone that she bursts into tears. "And he burst out crying like a baby! While the brave mother forgets her grief and consoles him! After which she retires to burst out crying." What is interesting about this passage is the tense of the verbs used. Thus, while the verb "burst," in relation to the father, is used in the perfect tense as an accomplished act of the past describing one particular event, the other verbs, in reference to the mother *(tanfagir, takhlu, tu'azzi, tansa)* are all in the present, signifying a continuous and permanent state of affairs describing the personality of the mother rather than the outcome of one event.[72]

While Qutb is categorical about Divine Law and the divine right of legislation, he admits the flexibility of the general principles therein and their comprehensive ability to meet all the needs and conditions of life. He therefore advocates codification of legal articles from these general principles in the light of temporal and spatial changes in everyday life. Thus, regulations and procedures are always subject to change and development to meet the needs of both people and government. Qutb distinguishes between Divine Law, the Qur'an, and the Sunna, which are permanent and immutable, and jurisprudence, which is the human understanding of the Divine Law. Since the individual's knowledge and understanding are finite and God's Law is infinite, the individual is bound to err in interpretation. This, in addition to historical changes and limitations, makes total reliance on jurisprudence unwise and subject to error. Hence, since human material and social needs are always in flux, contemporary jurisprudence should not rely on tradition. The establishment and development of new Muslim societies should not be encumbered by the past. Thus, Qutb maintains that, while the divine concept itself is perfect, human understanding is subject to fluctuation, incapable of transcendence, and highly impressionable, modulated by its environment, emotions, and desires. Human knowledge then is composed of mere allusions *('iyha'at)* to the divine truths, rather than the truths themselves. Therefore, a periodic *ijtihad* in jurisprudence is necessitated by new circumstances, needs, and challenges facing Muslims in the modern world: "The attribution of sacredness to the old stands always in the path of every renaissance."[73]

Qutb, like al-Banna before him, proposes a new, comprehensive reading of Islam, based on the individual's interpretation of the text without any authoritative human guide, albeit after having mastered the disciplines of linguistics and grammar among others. Thus, he confirms the notion that Islam is eternally valid, its principles capable of accommodating diverse conditions and changes.[74] With this view of tradition and jurisprudence in mind, coupled with his belief in the finiteness of man, it is amazing that, although he revolutionized Islamic political theory and called for liberation, freedom, and equality, Qutb, just like Mawdudi, keeps women chained to their past. And, despite clinging to Islam as a liberating force, he keeps women languishing in their chains and seclusion.

Social justice, according to Qutb, is based on three Islamic principles: absolute freedom from all limitations, such as the *zakat* that eases economic need of the poor while not overtaxing the affluent; absolute equality between Muslims, including gender equality; and mutual responsibility, which may limit one's freedom within the family and the community. Sexual equality, however, is qualified by Qutb to the extent required by physical difference, social customs, and family responsibilities, such as breast-feeding for women and family income for men. Qutb writes, "As for the relationship between both sexes, woman has been guaranteed complete equality with man . . . There is no superiority, except in some incidental matters, which are associated with natural aptitude, training, or responsibility, wherein the privileges of both sexes are not affected. But, whenever the natural aptitude, training, and the responsibilities are equal, the two sexes are equal; whenever they differ in any of these respects, the treatment will differ accordingly."[75] Qutb here seems oblivious to the fact that these exceptions may keep women in the same position they have been in for centuries. In addition, he does not specify who is to determine these "differences" or "incidental matters," which seem to be responsible for the perpetuation of gender inequality, keeping in mind that they are nowhere to be found in the Qur'an itself. He seems confident, though, that justice would prevail if the Qur'anic exhortations to enjoin good and forbid wrongdoing were applied and the government implemented the Shari'ah. But, again, Qutb seems to forget that, although individuals may be aware of their duties, true to their human nature they continue to avoid fulfilling them, despite all exhortations and inducements.

A careful study of history and personal behavior shows that no idealist system was ever implemented through exhortation alone. Qutb himself, unaware or unconsciously, endorses this when he describes modern society as *jahiliyyah* despite fourteen centuries of Islamic rule. Yet, he is content to leave women's fate dependent upon human whim and Qur'anic exhortations. He further adopts the traditional interpretation of gender as "physical differences," despite the fact that the Qur'an itself is either silent on this subject or states the exact opposite. Women thus continue to be outside Qutb's universal Islamic vision, even though he declares that Islamism is "a movement to wipe out tyranny and introduce true freedom to mankind . . . The jihad of Islam is to secure complete freedom for all individuals throughout the world, by releasing them from servitude to other human beings, so that he may serve God." He also describes Islamic society as not "a mere historical form that is hidden in the memories of the past, [but] is the demand of the present and the hope of the future."[76] Thus, Islamic society, while grounded in eternal principles, is not a fixed historical entity but is subject to the vagaries of circumstances and should, therefore, be able to adapt to any change in customs and lifestyles. Qutb thus extols the freedom of the individual from servitude to other human beings and calls on jihad to achieve that, yet he confines women to permanent servitude to their husbands and families, glossing over the fact that women, as individuals, crave freedom as much as their male counterparts do. However, instead of devising a system capable of meeting the challenges of the twentieth century in assuring the benevolent treatment of women, he nonchalantly avoids these issues by attributing any mistreatment of women to the lapses of men in authority and not to Islam.

Qutb affirms that God created humans with a natural desire for good things for themselves and their posterity, their amassed wealth to be passed on to their children. By fulfilling these natural tendencies, individuals will expend their energy in productive activity neither exploited nor lacking in hope for a better future.[77] Yet, once again, women who are created from one and the same soul (sura 4:1) are deprived of this "natural" right of self-fulfillment; and their "natural and reasonable incentives," which can be employed for the general good of the community, are aborted. This is true even though, as Qutb states, the validity or invalidity of any social order depends upon the fulfillment of human needs, and justice and happiness can only be achieved when the individual lives according to nature and is able to realize his or her potential by being in harmony with the universe.[78] Qutb himself declares that the equality of the human race has existed from "its beginning and fate, in life and death, in duties and rights, before the law and before God, and in this and the other life."[79] Again, while Qutb admits that the origin of inequality is in the soul or the conscience, not in institutions, and the only remedy is to eradicate it by the roots and then move on to its secondary manifestation, he makes no corrective moves in theory or practice, keeping in mind, of course, the virtual impossibility of such reform.[80] One wonders at this point whether Qutb had any intention of including women in his vision of humanity as a whole or as an individual entity. In his arguments for natural rights and freedom, he seems to address the male population exclusively. And although he affirms that men and women were created of one soul, he appears content to leave women stagnant at that stage, while he takes men by the hand to new roads of freedom and hegemony.

Another discrepancy in Qutb's thought, similar to that of al-Mawdudi, is his emphasis on the comprehensiveness of God's *hakimiyyah*, precluding all human sovereignty and authority. In fact, he maintains that any nondivine authority is *taghut*, that is, tyrannical, irreligious, and illegitimate. Since all humans are equally God's slaves, no one has the right to exercise authority over another. Yet, we find Qutb once again not only accepting a wife's subjugation to her husband but even confirming it. He bases his argument on the natural biologic differences that dictate the wife's domestic duties, an argument once again not found in the Qur'an. Thus, not only does he leave women stranded at the postcreation stage, he proceeds to subjugate them to the will of their husbands, relegated to housework and the care of children. Yet, even then, mothers are not to be guardians of the children, lest the children become perverted in one form or another.

Furthermore, Qutb's definition of *tawhid* consists of three principles: the principle of *hakimiyyah* and man's freedom from subordination to any human authority; the principle of revolution against tyrannical lords; and, finally, the principle of declaring un-Islamic any negation of personality and loss of freedom.[81] All three principles are in direct contradiction to the status of women as defined by Qutb himself. If the individual is free from any subordination to human authority, then a wife should be her husband's partner and not his "obedient" subordinate; if the Muslim is to revolt against the tyranny of his lord, a wife should, at least, have the right to divorce, even if she is unable to "buy" her freedom from her husband. This is especially so since Qutb himself blames the oppressed for their condition, which he attributes to their weakness in following their oppressors. In fact, they deserve punishment for their indolence (40:47; 34:32). It is their own "subservience, submission, and degradation that has kept them" from taking their proper place in society.[82] And, finally, if the negation of personality and loss of freedom are un-Islamic, then a woman or wife should have the right to free movement, education, and work, enabling her to own property. Private property, according to Qutb, is the balance between effort and reward, is in accord with human nature, and encourages the individual to maximize his or her effort for advancement, generates self-respect, honor, and independence, and bolsters one's personality.[83] Yet Qutb prohibits women from fulfilling the third principle of *tawhid*.

Qutb further admits that the restriction of women to their domestic duties reduces their rational and deliberative acuity and enhances their emotional and sentimental traits, hence keeping them permanently out of the public arena. However, instead of allowing them to join men in the public arena to sharpen their rational and deliberative faculties, which he admits they possess, he keeps them at home as caretakers of children. Moreover, while Qutb describes a human being as "one who eats, marries, procreates, loves, hates, hopes, and fears," with no differentiation between men and women, he elevates the role of men in society at the expense of that of women and, simultaneously, admits that the renaissance of the *ummah* and the preservation of Muslim society would be impossible without a fundamental concern for the condition of the individual.[84]

Finally, while Qutb conceives of Islam as conforming to human nature *(fitrah)* and the whole universe, humans, being part of this universe, can only be happy when harmony is achieved between the part and the whole. Conversely, unhappiness and misery prevail when conflict between society and the universe arises. Thus, happiness to Qutb is "the conformity to and fulfillment of human *fitrah* in nature itself."[85] However, since men and women have the same *fitrah*, are women to be condemned to perpetual earthly unhappiness due to their "ordained" domestic duties and restriction from uniting with the universe?

In his discourse on women, Qutb, like al-Mawdudi, emphasizes their domestic role of childbearing, child rearing, breast-feeding, and housework, which enhance their emotionality, spontaneity, and temper at the expense of their deliberative and rational faculties, thereby ostracizing them from the rest of society and preventing them from entering into any form of business or testifying in court alone in matters of finance or murder. Such allegations contradict the Qur'anic text, which only requires women to satisfy their men sexually and bear their children. Child rearing, breast-feeding, and housework are not obligatory, as ordained by God. In fact, should the wife perform such duties, she should be recompensed financially. Moreover, women, according to the Qur'an, are allowed, like men, to own and administer property, which implies equality in intelligence, memory, and, above all, rationality and deliberation, traits denied them by Qutb. Hence, just like Mawdudi, in Qutb's zeal to keep women at home isolated from the affairs of society, he glides over the clear instructions of the Scripture.

Qutb claims that "when man is made to be overseer (guardian) over woman [4:34], this directive stands so, because of his natural aptitude, position and honor." Yet, he himself admits that "[man] is charged with the financial responsibility," and since there is a strong link between "the financial aspect with that of guidance, . . . the acceptance of that responsibility" is essential.[86] Thus, Qutb, once again, does not restrict himself to the Qur'anic text, which says nothing about man's superiority in aptitude or honor, and limits the distinction to financial superiority only. Nor does he attempt to explain such a verse in cases where women are financially independent and at times actually superior to men.

While Qutb and al-Mawdudi would limit women's education, prevent them from working outside the home, and confine them to it, they do not explain Qur'anic verses that equate men and women in education, knowledge, the earning of wages (4:32; 96:1-4; 16:97; 3:195), and the paying of *zakat* (57:18). The latter two, in fact, demonstrate the Qur'anic approval of women's work, since wages are earned for work performed and *zakat* is paid from wages earned. Once again both ideologues seem to disregard the instructions of the Qur'an in an effort to subordinate women to men in the name of God.

As for inequality in inheritance, Qutb attributes this to the responsibilities borne by men that outweigh those of women, to the *mahr* a woman is paid upon marriage, and to the fact that she is supported by her husband or her male relatives. Again, Qutb seems oblivious to the problems women may face and refuses to address them: a woman may not have male relatives to take care of her, or an inheritance to speak of, or a sizable *mahr*, which would then leave her without support. Qutb further explains the inequality in testimony in court as due to the forgetfulness brought upon women by the nature of their motherly duties, which automatically enhance their emotional and passionate side and suppress their reflective and deliberative side. Yet, he ignores the existence of single working women or childless women, whose deliberative acuity and sharpness of memory should therefore be as good as that of men.

Qutb, in his zeal to elevate motherhood, attributes the full growth and development of women to the first two pregnancies. In doing this, not only does he contradict the Qur'anic text that stipulates the natural equality of men and women, but he also incapacitates single and childless women and reduces them to an inferior position plagued by imbalance and neurological instability. He thus contradicts his earlier stand where he described women (without exceptions) as being capable of drawing up contracts, entering business ventures, drawing up wills, owning property and administering it, and amassing wealth.

Finally, although any interpretation based on the Sunna or Hadith is void if contradictory to the Qur'an, Qutb, just like Mawdudi, affirms the stoning of adulterous women, a punishment not prescribed by the Qur'an, violating thereby the principles of jurisprudence and his own fragile and delicate nature, as reflected by his earlier writings! Unless, of course, one is to separate men from women and then divide women into two classes: the subordinate, submissive, and quasi-human woman, whose place is at home bearing children and caring for them under the guardianship of men; and the "third sex," coined by him to describe those women who work outside the home and deserve to be stoned if they commit adultery. Hence, if adulterous women belong to his "third sex," they would not, I imagine, fall into the class of being human. His flagrant disregard of the stipulations of the Qur'an concerning women would then be justified.

The preceding analysis thus leads to the following postulates: Qutb's personal disappointment in love and possible disillusionment with women led him to digress from his liberal views of women as portrayed in his novels, to adopt a more restrictive female ideology. Or, his immersion in radical political Islam and desire to attract numerous followers made him relegate his compassion, romanticism, and tenderness to the background and adopt a harsh interpretation of women's role in Islam to appease men and ensure a massive following. A third alternative is that he came to a "fork in the road" in his views on history, *ijtihad,* and revolution: The principles and ideals he fought for within the context of his universal Islamic concept were directed at men and withheld from the female half of the population, whom he relegated to an inferior position contrary to the stipulations of the Qur'an. Thus, while he campaigns for dynamism, freedom, and progress for the Muslim male, he denies them to women.[87]

In conclusion, what seems to be at stake for Qutb is not the role of women as such but the validity of the Islamic vision, where no differentiation between the sacred and the secular is permitted. The role of women as prescribed by the Qur'an and the Sunna is part of God's general plan for human happiness in this world and the next and can, therefore, neither be changed nor altered. The only permissible thing is that which would remove all remaining vestiges of Western customs and innovations in the effort to purify society and guide it back to the path of God. Thus, we find that at the heart of Qutb's debate is the limitation of a woman's duties in society to that of wife and mother. This is not only her role but her sole identity, for marriage in Islam is seen as a pivotal institution in the building of society and civilization.

As is the case with most polemicists, Qutb selectively cites passages from the Scriptures whose interpretation justifies his stance with regard to the role of women in society. This has been done to the exclusion of other Qur'anic passages that clearly assert the equality of all believers and historical facts that reflect the proliferation of women saints, mystics, and warriors in early Islam. Thus, whereas Qutb emphasizes the *qiwamah* [protection/guardianship] of men over women, he simply glides over passages that speak of "love and mercy" and the wife's role as the "moral support" for the husband (30:21), as well as the mutual support of husband and wife—"They are garments unto you and you are garments unto them" (2:187), taking the term "garments" to mean that which covers up one's weaknesses or to become one by fitting each other the way a garment fits its owner.[88] And, finally, he willfully overlooks clear and unambiguous verses concerning the punishment of the adulteresses, to ensure the further subordination of women.

To sum up, contrary to al-Mawdudi, who dedicated two books to the subject of gender relations, Qutb's elaborate views on women are to be gleaned from scattered references in his various writings. Like al-Banna, his primary focus was on the movement itself and his ideological views of Islam, with little attention to women's affairs. In this he runs contrary to Mawdudi, who dedicated a good part of his output to a description of the role of women in Muslim society. Qutb, on the other hand, attempts to use biologic and scientific data, albeit distorted, to reinforce his Islamic view of women's role in society. It thus becomes evident from the preceding that despite the fact that the three ideologues did not necessarily address identical issues pertaining to women, they shared the same traditional views on gender relations despite their modern and liberal stance in the interpretation of Scripture for the founding of their proposed ideal Islamic state.

Chapter 5

Ayatollah Ruhollah Khomeini

The Iranian Revolution marked a turning point in the history of twentieth-century Islamic fundamentalism and the consequent history of many Muslim countries. Bernard Lewis, in fact, maintained that it constituted "by far the most powerful and significant movement within the Islamic world for more than a century."[1] With the deposition of the shah and his monarchy, a whole era, characterized by important "modernizers"—Atatürk, Bourguiba, Boumedienne, Nasser—came to an end. The Iranian Revolution also triggered in the Muslim world a series of aggressive militant Islamic fundamentalist movements and revived the idea of Islamic jihad. Moreover, it set the example of using Islam as a mobilizing force of the masses. The 1979 Iranian Revolution thus became a landmark in the implementation of revivalist Islamic policy, the establishment of the Islamic Republic, and the claim to be the first real populist rule since the death of the first Imam, Ali Ibn Abi Talib. The revolution, moreover, proved to be a cataclysmic event transforming the country's political, social, economic, and legal structure. It also succeeded in mobilizing millions, overthrowing a strong and autocratic government, "humiliating the West," defending its frontiers, and waging a foreign war. Most importantly, however, it brought the concept of an Islamic state to fruition.[2]

Shiʿism in Iran had undergone a tremendous transformation in the 1960s, catapulting it into a political force. It asserted a holistic approach to Islam and implemented itself as an ideology and a way of life. This resurgence of Islam in Iran is not to be seen as a return to the old religion but rather as a transformation of Shiʿism and its message from a state of dependency and inferiority to one of self-sufficiency, self-confidence, and national pride. It was this transformation, with its ability to meet the needs of the population, that drew Iranians to it by the millions.[3]

Within Islamic discourse, the Shi'ites may be described as the most ardent opponents of secularism. Islam is envisaged as a political order with God as its only legislator. The state exists only to protect and implement the law of God as defined in the Qur'an and the Sunna. However, the Shi'ites, contrary to the Muslim Sunnis, have always had difficulty recognizing the legitimacy of temporal rulers subsequent to the Prophet, with the exception of Ali Ibn Abi Talib. The subsequent Imams are perceived as divinely inspired, infallible (just like the Prophet and his daughter, Fatimah), and protected against sin. They are, therefore, able to delineate the path of God and are the legitimate rulers. The imamate thus provided an alternative divinely inspired government for the Shi'ites, although none of them ever held the reins of power. The line of succession of the Imams came to an end with the occultation of the twelfth Imam, Muhammad al-Mahdi, in 874 A.D., and with him disappeared the possibility of ever exercising legitimate worldly power, since universal authority rests only with the Imam, the government being only the protector of Muslim lands. Shi'ites, however, have opted to obey the Qur'anic commandment enjoining believers to obey God, the Prophet, and "those in power." The caliph, according to the Shi'ites, could issue decrees within the framework of the *Shari'ah*, but never legislate. The ruler was to be obeyed only as long as he continued to protect Islam and maintain social justice. The Shi'ite ulema, however, never exercised this potential of rebellion when the ruler overstepped his bounds to legislate, but retained, instead, a distance from the state.[4]

Following the lead of the twentieth-century philosopher Ali Shari'ati, Ayatollah Ruhollah Khomeini reinterpreted and developed the long-standing but neglected doctrine of the *wilayat al-faqih* [guardianship of the jurist], creating thereby an absolute theocratic rule in Iran. Thus, Abdulaziz Sachedina comments that the teachings of the Shi'ite fundamentalists "can be designated as an activist type of reaction involving creative interpretation of religious ideas and symbols to render them applicable to contemporary Muslim history."[5] However, in creating the Islamic Republic, Khomeini had tacitly accepted the legal existence of the modern nation-state and carried out his "most daring and perhaps most lasting innovation."[6]

Ayatollah Khomeini is clearly the most prominent religious leader to emerge from the revolution. He symbolized the whole revolutionary process and became its focal point and the dominant political force in the Islamic Republic. He secured the respect and obedience of all groups, including those who differed with him ideologically. Khomeini also assumed the role of advocate par excellence for an active political role for the ulema. He thus emerged not only as the role model of militant Islam but also as the defender of Islam, who restored it to its old power and puritanism in the face of "Western decadence and corruption."[7]

Khomeini merged, in his person, the roles of the contemplative, teacher, scholar, and activist. He began his career in 1928 teaching Islamic philosophy and mysticism. It was not until 1944 that he started teaching advanced courses in the canonical sources of Islamic law. His writings, which began to appear in the late twenties, cover a wide spectrum of subjects, ranging from Shi'ite jurisprudence, Islamic philosophy, and mysticism to Persian poetry and political polemics. Some twenty-five books and treatises have been identified as his work.[8]

Khomeini's first political statement appeared in his book *Kashf al-asrar* [Revelation of secrets], published in 1941.[9] His interest in politics continued to widen until Borujerdi, the chief Iranian theologian, died in 1962 and the task of fusing religion and politics fell to Khomeini. He undertook a one-month "mystical retreat" from which he emerged convinced that God wanted him to eliminate all corruption from the face of the earth. In 1963, the shah started pushing ahead with his secular reforms known as the "White Revolution," including women's suffrage and a land reform bill that would cut into clerical income. This resulted in a confrontation between the clerics and the government, bringing Khomeini to the fore as a militant leader who branded the government as a threat to Islam. Soon after, the shah realized that Khomeini could not be intimidated into silence, and on November 4, 1964, he was arrested and sent into exile in Turkey. In October 1965, he was allowed to move to Najaf, one of the Shi'ite shrine cities of Iraq. He was to stay there for thirteen years.[10]

During his stay in Najaf, he issued periodic statements, smuggled into the country and clandestinely circulated, denouncing the Iranian government. In September 1978, the shah's government requested that Iraq expel him from its territory, in the hope of depriving him of his base of operations. No Muslim country would grant him asylum, but France did, and he moved to the hamlet of Neauphle-le-Chateau near Paris in early 1978, where his line of communications with his followers in Iran proved to be more open. While there he spoke of a "progressive Islam" in which even women could become president and in which "Islamic rules of retribution would not be applied unless sufficient preparations had been made to implement Islamic justice in its totality." The month of December 1978 was rife with demonstrations against the shah, with strident calls for an

Islamic republic under Khomeini. The shah abdicated and left Iran on January 16, 1979. Khomeini returned to Tehran on February 1, 1979, in fulfillment of an oft-repeated Iranian prophecy of one of the Shi'ite Imams that "a man will rise from Qom [as a precursor to the Mahdi] and he will summon the people to the right path. People will rally to him like pieces of iron [to a magnet], not to be shaken by strong winds, free and relying on God."[11] Shortly afterward, the Islamic Republic was born, Khomeini withdrew to Qom, and died there on June 3, 1989.[12]

Khomeini developed his distinctive vision of Islam as encompassing spiritual, intellectual, social, and political dimensions at a fairly early age. His designation, therefore, as "leader of the Islamic revolution and founder of the Islamic Republic" is a true description of his person and message. He had a firm belief in the role the ulema should play—to guide, lead, purify, and defend Iranian society; a conviction that the spiritual and gnostic aspects of Islam should be cultivated; a rejection of the Pahlavi state; a determination to liberate Islamic lands from Western control; and a deep distrust of secular intellectuals. Ervan Abrahamian described Khomeini as having "transformed Shi'ism from a conservative quietist faith into a militant political ideology, that challenged both the imperial powers and the country's upper class."[13]

Khomeini exercised dictatorial powers by imposing his will on different branches of the government and taking decisions without consulting the authorities in charge. It was his conviction that, unless power was consolidated, "evil could not be eradicated, truth could not be established and Islam could not be implemented," and in January 1988, Khomeini declared his *wilayat al-faqih* [guardianship of the jurist].[14] He was intent on bringing Iranian society into conformity with what he perceived to be the full application of the *Shari'ah*, including the imposition of its penal code regarding adultery, theft, and other criminal acts. His second priority was to export the revolution and his understanding of fundamentalism to the rest of the Islamic world, which had been under the sway of Saudi Arabia for too long.[15]

Unlike the two founders of Sunni radicalism, Sayyid Qutb and Abu al-'A'la al-Mawdudi, Khomeini was a cleric with a distinct rank and defined role; and while the former two concerned themselves primarily with a comprehensive ideology based on their concept of God's sovereignty, Khomeini's main task was the positing of the clergy as the executors of God's law. His ideological world, hence, envisioned a theocratic state in which a priestly order, organized according to rank, would exercise absolute power.

His revolutionary ideology was, thus, not in proclaiming the Islamic state that all fundamentalists desired, but in enforcing his principle that only those most learned in Islamic law could rule: "Since Islamic government is a government of law, knowledge of the law is necessary for the ruler, as has been laid down in tradition." The ruler "must surpass all others in knowledge" and be "more learned than everyone else."[16] Since the clergy in Iran had been completely independent of the state for a long time, this ideology automatically transformed them into a revolutionary class intent on the seizure of power and its implementation. When Islam is threatened and endangered, it can be saved by the jurists, whose duty would be to establish an Islamic state on the model of that of the Prophet himself, who had established a government to implement laws and administer society. It is the only way to prevent anarchy and protect society from corruption.

The denial of the necessity of a government is a denial of the necessity of the implementation of Divine Law, its universality and comprehensiveness, and the eternal validity of Islam itself. To that end, Khomeini declares, "We believe in the Imamate; we believe that the Prophet appointed a successor to assume responsibility for the affairs of Muslims, and that he did so in conformity with the divine will. Therefore, we must also believe in the necessity for the establishment of government, and we must strive to establish organs for the execution of law and the administration of affairs."[17] The successor should, therefore, be a jurist capable of maintaining and protecting the achievements of his predecessors and, simultaneously, guaranteeing the security of Muslim society. The jurist would surely not legislate, since this is solely God's domain, but he would carry out and execute God's rules and regulations and ensure obedience of the community. The jurist governor would then enjoy the same powers and inherit the same authority as the Prophet and the Imams, but without their perfect eminence, and people would have to obey them accordingly. In the absence of the Twelfth Imam, the jurists, argues Khomeini, are of central authority in all matters pertaining to the community. The *faqih*, in turn, if he is to be true to himself and to Islam, should concentrate on the restoration of religious values and Islamic practices. In fact, this duty is so important that Khomeini equates it with the five daily prayers and the fasting of Ramadan. There must, therefore, be a state based on Islamic *Shari'ah* that can provide for all the needs of the community ranging from problems of personal status to issues of international relations. The ultimate purpose, then, of assuming the supreme political authority is to provide justice for all and guide society to perfection. A just society would be one in which the

Shari'ah is implemented without privilege or discrimination.[18] Khomeini elucidates, "If a deserving jurist is endowed with these two qualities [justice and knowledge of Islamic law], then his regency will be the same as enjoyed by the Prophet in the governing of the Islamic community and it is incumbent on all Muslims to obey him."[19] Thus, by shifting the emphasis from the Divine Law itself to the jurisconsult or *faqih*, any act of his, if deemed necessary, could be defined as Islamic.

In Khomeini's declarations of December 1987 and January 1988, he maintained that government has primacy over devotional matters such as prayers, fasting, and pilgrimage. The Islamic government can, therefore, according to him, break any contract or stop any activity based on the *Shari'ah* whenever it is in the interest (*maslahah*) of the state and Islam to do so. In his letter to President Khamane'i, he stated, "The [Islamic] government can unilaterally break [even] those contracts which it had made with the people on the basis of *Shari'ah* rules, whenever the contract may be contrary to the expedience or interest (*maslahah*) of the country and Islam. It can also stop any activity—be it spiritual or temporal—whose continuation would be contrary to the expedience or interest of Islam, for as long as this is the case."[20] The guardianship of the jurisconsult is, thus, absolute, even if it contradicts the *Shari'ah*, for it is now the state that is supreme, not the *Shari'ah* or ideology. Thus, when asked whether disobeying traffic regulations was a sin, Khomeini answered, "Obeying the rules and regulations of the Islamic government is a religious obligation and their violation is sin."[21]

The aim of the *Shari'ah*, maintains Khomeini, is to produce an integrated society consisting of virtuous human beings who internalize the law to attain happiness and perfection. Therefore, the Islamic Republic that emerged after the revolution set out to implement its laws and actualize the proposed ideal Islamic family. This was defined as the counterpart of the "Western" definition of family and sexuality and was hailed as the "culturally authentic and appropriate" form of the family that was to reflect the revolutionary and modern Muslim society. Gender was thus turned into a revolutionary discourse in the process of Iran's redefinition of its relations with the West. This was further accentuated by the participation of women in the revolution, the use of gender as symbols of the revolution, and the need of the revolutionary leadership to address gender issues and endorse women's "special worth and respect." The emancipated woman of the Pahlavi state, under the influence of Western culture, came to represent all the social ills of superconsumerism and dependence upon imperialistic foreign goods, propagation of corrupt Western culture, and the undermining of social morality. Male and female citizens were promised the fulfillment of their "natural" rights. Women were to obey their husbands, who in return would protect them in tandem with the state. The Constitution emphasized that "since the family is the fundamental unit of the Islamic society, all pertinent laws, regulations and programs must tend to facilitate the foundation of a family and to protect the sanctity of family relations on the basis of the law and the ethics of Islam."[22] This necessitated the establishment of a clear code of behavior to govern the various dimensions of Islamic gender relations. The first priority was, therefore, to define the "Islamic family," and policies were issued to cover marriage, family planning, familial relations, divorce, and custody of children. The second dealt with women's participation in the various fields of education, employment, and political participation. The third was to ensure harmony between the family and society through laws that would ensure gender segregation and the punishment of adultery.[23]

The process of the construction of the "Islamic family" was initiated by Khomeini's abolition of the Family Protection Laws of 1967 and 1975, just a few days after the victory of the revolution on February 26, 1979, which was put into effect on August 9, 1979, by the Ministry of Justice. The main objection was the extension of the right to vote to women, which Khomeini described as an attempt "to corrupt our chaste women." He also proclaimed that all women who had been divorced under the Family Act were still married to their former husbands. If they had remarried, they had committed adultery and their children were declared illegitimate, with no inheritance rights.[24]

Ayatollah Khomeini took pride in the women of the revolution—"Any nation that has women like the Iranian women will surely be victorious"—and promised them freedom, equality, and dignity, affirming that

> Islam has never been against their freedom. It is, to the contrary, opposed to the idea of woman-as-object, and it gives her back her dignity. A woman is man's equal; she and he are both free to choose their lives and their occupations . . . [It is the Pahlavi regime, in fact, that] has destroyed the freedom of women as well as men. Women, as well as men, swell the population of Iranian prisons, and this is where freedom is threatened. We want to free them from the corruption menacing them.[25]

While addressing a group of Iranians in Paris, he extolled the role women played in the "glorious" days of Islam, when they also served in the army.

Today women should be equal, free to choose their careers and activities and go to universities. They should be free to vote and be elected and play an active role in the society. It is not true that Islam discriminates against women. What Islam is against is immoral practices. We want to free women from the role forced upon them under the Shah in the name of modernization. Islam is not opposed to any positive aspect of modernization involving women. We want them to be human beings and not means of entertainment and lust.[26]

Such statements, vague as they may be, gave women feelings of security and importance. Khomeini, however, was quite specific on other issues. In one interview, he emphasized the freedom of women in choosing their dress within the framework of decency, while the imposition of the veil was considered inconceivable. On March 31, 1979, Khomeini issued an appeal to Iranian women, urging them to vote in favor of an Islamic republic. He argued that Islam had granted "greater consideration to women's rights than men's rights." In Islam, he maintained, "our women have the right to vote and the right to get elected. They have the right on all affairs relating to them. They have the right to freely choose many professions." "[I]n the Islamic government," he promised, "each and everyone will be free, and all people will attain their rights."[27] Yet, as soon as the Islamic Republic was declared, the Retribution Bill was passed, setting the *diyyah* [blood money] for a murdered woman to be half the amount of that of a murdered man. Also, and in accordance with the *Shari'ah*, women witnesses in murder cases, irrespective of their number, were to carry no legal weight. Moreover, since their right to give any form of judgment was not recognized, they could not join the legal profession. Khomeini even asked women to accept the limitations imposed upon their individual freedom for the benefit of society and explained, "Islam's limitation on you is in your interest."[28] Islamic jurisprudence, Khomeini continues, comprises a complete sociolegal system that meets all human needs and regulates all facets of life, be they social, political, commercial, educational, or marital. It further offers detailed guidance in matters such as sex, pregnancy, and nursing. It thus makes the individual's existence clear and orderly from before birth through death and beyond and defines all aspects of life.[29]

Like the three previous Sunni fundamentalists, Khomeini views Islam as having elevated women beyond measure and equated them with men. It becomes their duty to maintain this stature and safeguard their rights, for without women, nations would collapse, since women are responsible for the rearing of future generations. The well-being of society, therefore, rests on women who are the source of all that is good. The first stages of learning and guidance take place in the mother's lap, so that children learn more from and are influenced most by their mothers. Thus, women are more valuable and influential than men, their children looking up to them as prophets. This requires that women be well educated, especially in that learning is a form of worship.[30] Thus, Fatimah al-Zahra', a woman equal to any man and an embodiment of all perfect human attributes, was born in an age when women were considered inferior and valueless. The Prophet held her in high esteem, and her birthday came to mark the rebirth of all women and should rightly be considered Woman's Day. She was the equal of an Imam in stature, a divine being in human form, possessing all the attributes of a prophet. Had she been a man, she would have been a prophet of the stature of Prophet Muhammad.

In the pre-Islamic era, Khomeini argues, women were treated like animals. After being freed by Islam, they were again reduced to the status of commodities during the reigns of Rida Khan and his son and successor in Persia. Women who followed the shah's directives did so because they were poorly brought up, removed from all Islamic values. However, women who adopted Islamic teachings are credited for the Islamic upheaval pioneered by them to be later emulated by men. During the jihad, women proved equal to men and were the vanguard that stimulated men and drove them to superhuman efforts for the revolution. They then provided them with all necessary support in the defense of Islamic culture against the shah's tyranny. Earlier, the shah had forced eighteen-year-old girls into military service, which was tantamount to prostitution.[31]

While jihad is not compulsory for women, Khomeini argues, defense of the revolution is mandatory for all. Since Islam does not shackle women but only seeks to preempt decadence and sedition, women may enroll in the Revolutionary Guard and the army, vote, take up government posts, and act as guardians of the Islamic revolution, all the while observing Islamic regulations of dress and behavior. Women thus remain free like men and not mere prisoners of the home. This is evidenced by their participation in revolutionary activities, combat, and education. Islam bans moral degeneration for both men and women. Thus, Khomeini claims, women enjoy their full freedom in post-shah Iran: they participate in the struggle against the shah, in political rallies, and in public and private domains, and they run for political office just like men, always, however, observing the Islamic dress code (*hijab*). This does not limit their freedom but guards their honor and prevents unwanted male arousal. The *hijab* is not necessarily the *chador*, but rather any dress that meets the requirements of the Islamic code. Yet, women voluntarily choose the *chador* over all other forms of dress. Women who repudiate the Islamic dress are neither punished nor chastised. They instead are automatically and voluntarily ostracized by their peers. Furthermore, Islam does not allow women to bare their bodies and mix with men on beaches. Culture and civilization are not demonstrated by semidressed women parading in the streets. This only succeeds in encouraging depravity and the collapse of the family unit.[32]

Upon marriage, Khomeini explains, in agreement with the Sunni ideologues, women may stipulate certain privileges in the marriage contract, such as the right of divorce if their husband mistreats them. They should take advantage of *wilayat al-faqih*, which is their protector. Thus, if a man mistreats his wife, she may appeal to a judge who will counsel the husband, then admonish him, and if all fails, force him to divorce her. However, married women are bound to obey their husbands and leave the home only with their permission. Since the primary function of the married woman is caring for home and family, outside employment can only abort this sacred duty to the detriment of her children. Thus, employment only serves to destroy family foundations and deprive children of their mothers. Furthermore, the smooth functioning of governmental departments was disrupted with the advent of women employees. Thus, women's employment may keep the country backward and underdeveloped by preoccupying youth with women and causing them to neglect their duties.[33]

Khomeini explains in his book *Tawzi' al-masa'il* [A clarification of questions] that marriage can be either permanent or temporary. The permanent contract is that in which the duration of matrimony is not specified, and the temporary is that in which longevity is defined. It can be for one hour, a day, a month, a year, or more. The woman who is contracted for such a marriage is called either a concubine (*mot'eh*) or a formula (*seegheh*). The consent of both partners is necessary. However, if the woman appears dismayed or disgusted but evidently pleased at heart, the contract will still be valid. No age limit is set, although "it is one of a man's good fortunes that his daughter does not see menses in his own house."[34]

Mut'ah, or temporary marriage, according to Khomeini and contrary to Sunni doctrine, is ordained by God for sexual gratification and to prevent adultery, fornication, and prostitution. In prostitution, it is argued, women are forced into humiliation, degradation, and exploitation, while in *mut'ah*, women enter into marriage voluntarily with the man of their choice. *Mut'ah*, however, need not be only for pleasure. If a woman who becomes a formula (*seegheh*) stipulates that the husband has no rights to intercourse, he may derive "other pleasures" from her. She, on the other hand, cannot require her husband to have sexual intercourse with her; she is there for his pleasure and not hers.[35]

In agreement with the previously studied Sunni ideologues, Khomeini explains that "the law of the four wives is a very progressive law, and was written for the good of women, since there are more women than men. More women are born than men, and more men are killed in war than women. As a woman needs a man, so what can we do, since there are more women than men in the world? Would you rather prefer that the excess number of women became whores—or that they married a man with other wives?" Wives, however, must be treated equally.[36]

In step with al-Mawdudi and Qutb, Khomeini enumerates the duties of a wife to her husband: "A woman who has been contracted permanently must not leave the house without the husband's permission, and must surrender herself for any pleasure that he may desire and must not prevent him from having intercourse with her without a religious excuse. If she obeys the husband in these, he is obligated to provide for her food, clothing, dwelling and other appliances mentioned in books, and if he does not, he is indebted to her, whether or not he can afford them."[37] If the wife does not obey her husband in these matters, "she is a sinner and has no right to food and clothing and shelter and sleeping with the husband."[38] Although a woman may refuse her husband's sexual advances on religious grounds, Khomeini grants her husband permission to forbid her from fulfilling her religious obligations, like fasting, pilgrimage, or prayer. A wife is also prohibited from making a religious vow to do a good deed unless she obtains her husband's permission, for only the sane and mature can make such vows. Yet, children are allowed to carry out their vows, even without the permission of their fathers.[39]

The view that emerges from Khomeini's writings is that the role of women in society is that of mother and educator of children. Since the family is viewed as the fundamental unit of Islamic society, women, being the "strong forts of virtue and chastity," are considered "the pillars of the nation," "raising brave and enlightened men and meek and united women." Motherhood, argues Khomeini, bestows on women "a special rank in society which is not less than a man's, if not greater," because it is "a task nobler than all other tasks," and "child rearing is the most difficult, the most challenging, but one of the sweetest ordeals. This crucial responsibility is exclusively reserved for women." He argues that mothers become "invaluable" by raising martyrs and educating children to be good Muslims and dedicated soldiers. He says, "Our women comprise half of our nation [and] are entrusted with the task of giving an education to the other half . . . in the school of the family." A woman's status is, therefore, enhanced if she fulfills her role as mother. Moreover, the role of rearing children is viewed by him as "a source of support for the country" in the future, because it ensures new generations of "great men and women." By fulfilling this role, women will emerge as "the foundation of the nation." He reiterates that motherhood is the epitome of a woman's life, calling women "mothers-to-be of the next Iranian generation." He extols their role further by praising their ability to offer their sons as martyrs to the revolution: "[W]omen are the foundation of this country . . . and this revolution. They raise their youths to send them to the front." Elsewhere, he goes on to stress the importance of mourning to women and teaches them how to observe it. It is "unlawful" for them "to wear colorful clothes or jewelry or to use makeup" during such circumstances.[40]

Khomeini sets down the precepts of divorce in *Tawzi' al-masa'il* and cautions that to divorce his wife a man has to be sane and at least of pubertal age, or else his divorce will be void. The wife, at the time of divorce, must be clean of menstrual and childbirth blood and should not have had intercourse with her husband while clean. The divorce must be declared in front of witnesses, but not necessarily in the presence of the wife, and should follow a correct Arabic formula. In cases of revocable divorce, the husband need not inform either the witnesses or the wife of his return. It is enough for him to say to himself, "I returned to my wife." A woman, on the other hand, may go to court for a divorce if her husband is insane, impotent, or infertile, imprisoned, away from the home without any reason and for a protracted period of time, or if he is unable to support her financially. She may also obtain a divorce if she pays him a certain amount of money, usually the dowry he paid her at marriage. A divorced woman whose marriage has been consummated and who is over nine years of age and not menopausal must observe a waiting period (*'iddah*) of three months before she may leave her marital home (unless her husband evicts her) or remarry. The waiting period of a pregnant woman ends with delivery. The woman need not know of her divorce until the end of her waiting period. However, a widow needs to observe a waiting period of four months and ten days, even if she is menopausal or her marriage has not been consummated.[41] If the deceased husband contracted a woman in marriage while suffering from a disease of which he died without having had intercourse with her, she will have no inheritance rights and may not retrieve her dowry. Yet, if the reverse is true and the wife dies without having consummated the marriage, the husband is entitled to his inheritance.[42]

The first directive requiring women to wear the veil was issued on March 7, 1979, shortly after Khomeini's return to Iran. Shops, restaurants, cinemas, and all other public areas, including offices, were instructed not to receive or serve unveiled women. The open defiance of this directive was to be immediately punishable by seventy-four lashes without court action, the offense being self-evident.[43] Khomeini devotes about ten sections of his *Tawzi' al-masa'il* to the rules and regulations dealing with the act of looking at women. The only parts of a woman's body permitted to be seen by strange men are the oval of the face and the hands. Men are forbidden to look at the covered body of a woman. He also advises against the innocent look at the face, body, and hair of a minor girl to preempt temptation. Men should "not look at such places as the thighs and abdomen, which are usually covered." A man and a woman, however, who are intimates (*mahram*) of one another may, if not with the intention of pleasure, look at all of each other's bodies, except for the private parts. Moreover, a man may not even look at the picture of a "strange woman who is not disreputable." Contrary to Qutb and Mawdudi, a doctor is not allowed to touch and look at the body of his female patient: he either touches her without looking, or simply looks without any contact.[44] Khomeini announced that women "are now ashamed of corrupting, extroverted behavior; they have become modest and have given up Western clothes to follow the example of Fatimah."[45]

Although Khomeini supports the education of women in general, he limits the fields they may choose to what is beneficial to their role as mothers, housekeepers, and devout Muslims, and he proposes segregation in schools, the professions, and in society as a whole. He expelled all women law students, and, in 1979, fired all women judges, while the minister of defense, General Ahmad Madani, dismissed all women conscripts and relieved them of military service.[46] The process of segregation included all games and physical activities, leading to the exclusion of women from all sports, since they would have to share the same coaches while traveling and use the same facilities. With the segregation of schools, many technical colleges had to expel their women students, and in June of the same year, married women were barred from attending high schools. In the summer of 1979, beaches were segregated and women transgressors were publicly flogged. Women accused of prostitution or "corruption" were summarily executed.[47]

To guide believers until the reappearance of the Imam, *mujtahid* [interpreters of Scripture], through their knowledge of Islamic rules and regulations, traditions, and precedents, took upon themselves the task of interpreting the Qur'an to fit the exigencies of the present. As such, they can exercise considerable authority over the community, especially so since they attain their position not by appointment or election but by virtue of the acclamation of their peers and followers. This makes them *marji' taqlid* [authority on tradition], but unlike Imams, their judgments are fallible and they are totally human. Therefore, it is forbidden to follow the fallible judgments of dead *mujtahid*. This resulted in assigning the *mujtahid*, who, in time assumes the title of ayatollah, tremendous powers over the community. Khomeini warned that man's reason ultimately fails him, and formal learning is "the thickest of veils." Man can only try to grasp just one dimension of God's reality, such that the interpretation of the Qur'an merely suggests possibilities, rather than proclaims ultimate truths.[48] Again here we find Khomeini in agreement with his Sunni peers regarding the finitude of man's reason and understanding and, therefore, his fallibility.

Khomeini emphasizes man's inability to fathom the truths of the Qur'an and the importance of the exigencies of the times in interpreting it, and he accords great latitude and authority to the *mujtahid, faqih*, and the Islamic government as a whole, to the extent of going against the *Shari'ah* if need be. In fact, he himself took several brave and revolutionary steps vis-à-vis tradition and Islam as a whole in incorporating modern concepts and terminology into his own religio-political ideology. For example, he allowed the use of banks, knowing that "usury," condemned by Islam, is involved in bank transactions, and he reformulated the banking term "interest" to become "risk sharing," to assure its being condoned by Islam. In view of all of this, one cannot but be confounded by his rigidity and inflexibility with regard to women and their role in society. Although he does not necessarily support his rulings in *Tawzi' al-masa'il* by any particular hadith, his rulings, like those of other ayatollahs such as Mutahhari, Milani, Khu'i, and Tabtaba'i, are almost replicas of Majlisi's, who died in 1699. We must assume, however, that this rigidity has nothing to do with religion and everything to do with political or personal motives. The same rigidity or traditionalism with regard to gender relations is also encountered in the discourses of al-Banna, al-Mawdudi, and Qutb.

Yet, even this rigidity was not apparent in his prerevolutionary discourse, with the exception of his book *Tawzi' al-masa'il*. He claimed that women had been victims of the shah's regime and the revolution was to give them back their integrity and true value. In countless interviews, he declared that Islam valued women above men; women would, henceforth, be able to walk the streets unmolested and mingle with men in huge mixed demonstrations, when previously they dreaded using mixed public transportation. Overnight, women were treated and addressed as "sisters." They were not subject to any form of division of labor within the revolution and were free to make their own choices with respect to their struggle against the shah. Thus, if women opted to dig trenches and carry arms, it was their choice. In fact, the religious leadership went so far as to encourage them to disobey their husbands and fathers for political reasons, pointing to historical Shi'ite female role models, such as Zaynab, who divorced her husband to support the struggle against the Sunni Muslims. Thus, participating in the revolution proved to be a rich and liberating experience for many women. It gave them, along with men, a sense of solidarity, communalism, and pride in embarrassing the shah's regime and his Western allies. Men and women joined in the search for a new national and gender identity, and the revolution promised them that.[49] Khomeini encouraged and urged women to come out into the streets and join the demonstrations against the shah.

In the referendum of April 1979, to determine what form the postrevolutionary government should take, he urged women to go to the polls and cast their votes in favor of the Islamic Republic, countermanding his own position in 1963, when he denounced women's enfranchisement as totally un-Islamic and against the Shari'ah: "This violates the fundamental principles of Islam and the Qur'an."[50] Another contradictory action taken by Khomeini is his stand regarding women's participation in demonstrations, carrying arms, and participating in combat. Thus, as soon as the Islamic Republic was established, all women conscripts were released from military service and were sent back home in accordance with Shari'ah precepts. Yet, in a speech in April 1985, he asked women to be ready to carry arms in defense of Islam, explaining that,

[W]hat is not accepted in the Shari'ah is women's participation in primary jihad. But when it comes to the question of defense, there is consensus in Islam that women are obliged to take part in every possible way, including military [activity]. Women should [therefore] receive military training . . . With their presence at the war front, women not only bring extra human power, but they also create a special sensitivity in men to fight even harder. Men are sensitive towards women and react more strongly against seeing one woman hurt than a hundred men killed. So, if . . . [women] participate in the defense of Islam in military and nonmilitary ways, . . . [they] will create great strength in our soldiers.[51]

This further contradicts his stand on segregation and the distracting influence women have on men. Thus, we see that in this instance and in situations involving watching seminude athletes on television and in the cinemas, where "the spectator must not watch these films with lustful intentions," contrary to Khomeini's previous assertions, men are capable of exercising control over their "animal instincts" and are able to cooperate with women, or simply watch them, without being overcome by any sexual urge.[52]

In his writings, Khomeini, in agreement with Qutb and Mawdudi, endorses total patriarchal control of women on the psychological, economic, religious, and physical levels. His interpretation is the most restricting variant of the Qur'an. Women, he argues, being deprived of much of the economic independence granted them in the Qur'an, are rendered entirely dependent upon men. He further affirms the Shi'ite practice of forbidding women to inherit any real estate or any income that may accrue from it, and he goes even beyond this to dictate that all of a wife's possessions, including the clothes she wears, are the property of her husband. He can, therefore, reclaim them upon divorce, and in case of death, her clothes should be included in all materials and funds to be inherited.[53]

Khomeini, in his March 13, 1979, speech urging women to vote, promised men and women that "in the Islamic government, each and everyone will be free, and all people will attain their rights." Yet, the Retribution Bill passed by the Islamic Parliament discriminated against women by fixing the *diyyah* [blood money] for a murdered woman to be half that of a murdered man. It also banned female testimony in murder cases and prohibited women from studying law or being appointed as judges. Men reclaimed their right to unilateral divorce and polygamy, and *mut'ah* marriages were encouraged. Thus, women reverted to the state they were in during the Pahlavi regime, namely, their reification into sex objects—the very thing Khomeini claimed to oppose.

This is further reflected in Khomeini's view of women's sexuality, similar to that of al-Mawdudi and Qutb. He views them as sexual beings bound to corrupt and tempt men into adultery, promiscuity, and moral corruption. Hence, we find Khomeini's teachings rampant with detailed but inaccurate descriptions of menstruation, such as "false menstruation," postnatal, and other vaginal discharges, and the menopause. All this is to assist husbands to recognize the times during which women are "impure" and to instruct them in the ways and means through which they can detect their wife's prevarication. His distrust of women is further underlined when he warns men not to believe their wives when they claim to be menopausal and advises men to follow his guiding principle: "All women menstruate between the ages of nine and fifty, sixty for the descendants of the Prophet." He then goes on to teach women how to recognize menses and distinguish it from abscess blood and instructs them that "menstruation must last at least three days and no more than ten days." Although this is one of the very few instances in which a wife may refuse the sexual advances of her husband, should he insist, however, she must not abstain. In that instance he has to pay a specified sum of gold to the poor. Otherwise, he may opt to practice sodomy instead.[54]

Moreover, while the Qur'an specifies women's equality before God, their responsibility for their own sins and good deeds, and their freedom to fulfill their religious duties with or without their husband's permission, Khomeini does not concede such independence. Instead, he permits the husband to prevent his wife from fulfilling her religious duties and forbids her from fasting when it is only desirable (*mustahab*) and not required. Nor does he permit women to make religious vows without their husband's permission. Finally, while praying, "A woman must stand behind the man and must place her forehead on the ground behind the man . . . Should a woman stand beside a man to say her prayers, it is preferable that she repeats that prayer," otherwise, it is deemed invalid because the woman assumed an apparent equality with men.

Again, in a discriminatory reinterpretation of the Qur'anic statement "Lodge them in your homes according to your means," Khomeini, contrary to Mawdudi and Qutb, allows the husband to force his wife out of her marital home but forbids her to leave the same home of her own free will during the waiting period. He even allows a man to have intercourse with his divorced wife during the waiting period, thus postponing the actual divorce for another three months and preventing her, thereby, from remarrying. Further, while the Qur'an specifies that "it is unlawful for husbands to take anything they had given them" (2:229), Khomeini allows a man to divorce his wife without notifying her and to repossess all he has given her during the period (possibly years) between the divorce and its announcement to the wife. Other discriminatory practices adopted by Khomeini in contradistinction to the clear commands of the Qur'an are seen in the fields of education and economics. Thus, while the Qur'an is quite clear in equating the two sexes in these realms, Khomeini, in agreement with Qutb and Mawdudi, not only segregates schools but also goes on to segregate school curricula as well and limit the fields women can pursue at the university level. As to women's economic independence, Khomeini dismissed many from their positions and made it very difficult for others to continue working by requiring unmarried women employees to submit a physician's certificate stating their virginity status and summarily dismissing any nonvirgins. He also encouraged women with fifteen years of service to retire without loss of benefits and paid married women a full salary if they stayed at home. In addition, many day care centers were closed.[55] Also, in his criticism of the West and its lifestyle, he points to the economic independence of Western women as being the major cause of the downfall of the family unit, the loss of love, and the prevailing immorality. He declares that it is the man's duty to provide for the family, making women's economic independence unnecessary. Instead, women are encouraged to save from the household budget, provided by their husband, toward their future financial security;[56] in effect, he is instructing them to cheat and steal from their husband. Women who follow his suggestion would actually be subverting the marital harmony Khomeini so fervently advocates.

The two matters this survey brings to the fore are the possible explanation(s) of Khomeini's erratic or contradictory behavior and the etiology of the female support Khomeini managed to garner before and during the revolution. There is a major discrepancy between the content of Khomeini's address to women, as well as various statements made during interviews, on the one hand, and the content of his book *Tawzi' al-masa'il*, written in his capacity as *marji' taqlid*, often in direct contradiction of Qur'anic instructions and lacking any supportive references. While he resorts to *ijtihad*, modernization, and *maslahah* in formulating many of his views, he seems to stray to an extreme, traditional position where women are concerned. Thus, following in the footsteps of Mawdudi and Qutb, women accrue no benefit from his liberal *ijtihad*. In fact, he resorts to the most constraining interpretations of Qur'anic dicta in some cases and remains conspicuously silent with regard to other, more liberal verses difficult to mold into an interpretation more suitable to his purposes. One thus gets the impression that Khomeini harbors a deep-seated conviction of women's inferiority, deceit, treachery, and lack of moral fiber. They are seen as the natural symbol of *fitnah* [chaos] and disorder in society and hence are to be controlled by masking and segregation. Thus, in 1981, contrary to his Paris interview, he declared that "one of the biggest achievements of the Islamic Revolution was the return of the veil. . . . If the Islamic Revolution had no other outcome but the veiling of women, this, in and of itself, is enough for the Revolution."[57] It is interesting at this point to compare this statement with Mawdudi's confession that it was the sight of unveiled women in Delhi that brought him back to Islam.

Despite the deep convictions of the malign female influence on men and society underpinning his strictly traditional stand, Khomeini realized that making these basically fundamentalist views public would cost him the support of secular intellectuals, those who believed in secular democracy, the Left, and women themselves, which would, consequently, cost him the leadership of the revolution. Furthermore, he needed women in his political program: he had exploited women's issues for political purposes since 1963, vehemently opposed the enfranchisement of women, and remained silent on the matter of the government's land reforms, which directly affected the clergy. Also, despite pressures by the conservative clergy to separate family and society and confine women to child rearing and domestic chores, and despite his implicit agreement with such views, he refrained from endorsing them. He realized that the political imperatives of the Islamic Republic and its survival in its formative years necessitated the involvement and active participation of both sexes in the social and military domains. Moreover, he thought it politically expedient to place women supporters of the revolution in offices and factories to replace or silence those who opposed the Islamic government. Khomeini thus needed the support of women at the religious, cultural, political, social, and economic levels to "purify . . . [and] reconstruct" a country ruined by the Pahlavi regime. Finally, just as in his anti-Western discourse, like other fundamentalist ideologues Khomeini transformed the political conflict with the West into a "timeless cultural and religious conflict with the 'enemies of Islam.'" He turned women into the symbols of the revolution and the protectors of Islamic values. Thus, women and their garments became "the public face" of the revolution.

A last and final rationalization of Khomeini's apparent equivocation regarding gender issues is the consolidation of his power and that of the Islamic Republic. During the transitional period between the ratification of the Constitution of the Islamic Republic in December 1979 and the final establishment of the Republic, a struggle raged for the new seats of power and the consolidation of clerical rule. The most expedient demonstration of power was, I believe, the Islamization of society and the ending of all internal political opposition. This was accomplished by the drastic measures taken to constrain women and the imposition of the *chador*. Thus, on February 26, 1979, the Family Protection Law was abrogated; on March 3, 1979, women were barred from the judiciary; on March 26, 1979, Khomeini announced the obligatory *hijab* in the workplace; on March 29, 1979, beaches were segregated, and a few weeks later, coeducational schools were abolished; on March 30, 1979, the first public flogging of a man and woman accused of adultery took place, and a couple of months later, the first woman was stoned to death for adultery. In this manner, Khomeini was the first to delineate the markers of his revolution, preempting any competition by other ideologues.

Moreover, women are usually seen as the weakest link in society and, therefore, the easiest to subdue. They are also the most visible, thereby making their subjugation readily observable, giving the false impression that the whole society is under control. This political manipulation of women and their role in society is made clearer when Khomeini's approval of women singing in groups on radio and television was criticized. "I feel it necessary," he wrote, "to express my despair about your understanding of the divine injunctions and the [Shi'ite] traditions. . . . The way you interpret the traditions, the new civilization should be destroyed and the people should live in shackles or live forever in the desert."[58] Liz Thurgood of *The Guardian* put it succinctly when she wrote, "Women are the barometers of Iranian politics."[59] This is made more evident by the return of women to the workplace during the war with Iraq (1980–88) to fill the need of the government for more nurses and physicians to back up the war effort. Placing a child in the custody of a deceased father's family when his widow remarried, in accordance with *Shari'ah* laws, was also abrogated to quell the public outcry. This became necessary in view of the increasing numbers of martyrs' war-widows, who were appeased by being allowed to retain custody of their children.[60] This, in addition to political expedience, also demonstrates the flexibility of Islam and the *Shari'ah* in meeting the exigencies of the time, should the clergy choose.

Moreover, Islam, in accordance with its flexibility, provides such ordinances as the so-called "rule of emergency," when "emergencies make it permissible to do what is forbidden," and transcend any religious obligation. This is based on the Qur'anic verses 2:173 and 6:145: "But if a person finds himself in a dilemma, without desiring," he is not guilty if he eats forbidden meat, albeit "account must be taken of the extent of the emergency in question." This is referred to as a "secondary ordinance," the primary ordinance being the *Shari'ah*.[61] Another method by which *Shari'ah* may be circumvented is "secondary contractual conditions."[62] Moreover, although *maslahah* was established in 1988 as the final decisive principle of legislation, it had been used before in the Islamic Republic, when religious taxation was abandoned and direct and indirect taxation imposed. The Islamic regulation of banking and the banning of interest as "usury" were circumvented by the use of such terms as "handling fee," "fixed earning," and "expected earning," and the term "payment facilities" replaced the word "loan."[63]

Finally, by subordinating women to their husbands and removing them from the public sphere, the government immediately won the support of the male population. Ceding them total and absolute authority over the other half of the population, their ego, lust for power, and need for social change were automatically assuaged. The exit of women from the public sphere gave males the illusion that the economic situation was improving by their becoming the sole economic agents in the arena with no obvious competitors.[64] In short, this approach to the status of women fully illustrates the principle of *maslahah*: despite many declarations to the contrary amply evident in many of his writings and sayings, Khomeini decided to appease his intensely patriarchal society to safeguard his power base. He simply granted the male population complete hegemony over their women, thereby ensuring their loyalty and support for his Islamic state and buying the needed time for promised reforms. This is alluded to by Ayatollah Yusef Sane'i, who describes Khomeini as being afraid to voice his true beliefs and ideas for fear of arousing the narrow-minded but powerful group of patriarchs and clerics.[65]

A final question to be answered is why women were such ardent supporters of Khomeini and the revolution. Several reasons may be advanced for this curious phenomenon. Khomeini's directions that the husband should "feed, house, and clothe [his obedient wife] whether he has the means or not" relieved the lower-class women who had been forced into the workplace. They were happy to return to their homes and have their husbands support them. The encouragement of women by the religious leadership to disobey their husbands and join the revolution gave them a feeling of independence, freedom, value, and respect. They found in the revolution a curious sense of security and a respected status within the revolutionary culture, elevated by the sacrifices they were making and the martyrs they were producing for the revolution. Both men and women found themselves searching for "a new national and gender identity" the revolution was able to provide.

Moreover, Khomeini himself in his prerevolutionary speeches promised all women that they, "like men, [would] participate in building the future of Islamic society. They [would] have the right to vote and to be elected. Women [had] contributed to the recent struggles in Iran alongside men." And, finally, he promised, "We will give all kinds of freedom to women."[66] In his *Le Monde* interview in May 1978, he declared, "As for women, Islam has never been against their freedom. It is, to the contrary, opposed to the idea of women as objects and it gives them back their dignity. A woman is a man's equal; she and he are both free to choose their lives and their occupations. But the Shah's regime is trying to prevent women from becoming free by plunging them into immorality. It is against this that Islam rears up. This regime has destroyed the freedom of women, as well as men,"[67] and women believed his every word. Thus, many women who wore the *chador* during the revolution thought they would remove it as soon as the revolution was over, since it was only a political symbol. While in the past *hijab* signified inhibition for women, it was regarded at the time of the revolution as enabling and empowering: it allowed them access to the public sphere free of any molestation or harassment, and it portrayed them as "free, non-sexual, politically aware, and in solidarity with the Revolution." Khomeini, viewed as a savior from the tyranny of the Pahlavi regime, was hailed by literate, educated, and intellectual women who got caught up in the fervor of the revolution and its promises of liberation. Conservative or traditional women supported the revolution possibly motivated by the existing gap between their traditional atmosphere at home and the growing Westernization in the external world, generating an imbalance in their lives and a sense of dissatisfaction with their mode of life. Religious revivalism thus seemed to be the answer to all these problems and, therefore, their only refuge.[68]

It is thus evident that, in several aspects of his doctrine, Khomeini is in agreement with the previously studied ideologues. All four have proven their traditionalism with regard to women's issues and women's role in Islamic society. All have manipulated these issues to further their own ends. However, unlike al-Banna, al-Mawdudi, and Qutb, Khomeini was actually able to establish his ideal Islamic state and to put his beliefs and teachings into practice in the interest of his ideal state.

In contrast to the three Sunni ideologues, however, Khomeini refused to recognize women witnesses in murder cases irrespective of their number, whereas the Sunnis allowed such testimony when rendered by two women. He endowed women with great stature when his interests dictated and to that end drew on great women from Shiʿite Islamic history. He went on to call on women to join the jihad and extolled their military virtues.

Khomeini takes his restrictions on women further than do al-Mawdudi and Qutb. He thus forbids them to inherit any real estate or any income that may accrue from it, and dictates that all of a wife's possessions, including her clothing, belong to her husband. Moreover, Khomeini, contrary to Qutb and Banna, but like al-Mawdudi, though more so, immerses himself in all the intimate details of a woman's physiology and marital sex.

However, despite these differences, it is clear that all four ideologues share the same traditional views of women, with Khomeini being more strident in his views except, of course, when the interest of the state dictates otherwise, as in matters of work, voting, or jihad.

Chapter 6

✳

Ayatollah Mortaza Mutahhari

Mutahhari's contribution to the exposition of Islamic doctrine and his delineation of the ideology of the revolution are unique in their scope and volume. His books were written in response to what he felt was of concern to Iranians. Ever since he wrote his commentary on 'Allamah Tabtaba'i's *Principles of Philosophy and the Realistic Method,* Mutahhari made it his mission to target contemporary political issues and subject them to an intellectual and ideological analysis rarely attempted by a legitimate cleric before—an amalgam of theological discourse interspersed with a radical analysis of Iranian society and Westernization. Mutahhari came to be known as one of the most significant thinkers of the Iranian clergy and the foremost ideologue of the revolution, thus securing a permanent niche in the annals of the Islamic Republic of Iran. One of his major concerns was the question of the rights of women.[1]

Mortaza Mutahhari was born on February 2, 1920, the son of Sheikh Muhammad Hussein Mutahhari, in the village of Faryman of the Khorasan province, and he began his studies there. Later on, he moved to Mashhad, and in 1936, he moved on to Qom for advanced religious studies. During his stay there, and while holding classes of his own, he attended Imam Khomeini's lectures on philosophy and epistemology, which "had a great influence in shaping my personality and thinking," and took part in the burgeoning Islamic movements.

Mutahhari joined the Islamic Movement led by Khomeini and participated in the uprising of June 6, 1963. He was arrested alongside other religious leaders and jailed for forty-three days, only to be released under mounting public pressure. Following Khomeini's exile to Turkey, and then to Iraq in 1964, the Society of Religious Mujahidin was formed with

Mutahhari a prominent member. He also acted as Khomeini's representative and liaison, and was arrested again with other society members following the assassination of Prime Minister Mansour. Following his release, he continued to be closely monitored by the Savak.

In 1978, Mutahhari directed all Islamic revolutionary activities in Iran as Khomeini's representative. He later joined Khomeini in Paris and was commissioned to form a revolutionary council to direct the Iranian uprising. He remained a close friend and companion of Khomeini after the latter returned to Iran. He was martyred on May 1, 1979, having amassed an impressive opus comprising thirty books and articles. Khomeini wept publicly at his funeral, calling him "the fruit of my life," and eulogized him as a "noble martyr, a distinguished thinker, philosopher, and jurist." Khomeini proclaimed a national day of mourning for him and personally received condolences at the Feyziyyeh Seminary.[2] President Ali Khamane'i described his works as "the intellectual infrastructure of the Islamic Republic."

Taken as a whole, Mutahhari's legacy demonstrates how an individual cleric, well-versed in traditional learning and concerned with contemporary issues and problems, with a comprehensive vision of Islam as a total system of life, was able to contribute to the creation of the intellectual atmosphere of the Iranian Revolution of 1979.[3] He views Islam as a dynamic system, able to metamorphose and acclimate to change, and encompassing a set of regulations governing the stable, unchangeable needs of mankind, constant through time. Other needs may be of a temporary nature and, therefore, subject to change. Accordingly, Islam provides a set of supervisory laws designed to alter or negate other regulations. In addition, Islamic dynamism is reinforced by allowing its laws to be reinterpreted by learned experts.[4] Mutahhari believed that the laws of God were eternal, not subject to any form of change. Hence, there was no room for evolution, development, or improvement upon them. Nor were people necessarily the best judges of what laws should govern them. The laws of Islam were absolute and irrefutable, to be obeyed until the end of days.

> If the laws obey the times, then who should the times obey? That would imply that laws should follow the wishes of the people. But one of the functions of the law is to control and conduct society. . . . Humanity is capable of moving forward, or veering to the right or left, or stopping and regressing. . . . This free will means that humanity is capable of making many mistakes. . . . This is precisely why we must not be submitted to the will of the times. We must rely on

absolute values ... We have faith in and rely absolutely on the knowledge that our series of laws and practices are eternal ... We regard religion as an absolute, and as independent of the economic and political circumstances of the time.[5]

Mutahhari, like his mentor Khomeini, believed that only the clergy were fit to be the leaders of an Islamic government. "It is the rich and magnificent Islamic culture that can and must be the foundation of our movement. It is the Islamic clergy who know this magnificent culture and have been educated by it and who are able to understand our contemporary society, who could and should be its leaders ... The leadership must be cognizant with true Islamic vision, only those who have been raised in the heart of the Islamic culture ... Only the clergy have the necessary quality and ability to lead the Islamic movement." In this context, intellectuals can only be followers, never leaders.[6]

Yet, Mutahhari's chief concern was to challenge the validity of taqlid [emulation, tradition], according to which Shiʻites are expected to follow in the footsteps of a religious authority of their own choice. "The basis of the Qurʾan," he explains, "is on admonishing those who are bound by emulation following their ancestors, and without thinking [for a moment] to rid themselves of slavery to rotten opinions, which, like a chain, ties their arms and legs ... The Qurʾan wants to teach us that the measure and criterion ought to be the judgment of the intellect and thought, not merely doing what our fathers did."[7] He assumes a certain superiority of the mind and rationality against blind obedience. "In Islamic traditions," he argues, "it has been emphasized that one should not pay attention to people's judgment. It has been repeatedly asked to [heed] the independence of intellect and that of the mind."[8] Mutahhari quotes sura 39:17–18, "Therefore, give good tidings to my bondmen who hear advice and follow the best thereof. Such are those whom Allah guideth, and such are men of understanding." To confirm his view of the superiority of intellect, he quotes countless prophetic and imami traditions in support of rationality and judicious reflection: "One hour of thinking is better than one year of prayer ... sixty years of prayer ... seventy years of prayer. ... Thinking itself is prayer."[9]

The authoritative spokesperson on the question of women can be either Khomeini or Mutahhari. However, although Khomeini is better known, Mutahhari is certainly the ideologue of the revolution and the one who systematically delved into the matter of women and their role in society, and his writings afford an accurate insight into the clerical view of women in Iran. He has been described as the most complete and comprehensive interpreter of Shi'ite views on the role of women in society. His writings are to be seen as those of a reformer opposed to Western infiltration of Iranian Shi'ite society and who, consequently, tried to establish a rational Islamic system clearly delineating male-female relationships within the ideal Shi'ite family. To this end, he used state-controlled media and any other available means to expound and popularize his views. He thus published several articles in *Zane Rooz* [Today's woman], condemning the government's family law reforms of the 1960s and defending Shari'ah regulations. He made extensive references to Western sources in philosophy, psychology, science, and even cinema and filmmaking to substantiate his views. His method and style appealed to the young and made Islamic dictates more palatable.[10]

In defending the position of women in Shi'ite Islam, Mutahhari attacks Western feminist movements by demonstrating their irrelevance to Islamic society. He argues that Western women acquired their economic independence only when cheap labor was in demand, while in Islam this was achieved for purely humanitarian reasons and in the interest of justice fourteen centuries ago. The Declaration of Human Rights, based on the philosophy of individualism, cannot but be rejected by Islam. For society, in Islam, is given precedence over the individual and his rights, such that the call for "equal rights," irrespective of gender, is untenable in Islam, since the term "equality" is easily confused with that of "similarity" of rights. Thus, women in the West are vying for similar rights to men, rather than true equality. In Islam, on the other hand, men and women are equal in their humanity, and, although they have different rights, they do not have a preferential status one over the other, nor is one more valuable than the other.[11]

Mutahhari urged Iranians not to ape the West in matters pertaining to women and the family, since Islam has always supported the rights of women as evidenced by the flexibility, elasticity, and compatibility of its laws with contemporary realities. Western philosophies, he declares, have diminished the status of human beings, and their views are self-contradictory. It is, therefore, only in the Qur'an that the true human rights of men and women are to be found. Mutahhari went to the further extreme of describing demands for gender equality in Iran as a Western plot, and all those, particularly women, who advocated secular reforms were branded as agents of the West. He resorted to history and tradition to demonstrate the insidious intrusion of imperialism implicit in the demands for modification of the family law. "Equal rights," he explained, was a misnomer for "similarity of rights," which is illegitimate in Islam. Equality, in Islam, cannot be discussed without the admission of biologic differences between the sexes. Given such natural differences between men and women and their different mental capacities and needs, "The only path to happiness and peace of mind for both sexes is to remove the similarity of rights."[12]

In the area of family relations, Islam provides a set of regulations that equate men and women in certain fields but differentiate between them in others: men and women are equal in human rights but differ in all else, according to their different natures. The Qur'an states that women were created from men and share the same soul. Islam declares men more suitable for prophecy and leadership but honors women as beloved of prophets, never despising or belittling them. The ban on sex during menstruation is not meant to reflect badly on women, the problem being merely the lack of cleanliness, a condition in which prayer or fasting are banned as well. The social rights of marriage partners are equal in education, politics, and employment, differences lying in ability and productivity, which propel some to higher positions and stature. In the family sphere, things are different. Mutahhari here argues for natural distinctions between men and women on the physical, emotional, and psychological levels. Women, according to him, were created to be unlike men and programmed for different roles. Thus, men and women possess different reproductive systems that control physical and mental functions: Men are stronger, taller, and coarser; their brain is larger, and they lean toward sports, hunting, and fighting and are easily aroused. Women attain maturity earlier but experience menopause, unlike men; they are calmer, more patient, but emotionally labile and unstable; they are more careful and cautious, religious, courteous, talkative, and fearful; they are motherly and family oriented; they are mentally inferior to men but equal in culture and art. Men are more secretive and are slaves of their lust, while women love men who show them attention and love; men want to lead and control women; women seek to capture men's hearts, while men prefer to control them forcefully; women admire courage and aggression in men, while men are attracted by women's beauty and coquetry; women need the protection of men but are more adept at curbing their appetites, which require stimulation for arousal, while men's appetites are rampant and aggressive.[13]

The family, Mutahhari maintains, is a natural institution where the natural differences between men and women are crystallized, for it is there that sexual activity, that continuous threat to social harmony, has to be harnessed. It is there that the two sexes can meet safely and productively, as stipulated by Divine Law. It is there that sexual desires are fulfilled and disciplined and the quality of future generations determined. "Mutual affection and sincerity, as well as human compassion and tenderness, are highly desirable attributes in married couples, in the context of their mutual social interactions."[14]

Upon marriage, the husband pays his wife (or her father, according to Mutahhari) a sum of money (*mahr*), symbolizing that she does not surrender herself easily and as a token of his love. The custom of paying a *mahr* to one's bride, explains Mutahhari, goes back to the beginning of human history, with gradual modification, up until the age of Islam. In the first phase of development, society was matriarchal with men subservient to their sovereign wives. During the second phase, men had grown in strength and abducted their brides from other tribes. In the third, a man won the hand of his beloved in marriage by working for her family for a number of years. In the fourth, a man would give the bride's father a sum of money in the form of a "present." Since men are stronger physically but weaker instinctually, it is they who have courted and offered women presents in the hope of winning them over. Women quickly realized their worth and upped the ante. This "present" came to be known as *mahr*, thereby crystalizing the natural differences between the two sexes. The Qur'an describes the *mahr* as a token of trust between the couple, to be paid to the bride, not to any other member of her family. Thus, God ordained the *mahr* to elevate the position of women in society. It reinforces a woman's personality, its spiritual value being far more important to her than its actual material worth. The *mahr*, then, is in harmony with nature in declaring the inception of a man's love of his woman. Moreover, Islam has taken into consideration women's diverse problems with regard to pregnancy and the rearing of children, their inability to compete in the domains of productivity and earning power, and their inexhaustible desire to spend money, in addition to certain characteristics peculiar to the sexes, such as man's urge to provide for his wife. These factors, combined, played a major role in imposing the *mahr* and financial support on the male.

The husband does not share in his wife's wealth or income and has to provide for her and his family, especially since periodic menstruation and childbearing reduce the wife's capacity for work. Furthermore, women's expenses are far more extravagant than men's, since their beauty requires rest and security and their demands for apparel and adornments exceed the expenditure of several men. Thus, Islam affords women economic independence and equal rights of employment, while the West frees them from the home only to enslave them in the marketplace.[15]

Based upon the marriage bond, Islamic law decrees "that the woman should be loved and respected within the family, [for] if she is no longer desired and loved by the man . . . the foundation of the family is shaken . . . From the point of view of Islam, the greatest insult to a woman is for her husband to say 'I do not love you; I hate you.'"[16] For a woman to remain loved and respected, Islam commands her to adorn and beautify herself for her husband, to devise ingenious ways to appeal to him and be attractive, to satisfy his sexual needs and preempt any possible complexes that may accrue as a result of her failure to do so.[17] If a woman's love for a man is not reciprocated, she remains fickle, but if her love reciprocates his, it remains stable for as long as he continues to love her.[18]

Men prefer their women pure and virtuous, out of envy and jealousy, while women's virtue emanates out of envy only. Envy is selfish, while jealousy is a beneficial social trait that provides protection for men to ensure the purity of their line, which, if tainted, may result in drastic social changes. In women, purity of line is always assured, since the offspring is always theirs. Thus, their need to monopolize their husband is selfish, while a man's monopoly of his wife has a social background. Further, jealousy is a facet of a man's honor and has a collective social color, and, as such, is not selfish.

When a married woman goes to work, with her husband's permission, and provided this does not interfere with her duties to home and husband, any accrued income is hers alone. In fact, her housework is strictly voluntary and she can demand payment for it. Thus, women need men materially, while men need them spiritually. If this marriage equation is disturbed, Mutahhari warns, it may lead to serious consequences: women will desert their homes for employment as breadwinners, which will nullify their role as mothers and lead to a breakdown of family structure with grave social repercussions.[19]

Mutahhari claims that monogamy is the "natural" form of marriage. A single wife is, undoubtedly, preferable, since monogamy reinforces family unity. However, this is not always possible as a result of economic and biologic necessities and the fact that women outnumber men. Also, a man is a slave of his passions and may not be able to restrain himself during his wife's menstruation or pregnancy and thus will be drawn into extramarital relations. Women also reach menopause at a time when their husbands require more children. Moreover, some women may be ill, frigid, or sterile.

Mutahhari explains, further, that because the death rate of men is higher than that of women, men being further decimated by wars, and women's immunity to disease is greater than that of men, and since it is the natural right of all women to marry, it is the duty of society as a whole to provide a suitable outlet whenever there is a shortage of men. It thus becomes a social duty for men to marry more than one woman to preempt illegal liaisons and extramarital relations. Men who are physically and financially able should take more than one wife, the first wife having to sacrifice some of her rights and privileges as a matter of social obligation. Further, the practice of polygamy becomes the only means by which monogamy itself is reinforced, since men, faced with an overpopulation of women, would prefer not to marry at all. Thus, the outcry against polygamy is simply a ploy of twentieth-century men to avoid the social responsibilities of marrying more than one woman, preferring to indulge in illegal sexual activities, instead. Since love and emotion are difficult to maintain in polygamy, polygamy should not be practiced unless certain conditions are met. Only those with a high level of social consciousness and an excellent Islamic education are eligible to practice it. If, with all these precautions, polygamy is abused, it would be through no fault of Islam. Islam's involvement is merely regulatory, limiting polygamy to four wives and insisting on equal rights and privileges for all wives, especially in financial and sexual aspects. Today, Mutahhari argues, polygamy has been replaced by retaining mistresses who are less demanding and burdensome.[20]

Hence, to discourage polygamy, Mutahhari argues, certain conditions have to be met: First, social justice should be ensured, such that ample employment opportunities affording decent wages are made available, to allow every eligible male to marry. Second, eligible women are to be allowed the freedom to choose their own husbands, eliminating, thereby, the possibility of a woman choosing a married man for a husband, since women prefer to monopolize their men. This is a factor that helps reduce the elements of seduction and sexual arousal in society. If these conditions are not met, many women would be deprived of marriage and driven into illegal sexual liaisons, dangerous to the marital state and family structure. Happiness in marriage depends on faithfulness, forgiveness, sacrifice, and unity, all of which are endangered by multiple wives with their attendant financial burdens. For the husband to be happy in a polygamous marriage, he usually immerses himself in caring for the new wife, neglecting the older ones.[21] Historically, the system of multiple husbands failed dismally because of the inherent nature of men and women. Women did not derive adequate care and protection from their multiple husbands, nor could they win their love, and they became, therefore, repelled by the whole arrangement, especially in that women are more interested in capturing men's hearts and enjoying the sacrifices they offer them. Men, on the other hand, seek possession of women's bodies and insist on definitive lineage. Men are, therefore, concerned with the physical attributes of women and their sexuality, which fade with time, while women seek emotional and spiritual attributes, which keep on growing. Hence, in multiple marriages, Islam reinforces women's rights in providing husbands for supernumerary women.[22]

Mutahhari also proposes temporary marriage or *mut'ah* as a complement to permanent marriage, at a time when "the gap between natural puberty and social puberty, or the ability to start a family, has widened." He is credited with being the first to conceptualize *mut'ah* in its contemporary form. He shifted the emphasis from the defensive traditional Shi'ite stand to declaring it a modern, functional institution on the social and psychological levels. He describes it as "one of the brilliant laws of Islam," timeless and universal. It is now unique to the Ja'fari sect, but it is universally agreed that it was prevalent at the time of the Prophet, especially during extended travel. However, it was later banned by 'Umar Ibn al-Khattab for political rather than legal or religious motives. It is still banned by Sunni Muslims, but not by the Shi'ites.[23]

Because of the financial burdens of permanent marriages, Mutahhari explains, Islam legislated the entity of temporary marriage. This, like regular marriage, is legal, contractual, and requires a *mahr*. It differs by being finite, with more freedom in setting the marriage contract, and in its *mahr* being mandatory, its absence voiding the contract. The wife has no inheritance rights, but her children, if any, are legitimate and do inherit. Temporary marriage is, otherwise, similar to regular marriage in rules and regulations, except for the duration of the *'iddah* [waiting period] which is limited to two months, instead of the three required in permanent marriages. *Mut'ah* is useful for young men who have not yet completed their education, are unable to enter into permanent marriages, and cannot contain their sexual needs; or for couples who cannot resist their physical attraction to one another prior to permanent marriage. It is also a deterrent against homosexuality, fornication, and adultery, since Islam opposes sexual abstinence and advocates a regulated satisfaction of all natural urges and needs. Furthermore, Shi'ite jurists maintain that permanent marriage is designed for the creation of a family unit with children, while temporary marriage serves to satisfy the partner's sexual needs legally but is not a means of providing simple pleasure and entertainment.[24]

Mutahhari draws on what he considers natural differences between men and women to justify differences in rights and duties. Thus, "It is nature that has placed the key to the dissolution of marriage in a man's hand." Marriage, he argues, is a natural bond, rather than a simple contractual relationship, sustained by mutual love and respect. When these are no longer present, the basis of family life is destroyed and marriage is, thence, best dissolved, especially so since Islamic laws are not empowered to restore normal relations. Moreover, while the cessation of the husband's love leads to the cessation of his wife's love, the opposite is not true, since the husband's love only intensifies when his wife's love wanes, and he would do the impossible to win her back. Thus, it is the husband who sustains the marital relationship and nurtures it, especially since a woman cannot but reciprocate her husband's love. It is, therefore, natural that "the extinction of a man's love results in the death and end of marriage, whereas extinction of a woman's love simply turns the marriage into a sick being who is curable." As such, "Nature has given the key of the natural dissolution of marriage to the man."[25] However, divorce simply for the love of another woman is opposed by Islam but not forbidden, since no one should be coerced into living with another. Nevertheless, on occasion, some husbands refuse to divorce their wives, simply to punish them, which is not acceptable. Although divorce is man's natural right, he may agree to relegate it to his wife if so stipulated in the marriage contract. A woman may also resort to a court for a divorce if her husband abuses her and refuses to divorce her. This, however, is not encouraged and is rarely done.[26]

Islam, continues Mutahhari, abhors divorce and tries hard to forestall or prevent it: two fair witnesses are required to act as intermediaries to attempt to reconcile the couple; a husband may not divorce his wife while she is menstruating, since this deters intercourse, which may bring the partners closer to each other; the 'iddah period of three months following pronouncement of the divorce may also provide another opportunity for reconciliation; and, finally, representatives of both partners may intercede to bring about a reconciliation.[27]

The matter of the veil, Mutahhari asserts, is incontrovertible, being clearly stated in the Qur'an. Several studies have attributed its origins to philosophical, social, moral, economic, and psychological factors. The philosophical trend describes it as a form of spiritual and religious exercise; the social stream sees it as a form of protection of women against insecurity and social injustice; the economic current attributes it to patriarchy and its concomitant subordination and exploitation of women's economic potential; the moralists trace it to man's egocentricity and jealousy; and, finally, the psychological school ascribes it to women's monthly menstruation, during which they feel inferior and discarded.[28]

Mutahhari explains that women are, by nature, modest and chaste and instinctively conceal themselves behind the veil in the presence of men, for added respect and dignity. Moreover, although they are inferior to men physically and, probably, mentally as well, they have always managed to overcome men emotionally and win them over. This becomes more effective when there is a barrier between them creating an air of mystery that enhances men's attraction.[29] Another determinant of the Islamic veil is the factor of psychological stability in society, since the free association of men and women enhances sexual stimulation to an unquenchable thirst and increases the incidence of venereal diseases. Hence, it is not permitted for men and women to stare at or examine each other, and women should not exhibit any bodily parts or provocative adornments that may arouse men, who tend to be easily aroused and are sexually insatiable. In this, women are always at fault, because they delight in attracting men through their beauty and nudity and are, therefore, culpable as the source of evil. The veil prevents all this and reserves women's talents of arousal for their husbands.[30]

A third determinant of the veil is the strengthening of family relations. Hence, contrary to a sexually free system, where the husband has to compete with outside interests, becoming, thus, burdened with guarding his wife against illegal liaisons, restriction of sexual activities to the legitimate marital bed strengthens the bond between the two partners. Thus, legitimate marital sex ensures happiness and contentment and does away with privation, while sexual freedom reduces marriage to imprisonment and deprivation, lowers marriage rates, breaks up marriages, impairs social and commercial productivity, and allows women to control men whenever they are unable to compete with them physically or mentally. The fourth and last determinant of the veil is the strengthening of the social fabric, since the extension of sexual relations from the family to the public sphere can only weaken social productivity and performance.[31]

The veil, which was never imposed by men, elaborates Mutahhari, not only solves all these problems but also increases men's respect for women. It does not "imprison" women, but, rather, acts as a protective measure, a shield, in the presence of men. To require women, in the interest of society at large, to wear a special dress or abstain from provocative movements in no way hampers their freedom or integrity; rather, it affords them free mobility alongside men in a safe environment for both. Women, according to him, have inalienable rights to enter into employment or business ventures with men, participate in societies or political parties, pray in mosques, take part in religious activities and festivities, seek education, and participate in the various fields of art, always with the permission of their husbands and properly veiled. The appearance of unveiled women in educational institutions, offices, and factories is bound to provoke men and divert their attention from productive activities. Unveiling, he argues, transforms half the population—the women—into idle creatures preoccupied with clothing and cosmetics and the other half—the men—into persons who are robbed of their willpower and turned into pleasure-seeking, lustful oglers.[32]

The veil, thus, does not shackle women but rather helps elevate desire to a pure level. Sexual desire is both physical and spiritual, the latter being heightened by the veil. Sexual deprivation and excess, explains Mutahhari, are equally harmful, contrary to Freud's contention that instincts may be controlled by satiation and that deprivation may cause mental illness. Sexual freedom, he goes on, can be just as destructive as privation. Only Islam provides the ideal solution by advocating sexual control through regulated satisfaction, avoiding excess, deprivation, and anarchy.[33] The Qur'an discusses this in suras 24 and 33 and warns that Muslims may not enter other homes without permission, to safeguard women's honor and protect personal and family secrets. Even *mahram* [unmarriageable men] should wait for permission before morning prayers, at midday (a time of relaxation), and after evening prayers when husband and wife are in intimate apparel. Muslim men and women should not examine each other lustfully, both remaining virtuous and women being properly covered and veiled to avoid arousing men. They should not expose provocative adornments or wear strong perfumes that may arouse men. They may unveil, disrobe, and exhibit their adornments (*zinah*) in the presence of their husbands and *mahram*. Old, sexually inactive women may be excused from the veil.[34]

A woman's disposition for love and her strong emotionality, Mutahhari expounds, prevent her from taking part in activities like jihad or occupying judicial positions. However, if the country is under attack, women may participate by providing support and care for the wounded. They may also participate in funerals, Friday prayers, and prayers of the two feasts, albeit in segregation. They may work, for social and economic reasons, in such fields as nursing, medicine, and teaching, provided they retain their veil and avoid close interaction with men. Muslim women are to have no relationship whatsoever with non-Muslim men and are not to unveil in the presence of non-Muslim women. They may not shake hands with men unless gloved, and their voices should not be heard if provocative.[35]

Thus, Islam, argues Mutahhari, has served women well, restored their freedom, assured their natural rights, and bolstered their personalities without treating them as sex objects, while preserving their respect for parents and husbands and protecting the sanctity of the family. Male and female children enjoy financial independence upon maturation without any family interference. The mature young man is free to marry whomever he wishes without interference. The mature young woman, if not a virgin, is similarly free, but if she is still virginal, her father has to approve the prospective husband, since she is still inexperienced and, therefore, impressionable and easily deceived. Women inherit half as much as men, only because they have the *mahr*, are financially dependent upon men, and are relieved of the duty of jihad and payment of the *diyyah* [blood money]. As such, this is not discriminatory and does not reflect negatively on women but instead represents a just and fair distribution of wealth according to each gender's financial obligations.[36]

Mutahhari's chief concern seems to be in challenging the validity of *taqlid* [emulation], emphasizing rationality and the superiority of the intellect. He maintains that "one hour of thinking is better than one year of prayer," thus elevating the thinking process above prayer itself. Yet, nowhere does he apply this to the question of women. His interpretation of the Qur'anic text on women is categorical and traditional in the extreme despite his admission of man's fallibility. Like Qutb, he uses the scientific, rational method only to substantiate preconceived traditional notions of women and their role in society. He describes Islam as dynamic and able to metamorphose and acclimate to change, but he comes up with a fixed, rigid system of rules and regulations whenever women and family matters arise.

Mutahhari's writings on women were a reaction to the attempts of intellectual reformers at emulating Western practices in an effort to secularize and reform civil code articles dealing with women's issues. He states that these articles are based on Qur'anic verses that define the role of women in society. He goes on to explain that God created men and women of the same material (clay), but he differs from other ideologues by interpreting sura 4:1, "who created you from a single soul and from it created its mate," in an ultraconservative fashion to mean that God created Adam first and, from him, created Eve. While he is categorical in this interpretation, the quoted sura lends itself to several interpretations, one of which actually holds that God created Eve first, since there is no gender specification anywhere in the text. Mutahhari moves on to quote other verses from suras 3 (al-'Umran) and 4 (al-Nisa') in an effort to demonstrate gender equality. He refers to the story of the Garden of Eden, where both Adam and Eve are held equally guilty of disobedience, with no reference to Eve being the instigator of Adam's fall (2:35; 3:20–22). Nowhere in the Qur'an, according to him, are women described as inferior to men. In fact, both were created for each other, "They are garments for you, and you are garments for them" (2:187). Moreover, the Qur'an describes women as good for men and the source of their tranquility and contentment—"that ye might find rest in them" (30:21)—and "We have created you male and female, and have made you nations and tribes that ye may know one another" (49:13) demonstrating unequivocally the equality of the two sexes. He also draws attention to the fact that the final reward is not sex-specific but dependent upon faith and the good deeds of both men and women, and he identifies a number of women praised in the Qur'an as the equals of great men. The Qur'an, thus, mentions the wives of Adam and Abraham as well as the mothers of 'Issa and Moses, demonstrating that heroic deeds are not peculiar to men. Mutahhari goes on to draw upon history for examples of male and female saints, as well as great men and women, to demonstrate their equality in the path to God. Men alone, however, are chosen for prophethood. They alone are qualified to carry the message and provide religious guidance. All these declarations, however, become suspect when we see that in the bulk of his published works, Mutahhari considers women inferior to men at the physical, emotional, and psychological levels.[37]

Contradictions are clearly observed in his vacillation in defining the relationship between men and women, whether physical or spiritual, depending on the point he is trying to prove at any particular time in his argument. Thus, when he quotes the Qur'an to define the relationship between husband and wife, he describes it as one of "love and mercy," contradicting earlier statements specifying the motives for marriage as sex and procreation.[38] He further affirms that legitimate marital sex ensures happiness and contentment and does away with privation, while sexual freedom reduces marriage to a state of imprisonment and deprivation. Yet, in flagrant contradiction, he encourages the unlimited practice of *mut'ah* marriage. Moreover, while he admits the possibility of men oppressing women, due to their superior physical strength, nowhere does Mutahhari recommend any measures to prevent such oppression or preserve women's God-given rights,[39] although nothing in the Scripture hinders his promulgation of such safeguards. Finally, although he draws on history to claim that in the first phase of development, society was matriarchal with men subservient to their sovereign wives, thus implicitly admitting the rational and possibly physical superiority of women, he asserts the physical and rational superiority of men over women, in general, in his eagerness to rationalize the custom of *mahr*.

In his argument to enforce the veil, Mutahhari explains, "It is a mistake for us to imagine that a man's sensuality, when satisfied to a certain limit, will attain rest. In the same way that a person, whether male or female, cannot be satisfied with wealth and power, no man ever has enough of possessing beautiful women, and no woman enough of attracting the attentions of men and possessing their hearts. Finally, no man's heart is satiated by sexual pleasure."[40] The implication here is that men are weak, unable to control their desires and sexual needs, and, therefore, they need to be protected against the charms of women and their own dangerous instincts, which, unless checked, would lead to extramarital sex. This is best achieved, according to him, through the enforcement of the veil, the wearing of gloves when shaking men's hands, and the muting of provocative voices. He is, however, quite vague in defining what actually constitutes a "provocative voice," unless, of course, he prefers the total muting of the female voice. Moreover, Mutahhari seems to have forgotten that he has provided men with several drive-release mechanisms, such as unilateral divorce, polygamy, and *mut'ah* marriage, which is allowed to take place in tandem with polygamy without any limitation of number, frequency, or duration.

In Mutahhari's own words, "Where would a man be more productive, where he is studying in all-male institutions or where he is sitting next to a girl whose skirt reveals her thighs? Which man can do more work, he who is constantly exposed to arousing and exciting faces of made-up women in the street, bazaar, office, or factory, or he who does not have to face such sights?"[41] Claiming such assertions to be factual, he declares that, in the interest of society in general, women are best kept at home out of men's sight. Yet, in a final argument to persuade women to wear the veil, he resorts to playing on their emotions: Assuming their main concern lies in attracting men, he explains that the veil is their best ally in ensnaring husbands, since they are much more alluring when they are mysterious, the veil hinting at hidden pleasures! Seeing a veiled woman only heightens men's desires and intensifies their passion, especially in that women's modesty provides a further incentive for men to pursue them.[42] Mutahhari, here, seems oblivious to the fact that the reason he advanced earlier for wearing the veil was, in fact, to keep women from being alluring to men and not to attract them. Hence, one would think that, if the veil is actually more seductive to men, it is in the best interest of society to do away with it entirely and spare men its "magical" attraction. Or could it be that Mutahhari, believing women to be intellectually inferior, thinks he can persuade them to wear the veil through such simplistic and self-contradictory arguments?

Mutahhari's discourse on the veil displays many more fallacies. Like other ideologues, his concern for the veil is confined to urban women. But, while other ideologues, with the exception of Khomeini, remain mute on this point, Mutahhari tackles it head-on: "Except in villages, and among the pious families, no woman can be found whose energy is spent on useful social, economic, or cultural activities . . . half the population has been transformed into idle creatures preoccupied with clothing, cosmetics, and attracting men."[43] His arguments have several implications:

1. Only rural women are virtuous and can be trusted to move about unveiled and work side-by-side with men in the fields. Mutahhari here seems oblivious to his earlier description of male and female sexual instincts, which men can never satiate and women can never curb. Are we to believe that rural women do not have the impetus to seduce and attract men? And do rural men not yearn to satisfy their desires? And, if both can control these urges, why can't urban men and women?

2. Mutahhari lauds the cooperative efforts of rural men and women outside the home but denounces urban women for being idle, interested only in minor, superficial occupations. He seems to forget that he himself relegated women to the home sphere and barred them from joining men in the workplace, on the pretext that they would distract the men. As to women being interested in cosmetics and wasting valuable time on makeup, he also seems to forget that he required this of all dutiful wives to help preserve the interest of their husbands, prevent divorce, and discourage polygamy. Is one to understand, then, that rural and urban people are different by nature, rural

men being able to control their instincts in the presence of unveiled women, and rural women their seductive powers? Or does this discrepancy depend upon the particular aim of his argument? And, if so, doesn't the whole edifice of his discourse collapse?

3. Could Mutahhari's aim here be to encourage agriculture and discourage urbanization? And, if so, wouldn't he be going against Islamic injunctions for purely economic and political reasons? In the same vein, could the veiling of urban women, then, be motivated by political and economic reasons as well?

4. His argument is also in peril when he attempts to disprove Freud's theory on the satisfaction of instincts: he quotes a poet claiming the soul (al-nafs) to be like a baby, who, unless weaned, would continue to breast-feed; and another who declared that the soul is as desirous as you allow it to be but can be content with very little if so trained.[44] These quotations, explicitly admitting the ability of all humans to control their passions if they so desire, defeat his earlier arguments about men's and women's instincts that can neither be curbed nor controlled except through the veiling of women.

5. Mutahhari explains that women are, by nature, modest and chaste, instinctively concealing themselves behind the veil in the presence of men for added respect and dignity. Yet, he goes on to prohibit women from staring at or examining men or exhibiting any bodily part or provocative adornments that may arouse men. He even accuses them of delighting in attracting men through their beauty and nudity, being, therefore, culpable as the source of evil. Here, once again, to rationalize the desirability of veiling by reminding women that they naturally crave modesty and chastity, he goes against his own arguments that women's natural instincts drive them to seduce and attract men. Moreover, if women are by nature modest and chaste, there would be no need to veil them.

6. Finally, by denying men the ability to control their sexual instinct, Mutahhari is actually denying them their will power and rationality, which, according to him, are the basis of their superiority over women, who are, by nature, emotional. In effect, Mutahhari, in his zeal to veil women, reduces men to a level below that of women, who seem to have the ultimate power of manipulating men.

Moreover, the categorical tone of his argument for the veiling of women and for the design of the veil automatically loses its credibility once he tries to explain the relevant Qur'anic verses. His interpretation only serves to demonstrate the controversial nature of the subject matter: The uncertainty revolves around the identity of the women to be veiled and the nature of the veil itself—does it entail covering women's bodies or does it involve actual segregation of the sexes? What do the Arabic words *jilbab* [loose garment] and *khimar* [veil] actually mean, and, more importantly, what does the word *zinah* [adornment or ornament] refer to? In view of the difficulties involved in deciphering Qur'anic texts, Mutahhari's argument in favor of the veil becomes tenuous, if not totally superfluous. He explains that covering one's private parts was not known in pre-Islamic Arabia, and, thus, when the Qur'an requires this, it is to be taken literally for both men and women—to cover their private parts and avoid staring at them. Mutahhari, however, elaborates further that women were singled out later on because of their beauty and its effect on men.[45] He attempts to explain the meaning of *jilbab* and *khimar* but admits the difficulty in that, especially in the light of previous interpretations by early jurisprudents.[46]

What is being overlooked in this discussion is the fact that *jilbab* and *khimar* simply describe the fashion of the time, which apparently covered very little of a woman's body, as inferred from the Qur'anic directives to cover all private parts. Thus, wearing a *khimar* or *jilbab* today need not be a requirement, just as men today are not required to cover only body parts between navel and knees. This becomes even more important when one notes the difficulties faced by jurisprudents in trying to determine the meaning of *zinah* [ornaments]. The conclusions of Mutahhari and other jurisprudents are, therefore, completely arbitrary and are not substantiated by any solid evidence from the Qur'an or Sunna. The definition of *zinah* remains totally arbitrary and speculative, especially given that the nature of visible and/or covered ornaments was dictated by the dress of the time and relative to it—and this remains unclear. Thus, while *zinah* in Arabic denotes visible ornaments, Mutahhari concludes that women's ornaments may be visible or covered, unless willfully exposed by them. He then stipulates, like others before him, that ornaments are to be limited only to the uncovered parts of women's bodies—the face and hands. My contention is that this interpretation remains quite arbitrary since we are ignorant of the mode of dress of the time and the type and location of worn ornaments. It is quite possible that ornaments were worn on all parts of the body, especially so since it is clear from the Qur'an itself that the whole body could be discerned through presumably diaphanous dresses. This further explains Qur'anic directives that women avoid stamping their feet while walking so that ornaments worn on sensitive and suggestive areas are not heard, and not, as Mutahhari sweepingly claims, that ornaments are to include perfume, makeup, and anything else that might unduly attract men. Moreover, one cannot deny the beauty and attractiveness of the face. Thus, if the arms and neck are to be covered as seductive, then, following Mutahhari's own logic, the face should be covered as well.

In short, determining the exact definition of the *zinah*, *jilbab*, and *khimar* of women and their extant dress fashions is purely arbitrary with no basis in sacred texts. The narrowness of Mutahhari's vision in this matter is best demonstrated when he allows women to appear before their *mahram* [father-in-law, brother-in-law, son-in-law, male servants, sons, nephews, among others] totally uncovered, except for the area between navel and knees.[47] Interestingly enough, he explains away exceptions to his strictures on dress and behavior, including the identity of those allowed to enter a woman's room unannounced, as a matter of convenience. If convenience may be used as a basis of exceptions, couldn't its area of influence have been extended further? Mutahhari also fails to justify his adoption of traditionally imposed limitations as in including the poor among the *mahram*, though he himself does not subscribe to this ruling. Moreover, if men are controlled by their instincts to such an extent, shouldn't the *mahram* be similarly aroused in the presence of women clad only in garments covering the area between navel and knees? If they are able to control their instincts under these circumstances, why can't they under all circumstances?

In his zeal to defend polygamy, Mutahhari declares it to be in women's best interests, since it would ensure each woman the pleasure and privilege of having a home and family through marriage. It would satiate their sexual needs, which may not be satisfied extramaritally; and make it possible for them to enjoy the security, protection, and love of a superior (*ra'is*) unavailable outside the marriage bounds. The imposition of monogamy as the only legal form of marriage can deprive many women of their natural right of marriage. However, Mutahhari takes care to avoid mentioning the many advantages men derive from polygamy, as he describes elsewhere,[48] and concentrates instead on convincing women that polygamy is in their best interest and not men's.

In the past, commentators simply accepted *mut'ah* as a religious sanction for alleviating men's urges in times of need. However, contemporary advocates of the practice have made great effort to provide socially and morally acceptable arguments for this type of union and have explained away 'Umar's suspension of the practice on the grounds of sociopolitical reform, and, as such, this suspension is not to be considered categorical. Mutahhari has been an ardent supporter and advocate of this practice. He argues that it demonstrates the awareness of Islam of the emotional and psychological needs of adolescents, proving, thereby, its progressiveness and compatibility with modern times and needs. He even quotes Bertrand Russell on the advantages of temporary marriage for the young. However, he glosses over the fact that Russell suggested such an arrangement only as a premarital experiment of compatibility. He also avoids noting the male privileges in temporary marriage, where a man with four wives, and no age limit, may contract any number of additional temporary wives.[49]

Mutahhari emphasizes that Islam considers divorce an abomination to be undertaken only under extreme circumstances, and he quotes al-Tabarsi in his book on ethics *(Makarim al-akhlaq)*, who in turn quotes the Prophet as having said, "Marry and do not divorce, because the throne shakes upon divorce."[50] However, he then goes on to explain that divorce is permissible in Islam and contends that marriage is a natural, rather than circumstantial *(wadʿiy)*, relationship and is, therefore, governed by natural laws contrary to all other social contracts. The natural law prevalent in a civilized society is that of equality and freedom, which governs all social actions except marriage. Since marriage is built on the principles of love, unity, and compassion, rather than friendship and support, and since the wife is the center of the family with man revolving around her, divorce must necessarily follow the natural laws appropriate to it. Thus, a marriage built on love and unity cannot be sustained by legal coercion.[51] However, the "natural" laws governing marriage and family life are weighted in favor of the husband: when he stops loving his wife, he should not be forced to remain married to her. The wife, on the other hand, cannot divorce her husband if she stops loving him, irrespective of how unbearable her situation may be, although she may appeal to the courts in certain circumstances. Mutahhari even admits the existence of cases where a virtuous wife is unilaterally divorced and evicted from her marital home for no legitimate reason. Yet, he goes on to remind women that Islam has given them autonomy and placed the burden of their financial support on their husbands, hoping to make such unjust divorces palatable. Upon such divorce, the woman may subsist on any monies she saved from her household allowance, such savings being legally hers, not to be confiscated by her husband.

However, Mutahhari's awareness of the problems emanating from unilateral divorce or repudiation does not impel him to suggest viable solutions. In fact, like Khomeini, he claims that such tragedies are not the result of divorce per se, but of the wife's shortsightedness in being overly loyal and self-sacrificing instead of saving enough to ensure financial autonomy. However, in such cases, it would be appropriate for the husband to compensate his wife, although alimony as such is not acceptable. It is amazing that Mutahhari refuses to recognize that Islam never prohibits a husband from compensating his wife in case of divorce, nor does he consider the fact that the household budget may be too modest to save from unless the wife resorts to stealing from her husband. This is especially relevant since, while the Qur'an specifies a wife's right to earn money and save it, Mutahhari does not allow her to work outside the home except in extreme cases.[52] In addition, he rejects the proposition that the state pay the wife for her household duties (which are completely voluntary) on the grounds that this may disrupt family relations by undermining the husband's authority (through financial dominance) and rendering motherhood a business venture. In short, Mutahhari is explicitly advocating the total subordination of women to their husbands by denying them outside work, remuneration for housework, and alimony.[53] He also seems to have forgotten his own prescription for a harmonious marriage: love, harmony, autonomy, and dignity. Instead of requiring the husband to treat his virtuous wife fairly and compassionately, Mutahhari indirectly asks her to steal from her husband to ensure financial security in case of an unjust divorce.

Also, in defending the male's unilateral right of divorce, Mutahhari describes, at length, the importance of love and harmony between husband and wife and the necessity of maintaining the wife's integrity before her children. For, without her husband's love, the wife will lose the respect of her children, as well as her motherly feelings, which are not instinctual, as some may tend to believe, but derived from the love and warmth of her husband. Thus, in his partisan defense of unilateral divorce, Mutahhari ignores the importance he relegated earlier to motherhood, as an instinct preordained by God to supersede all other interests and values. However, he hastens to maintain that enough obstacles have been designed to deter unjust or capricious divorces, such as marriage expenses, 'iddah expenses, custody of children, as well as mahr of the new wife and expenses of the new family, and so on.[54] But, contrary to Mutahhari's vision, these "obstacles" do not constitute deterrents to divorce. Rather, they may only deter the husband from marrying again if his finances cannot withstand the burden, but they remain of no consequence if he is well off.[55]

In conclusion, we find that Mutahhari, like other ideologues, considers himself an expert on women's nature and needs: he holds them to be untrustworthy, unintelligent, and inferior to men, yet to be feared by them. But, despite their inferiority and simplistic nature, he makes no effort to provide women with the security and care such vulnerable creatures need, nor does he explain how such inferior beings can instill fear in their superior male counterparts. In fact, he reserves all benefits and privileges for the exclusive benefit of men. Moreover, while his ideas on women are wholly traditional and almost completely derivative from Tabtaba'i's views in *al-Mizan* [The scales], he differs from al-Mawdudi and Khomeini in employing modern, "rational," and scientific reasoning to demonstrate the veracity of a traditional stand or belief and affirm all traditional Islamic laws and practices concerning women and family life. This dichotomy between form and content may account for the numerous contradictions encountered throughout his discourse.

Chapter 7

Zaynab al-Ghazali

The reputation of Zaynab al-Ghazali as "soldier of God" is almost legendary among male and female Islamists, to whom she refers as her children because of her elder status and her leading role as teacher and propagator of the *da'wah* [Islamic call or mission], the Muslim Brotherhood's cause in Egypt. Due to her experience, position, connections with the Brotherhood, activism, and ideological views, al-Ghazali may be looked upon as an ideologue and an archetype for the young Islamist woman.[1]

She was born on January 2, 1917, the daughter of Muhammad al-Ghazali al-Jubayli, an Azhar-educated cotton merchant. He was an independent religious teacher who privately tutored her in Islamic studies while she simultaneously completed her secondary education in the public school system. She obtained certificates in Hadith, preaching, and Qur'anic exegesis.

At the age of seventeen, full of dynamism, ambition, and idealism, she joined Huda Sha'rawi's Egyptian Feminist Union, but she resigned at the end of the first year, claiming it was the wrong path for women, especially because Islam guaranteed their rights. Her father, I believe, fearful of her charisma and hot-bloodedness, decided to channel and direct her strong personality in her own interest and that of Islam. He therefore encouraged her to become an Islamic leader and emulate Nusaybah bint Ka'b al-Maziniyyah, a woman who fought side by side with the Prophet and shielded him with her own body at the Battle of Uhud. Al-Ghazali quoted her father, guiding her, saying,

> "Huda al-Sha'rawi does this and Malak Hifni Nassif does that, but among the Companions of the Prophet there was a woman named

Nusaybah, the daughter of Ka'b ibn 'Amr al-Ansariyya, [who] . . . struggled in the path of Islam . . ." He would then ask me, "whom do you choose? Do you choose Huda al-Sha'rawi, or will you become Nusaybah?" And I would say to him, "I will be Nusaybah."[2]

The constant encouragement of her father and his fueling of her ambition and religious zeal, together with the temptation of founding her own organization with her father's financial support, all played a role, I believe, in her final decision to quit the feminist movement of Sha'rawi. She founded the Jama'at al-Sayyidat al-Muslimat [Muslim Women's Association] in 1935, at the age of eighteen, which, according to her, peaked at a membership of three million and had nearly 120 branches throughout Egypt by the time it was disbanded by Nasser's government in 1964. The association, less concerned with the liberation of women than with social welfare, espoused the teaching of women, published its own magazine, maintained an orphanage, gave financial aid to poor families, and mediated family disputes.

Al-Ghazali slowly but surely drifted away from women's liberation to embrace once again the traditional, patriarchal values of her society. She claimed, twenty-three years after the publication of her memoirs, that she quit the feminist movement because she was suspicious of its goals, which she believed to be establishing "the civilization of the Western woman in Egypt and the rest of the Arab and Islamic World." Al-Ghazali described Sha'rawi's feminism and her call for the liberation of women in an Islamic society "a grave error." Islam, according to al-Ghazali, provided women with "everything—freedom, economic rights, political rights, social rights, public, and private rights," even if these rights were not practiced in contemporary Islamic societies.[3]

Due to the similar goals shared by the Muslim Brotherhood and the Muslim Women's Association, Hasan al-Banna approached Zaynab al-Ghazali in 1939, proposing a merger of her organization with that of the Muslim Sisters, the women's branch of his organization.[4] Fearing, I believe, the loss of her power base and, therefore, independence and leadership, which she seemed to cherish deeply, she rejected his offer. In 1948, however, realizing the importance of unity under the banner of al-Banna's Islamism, she gave him her oath of allegiance but kept her association independent. She wrote him saying, "Zaynab al-Ghazali al-Jubayli approaches you as a slave, who has nothing but her worship of God and her total devotion to the service of God's call. You are the only one today who

can sell this slave at the price he wishes for the cause of God the Exalted."
On their second meeting, and as she was going up the stairs, she stopped
and said, "By God I pledge allegiance to you to work to establish the state
of Islam. The least I can offer you to achieve [this] is my blood, and the
Muslim Women's Association with its name." He replied, according to her,
"I accept your pledge of allegiance. The Muslim Women's Association may
remain as it is."[5]

This was maintained even after ʿAbd al-Qadir ʿAwda delivered a message to her on behalf of the Brotherhood: "It would please us if Zaynab al-
Ghazali al-Jubayli were to become one of the Muslim Brotherhood." She
accepted the invitation as an individual but retained the independence of
the association.[6] However, on the inauguration of the general headquarters of the Muslim Brotherhood under Hasan al-Hudaybi, she donated,
according to her, "the most expensive and precious piece of furniture in my
house, an arabesque parlor set inlaid with the mother of pearl, to furnish
the office of the General Guide," as a token of her loyalty to the Brothers.[7]
However, the two women's organizations continued to cooperate in alleviating the suffering of the Islamist families during the Nasserite persecution of the Brotherhood. When the Egyptian government dissolved the
Muslim Women's Association in the late 1940s, al-Ghazali contested the
action in court and won.

In the wake of the attempted assassination of Nasser and the subsequent crackdown of the Egyptian government on the Brothers, al-Ghazali,
together with ʿAbd al-Fattah Ismail, was permitted by the then-leader, al-
Hudaybi, to reorganize the Brotherhood as an underground movement.
She had met with Ismail while on pilgrimage in Mecca, and together they
took an oath: "We must be linked here by a vow with God to struggle in
His path and not to waver until we gather the ranks of the Brotherhood
and separate out those who do not want to work, whatever their circumstances and status."[8] Her home, as a result, was turned into the clandestine
meeting place of the younger generation. By 1962, she was already in
touch with Sayyid Qutb in prison through the mediation of his two sisters.
He had approved a course in Islamic readings, based on commentaries on
the Qurʾan and the Hadith, and Islamic jurisprudence. She had also managed to receive excerpts from the book Maʿalim fi al-Tariq, which he was
writing in prison.

This material, together with set Qurʾanic verses and instructions from
Qutb, was studied by groups of five to ten young men who met at night at
al-Ghazali's home. Discussions would usually follow to help the young

formulate their own opinions and beliefs. This training was set for a period of thirteen years, symbolizing the thirteen years spent by the Prophet Muhammad in Mecca spreading his message before he left for Medina and established his Islamic state. Al-Ghazali had met frequently with Ismail to organize the program and to plan "to restore this nation to its glory and its creed." After the thirteen years of study they would conduct a survey to evaluate the extent of support for an Islamic state. If 75 percent or more were in favor of the formation of such a state, they would go ahead with the plan, otherwise, they would repeat the program for another thirteen years and try again. Time was therefore of no import. Of paramount concern, however, was the continuation of the struggle to the last person, who would then pass the "banner of Islam" to the next generation.[9]

After al-Ghazali repeatedly resisted the overtures of the Nasserite government to spy on the Brotherhood, her association was disbanded on September 15, 1964, and her headquarters shut down, but the association continued to function clandestinely by holding meetings in the homes of the members. However, her resistance to the government, coupled with her underground activities, led to her arrest in 1965, along with many members of the Muslim Brothers and Sisters. She was brought to trial in 1966 and sentenced to hard labor for life, and her association was banned permanently. In 1971, she was released, along with a number of colleagues, by President Anwar Sadat, as a gesture of goodwill after she had spent six years in prison. She never ceased to disseminate the Islamist message and call for the establishment of the ideal Islamic state divinely guided by the Qur'an and the Sunna, through teaching, public lectures, and writing in *al-Da'wah*, the magazine of the Brotherhood until it was banned in 1981, and in *Liwa' al-Islam* thereafter.[10]

Al-Ghazali was sent to Qanatir Prison (a women's prison) after spending one year in the Liman Tura Prison with the Muslim Brothers, like Sayyid Qutb and many others. She recounts her prison experiences in her famous book *Ayyam min hayati* [Days of my life]. She describes all the terrible forms of torture she had to endure and her fortitude in withstanding them, which, according to her, transcended that shown by men in the same prison. She also attests to miracle visions that helped her survive almost unscathed. She further denies having ever broken down or confessed to any guilt but condones the failure of others to do so, due to human frailty.[11] Whereas at the Liman Tura Prison al-Ghazali had to face men alone, in Qanatir Prison she was surrounded by what she described as a "lost troop of wandering humanity in the depths of ignorance [who have] forgotten their humanity, purity, chastity, and nobility, and become animals." She is, thus, disdainful of these women and shows them no compassion or sympathy but rather condemns them for their weaknesses.[12]

Zaynab al-Ghazali married twice but had no children. Her hyperactive political life and her dedication to the Islamic cause took precedence and proved problematic to her first marriage, which ended in divorce. Her second husband, according to her own account, was more understanding and pledged in writing, as a precondition to marriage, to help her in her political endeavors and never to hinder her Islamic mission and cause. "I know," she writes, "that it is your right to order and my duty to obey you, but God is greater than us, and his mission is dearer to us than ourselves."[13] She claims, in contradiction of her statement regarding her first husband, that she never neglected her second husband or her family duties, even during her tenure as president of the Muslim Women's Association, and despite her long hours of work outside her home and her involvement in the clandestine activities of the Brotherhood. In fact, al-Ghazali comments on the nobility of Muhammad Salim Salim, her second husband, manifested during the frequent visits of ʿAbd al-Fattah Ismail and the young Brothers to their home often in the early morning hours. She says,

> My believing husband would hear the knocks on the door in the middle of the night and get up to open the door. He would escort the visitors to the office, then he would go to the maid's room and wake her, asking her to prepare some food and tea for the visitors. Then, he would come to me and wake me gently saying, "some of your sons are in the office. They look like they have been traveling or working hard." I would dress and go to them, while he went back to sleep, saying to me, "Wake me if you pray the morning prayer together, so I can pray with you, if that is no bother" . . . Then he would leave, greeting those who were present in a fatherly way, full of warmth, love, and compassion."

She talks of the understanding she had with her second husband after explaining the role she was playing for the Islamic cause:

> "[I]f your personal welfare and economic work conflict with my Islamic work, and I find that my married life interferes with the way of the call and the establishment of the Islamic state, then we will separate . . . I cannot ask you today that you join me in this struggle, but it is my right to stipulate that you not interfere with my struggle in

the path of God, and that the day that responsibility places me in the ranks of the strugglers, that you not ask me what I am doing . . . If there is a conflict of interests between marriage and the call of God, then the marriage will come to an end and the call will remain in my whole being."[14]

Al-Ghazali and her second husband were separated only when she was imprisoned. They were divorced at her own request, but she seems to have resented his prompt acquiescence. He died twenty-one days later. Al-Ghazali never remarried, believing she had fulfilled her Muslim duty twice and it was time for her to dedicate the rest of her life to the cause. She describes her marriage as "only a contingent worldly event, but brotherhood in Allah is everlasting: it does not elapse nor can it be measured in the world and all that is therein."[15]

In 1977, Zaynab al-Ghazali published her book *Ayyam min hayati* [Days of my life], described as "a legend of torture and hardship." She writes of her prison days, her relationship with the Muslim Brothers and her leadership of the Muslim Women's Association. Miriam Cooke explains that her autobiographical style is masculine, reflecting feelings of "self-confidence and a sense of empowerment." Contrary to a diary or journal, it has a unified theme or message portraying the author as playing a transforming role in society.[16] However, since al-Ghazali played the role of a Brother outside prison and inside (Liman Tura Prison), she feels justified in not only comparing herself with them but actually regarding herself above them in loyalty and endurance of torture and pain. And while she, like several others who had been severely tortured, according to Saad Eddin Ibrahim, "reported having images and dreams of prophets and saints welcoming them to the Garden of Eden, or images of the just Islamic society being established upon their martyrdom . . . [and] perceived their present prison sentences as an integral part of their struggle (jihad) [and] God's testing of their faith and perseverance,"[17] al-Ghazali saw herself as having been unique, chosen by God for such a role. Thus, while her book may have been intended as a guide for others, the "others" were men and not women, whose role, according to al-Ghazali herself, was domestic.[18]

Al-Ghazali's writings are not limited to her prison memoirs. She also published *Nahwa ba'thin jadid* [For a new resurrection] and *Nadharat fi Kitab Allah* [Views on God's Book], and was working on others: *Asma' Allah* [Names of God] and a book on women's instincts. She contributed many articles to Islamic newspapers and magazines throughout the Muslim world and edited the section "Toward a Muslim Home" in *al-Da'wah*. This includes a subsection dedicated to children and consisting of a feature titled "Know the Enemies of Your Religion," in which al-Ghazali warned children against Zionists, evangelists, and imperialists, who were intent on destroying Islamic religion and society. She also toured and lectured extensively in Egypt, Pakistan, Saudi Arabia (sixty times), Algeria, Jordan, Kuwait, India, Spain, Afghanistan, Sudan, and even the United States, England, France, and Switzerland. She performed the *hajj* thirty-nine times and the *'umra* [minor pilgrimage] one hundred times.[19]

Timothy Mitchell, in his critique of *Ayyam min hayati* as an example of fundamentalist discourse, maintains that "the description of prison life becomes a detailed diagnosis of the state's methods of control. Thus, such memoirs can themselves show how these methods actually participate in producing the political discourse of Islam . . . these forms of opposition were not something external to the system of power, but the product of techniques and tensions within it."[20] Al-Ghazali denies any role of the Muslim Brothers in the attempted assassination of President 'Abd el-Nasser. She maintains that "killing the unjust ruler does not do away with the problem" of a society in dire need of reeducation in Islamic principles. While condemning acts of murder, torture, and terrorism as means to power, she justifies the use of force against unbelievers as necessary to lead them "from darkness to light" and compares such methods to "snatching poison from the hands of a child."[21]

She saw the Muslim Brotherhood as inclusive of all Muslims and branded all those who were not members as "deficient." The goal of the Brotherhood is the reestablishment of the Islamic state and rule by the Qur'an and the Sunna. Practically speaking this should not be impossible since the Islamic nation dominates one third of the world and is richer than the rest of the world geographically and in oil production. Hence, the backwardness of Muslim societies is due to their straying from Islam and its constitution. Once they return to Islam and live according to its principles, they will rule the world. Countries will retain their individualism but will form a union like that of the United States. This will be achieved when all children are taught the Islamic religion and the necessity of being governed only by the Qur'an. Once this is accomplished, no ruler can reject Islam as a state and religion. The trials the Brothers have gone through have only made them stronger, more profound and enduring, refusing to accept anything less than the fulfillment of their goals and the establishment of the Islamic state.[22]

Al-Ghazali, following in the footsteps of Hasan al-Banna, calls on women to join the Brotherhood, emphasizing their central role in the political campaign of the Islamic movement. She told Valerie Hoffman, in a 1981 interview:

The Brotherhood considers women a fundamental part of the Islamic call. They are the ones who are most active, because men have to work. They are the ones who build the kind of men that we need to fill the ranks of the Islamic call. So, women must be well educated, cultured, knowing the precepts of the Qur'an and Sunna, knowing world politics, why we are backward, why we don't have technology. The Muslim woman must study all these things, and then raise her son in the conviction that he must possess the scientific tools of the age, and at the same time, he must understand Islam, politics, geography, and current events . . . Islam does not forbid women to actively participate in public life . . . as long as that does not interfere with her first duty as a mother, the one who first trains her children in the Islamic call. So, her first holy and most important mission is to be a mother and a wife.[23]

Women's access to the political world will, thus, be through their domestic roles. They should be educated, not to compete with men in the marketplace but to be better mothers, properly qualified to educate and bring up their sons. Thus, according to her, Islam welcomes women in the public sphere, but only after they have perfected the roles of mother and wife in the private sphere.

Al-Ghazali, like al-Banna before her, argued that men and women had different natures that determined their distinct activities. She emphasized the dynamic role of women in raising families and the importance of abstaining from public work unless absolutely necessary. There are movements, according to her, that call for absolute equality between men and women, resulting in the desertion of home and family to compete with men in their work milieu and rejection of dependency on men, leading thereby to moral decadence. This also has resulted in men taking on women's work, forgetting the hadith that says, "Accursed are men who emulate women and women who emulate men."[24] Both men and women —shaqa'iq al-rijal [sisters of men]—were to contribute to the alleviation of the "under-development of the Islamic nation," each according to his or her natural qualifications. However, should it be in the interest of the Islamic state, Muslim women may be required to play a role outside the home, provided, of course, they are dressed properly and are able to manage their domestic and public roles efficiently.[25] Also, like al-Banna, she does not make allowances for single women or efficient wives (like herself) and mothers, who are able to fulfill their domestic roles and find the time to obey the demands of Islam and fight for the establishment of the Islamic state.

Women, according to al-Ghazali, have so far been unwilling or unable to turn themselves into good wives and mothers, thus playing havoc with the Islamic family, home, and society as a whole. The implication here is that all shortcomings of the Muslim world are to be attributed to women's inefficiencies. "What kind of society," she asks, "is this where the home that forms the seed of the society has been ruined by tearing women between the home and workplace?"[26] It is, therefore, imperative that women shoulder their duties as wives and mothers, which far outweigh their contribution to the marketplace. "God, in his infinite wisdom, has created . . . the woman's natural disposition in such a way that she specializes in making a man happy and comfortable, so he can improve his productivity and do his duty wisely and observantly by her, and she will not find this man unless we find him the protective family which is clever with its capabilities."[27]

Al-Ghazali points out that "it is the duty of the Muslim girl to diligently attend to performing her prayers at the right time. To make sure she respects and obeys her parents and treats them well, because obedience to them is obedience to God almighty. Also, to wear the proper and [religiously] ordained dress . . . In school or university, to be the good example of her colleagues, so she makes sure she achieves the highest of grades in her lessons and, thus, becomes an example in positive achievements and practical achievements."[28] The goal of the Muslim Women's Association was, thus, "to acquaint the Muslim woman with her religion, to convince her through study that the women's liberation movement is a deviant innovation that took root, because of the backwardness of Muslims."[29] Although al-Ghazali stresses that women's rights and liberation would be accomplished upon the establishment of the Islamic state, she does not specify how this would come about. "It may take generations," she says, "for Islam to rule. We are not rushing ahead of ourselves. On the day that Islam rules, Muslim women will find themselves in their natural kingdom, educating men."[30] However, she fails to explain or justify why women should continue in subordination until that time.

Even though Zaynab al-Ghazali achieved her political heights as president of the Muslim Women's Association, she does not seem to be able to tolerate secular women's organizations and condemns their feminist demands for equity in the Shari'ah laws. She asserts that Islam has given women all their rights. Quoting a verse from the Qur'an, she assures women they are equal to men in faith and belief, superceding all other forms of equality. God, according to her, has proclaimed "men responsible for women" because men are better than women and supercede them in intelligence, planning, and physical prowess. This fact is demonstrated by God's allowing men to marry four wives, granting them the exclusive right to divorce, and requiring women to assume their husband's identity. Men are the sole rulers, imams, and leaders. They are dependable witnesses in court, enjoy a double inheritance share, and are obligated to go to jihad. Moreover, al-Ghazali quotes Ibn Kathir as saying, "Man is responsible for his woman. He is her leader, elder, ruler, and punisher if she deviates."[31] Thus, instead of stressing women's prowess and potential to work alongside men on equal footing (as she herself did) by interpreting these Qur'anic references to the advantage of women, as some male ideologues have indeed done, she adopts the strictest and most traditional of interpretations contributing, thereby, to the further subordination of women.

The new Muslim woman, al-Ghazali argues, must be aware of the unity of the Islamic faith and, therefore, the "indivisibility" of matters of state, all of which emanate from the Qur'an: the political, social, domestic, individual, and communal. The genuine Islamic woman is, therefore, she who pursues the unity of the community guided by Qur'anic principles. Politically, she is equal to her male counterpart and should, therefore, educate herself to increase her awareness of the political rights, such as voting, representation, and consultation (shura), awarded her by Islam. Thus, while women may speak of "liberation" in Jewish, Christian, and pagan societies, Muslim women had already been emancipated by Islam centuries earlier. This, of course, contradicts her clearly stated views on women as inferior to men in all things, subject to their leadership, to be punished if they deviate, unless she means that women are to obey their husbands even in fulfilling such rights as voting.

Al-Ghazali assures women that "Islam does not forbid women to participate actively in public life. It does not prevent them from working, entering into politics and expressing their opinion, or anything else, as long as that does not interfere with their first . . . holy and most important mission [of being] a mother and wife . . . If after that she has the time, she may participate in public activities."[32] But, she states elsewhere that working outside the home is contrary to women's nature (*fitrah*) unless, of course, "an urgent need arises," whereupon women should work in the field of education. Otherwise, they should stay at home and obey their husbands as they obey the Prophet, an action they will be rewarded for in the hereafter.[33] She accuses the West, "which has lied and fraudulently claimed that they have liberated women" and encouraged them to work outside the home, of destroying the home unit and betraying the world. The workingwoman has become "a human distortion and an available commodity for the last of the wolves." She reminds her readers that women's skills lay in rearing their sons and "preparing them for their leading and productive roles in society," which is far more "valuable and useful."[34] In following the divine commands and emulating the Sunna of the Prophet, a mother lays the foundation of a strong household. Due to her central role in the family, a mother could instill in the hearts of her children the love of Islam and its practice and guide her children to be well-behaved and devout Muslims. However, this important role should be enhanced by grounding potential mothers in scientific knowledge and training as well as the Islamic sciences early on in life, thus, guaranteeing an education that is both modernist and Islamist.[35] She further asserts that "a wife should be an elegant flower . . . Only fools will equate the education of women with the education of men . . . We need special programs that will prepare women for their tasks . . . to create a loving motherhood . . . and build happy families."[36]

In her argument for building a cohesive Muslim family, al-Ghazali stressed the centrality of marital relations in ensuring a happy, stable, and secure home. The wife should never complain to her husband of being tired, rather, she should let him come to this realization on his own to better appreciate the hard work endured for his welfare; she should actually downgrade her pain and belittle it before her husband to win his solace and compassion; and most importantly, she should never arouse his jealousy to avoid conflict. Furthermore, to earn the love and respect of her husband, a wife should carry out all her responsibilities, such as cooking, cleaning, and child rearing. She should create a beautiful environment and atmosphere to the minutest detail, in an effort to ensure her husband's comfort and happiness and to manage his income efficiently. Moreover, a wife should be careful to select only the most respectable, virtuous, and well-behaved female friends. Their visits should be well planned and beneficial, geared toward religious readings on matters concerning family affairs, religious practice, or even male-female relations. Al-Ghazali encouraged a wife to be honest with her husband, keeping no secrets from him. A wife should keep all her marital problems to herself and should share them only with her husband, and any complaints about her in-laws are unacceptable. Finally, it is up to the husband to determine his wife's dress outside the home, as long as it is within the boundaries set by Islam, but the wife may share in the decision regarding the mode of dress she adopts at home.[37]

Marriage, according to al-Ghazali, is "a mission and a trust in Islam."[38] Thus, a woman's "first, holy, and most important mission" in life is to be a wife and a mother. Inasmuch as sex is important in one's life in Islam, the primary and most important objective of marriage is conception and the preservation of the human race, rather than the satisfaction of one's instinct. "Marriage is to preserve the human race, establish the family, and build the man and the woman, . . . to build the ruler, [and] to bring about righteous government." Thus, contraception is prohibited in Islam.[39] Needless to say, "Any sexual relations outside marriage are totally prohibited." Al-Ghazali reminds women of the ritual to be carried out before a man approaches his wife: He has to say, "In the name of God, the Compassionate, the Merciful. God, protect us from Satan," thereby fulfilling his duty as ordained by God.[40] Finally, al-Ghazali, instead of assisting women in escaping an oppressive marriage, defines her emphatic position on divorce saying, "A woman asking her husband for divorce is a crime that deserves punishment, for is there anything more terrible than a woman threatening the nest of her marriage and her motherhood?"[41] The ten commandments of marriage, according to her, are therefore obedience, willingness to have sexual intercourse on demand, avoidance of looking ugly or emanating bad odors, ensuring peace and silence while the husband sleeps, preparing his food on time, protecting his wealth, family, and honor, refraining from revealing his secrets, and never being happy when he is sad or sad when he is happy.[42] Disobedient and recalcitrant wives, warns al-Ghazali, are punished by God for disobeying His dictates. They are admonished first, then deprived sexually, and, finally, beaten without the infliction of bodily harm to bring them back to the right path.[43]

As to the oft-reiterated question of the *hijab*, al-Ghazali explains that "the veil that covers the face is a *fard* [obligation] for the Prophet's wives, who are the mothers of the early believers. As for the other women of the Islamic nation, it is optional. There is no obligation to those who wish to follow the example of the Prophet's wives, and any woman who wishes to abide by the *fard*, that guides the Muslim woman, may do so. The *fard* states that all the woman's body, except for the face, which should not be made up, and the hands, should be covered; the dress should be large and opaque to avoid outlining the body. It should not be perfumed or outstanding and her feet should be covered as well."[44] "The Prophet's wives," al-Ghazali continues, "were obliged to converse from behind the veil, and whoever wants to follow their example may do so, because it is a virtue. And if a woman wants to rise up to that virtue and follow it, nobody can oppose her for doing so, as this is her personal right." The *hijab* and *niqab* [veil covering face] may be adopted at puberty. However, al-Ghazali goes on to describe how "today's declining society allows women to wear clothes above their knees," which, upon sitting, exposes their thighs and private parts. She brands such women who uncover their bodies to show their "thighs and legs and breasts and back" as bad, "rejected by Islam and . . . condemned for not abiding by the teachings of Islam."[45] Finally, al-Ghazali asserts that whenever Islamist women leave the home and participate in such activities as public prayer, political work with men, or productive or administrative functions, segregation of the sexes must be practiced.

Although the Islamist movement throughout the Muslim world has attracted huge numbers of women like Safinaz Qazim (b. 1939) and Hiba Ra'uf (b. 1965), Zaynab al-Ghazali stands tall, having distinguished herself as one of its prominent leaders. Her life, suffering, dedication, and accomplishments have been the subject of discussions by Muslim and non-Muslim authors alike and continue to be the subject of research of many academics. My concern here, however, is not her life or her innumerable contributions to Islam and the Muslim Brotherhood, but her position on the question of women and their role in society. Her life, activism, and political involvement propose an agenda that speaks for the empowerment of women beyond the home, yet a closer look at her writings, interviews, and lectures portrays a patriarchal traditionalist who favors her own transcendence of the traditional female role but discourages other women from participating in public life and restricts them to the private sphere, exceeding thereby the zeal of the most conservative Islamist male or ideologue throughout Muslim history.

She used the Islamic legal system to empower herself by dictating her own conditions in the marriage contract, but she would deny other Islamist women similar privileges, as well as the right to petition for divorce. She regards the current situation in Muslim history as conducive to jihad for an ideal Islamic state. This would permit the enactment of the rules of war, which allow for adjustments in gender roles, to enhance her own activism. Yet, she simultaneously imposes domestic roles on her peers. Thus, while she emphasizes women's political centrality to the *da'wah* [call] to enhance her own position, she lulls her female associates and disciples into believing that their jihad lies in the home front. They would have access to the masculine world of politics by raising their sons to be the future *mujahidin* [fighters], who will, in turn, establish the ideal Islamic state. The founding of the Islamic state would then guarantee the implementation of women's God-ordained Islamic rights.

Leila Ahmed draws attention to al-Ghazali's lack of spiritual commitment to Islam, which is only used as "a path to empowerment, to glory, to a properly regulated society—but not as a spiritual path."[46] Although al-Ghazali writes of "good nights and unforgettable days, holy moments with God,"[47] these experiences, I believe, are recounted to demonstrate her unique role in the Islamic movement, thus shunning any vestiges of femininity that may have played a role in her Islamic mission "to purify the world of unbelief, atheism, oppression, and persecution."[48] She believes herself, as is evident from her book *Ayyam min hayati*, to have been called by God to carry on the *da'wah* and to sacrifice herself for the redemption of Egypt and possibly the whole world. She sees herself as superior to those men who could not withstand torture and broke down; the men in official positions who abused their subordinates; and the husbands of the Muslim Sisters, including her own, who could not withstand the pressure and divorced their wives. Thus, having succeeded where men had failed, she declares herself a *mujahidah* [fighter] or a *mujaddidah* [renewer/reformer].

She sees her name as indicative of her unique role and power: Zaynab was the name of the Prophet's granddaughter, who fought alongside men in the battlefield; and al-Ghazali was the name of the eleventh–twelfth century imam who wrote his autobiography, *al-Munqidh min al-dalal* [Deliverance from error], to define the pathway that would save the world and transcend it at the same time. She saw herself as having come to this world to continue his message and save the world from tyrants like Nasser. She describes a vision she had in prison in which she saw herself climbing a mountain along a path that took her to the top. On her way up, she could see no men, but she met five women—Aminah and Hamidah Qutb (Sayyid Qutb's sisters), Khalidah and 'Aliyyah al-Hudaybi, and Fatimah 'Issa—who assured her she was on the right track. She found the top of the mountain to be a plateau covered with carpets and couches, with al-

Hudaybi (leader of the Brotherhood) standing there. She approached and conveyed to him the greetings of the Prophet. As she stood next to him, she saw a train with two naked women aboard, passing by at the foot of the mountain. She was surprised at al-Hudaybi's lack of reaction, but he advised her not to concern herself, since she had nothing in common with them, and to content herself with having gained the top of the mountain next to him, both of them having earned this position through their good works and God's grace. Al-Ghazali, however, insisted that the women be admonished and reformed.

It seems to me that this vision reflects her own vision of her exalted position in the Brotherhood, equal to that of the leader, if not his superior. For it was she who had been sent to deliver him a message from the Prophet. The nakedness of the women reflected their freedom, and her inquiries of the other women for direction reflect her ambivalence regarding the role she had chosen for herself in contrast to the steadfastness of al-Hudaybi, oblivious to her vacillation. The affirmative answers of the five women and the assurance of al-Hudaybi that she was indeed on the right track and had in fact reached the top represent a vindication of her travails. This is further confirmed by the women's names: Zaynab al-Ghazali is a fighter with a mission to change the world; Aminah is loyal and trustworthy; Hamidah is praiseworthy; Khalidah is immortal; 'Aliyyah is exalted; and Fatimah is the daughter of the Prophet, whose name also denotes one who weans, thus indicating maturity, implying that Fatimah helped her reach maturity and end her equivocation. Thus, we find Zaynab al-Ghazali seeing herself as a "woman-man" with a divine mission from the outset; she compares herself with men, equates herself with them, and at times places herself above them. In her vision, all the women she sees are either at the bottom of the mountain or on their way up, while she alone is at the top in the company of a male leader of men.

Although the example Zaynab al-Ghazali sets for women is that of a free, strong, and independent woman, she never calls for gender equality nor does she advocate women's causes. Her main concern is the establishment of an Islamic state, where all citizens, male and female, will have their natural rights. In fact, she is a fierce opponent of all secular or feminist movements and a champion of all patriarchal and traditional values for both men and women. This is all the more interesting in view of the role the Egyptian feminist movement played in catapulting her to her current position. Had it not been for that movement, would her father have helped her found her women's association? Would Hasan al-Banna have approached her to head the Muslim Sisters?

Zaynab al-Ghazali's narrative of sainthood and jihad, in fact her whole life, may very well be used by feminists to demonstrate women's endurance, independence, and unshakable determination to achieve their goals. Her writings and teachings, however, speak of something totally different and quite contradictory. She seldom practiced what she preached. Although her public statements stressed the primary role of women as wives and mothers, and although she claims that her public life never kept her from fulfilling her marital duties, her personal life reflected exactly the opposite: she opted for a public role for herself, which inevitably led to her two divorces, albeit for different reasons, and possibly motivated her remaining childless, thus failing or violating the very principles she advocated for women. She shunned the domestic role she prescribed for women and ignored the commandments she herself imposed on "virtuous" wives, and she proclaimed that "a woman asking her husband for divorce is a *crime* [my emphasis] that deserves punishment." As for obedience to one's husband and the sharing of all one's secrets with him, duties she had imposed on all Muslim wives, she carefully stipulated in her marriage contract that her husband was not to interfere in her mission and was to abstain from asking any questions relating to it. She also admitted to her interviewer that she divorced her first husband because her marriage "took up all [her] time and kept [her] from [her] mission" and because "[her] husband did not agree with [her] work." However, her second husband, contrary to all conventions, "agreed . . . to help [her] and to be [her] assistant."[49] This was in direct contradiction to her teachings, especially when she quotes Ibn Kathir as saying, "Man is responsible for his woman. He is her leader, elder, ruler, and punisher if she deviates," thereby proclaiming him to be her God on earth. Can she, therefore, be described as the ideal, virtuous wife whose major role in society is devotion to her husband and children, when she controlled and ignored her husband and plunged herself into the complex world of power politics?

Or, has she set herself up as a "chosen one," above the reproach and punishment due other women who bypass their prescribed limits? Al-Ghazali rationalized this contradiction away by claiming that she was compelled to set aside her domestic duties in favor of her jihad for the establishment of the ideal Islamic state that would ensure equal rights for men and women. She further explained that she had no children to tie her down; her husband was wealthy and could, therefore, afford to have servants do the housework. Moreover, he was polygamous and thus freed her from her wifely duties. This justification, of course, does not explain away her assertion to her colleagues that women are naturally determined to play a domestic role just as men are preordained to play a public role in society. Nor does it explain her belittlement of the fitness of women, whose education she claims "only fools" could equate with the education of men, especially when they have to rear their sons and prepare them for "their leading and productive roles in society." Moreover, she claims that men are superior to women in intelligence, planning, and physical prowess as evidenced by the rights granted them by God. Al-Ghazali's contradictory behavior is further highlighted when she requires the complete segregation of the sexes and the implementation of full *hijab*, including the *niqab*, yet, she meets with Hasan al-Banna in private, goes on the pilgrimage and meets with ʿAbd al-Fattah Ismail alone, and holds regular meetings with him and other young Brothers in her home, at night, in the absence of her husband. This leaves one wondering whether al-Ghazali considers herself of a different nature or breed than those other women whom she describes as inferior to men in intelligence, planning, and physical prowess. What she, finally, fails to explain is why other married women could not have access to these same rights and privileges.

Contradictions abound not only between her teachings and personal life, but within her teachings as well: Thus, the ideal woman that emerges through her teaching is obedient, submissive, passive, educated only in matters that concern her home and family, and completely veiled, especially if beautiful. Yet, this same benign woman is expected to leave home and family, should the need arise, and either help her husband financially by working in the public arena or help defend Islam and propagate its message. Moreover, the historical models of women she provides are those of women warriors of the likes of the Kharijite Layla bint Tarif and Nusaybah bint Kaʿb al-Maziniyyah, the Prophet's woman companion who "sacrificed herself, her husband, [her] children, while the male companion [of the Prophet] sacrificed only himself."[50] Furthermore, while she instructs wives to obey their husband and never complain of any physical pain or discomfort and even to acquiesce to their husband's choice of dress for them, she reassures them that they can still participate in the affairs of their society and are free to express their views and opinions. One is thus left to wonder how these women can form opinions and express them, when they cannot choose what dress to wear. What is also unclear in her discourse is the identity of those who are to oversee the "production" of this ideal woman/wife/mother.

Given the high regard in which the Brothers and other prominent patriarchal leaders of the Arab and Muslim world hold al-Ghazali, it can be safely assumed that not only does she not challenge male authority over their female counterparts and children, but, also, she indoctrinates the female to be totally submissive to the male. To substantiate her views, she quotes from the Sunna and Hadith only such passages as would strengthen her arguments and omits others that would weaken them. Thus, she quotes the Prophet to have forbidden the sexes from emulating each other, but she fails to mention that on one occasion the Prophet asked Ali to help his wife in her domestic chores.

Moreover, al-Ghazali promises that the liberation of women would be achieved once the Islamic state is established. "On the day that Islam rules," she declares, "the Muslim women will find themselves in their natural kingdom, educating men." However, if this is true, why does she impose so many strictures on women's dress, lives, and roles while waiting for that ideal society, instead of initiating the promised reforms in gradual stages and training women to be ready for the forthcoming freedom with all that it entails? Or is this a disguised omen of things to come?

In conclusion, what is it exactly that Zaynab al-Ghazali is trying to impart to her followers? Is it that their feminine nature determines their domestic role and renders them, therefore, incompatible with the outside world? Or is it that women can in fact work outside the home, participate in the spreading of the da'wah, fight as warriors, and withstand torture and imprisonment like the best of men? Are women to obey their husbands, or is the Islamic cause their "first and most holy" duty superceding all other obligations toward their husband? Should women concentrate on raising the future "Qur'anic generation" in the home, or is it far better for them not to be blessed with children at all so they may be free to follow their ambitions, albeit in the course of the Islamic cause? And, finally, is one to conclude that Islamic values are labile? That privileges are doled out to a select few while the rest remain suppressed and deprived?

Many have attempted to interpret her ambivalence, the most important of whom is Miriam Cooke, who attributed it to an ingrained feminism and the inherent goal of women's liberation. What causes this ambivalence, Cooke argues, is the covert action of al-Ghazali, where she poses for the Muslim Brothers and the prominent patriarchs of the Muslim world as patriarchal and traditional as they themselves are, if not more. She then hopes that through her emancipated role, activism, imprisonment, suffering, torture, and sacrifice, she would prove to Muslim women first and the rest of the world as well that women are just as capable as men and, therefore, as worthy of independence and leadership. This, then, should effect the liberation of women slowly but surely, rather than in a confrontational manner, provided the whole population becomes appreciative and convinced of women's worth.[51]

Inasmuch as I would like to adopt such a stance, assuming that all women desire the liberation of womankind from oppression, I cannot agree with Miriam Cooke or others who may share her interpretation. Rather, I see in Zaynab al-Ghazali a young woman of seventeen, full of ambition, fire, and dynamism, "a political animal," as she called herself, who wanted to liberate herself from the oppression of tradition. Her first step toward that was in joining the feminist movement of Huda al-Sha'rawi. The astuteness of her father, his love, and compassion, as well as his admiration of her personality, his love of and dedication to Islam, and his fear of losing his daughter to the perils of modernism and the West, made him contain her dynamism, while simultaneously lighting the spark of her desire for leadership. This, in addition to his tutoring her in the Islamic sciences, effected her diversion from secular feminism to Islamic feminism to establish her own Muslim association. It was not long afterward, however, that she met the charismatic Hasan al-Banna, who not only left an indelible impression on this young woman but also made her appreciative of her own importance and worth.

Intoxicated with her position and the attention lavished upon her by Hasan al-Banna, she swerved from her original path to another that assured her access to the top. She slowly came to realize that she could not speak from within the Islamic movement against religiously sanctioned gender norms without incurring the anger of the Brothers and the possible charge of apostasy. She therefore adopted the Brothers' conservative stance. In time, this approach earned her an invitation not only to join the Muslim Brotherhood but also to play a major role in the restructuring of the whole organization.

Having thus chosen this route, she had to suppress her feminism, while still allowing it to propel her to freedom, independence, and power at the expense of her fellow sisters in the struggle. Like other women in her position, in other religions, she argues for a renewed emphasis on patriarchal gender norms and women's submission to male power in general, seeking to excel in the power game by sacralizing the patriarchal norms and emphasizing them with more force than any male had ever done before. Such a conservative attitude ensured her a secure place in the exclusively male organization and access to the ladder of power. Her disdain of her own kind is clearly expressed in her prison memoirs, when she describes her fellow inmates in Qanatir Prison as a "lost troop of wandering humanity in the depths of ignorance [who have] forgotten their humanity, purity, chastity, and nobility, and become animals."[52] She, like others before her and since, identifies herself with the "patrician" class, sees herself as unique, and turns upon her own kind with a vengeance to keep them in their subjugated position. This assuages the fears of the dominant class and encourages them to use her as their best ambassador. Thus, while she sits alongside her male compatriots reveling in her freedom, independence, dignity, and power, she indoctrinates her "sisters" into confinement, dependence, submission, and passivity.

To sum up, Zaynab al-Ghazali saw herself as "unique," certainly different from other women, and sought liberation from the shackles traditionally imposed on women. To that end, she had to "lose" her feminism and don "male" clothing. This was made doubly attractive given her disdain of women and her firm belief in her "uniqueness." This and the resultant assumption of a quasi-male persona explains many of the discrepancies noted in her odyssey:

1. She declared that women who asked their husbands for divorce were committing a criminal act, yet she asked her two husbands for divorce.
2. She used her second husband as her "assistant," while teaching that men are the leaders, rulers, and punishers of women.
3. She stated that women were too inept and ignorant to be trusted with raising and educating children, yet she sacralized motherhood as an instinct ordained by God.
4. She repeatedly asserted that men were superior to women in all things and were, therefore, responsible for women and their rulers, yet she saw herself as a messenger of God with a preordained mission.

To reinforce her male alter ego, she identified with male leaders and curried their favor in exerting restrictions on women. At the same time, to garner the support and adulation of the women she actually disdained, she promised them freedom and security in the coming Ideal State, thus becoming their "patron saint" while actually condemning them to a permanently inferior state. In doing so she garnered the adulation of both oppressors and oppressed as a reformist and champion of women's rights.

Chapter 8

※

Hasan al-Turabi

Although Sudan began its postindependence era as a parliamentary democracy, the military has been in power for much of that period. The military was invited into power in 1958, then overthrown in 1964. In 1969, the
military, under General Ja'far Numayri, overthrew the civilian government and resumed power until 1985, when Numayri was, in turn, overthrown by a civilian coalition of students, factions from the South, trade,
and professional unions and intellectuals. Sadiq al-Mahdi, head of the
Ummah Party, and the Ansar Brotherhood established an "Islamic Trend"
government inspired by elements of the National Islamic Front (NIF). Its
tenure was brief; in 1989, a "National Salvation Revolution" led by Lieu-
tenant General 'Umar al-Bashir replaced it with an NIF government, with
Dr. Hasan al-Turabi, leader of the Muslim Brotherhood, as its de facto
ideological guide.

On June 30, 1989, a group of military officers seized power and ush-
ered in an ideological orientation in harmony with the NIF. With this
coup d'état, Sudan, a century after the Mahdiyyah (1882–98), was able to
proclaim the establishment of the first Arab Islamist state in the twentieth century, based on the Sunni fundamentalist ideology of the Muslim
Brotherhood.[1] The coup d'état realized what one of al-Turabi's followers
predicted before 1989: According to him, the NIF leaders were preparing
"to make a bid to control the state and impose their norms on society,
hoping to succeed where their opponents had failed by defining a new
Sudanese community based on Islam."[2]

After World War II the influence of political Islam, spearheaded by the
Muslim Brotherhood, spread in Sudan. The Brotherhood, partly an off-
shoot of the Muslim Brotherhood in Egypt, made its appearance in the

1940s, partially in response to the rise of the Sudanese Communist Party and nationalism. It proved attractive to intellectuals and quickly established a strong base at the University of Khartoum. It produced a dynamic leader in Hasan al-Turabi, who had returned to Sudan in 1962 after having studied law at the University of London and the Sorbonne. He became dean of the law school at the University of Khartoum and was elected secretary-general of the Brotherhood in 1964.

Al-Turabi, the architect of Sudan's Islamization, is described as a man of high intellect and incredible charisma. He is articulate in English, French, and Arabic and at ease in both Western and Sudanese dress. Milton Viorst describes him as being slim and of small stature, with dark features and delicate hands. He is soft-spoken and smiles readily. His students, according to Viorst, claim that al-Turabi changes his tone, if not his argument, to fit his audience; and the Sudanese joke that "there is an 'al-Turabi for domestic consumption' and an 'al-Turabi for export.'"[3] Al-Turabi is a highly controversial figure "who excites passionate hostility and support in equal measure" and is, according to Peter Nyot Kok, "a villain, Machiavellian, dynamic, and ruthless, forceful and charismatic personality."[4] One of his followers is purported to have said, "Al-Turabi's genius is most apparent in his ability to hover on the borderline between numerous antagonistic positions. He sits astride modernity and tradition, pragmatism and idealism, calculation, and faith."[5] A charismatic leader, al-Turabi masters the game of power politics. In his appeal to the educated elite, he resorts to reason and, when necessary, "moral persuasion."[6]

Hasan al-Turabi was born in the town of Kassala in eastern Sudan in 1932. He graduated from the Faculty of Law at the University of Khartoum in 1955 with a bachelor's degree. In 1957, he obtained his master's degree in law from the University of London, and in 1964 he received his doctorate from the Sorbonne in Paris. In the mid-1960s, he served as dean of the law school at the University of Khartoum and was appointed attorney general of the Sudan. He was later elected to Parliament and coauthored the constitutions of Pakistan and the United Arab Emirates. During the period of 1964–69, he served as secretary-general of the Islamic Charter Front, which first appeared on December 6, 1964. The formation of this front heralded the triumph of his ideology and launched him as the pundit of the movement.

In 1986, Sadiq al-Mahdi, brother of al-Turabi's wife, was elected prime minister, and al-Turabi was appointed minister of foreign affairs. The National Islamic Front, a coalition of Islamic parties dominated by the Muslim Brotherhood, founded by al-Turabi, remained in the opposition since the new regime failed to reform the deteriorating economy and put an end to the rebellion of the non-Muslims in southern Sudan. The government was overthrown in June 1989 in a coup d'état by General 'Umar Hasan al-Bashir. Al-Turabi was imprisoned, only to reemerge as the regime's supreme ideologue and Sudan's de facto ruler. He was elected speaker of parliament and became secretary-general of the Khartoum-based Popular and Islamic Congress, whose membership included nationalist parties, groups, and personalities from fifty-five Muslim countries.[7] He was in contact with all the leaders of militant Islam and stated, "Revolution would be the fundamentalist's only resort if other means of coming to power were denied to him, or otherwise blocked." Ultimately, according to him, it did not matter how power was attained, "What matters is that history be permitted to take its course. Islam is the future."[8]

Because the new regime's creed was "homogenization" of Islamic faith and practice, all political parties, trade unions, women's organizations, and nongovernmental media were proscribed, political opponents were arrested and imprisoned, and an Islamic restructuring of Sudanese society was embarked upon. It soon became clear that the Islamist movement was not only the backbone of the revolution but was the real power behind the regime, whose ideology called for the implementation of Islam and Shari'ah, since democracy had failed the Sudanese people.[9] Milton Viorst quotes al-Turabi as having said that without Islam, "Sudan has no identity, no direction," and he called the new regime an "Islamic experiment."[10]

Hasan al-Turabi designed a harsher version of the 1983 Islamic penal code that had been enforced by Numayri. The new version was promulgated by the government on March 22, 1991, and was based on the Shari'ah, including sections that discriminated based on gender and non-Muslim status, as well as such penalties as flogging, amputation, and stoning to death. A further addition was the provision for apostasy (riddah). In November 1991, "The Islamic Fundamentalist military junta decreed . . . that, henceforth, all Sudanese women will wear long black dresses to their ankles and a black veil covering their head and face . . . those who disobey to be instantly punished by whipping."[11] Thus, the liberal intellectual atmosphere and political dynamism created by the downfall of Numayri changed abruptly with the military coup of 'Umar al-Bashir.[12]

Al-Turabi has been hailed as a hero by his fellow Islamists for establishing the first Sunni Islamist state of the twentieth century. He is seen as a mujaddid [renewer/reformer], a man who combines both theory and practice. He emphasizes *al-faʿiliyyah al-qutriyyah* [regional/national activism] to enable Islamists, through political participation, to Islamize Arab governments and pave the way for their unity in Islam.[13] Al-Turabi sees himself unique in his Islamist activism, ready to lead Islamism into a new era: he has managed to master classical Islamic learning, on the one hand, and the Western sophistication of the post-Enlightenment period, on the other. His experience in prison inspired him to view Islam "as a comprehensive way of life" and to "renew religion as a broad base from which to integrate society." He saw the "Islamic awakening" as the means by which Muslims could transcend their ethnicity, factionalism, and nationalism. He views himself as an exponent of moderation and gradualism: Islamic law will be implemented in a manner designed to ensure individual dignity and women's rights and to protect one's property and the rights of minorities.[14] According to al-Turabi, "The modern Islamist movement looks like the only hope for rescuing modern Muslim societies from the endemic cycle of instability caused by the inherent illegitimacy of the secular political systems ruling over them . . . For a worldview that remains unchallenged theoretically, that places its adherents at the center of the universe as the divinely sanctioned leaders of humanity, replacements are hard to find, especially if they all entailed third—or fourth—class membership in the community of nations." Al-Turabi claims that the movement is democratic in origin but "became revolutionary because there was very little option left." He advocated, instead, peaceful and protracted resistance.[15]

Al-Turabi's contribution to twentieth-century Islamism is his revolutionary shift from al-Mawdudi's and Qutb's rejectionism to political and ideological pragmatism. In contrast to al-Mawdudi's thesis of attacking society from the outside as a moral ideal, al-Turabi saw the Islamic movement as a force advocating Islam from within the system.[16] This was to be accomplished by addressing the concerns of the largest sectors of society, being an example of the ideal Islamic society, emphasizing the centrality of God in all domains of life, bringing about an intellectual renaissance, enabling women to participate "in the struggle for construction and progress, not as a favor or privilege, but as a duty and an obligation," basing economic progress on "sound economic systems with clear means and objectives indigenous to our people and culture and free from the rootless influence of capitalism and socialism, changing oppressive regimes through political action and the establishment of *shura* [consultation], and developing international relations based on Islamic principles.[17]

Al-Turabi believed in the possibility of a peaceful transition achieved from within Islam, and he discarded the use of coercion to achieve Islamic reform, since the role of the state in reform was to be secondary, even in the eradication of vice. The role of the state was to provide the right atmosphere for reform and virtue. Al-Turabi, in contrast to Sayyid Qutb, never required a withdrawal from existent society but encouraged cooperation with other organizations; Islamization was to be a gradual process, where the emphasis was to be on the transformation of individuals rather than transformation of society as a whole, revolutionary style.[18]

Al-Turabi's gradualism is further evidenced in his view of Islam and its interpretation. He describes the traditional ulema as having a virtual "monopoly over Islam" and being "conservative in their attitudes." According to him, "They are not conscious of developments, and they never renew religious spirit and religious thought from time to time."[19] In emphasizing the central role of knowledge in Islamism, al-Turabi expands the original meaning of *'alim* [religious scholar] to designate anybody "who knows anything well enough to relate to Allah." Since all knowledge is divine, specialists of all domains—medicine, engineering, chemistry, law, economics—are ulema. This definition expands the role of ulema, be they natural or social scientists, philosophers or administrators, to enlighten society.[20] Furthermore, al-Turabi rejects historical jurisprudence in favor of free thinking without the constraints of traditional jurists. He maintains that "no limits" should be imposed "on revolution and freedom . . . thus *ijtihad* rearranges *Shari'ah* without any institutional regulative principle."[21] Social adherence to the *Shari'ah* signifies the general goals of Islam and not the prohibition of all things un-Islamic. Thus, Islam's exhortation for justice does not negate the people's prerogative to interpret it. Both the individual and society are entitled to interpret and/or reinterpret, or even entertain new concepts so long as they do not directly oppose or contradict a Qur'anic text.[22]

Al-Turabi further emphasized the need for a wide-ranging *ijtihad* by stating that "the most serious thing we have found is that most of the Islamic literature has been written centuries ago, and much of it is not relevant today, in the fields of economics, law, politics, government, etc. Therefore, a great deal of *ijtihad* is required," for changes in circumstances necessitate changes in religious expression, the only exceptions to change being "the eternal components of the divine message." Muslims may vary the practices of the prototype community of the Prophet to meet the changing realities, but they must always retain the meaning behind the original model.[23]

Everyone can exercise *ijtihad*, which is "not the prerogative of a small select group, but a dynamic of the whole community ... *ijtihad* and knowledge are a collective social function."[24] In fact, al-Turabi describes *ijtihad* as a jihad and, therefore, it is the right of every individual and should not be restricted to a group of individuals. The people should be able to distinguish right from wrong in the words and actions of their leaders and ulema, and they should have the right to choose what they believe is right and adhere to the teaching of the sect (*madhhab*) of their choosing. Jurists or ulema have no right to impose their judgments on Muslims, it is only the Muslim people or *jama'ah* [community] that has the right to impose the decisions arrived at by consensus.[25] The *ijtihad* that al-Turabi espouses is that of *al-ra'y* [opinion] based on rational empirical thinking that would help the establishment of a modern and vibrant civilization reminiscent of a glorious past. Al-Turabi reassures those afraid of consequent chaos by emphasizing the roles public opinion and Islamic government play as safeguards against anarchy: public opinion, though uninitiated in the religious sciences, has always made the right decisions regarding what new ideas to accept or reject, and a Muslim government can assist the development of an educated public opinion through education and public awareness.

Tajdid, or renewal, the continuous striving to bring amorphous existence under the everlasting divine principles, is the central tenet of al-Turabi's outlook. According to him, Islam needs constant examination and reconsideration, for there is a stark difference between the eternal principles of Islam and human endeavor expressed in the *fiqh* [jurisprudence] handed down from earlier generations. Therefore, renewal should be an ongoing process to meet new circumstances. This, however, is the task of the whole *ummah*, and not individual reformers.[26]

Since human intellectual development, regardless of its prowess, is finite and confined to the irreversibility of time, the "truth" of the Qur'anic text becomes relative to time, space, and interpreter, making the original scriptural message beyond his or her comprehension. Therefore, a humanly developed doctrine, albeit based on the Qur'an, cannot be transformed into an infallible universal and eternal truth. Needless to say, the divine text itself remains permanent, immutable, and valid for all ages and places, because its truth is interpreted to fit different times and circumstances. Therefore, attempted interpretations over the ages are finite and should be transcended by new "theoretical roots" deduced from the sacred texts to meet the real conditions and ideals of existent society.[27] He expresses the dilemma of adapting the Qur'an and the Sunna to modern ways of life by explaining that "the basic doctrine in Islam is one that unites the relativity of human existence to the absoluteness of the divine. ... Islam, as a divine word, is the eternal embodiment of truth, goodness, and right. But, as a message, it is addressed to man in history."[28]

Al-Turabi has increasingly been seen as one of the most important and influential leaders in the world, as well as a controversial figure in the international Islamic movement and one of its most influential thinkers. Throughout the Middle East, young Muslims use his teachings as a model for synthesizing modernity and religious principles to bring about radical changes in their societies. For al-Turabi sees Islam as a "rebellious call to arms" to implement God's Shari'ah through the creation of authentic Islamic states.[29]

To encapsulate his own role in contemporary Islamism, al-Turabi says:

I have learned a great deal from the West, studied there, stayed there; I have visited every Western country. I know many languages: English, French, some German [and] a little bit [of] Italian. And I have learned a lot about original Islam, its history, the Qur'an itself, [and] traditional knowledge of Islam ... I have traveled a great deal and I am free now. I think there is a great need of reform now, and I am not bound by anything historical. I want to reform society politically, so that it is completely free, not just formally free; not just a form of representation and democracy. You can have a form of democracy without true democracy. And you have to have a free society, but also a very clean society. . . . I am a revolutionary, because the change I work for is a complete change of social structures. . . . I can persuade society [without] using force with the revolution. I can persuade women, I can persuade men to allow women to have freedom. I can persuade the government to give freedom to people. I can persuade rich people to share their wealth, persuade intelligent people to share their opinion with the masses.[30]

Al-Turabi almost provoked an uprising when, in 1957, upon his return from London, he publicly advocated the liberation of women. He declared that most of the repression of women "is only an expression of many other forms of religious life which are not necessarily true to Islam itself, but they are done in the name of religion."[31] In 1973, his first publication was a pamphlet titled Women in Islamic Teachings, in which he made an exposition of his "radical" views on the role of Muslim women in society. The oppression of women witnessed in the world of Islam is a reflection of the decline and decadence of religion, rather than the effect of Islamic principles. He outlined his rationale for the liberation of women as an emancipation, not only from conservative Islamic traditions but also from what he calls Western exploitation and enslavement as sex objects. Economic pressures in urban areas and the shedding of restrictions on education and employment led the Sudanese to an anti-Islamic social order, which, influenced by the West, transformed women from being slaves to men to becoming enslaved by material needs and sexual desires. Al-Turabi saw modern women as dehumanized, being manipulated commercially and sexually. The goal of women had shifted from the fulfillment of their humanity to the fulfillment of their womanhood.

Al-Turabi explains that, inasmuch as the *Shari'ah* is important and central to Islamic life, it is not free of external and non-Islamic influences. He reminds Muslims that concepts change meaning in time to fit new places and times. As such, individual interpretations must change accordingly, but always in keeping with the Qur'anic text. Thus, al-Turabi draws attention to the equal and independent position the Qur'an accords women. Accordingly, he attributes the historically lower status afforded women and their abuse to the misinterpretation of Qur'anic verses on the subject of women and the negative effects of contemporary social environments accumulated over the ages. These two factors, however, could be modified to restore women to their original status, through a reinterpretation of relevant Qur'anic verses and affording women their natural place in society. Such changes, however, require comprehensive mental readjustment through changes in the curricula and raising consciousness within society. The initial step of such a program should be freeing individuals and community from old and defunct beliefs and preparing them to develop and comprehend new visions to carve themselves a space in the new world. This needs the establishment of new jurisprudence based on modern experience and freedom of research without the restrictions imposed by traditional jurists.[32] Islamists should not fear the rapid changes taking place around them and cower behind conservative traditions, but, rather, rush to assume the leadership of a new renaissance and deliver women from the evils of traditionalism on the one hand and Westernization on the other, since it is their religious duty to "give guidance to humanity and save people from inherited deviations and novel aberrations."[33]

Hasan al-Turabi believes that Islam holds women totally independent. Qur'anic text addresses them independently without a mediator, their faith being authentic and uninfluenced, based solely on personal conviction. A woman, according to him, not only had the right but was actually obliged to defy her family, if need be, to fulfill her religious duties. Since the *Shari'ah* itself explicitly states this fact, al-Turabi finds it "very strange" that traditional Muslim societies have blatantly disobeyed not only the spirit of Qur'anic law but its letter as well. He maintains that "the Qur'an itself pronounces that men and women both have to help each other in public life," even in matters of defense. The model set by the Prophet's life shows the presence of women in public, social, and military life. Thus, although it may not be a duty, it is her right to be "everywhere." In fact, "It is a religious obligation for her to contribute," even though she may have extenuating circumstances that men do not have.[34] If women are isolated from public life, it is not due to Islamic principles but to social backwardness and the misinterpretation of textual authorities. What is needed, therefore, is not a rejection of Islam but a reinterpretation of that part of religion that has been abused by men for the exploitation of women and their isolation and the provision of an environment where women can reclaim their original rights and exercise their freedom and independence. The participation of women in public life, albeit with reasonable safeguards and the provisions permitted by the *Shari'ah*, is worth the potential damage that may ensue from the mixing of the sexes. The indisputable benefit that women may accrue from their participation in public life far outweighs the alleged danger. Muslims who see women's place at home raising children seem to forget that by leading an isolated life, women are incapacitated from fulfilling their role of rearing children and preparing them to face the vicissitudes of life.[35]

The *Shari'ah*, according to al-Turabi, considers women the sisters of men and their equal, except in some minor matters relating to their physical nature. The duties prescribed for women are identical to those of men in the domains of religion (prayer, fasting, pilgrimage), personal relations (truthfulness, justice, kindness, faithfulness), and public life (patience, avoidance of heretics, and obedience of believers). Women may not be denied any type of work, and while they are exempted from assuming financial responsibility for the family, warfare, and prayer in groups, they will have to bear these responsibilities if men are unable to do so for any reason. Women enter the faith voluntarily, as men do. Thus, some women have taken up Islam when their families did not, and kept the faith as émigrés when their husbands converted to Christianity; and still others took up missionary work.[36]

Al-Turabi went further in his exposition of women's independence and freedom in public life by saying:

> Nor is an Islamic democracy government by the male members of society . . . Women played a considerable role in public life during the life of the Prophet; and they contributed to the election of the third caliph. Only afterwards were women denied their rightful place in public life, but this was history departing from the ideal . . . In principle, all believers, rich or poor, noble or humble, learned or ignorant, men or women, are equal before God and they are his vice regents on earth and the holders of his trust.[37]

Al-Turabi maintains that this state of affairs existed at the time of the Prophet. Being a rural society, women were ubiquitous without segregation. They participated in elections and consultations. Ibn Kathir, according to al-Turabi, said: "And 'Abdul-Rahman bin 'Awf started consulting people, leaders and followers alike, including veiled women." Women were also permitted to participate in group prayer meetings, aided in wars by caring for the wounded (Aisha and Umm-Salim), and even participating in actual combat (Safiyyah bint 'Abdul-Muttaleb). They were allowed to trade in the marketplace, and their opinions were respected: Aisha gave formal legal opinions (*fatwa*), and women discussed a variety of matters freely with the Prophet and his successors.[38]

Al-Turabi claims that women in Sudan have played a more active role in the Muslim Brotherhood than men. "They came with a vengeance, because they had been deprived, and so, when we allowed them in the Movement, more women voted for us than men, because we were the ones who gave them more recognition and a message and a place in society." They played an important role in the election campaigns and did most of the social and charitable work conducted by the movement. Al-Turabi claims that women have even joined the "Popular Defense Forces." Although women are currently present in all fields, al-Turabi admits, they have not achieved parity with men, just as is the case in the West. Women are allowed into all faculties at the university, although they seldom practice their specialty after graduation, as in engineering. They do it to prove they are as good in the professions as men.[39] In 1993, there were about twenty-five women in the Sudanese Parliament, which had assigned women 10 percent of elected positions.[40]

It is unfortunate, according to al-Turabi, that people focus so much on women's Islamic dress. In the Qur'an and Sunna, there is a definite prescription governing personal dress but without specifying the mode. The Prophet at no time imposed a particular form of dress, although he advised modesty. Keeping in mind that men and women, in general, submit to fashion and are free to dress as they please, it should not be difficult to understand and accept the fact that Islamic society exercises measures of censure or encouragement for one particular form of dress. "But no one, I mean no organization like the Saudi 'amr bil ma'ruf wal nahi 'an al-munkar [enjoining good and prohibiting evil], would have a legal authority to stop women or to harass them. And no punishments can be attached unless someone goes completely naked; that would be obscenity."[41] Most women in Sudan, according to al-Turabi, are dressed in long sleeves and headscarves, while many others go to work dressed as they please. Al-Turabi maintains that in his "ideal Islamic state, Islamic dress will not be demanded by law, but by moral instruction."[42]

The veil, at the time of the Prophet, al-Turabi points out, was particular to the Prophet's wives to distinguish them from the rest: "O ye wives of the Prophet! Whosoever of you committeth manifest lewdness, the punishment of her will be doubled, and that is easy for Allah" (33:30). Thus, the wives of the Prophet were not to appear uncovered in public, including their hands and faces, while it was permissible for other women to do so, although modestly. They were to lower their gaze when out in the streets, and they were not to stare at men or mix with them in crowded areas, to avoid temptation, except during pilgrimage.[43]

After the Prophet's era and the gradual transition to urban social life, al-Turabi explains, important changes took place in Muslim society, among them the weakening of family ties, increased social indifference, economic pressures, and an increasing tendency for more personal freedom of women, together with the relaxation of the codes of safety and security.[44] This development naturally led traditional Islamic societies to seek the protection of women and, therefore, impose strict regulations. Al-Turabi argues that this deterioration in social conditions led to the segregation of women and the abrogation of their rights, which stands as a departure from historical ideals and explicit Qur'anic stipulations. Women subsequently became totally isolated on the pretext of full-time activity in the home.[45] "Segregation," al-Turabi asserts, "is definitely not part of Islam"; "the harem quarters is a development, which was totally unknown in the model of Islam, or in the text of Islam; it is unjustified."[46]

Yet, al-Turabi is for veiling, for, he says, "A woman who is not veiled is not the equal of men. She is not looked on as one would look on a man [as one would when veiled]. She is looked at to [determine] if she is beautiful, if she is desirable. When she is veiled, she is considered a human being, not an object of pleasure, not an erotic image."[47] Here one wonders whether the Prophet himself was remiss in failing to consider unveiled women as subhuman or whether al-Turabi is more knowledgeable in such matters. Thus, even the *tobe*, the traditional dress of the northern Sudanese, which covers women from head to foot in a wraparound veil of light fabric and is worn over other clothes, is regarded as too revealing. According to the Sudanese Islamists, the *tobe* does not cover the hair, forearms, and neck adequately and, therefore, leads to public disorder. Such traditional apparel should, therefore, be replaced by "proper Islamic dress."[48] Whereas in the past women objected to the veil on financial grounds, not long after the new regime assumed power loans of a value of thirty dollars were granted to women government employees to buy the appropriate Islamic dress, to be later deducted from their monthly salaries, and employed women students were given an ultimatum to don the Islamic dress or risk getting fired or arrested.[49] At a time when al-Turabi claimed in a May 18, 1992, lecture at the University of Southern California that the Islamic dress code was not enforced except by "peer pressure," the military junta had issued a decree, in November 1991, that "henceforth all Sudanese women will wear long black dresses to their ankles and a black veil covering their head and face . . . those who disobey to be instantly punished by whipping."[50]

While al-Turabi asserts that there are no barriers to women becoming judges or rulers or anything else they might aspire to, since sex does not determine qualifications, he admits that "there is something about advocacy perhaps, which is not very consistent with the female temperament."[51] However, in 1992, three years after his NIF had come to power in Sudan, al-Turabi insisted, in a lecture to an American audience at a think tank in Washington, D.C., that while women could be in charge of "smaller institutions and businesses," and even lead men in prayer, they could not head a state.[52]

Wisal al-Mahdi, al-Turabi's wife, in an interview together with her husband, asserted that Islam is the best system for the protection of women and society as a whole. But, while she admitted that women have social responsibilities like men, she agreed with the Qur'anic stipulation that it takes two women to testify compared to only one man. This, she explains, is due to the limited experience of women in public life—as evidenced by the number of illiterate women in many parts of the world who seldom leave their communities. Hikmat Sidahmed, NIF representative in the government, maintains that women are different from men and that women, by their nature, sometimes forget. Sometimes they sympathize. "When one of them forgets, the other will remind her, and if one of them sympathizes with the criminal, the other could correct her." Thus, she holds that it is not a problem for women to find themselves treated differently, because "[i]t is natural . . . the entire principle [in *Shari'ah*] is in accord with the way women are created, since women are naturally empathetic."[53] Wisal al-Mahdi concurs that women are "sentimental" and adds, "This does not mean that a woman is less than a man, or that her mental capacity is less than a man. It means that her disposition is different than [a man's]. We are equal in all rights in Islam."[54] Furthermore, according to Islamist Nagwa Kamal Farid, Sudan's first woman *Shari'ah* judge, inequities in inheritance are not detrimental to women since women never have to support themselves, this being the burden of men, and, therefore, it is right that men receive a larger share of inheritance.[55]

The National Islamic Front believes that, although Islam and *Shari'ah* allow women to work outside the home, only childless and needy women are to do so. Thus, women's jobs should not "threaten the power structure," they should only be extensions of their domestic work and, therefore, reflect the essence of women. Since 1989, "Women have increasingly entered the workforce as clerks and secretaries, in order to boost household income. After the 1989 coup, many were 'retrenched' for 'religious' reasons, but they have mainly been allowed back from many public positions, including the renowned judge Aminah Awwad."[56] Career development, while approved in principle, should not obscure or hinder women's primary role: "The woman's natural place is in the home, but if she finds that, after doing her duty in the home, she has time, she can use part of it in the service of society, on condition that this is done within the legal limits, which preserve her dignity and morality."[57] Nagwa Kamal Farid adds that, if a woman needs to go to work, "She should be well dressed, not too much perfume, so as not to attract attention . . . She has to go out respectably . . . to cover her hair, all of her face, and hands should be inside, not too colorful . . . When a man stands beside her, he should remember work and nothing else."[58] Islamist women are further seen as the potential means by which the NIF intends to lay the foundation of an authentic Islamic culture that is neither regressive nor fundamentalist.[59]

Moreover, al-Turabi maintained that, since the liberation of women is no longer subject to discussion due to modernization, growing economic pressures, and urbanization, which made it a reality through the inevitable exodus of women into the work community, Islamists should stop resisting the inevitable and attempt to ameliorate the condition of women "in a truly Islamic manner."[60] To be able to recreate the Muslim woman as "public servant" through her private life, and launch her as the "vanguard" of the Islamic movement, it was imperative to place her as organizer and socializer at the forefront, together with the family as the foundation of "authentic" culture based in the Islam of the past but far removed from past Arab culture, which is, more and more, being blamed for all the ills of the modern Sudanese woman. "To tell the truth," says Wisal al-Mahdi, "a woman in Islam . . . should first be responsible and care for her children, her family, because they are the ones who need her most. Because in caring for [one's] family and caring for [one's] children you care for the nation, and you care for the offspring which will come in later times to take care of the specialized jobs of the government and the specialized jobs of society."[61] In this way, women will realize that the discriminatory Islam that had been taught to them was an Islam sheathed in Arab culture, conventions, and customs, contrary to the pure Islam that will "liberate" women and propel them forward.[62]

In May 1990, eleven months after 'Umar al-Bashir and the Islamic fundamentalist regime assumed power, it was decreed that no Sudanese woman was to leave the country unaccompanied by a *mahram* [unmarriageable male] unless she could provide proper documentation of consent from a male guardian.[63]

Al-Turabi affirms that, while in the past Egyptian judges used the Hanafi personal status law with elements of the Sudanese Maliki practice, there is now in Sudan a new personal status code that draws freely on all sources of Islamic jurisprudence—Sunni and Shi'ite—in matters of marriage, divorce, parenthood, and inheritance. This new law, according to al-Turabi, "borders on being liberal."[64]

Legally speaking, al-Turabi maintains, a marriage contract can contain a host of conditions stipulated by the two parties as long as these are not contrary to the fundamentals of Islamic marriage itself. For just as an ordinary commercial contract cannot stipulate any terms contrary to state law, so it is with the Islamic marriage contract. Thus, a man, for example, cannot stipulate that his wife support him, since, according to the Qur'an, it is his duty to support his wife. Thus, once married, the law specifies that the husband, and not the wife, support the family, even if the latter is rich; and she may retain full control of her money. Because of this duty, al-Turabi explains, the husband is the one entrusted with the prerogative of divorce without referring to the courts, since he will suffer a financial loss by returning his wife's *mahr* [dower], while the woman stands to gain. Because a woman's judgment could be clouded by the prospects of financial gain, she can divorce only by going to court.[65]

Polygamy, according to al-Turabi, is categoric in the Qur'an, although it is discouraged unless fairness and equity are ensured in the treatment of the wives. Al-Turabi further claims that the world at present is going in that direction: "[T]he whole world is going polygamous, de facto if not de jure. English law now recognizes cohabitation as a legal relation with legal consequences."[66] He goes on to cite a number of benefits of the practice of polygamy and defends its legitimacy: since female fertility is limited to the period between the ages of fifteen and forty, while that of men is limitless after the age of fifteen, it is only natural to marry another wife for the sake of begetting children. Further, women, by nature, are normally more eager to have children than men, and it is, therefore, only fair to afford them the opportunity to fulfill this desire. This becomes even more important when one realizes that having only two children is enough to satisfy women, even if they never remarry after their husband's death. On the other hand, men are more interested in sex than raising families and, therefore, when sexually thwarted during their wife's menstruation, pregnancy, or delivery, they need to release their sexual urges elsewhere. This is compounded when women become forty years of age or more, become active in social affairs (hospitals, schools, and so on), and lose their interest in sex. It would then be only natural for men to marry another to satisfy their needs. Wisal al-Mahdi insisted that polygamy should be practiced for the development of Sudan. Although she is al-Turabi's only wife, she claimed she would welcome his taking another, rather than having several girlfriends. He should have "a clear wife there, whom he is married to by *Shari'ah* like me, and her children are the half-brothers of my children . . . Every man should marry more than one wife. We will have more children [and, therefore], more people to fill the Sudan and to make the Sudanese economic position better."[67] Finally, Islam's position on abortion, al-Turabi argues, is much more liberal than some Christian views. He says, "In the late stages of development, it's not legitimate, but in the early stages, it's not really a very serious offense. If there is any risk to the woman, definitely abortion is allowed right up to the end."[68]

Though influenced by such notable contemporary thinkers as Hasan al-Banna and Abu al-'A'la al-Mawdudi, al-Turabi has always professed liberalism and gradualism in his approach to Islamism. Among his more unorthodox views has been his vision of women and the role they may play in the transformation of society. Al-Turabi has further shown his liberalism in allowing all intellectuals, whatever their field may be, to exercise their own reason in interpreting and understanding Islam, as long as they use the Qur'an and the Sunna as their cornerstones. He thus never attached himself to any one school of law and was dismayed at the official ulema, whom he described as weak and ineffectual. Through his advocacy of non-violence and gradualism, al-Turabi opposes the implementation of the *hudud* [mandatory punishments] save in an ideal Muslim society.[69]

Renewal and revival (*tajdid*) are among his most cherished goals. Al-Turabi believes in the constant reevaluation and study of Islam and its openness to radical change to meet the exigencies of the present. He never doubted the eternal and immutable Islamic principles but insisted on the mortality and human origin of the classical exposition of Islamic law (*fiqh*), which, by definition, made it subject to reevaluation and change in accordance with present needs. The reopening of the doors of *ijtihad* becomes possible through al-Turabi's definition of the Islamic concept of *tawhid*. According to him, *tawhid* [unity/fusion, unicity] involves the union of the eternal divine principles with the changing conditions of the world and human life, and the reconciliation of reason and faith. Once this is accomplished, a universal method of reinterpretation of all human knowledge—religious, natural, and social—becomes possible through Islamic understanding.[70]

Based on these ideas and his Western education, al-Turabi was seen by many as a bridge between Islam and the West, since he was able to communicate with the West using their own language, as evidenced by his declaration, "I can persuade society, not by using force with revolution. I can persuade women, I can persuade men to allow women to have freedom. I can persuade the government to give freedom to people. I can persuade rich people to share their wealth, persuade intelligent people to share their opinion with the masses."[71] Abdel Wahhab Effendi describes al-Turabi's desire to "liberate" women from Arabic cultural constraints that are groundless in Islam as a "far-reaching revolution" within Sudan. The place of women in Sudanese society has been a vexing problem to Islamists, who were "torn between their sympathy for the demands for a better lot for women and their perception of what Islam taught and tradition dictated."[72]

Al-Turabi's vision of the future is admirable and enthralling. He speaks of "freedom for the people, an end to oppression and discrimination, elimination of national chauvinism, borders, wars, and tension among people."[73] His language is that of persuasion and reconciliation in the hope of achieving the unity of all mankind. He says, "Mankind is one community, and people can cooperate in the field of science and knowledge, and exchange ideas and achievements. National resources of different countries and regions of the world should be pooled."[74] But, enlightened and progressive as his views may be, contradictions between theory and practice abound. During a visit to the United States in 1992, he was accused of having become more authoritarian in his views than before the coup d'état of 1989. He replied, "They don't know me well enough to compare my position today to my position before, they barely *listened* to me."[75] The implication here is that all his apparently liberal statements were merely couched in moderation and no one bothered to read between the lines. The real al-Turabi was a master at the roles of the diplomat and *taqiyyah* [to act contrary to the principles of faith for the sake of expediency] interchangeably. Once in power, al-Turabi seems to have discarded the liberal ideas expressed in his lectures and writings. By 1994, he had even stopped rationalizing the glaring shift in his stand. Judith Miller says, "He simply denied things that he knew I had seen and heard firsthand and knew to be true, abuses that could never be defended by Islamic principles or any other moral standard."[76]

Amin Mekki Mandani claims that the new regime is "a reign of terror," and he states, "There is repression. There is intimidation. There is dismissal from service. There is detention. There is torture. There is restriction of movement. There is a reign of terror."[77] Rashid al-Ghannoushi, al-Turabi's follower and colleague, comments on the situation in Sudan, "As far as the political system in Sudan is concerned, I do not approve of it, I do not condone it, I call for the recognition of pluralism and I do not see that the Sudanese or Iranian models are models for us to follow, but we consider them experiments that may lead to something in the future."[78]

Thus, the contemporary condition of Sudanese women is highly complex, rife with contradictions and dynamism as their legal and political stature keep changing at fantastic speed. They keep receiving contradictory messages. They achieved universal suffrage in 1965, earned the right of equal pay for equal work in 1968, became entitled to pensions in 1975, and were given special benefits, such as maternity leave, by the Public Service Regulations; and they were granted equal rights to seek an education and to hold public office, and equal rights to freedom of association, unionization, speech and movement by the Permanent Constitution of 1973. Nevertheless, Sadiq al-Mahdi maintained that al-Bashir's regime failed to grant any civil rights to women, and many women feared their acquired rights could be revoked at any time. Lower-class women, who once were barely able to make a living selling local brew, tea, or trinkets, as well as prostitutes on the streets, were now harassed and co-erced by self-appointed morality officers. Some of the women have even been flogged in the streets, beaten by gangs of men, and jailed. Women's apprehension became even greater when they were reminded that their judgment could be clouded by financial gain, thus limiting their qualifications for employment to certain fields. Apprehension was reinforced further when domesticity and reproduction were romanticized and women manipulated out of the workforce and forced into "appropriate" jobs. This could bring to an end the "equal participation" women had worked so hard for during the past three decades.[79]

Even if one concedes, despite evidence to the contrary, that al-Turabi's views on women are liberal, this liberality is not reflected in the present regime. Some of the restrictions perpetrated by the al-Bashir government are the prohibition of free travel for women outside the Sudan; the segregation of public transport according to gender; the imposition of Islamic dress on women and public punishment of those who disobey, no matter how slight the infraction; and massive dismissals of women from public service. All these measures clearly demonstrate that al-Turabi, once in power, contradicted his former liberal views urging women to "escape social oppression and discrimination, and to play a full part in the building of a new society."[80] Wisal al-Mahdi herself, who considers herself a formidable force "behind" her husband and is herself an activist, resides in a house that is segregated into women's and men's quarters, wears the hijab, and molds her role in society to fit the dictates of Islam as perceived by the NIF. This becomes even more interesting when one recalls al-Turabi's stand on segregation prior to the 1989 coup d'état, that "segregation is definitely not part of Islam . . . and the harem quarters is a development, which was totally unknown in the model of Islam, or in the text of Islam; it is unjustified."[81] His contradictory stand on imposing the veil was unmasked when the new regime dictated that Islamic dress would be a long black dress with a veil covering the head and face, a requirement that he himself admits does not exist in the Qur'an, with all infractions being instantly punished by public flogging, a procedure he had condemned as practiced in Saudi Arabia and which he had vowed would not be practiced in Sudan.[82]

Although, in principle, women were not prohibited from participating in public life, the restrictions imposed on them by Islamic principles as understood by the new regime, such as the enforcement of *qiwamah* [male authority], hijab, and segregation between the sexes, made this very difficult to carry out. The imposition of the hijab at work automatically led to the displacement of many women from skilled and professional public employment.[83] The encouragement of women by al-Turabi to participate in public life and his spearheading of their liberation movement were forgotten once he came to power. The new regime, in depoliticizing gender issues, reaffirmed traditional Islamic concepts regarding the role of women. Thus, their activities and interests in the public arena were restricted, and gender became a secondary social concern of the government, a development that would eventually lead to relocating gender issues into the hands of the society's patriarchs and the families of the individual women.[84]

As usual, women were the main targets of the government in trying to establish an Islamic state and eradicate non-Islamic practices. Al-Bashir banned dancing between the sexes in November 1991 and decreed that all female government employees should be in Islamic dress. Women were flogged even before this law was decreed. That same year, the government announced a new criminal law based on *Shari'ah*. Married women convicted of adultery were to be stoned to death; abortions, contrary to what al-Turabi had declared, unless to save the mother's life or to end a pregnancy due to rape, could result in a prison sentence ranging between one and three years and the payment of a fine; "gross indecency," that is, "any act contrary to another person's modesty" or the wearing of an "indecent or immoral uniform which caused annoyance to public feelings," may result in forty lashes. The Public Order Act of Khartoum State, promulgated in 1992, forbids women from selling peanuts, making tea in street stands or any other form of small business between 5:00 P.M. and 5:00 A.M., thereby curtailing the extra income many women need to support their families; women could be prosecuted for "suspicion of intent to commit prostitution." The Personal Status Code, enacted in 1991, set the legal marriage age at ten for girls, legitimized polygamy, and asserted the husband's unilateral right to divorce. And, finally, all so-called rights accorded women, such as voting and running for office or elections, became void when it became necessary to solicit the husband's or guardian's permission to leave the house or participate in political activities, a permission that may be withdrawn at will.[85]

Although many restrictions have been imposed on educated and highly skilled women, including restricting fields of study, the uneducated and unskilled have gone unfettered, probably because they were not perceived to pose any threat to the power structure. Jobs usually filled by women are being withheld on the basis of the jobs being "necessary but not appropriate" or "appropriate but not necessary." This policy was coupled with campaigns to authenticate the Islamic revolution through the exaltation of the role of women in the home, thus pressuring urban women into leaving the public arena for the "worthier" domestic role. Furthermore, contrary to the declarations of al-Turabi and the NIF, women in well-paying jobs were suddenly seen as rivals to the seats of power, rather than contributors to such fields as medicine and agriculture.[86]

Al-Turabi is very subtle in his commentary on the role of women in Islamic society, and his statements need to be deconstructed carefully, as he himself maintained when accused of changing his views after the coup d'état of 1989, "They don't know me well enough to compare my position today to my position before, they barely *listened.*"[87] At a time when al-Turabi declares that women have invaded all public sectors "with a vengeance," he reminds his audience very discreetly that women have to recognize the fact that, although it is a religious obligation for them to contribute to society, there are extenuating circumstances (and not prohibitions) dictated by their "female condition." This "female condition" could prevent them from joining the military due to pregnancy; and prevents them from attending public prayers on Friday due to their maternal duties at home. Although they will be rewarded for fulfilling such duties, they are, by no means, "bound" to do them as men are. Wisal al-Mahdi insisted that woman's primary role was her home and her children, and the differences between the sexes in the *Shari'ah* were due to the fact that women were actually "different by nature." She elaborated on the emotional nature of women and, therefore, their inability to testify objectively in court without having another female witness. "After all, a woman is weaker than a man, and all her nervous system is made different [from a man's] . . . so she may say something that she believes . . . happened, not what she saw happen . . . Women are more sentimental, because they are the mothers who breed children . . . that is why, in *Shari'ah* law, we guard against the sentimentality of womankind." The prevalent female oppression, according to al-Mahdi, is due to Arab culture and the low opinion Arab men have of women.[88]

In January 1992, when interviewed by Judith Miller, al-Turabi insisted that only "moral education" was being used to encourage Islamic dress, and he called evidence, presented by doctors, of the lashing of young women for "improper attire" as "hostile propaganda and gibberish." As mentioned earlier, though he decries segregation and insists that the Qur'an describes which parts of the body are and which are not to be covered, he goes on to practice segregation in his own house and requires the covering of the face, contrary to Qur'anic injunctions. He further labeled as fictitious and untrue the charges brought against him by human rights organizations and the United Nations, as well as Western governments, that the rights and status of women have been compromised by his regime.[89]

Moreover, while al-Turabi insists on the practice of *ijtihad* and refuses to follow any one school of Islamic law, and despite the fact that the Qur'anic verses regarding polygamy may be interpreted as a call for monogamy, he maintains that no Islamic law could outlaw polygamy: "There is no way that can happen because it is categorical in the Qur'an." He also distanced himself from the present penal code, which he described as bordering "on being liberal," at a time when many believe he is a coauthor of the document.[90]

In the early 1970s, al-Turabi espoused the cause of women's emancipation and respect for individual dignity. He maintained that the individual had the right to education and a decent life of privacy, peace, and social well-being. This, of course, included freedom of religion and expression, as well as the right to revolution if the state transcended the *Shari'ah*, since a Muslim's ultimate obedience is to God alone. The ordinary Muslim citizen is obliged to practice *ijtihad* and to interpret Islamic principles himself. Thus, while a Muslim would not oppose the *Shari'ah* because he believes in it, if he does not agree with a particular interpretation of the law, he is entitled to his view.[91] According to him, it was the duty of all individuals, alone and in unison, to reform and change society to become conducive to a better, positive life. Freedom was to prevail on all levels of society, the intellectual, social, political, and religious, as a fundamental human right. Al-Turabi rejected the acquired right of governments to impose their views on their people, and he stressed that society must conduct its own affairs freely, without any interference. If, however, interference becomes necessary, the government should resort to *shura* [consultation]. Since the people have been given the authority to enjoin good and forbid evil by the Qur'an, this becomes, therefore, their prerogative and not the state's. Nor should they be subjected to any particular institution, be it political or religious.

Al-Turabi went on to state that democracy in Islam is not peculiar to society alone but should be practiced within the family unit as well. He further maintained that without freedom humans lose their essence and become indistinguishable from animals. The only normative commitment of the individual should be to Islam, which, in turn, guarantees his or her freedom from ever having to submit to imposed principles and ideologies. The Muslim community, according to al-Turabi, consists of free individuals associating together of their own volition under God's authority. The group helps the individual to locate his or her freedom and fulfillment and, thereby, achieve his or her full potential. The blind adherence to tradition contradicts one's religious obligations. Constant *tajdid* [reform/renewal] was, therefore, absolutely necessary.[92] Thus, "Freedom, according to the basic principles of religion, is the destiny of man, which distinguishes him from all other creatures . . . and just as this is man's natural destiny, so it is his lawful right. For God has given no Prophet or ruler authority to force him to accept true religion."[93] Freedom from all social, governmental, or religious scholars' constraints pave the way for true worship and *tawhid*; to achieve this freedom is not only a Muslim's right but an obligation. Differences in religious knowledge are comparable to differences in wealth and should not, therefore, be used as a means to subjugate people.

The freedom of the individual, al-Turabi maintains, ultimately originates from the doctrine of *tawhid*, "which requires [the] self-liberation of man from any worldly authority in order to serve Allah exclusively." Society and the government should help and support individuals in their endeavor to achieve their ideal. "To promote this cooperation, the freedom of one individual is related to that of the general group. The ultimate common aim of religious life is the unity of the private and social spheres; and the *Shari'ah* provides an arbiter between social order and individual freedom." The functions of the Islamic government are rather limited, and as such, not all aspects of Islam are to be enforced by the government, for society can manage in many areas without its interference. The Islamic government, however, is bound to provide "freedom, equality, and [unity] of believers."[94]

The classical Islamic definition of *tawhid* is the affirmation of the unity of God. A corollary of the belief in the unity of God is heeding the commands of God in all aspects of life. This is why life must, therefore, be ordered according to the *Shari'ah*. Al-Turabi, in addition to opining that *tawhid* requires the total submission of one's life to the rule of God, uses the term to refer to the "union of the eternal divine commands with the changing conditions of human life," or "the reuniting of the ideal with the actual." Furthermore, if man is created to worship and obey God, nature being created for him, he cannot allow himself to be enslaved by anything or anyone but God. *Tawhid* is, thus, the liberation of man from any form of enslavement to "one's own or other's whims and desires"; it is the total and absolute liberation of humans from humans.[95] The ideological conception, thus, of the Islamic state is based on the doctrine of *tawhid*—the unity of God and human life—as a universal form of worship. The state is, therefore, neither primordial nor absolute; rather, it is "the collective endeavor of Muslims. For most of it, the implementation of the *Shari'ah* is left to the free conscience of believers or to informal means of social control."[96]

After this lengthy discussion of the importance of freedom and *tawhid* in Islam and, therefore, their application in an Islamic state, one is bound to be confused by the apparent dichotomy within his own exposition and understanding of what Islam and Islamist ideology are, on the one hand, and the blatant contradictions between his theoretical views and their implementation in practice, on the other. This contradiction, no matter how subtle, affects the condition of women most of all. Thus, one wonders, if *ijtihad*, as al-Turabi claims, is an obligation of every Muslim for the purposes of *tajdid* and *islah* [renewal and reform], why it is that neither women themselves, nor men, including al-Turabi himself, have seen fit to utilize this tool for the liberation of women from the constraints imposed upon them by society. Yet, *ijtihad* has indeed been practiced by men, and in particular, by his own admission, by al-Turabi himself, but only to add more strictures and constraints than Scripture ever intended. This is despite the fact that al-Turabi not only views Islamic thought as human attempts at the interpretation of the Qur'an, but he declares the inability of man to give decisive interpretations of the divine text. Hence, Islamic thought can never be taken categorically, and all Islamic exegeses are tentative and subject to review.[97] In fact, he declared, in an interview, "Nous ne voulons pas répéter les formes historiques du passé de l'Islam. Je regarde le passé juste pour m'en inspirer, pour y prendre une certaine experience, non pour y trouver un modèle formel." (We do not want to repeat the historic forms of Islam's past. I look at the past to inspire me, to take from it a certain experience, not to find a formal model.)[98]

Al-Turabi, as mentioned earlier, emphasizes in his concept of the state and the role of the individual the importance of *tawhid* and the individual's freedom in society. Thus, although his own works portray *tawhid* as the total and absolute liberation of humans from humans, and he declares that individuals lose their essence unless they are free, since Islam guarantees their emancipation from any imposed principles or ideologies, women are publicly chained and flogged by the current regime and are oppressed by their husbands and male guardians in private, as previously shown. Thus, Islamic dress, as understood by al-Turabi and the new regime, is imposed on all women, infractions being punishable by flogging; and women's education is controlled to fit the roles preferred for them by men and the well-being of society as perceived by men. Although al-Turabi extols equality among individuals, women are ousted from the public sphere in one form or another and are forbidden from traveling abroad unless accompanied by a male guardian. In fact, once in power, al-Turabi claimed that the government had the right to restrict individual civil liberties in times of emergencies, as in civil war, and if deemed to be in the best interest of society. Thus, after initially denying the detention of political opponents, he justified the procedure of "preventive detention" on the grounds of safeguarding the stability of the state and the well-being of society.[99] The oppression of women during the present regime becomes even more curious in light of al-Turabi's position that "God has given man the freedom to believe or not to believe, and no human can force an idea or a point of view on another."[100]

Another inconsistency in al-Turabi's discourse has to do with his apparent liberalism and moderation vis-à-vis the radicalism of such fundamentalists as al-Mawdudi and Qutb. His "liberalism" and "modernization," in addition to his views on women, are best represented by the methodology he espoused for the dissemination of Islamism and the ultimate establishment of an Islamic state. He preached, to the chagrin of many other Islamists, the foundation of an Islamic state by the formation of a broad coalition of sympathetic forces, and the participation in government whenever possible, ostensibly to gain experience and develop useful contacts. Thus, soon after 1969, the Muslim Brothers had infiltrated the army, the security services, the bureaucracy, and many other sectors of government. This policy is also demonstrated by al-Turabi's joining Numayri's government and the enactment of the September Laws in 1983. However, his gradualist approach came to an end when he backed the military coup of 'Umar al-Bashir in 1989 and emerged as the ideologue of the new regime and its de facto ruler.[101]

Al-Turabi's apparent rigidity during his tenure, vis-à-vis women's role in society, becomes even more astonishing when one notes in many of his writings what he calls "jurisprudence of necessity" (*fiqh al-darurah*). This pragmatic interpretation of Islamic law and *ijtihad* is based on the priority of *maslahah* [self-interest, interest of state]. Its motto is "Necessity knows no law or rule," thus freeing al-Turabi and his followers from any fixed obligations and paving the way for a possible Islamist version of Machiavellianism. Al-Turabi further uses such terminology as "stage," "reality," and "status quo" to describe the flexible jurisprudence adopted by Islamists in matters of politics. He applied this method when he dissolved the National Front, which opposed Numayri, and joined the government after 1977. He called this step the "*fiqh* alliance." The criterion of evaluation for this kind of practice is called by al-Turabi "*kasb*" [achievement, gain].[102] With such a pragmatic outlook on Islamic jurisprudence, and his liberal and modern views, it is surprising that al-Turabi not only did not use this ingenious method to achieve the liberation of women from serfdom to tradition, which he so vehemently preached, but went on to shackle them with the most unyielding and implacable constraints.

Abdullahi An-Na'im appraised al-Turabi as "an outstanding lawyer, [who] knows that it is not possible to achieve these reforms in the *Shari'ah* without reformulating *'usul al-fiqh* [foundations of jurisprudence], which is the way in which *Shari'ah* principles are derived from the sources. Now, if al-Turabi, in forty years of scholarship and public life, had at any point articulated a different view of *'usul al-fiqh*, whereby the equality for non-Muslims and women that he is advocating and being criticized for is grounded in *Shari'ah* and jurisprudence, I would take his claims seriously. Until he does so, I will say that such claims are grossly misleading."[103]

As mentioned earlier, al-Turabi's contribution to fundamentalist discourse is his revolutionary shift from al-Mawdudi's and Qutb's rejectionism to political and ideological pragmatism. In contrast to al-Mawdudi, he saw the Islamic movement as a force advocating Islam from within the social system. This was to be accomplished, inter alia, by enabling women to participate "in the struggle for construction and progress, not as a favor or privilege, but as a duty and an obligation." Yet, as soon as he was in a position of power, he relegated women to the home and domestic duties. He further accused the traditional ulema, saying they are not "conscious of developments . . . and never renew religious spirit from time to time," and he extended the domain of ulema to include all those who know "anything well enough to relate to Allah," as long as their interpretation does not negate any Qur'anic text. Al-Turabi further emphasized that changes in circumstances necessitate changes in religious expression and taught that Muslims may vary the practices of the Prophet's prototype community to meet changing realities. He went even farther by affirming that jurists and ulema have no right to impose their judgments on Muslims. That prerogative belongs to the Muslim community as a whole in the form of consensus. Yet, none of these principles were put into practice once he assumed power.

Turabi, following in the footsteps of al-Mawdudi and Qutb in admitting the finitude of human intellect and its confinement to the irreversibility of time, asserts the relativity of the Qur'anic message to time, space, and interpreter and demonstrates the difficulty of transforming a humanly developed doctrine into an infallible universal and eternal truth. New "theoretical roots" should, therefore, be deduced from the sacred texts to meet the real conditions and ideals of the existent society. Thus, although "Islam, as a divine word, is the eternal embodiment of truth, goodness, and right . . . as a message, it is addressed to man in history." Yet, not only does al-Turabi not attempt any *ijtihad* to meet the exigencies of time and history, nor any liberalization or modernization of the role of women as promised, but, instead, he goes even further in constraining their role than any of the traditional ulema he so clearly disdains.

Moreover, al-Turabi explains that most of the repression of women "is only an expression of many other forms of religious life which are not necessarily true to Islam itself, but . . . are done in the name of religion." Their oppression is merely a reflection of the decline and decadence of religion rather than the effect of Islamic principles. He also stresses the impact of non-Islamic external customs and influences on the *Shari'ah* over time to meet new places and periods in history. Thus, al-Turabi blames these factors as directly responsible for the low status of women in Muslim society, but he assures the possibility of restoring women to their original Qur'anic social status. This, of course, is to be managed through the reinterpretation of relevant Qur'anic verses. However, instead of initiating the necessary programs for intellectual readjustment and modulation of awareness through changes in curricula to alleviate the existent oppression of women, he goes in a diametrically opposite direction.

Another set of contradictions is to be found in the wealth of material he draws upon from the early history of Islam to demonstrate the independent role of women during that period, the respect and dignity with which the Prophet held and treated them, and the variety of fields they excelled in ranging from the economic to the military. The factors responsible for their deterioration, he argues, lie in the faulty reinterpretation of the Qur'an and in social backwardness. Yet, al-Turabi never attempts to restore women to their original status in Prophetic society. Instead, he constrains himself and the regime he represents to an ultraconservative policy representing the traditional view regarding women's role in society. This dichotomy is never explained in any of his writings or declarations.

The questions to be asked here are twofold: why is al-Turabi inconsistent in theory and practice, and why do women receive all this attention from him and the Muslim Brotherhood or National Islamic Front? Al-Turabi's essentialist ideology is best captured by his attempt to create models of women and their role in society throughout history. The Muslim Brotherhood focuses its drive for authenticity on women more than any other group. One reason for this emphasis is that women are viewed as the "embodiment of culture" and are, therefore, expected to serve culture and/or society through distinctive forms of labor. Once seen from this perspective, it is easy to understand the centrality of women and the family unit in the Islamists' ideology and their integral function in the government's response to the ever-present economic crisis in Sudan. The state-sponsored Islamism of al-Bashir's government has been trying to maneuver its religious ideology into a more "legitimate" and/or "authentic" culture. Needless to say, the easiest road to take for the accomplishment of this task is through the authentication and purification of women's culture. The promotion of women's concerns for political purposes is not peculiar to the Islamists. In fact, ever since the independence of Sudan in 1956, the different consecutive governments have been disseminating gender ideology, either to "liberate" women from their traditional confinement to the domestic sphere for the development and progress of Sudan, or to "emancipate" women from Westernization and cultural imperialism for the foundation and development of the ideal Islamic state. Thus, in both cases, we see women constituting the central position in the male's political ideology, be it secular or religious.

Another manifestation of the Islamists' assumption of power is the intimidation and indoctrination of women in the hope of removing what the Islamists consider a major threat to their power. Thus, Richard Stevens notes that female suppression "has less to do with Islam in Sudan than it does with the fear that women, increasingly released from the shackles of tradition, will insist upon the totality of their rights."[104] Al-Turabi explains the regime's coercion of women as part of the effort to direct the weak civil society inherited from Ja'far Numayri in an Islamic direction. What he actually implies is that in subordinating women through the most obvious means, namely, Islamic dress, the state will have taken the first step in establishing its power. The male part of the population will be simultaneously subdued by the show of force and elated and gratified by the suppression of women, making them once again the masters at home and the unrivaled economic agents in the public sphere. The manipulation of women and their role in society for political purposes is further demonstrated by the Islamists' call for political activism on the part of women for election campaigns and the dissemination of the Islamist message, on the one hand, and by sending them back to domestic life in a very restricted Islamic dress when that served their purpose, on the other. Thus, although the traditional Sudanese dress of a head-to-foot wraparound veil was always accepted as modest and decent, the Islamists imposed a black robe that covered women completely from head to foot, including the face and hands. This move, I believe, clearly shows that veiling is not the issue, rather, it is demonstrating the power of the regime in controlling aspects of women's lives and behavior.

Furthermore, when five Sudanese women conducted a study of the Shari'ah and enumerated a number of points beneficial to women's status, granting them more rights, those rights were not adopted by the Islamists, nor were they publicized, indicating once again that the status of women and their role in society constitute political tools used by those aspiring to power, or consolidating a power already attained. Thus, using the rubric of "ideal woman" and "ideal family," women's role and behavior are ideologically manipulated by religio-political institutions dominated by men. Fatima Mernissi further explains this dichotomy in social role by attributing it to scarcity in economic resources and the construction of a moral framework. Muslim men, according to her, are challenged by any upheaval in gender roles that may challenge authority figures and put women in positions of power, thus transcending "authority thresholds." Conservative men see independent women as a threat to social order and to the status quo—as in the increasing number of female physicians who, despite the fact that more than 85 percent of male physicians were leaving the country for greener pastures, were directed in their fields of study away from surgery and obstetrics, subjects considered inappropriate and too strenuous for them. Considering the fact that women could not be examined by male physicians, making female obstetricians a necessity, the NIF, afraid of the economic power that might be wielded by women through such lucrative specialties, did everything within their power to shunt women away from garnering economic power.[105]

In short, Hasan al-Turabi, portrayed as a revolutionary in his writings and hailed as the hero of liberalism and modernization and a champion of women's liberation, in stark contrast to the radicalism of Qutb, al-Maw-dudi, Khomeini, and Mutahhari, proved to be a conservative traditional-ist vis-à-vis the gender issue once he was asked to put his teachings into practice, and as radical as the preceding ideologues. Thus, in reality he proved to be a dyed-in-the-wool conservative in liberal clothing who uti-lized the issue of women's rights and liberty in a demonstration of power and the appeasement of the male sector.

Chapter 9

✶

Rashid al-Ghannoushi

With the independence of Tunisia in 1956 and the rise to power of Habib Bourguiba, a secularist political strategy was undertaken. Among the policy changes were the secularization of the personal status code, dissolution of Shariʿah courts, and cancellation of religious endowments, as well as curbing of the influence of the Qurʾanic schools and the religious Zaituna University. Pilgrimages, Ramadan fasting, and other traditional practices were also toned down. This seeming Westernization alienated many Tunisians, particularly the less affluent and less educated.[1]

The resultant economic and cultural marginalization of a large segment of the Tunisian population by "modernization" and secularization led to an "occidental saturation" and a rebellion against everything Western or "modern." This was further fueled by the humiliating Arab defeat of 1967, the demise of the government's socialist program in 1969, the national strikes and food riots of 1978, the reemergence of Islam and Islamist organizations like the Egyptian Muslim Brotherhood and the Pakistani Jamaʿat-i Islami, and the Iranian Revolution. The natural counterreaction was the rise of an Islamic movement in Tunis that quickly grew in influence and appeal. Islamic discourse helped the disgruntled articulate their demands and agitate for a role in Tunisian politics. The religious revival grew informally during the 1970s, concentrating mainly on the dichotomy embodied in the coexistence of Westernized social institutions and the "collective consciousness based on an Islamic culture and spirit," resulting in "cultural dualism." In 1978, labor strikes and political violence spurred the Islamists into politicization, forming a loose coalition of Islamist groups known as the Movement of Islamic Renewal. Within a year of its inception, one of them, the Islamic Tendency Movement (ITM) (Harakat al-Ittijah al-Islami), led by Rashid al-Ghannoushi, emerged as the main-stay of the coalition and the Islamic movement in general. The ITM called for a more equitable economic policy, the end of single-party politics, a return to "the fundamental principles of Islam," and a purging of the social decadence prevalent in Tunisian society.[2] The spark for the politicization of Islam took place on the Night of Power in 1979, when Hind Cheibi appeared before Bourguiba in her own version of the Islamic *hijab*.[3]

Rashid al-Ghannoushi was born to a poor family in 1941 in al-Hammah, a town in the Gabès province in southern Tunisia. Realizing he needed to broaden his horizons, he left for Cairo with a "head full of dreams," where he studied agronomy. However, it was during his four years at the University of Damascus, studying philosophy, when he was exposed to Western thought and the secular social nationalism of Syria's Ba'th [Resurrection] Party, that he committed himself to Islamic reform. Thus, by the time he left Damascus in 1968 with a degree in philosophy and social sciences, he was already disenchanted with Arab nationalism, convinced, after the 1967 Israeli defeat of the Arabs, that it harbored major inherent flaws. The only viable social and political activism left open for him was that of the Muslim Brotherhood. He spent one year in Paris at the Sorbonne studying philosophy, working on farms and construction companies. He was also a member of the Islamist group al-Tabligh, helping poor Muslim immigrants confined to the slums of Paris. His disillusionment waxed at their plight, convincing him that Westernization was not the solution to the problems of the Arab world.

Family circumstances forced him to return to Tunisia to work as a secondary school teacher, and there he joined the Islamic movement. On his return, al-Ghannoushi viewed Bourguiba's attempts at Westernization and secularization of Tunisian society as a tearing "away from the winds of the East," a repudiation of Tunisia's Islamic roots and heritage, and a "capitulation" to the West and its so-called progressive ideas. As a secondary school teacher, he exposed his students to Islamic principles and the fallacy of all principles based on materialism.[4] He further sought to activate Islam and Islamic thought to become compatible with modern social and political life: "I wonder how our students feel studying 'Islamic philosophy' when it offers them only a bunch of dead issues having nothing to do with the problems of today . . . I propose that these should be returned to their graves, that these false problems be buried and that we deal with our real problems—economics, politics, sexual license." He gradually became more political and radical, emphasizing social injustice and Western domination.[5] In 1979 he founded the Islamic Association, which later came to be known as the Islamic Tendency Movement, symbolizing the transition from an Egyptian Muslim Brotherhood ideology to a more Tunisia-centered movement and from a radical Qutbian activism to a more pragmatic and moderate activism.[6]

In the hope of assuaging the new regime of Ben Ali, al-Ghannoushi changed the name of his movement to Hizb al-Nahda [the Renaissance Party] and redefined its goals, excluding all reference to Islam. Nonetheless, the new party was not recognized and, therefore, not allowed to run for elections. However, members of the party, running as independents, managed to garner 15 percent of the total vote. This invited the unleashing of a crackdown on al-Ghannoushi and his party, spurring him to flee to Sudan, seeking asylum in May 1989 from his friend Hasan al-Turabi. He declared, "Until now, we sought only a shop and we did not get it. Now it's the whole *suq* [market] that we want."[7] However, soon after, Sudan, afraid of jeopardizing its relations with Tunisia, refused to allow him to return. When France refused him entry, al-Ghannoushi was forced to seek asylum in the United Kingdom, where he has stayed in self-exile ever since.[8]

Al-Ghannoushi is a prolific intellectual who has written more than fifteen books and hundreds of scholarly articles and lectures. He describes himself as being of the generation of Zaituna students during the early years of independence: "We used to feel like strangers in our own country. We had been educated as Muslims and as Arabs, while we could see the country totally molded in the French cultural identity. For us, the doors to any further education were closed, since the university was completely westernized."[9] Like al-Turabi, and in contradistinction to al-Mawdudi and Qutb, he portrays a democratic outlook of reform and pluralism and champions women's rights and their equality with men. However, while he declares his acceptance of democracy and pluralistic politics, he opposes Westernized secularism in the Muslim world and brands Muslim secularist intellectuals "the devil's advocates . . . the pharaoh's witches."[10] Following al-Turabi's line of thinking, he argues for the importance of freedom and human rights, as prescribed in the Qur'an and ratified by the United Nations, the condemnation of violence and suppression of free thought and expression. He maintains that fighting for freedom and the elimination of oppression are Islamist goals, and he advocates, therefore, the empowerment of women, even to the point of using the quota system to increase their numbers in legislative bodies. Moreover, inasmuch as he would like to establish an Islamic state, he prefers to fight for a pluralistic democratic society and work for Islam from within the system.[11]

Addressing Muslim Americans at the Islamic Center of Los Angeles on January 1, 1989, al-Ghannoushi said:

> Your duty as Muslims is to entrench yourselves in the land, to assimilate the culture of your surrounding environment, to assimilate its language, its history and to consider yourselves as faithful patriots. No one asks you to import the Arab fashion of practicing religion. Your duty is to innovate your religious practice, to innovate a form of interaction between Islam and the reality of your environment, in order to produce something utterly new. We are asking you as Muslims living in a society that has reached the highest scientific level, to not imitate and reproduce the religious practices developed in under-developing environments. We ask you to be a new contribution to the Muslim notion of reform . . . You are living in a country that is closer to Islam than under-developed countries, because here . . . norms . . . [are] well respected.[12]

However, while there were lessons to be learned from the West, al-Ghannoushi preferred an Islamic order in the Muslim countries, where governments would not separate Islamic moral influences from politics. Separating state from religion, according to him, would rob the government of all moral practices, just as would separating religious practice from the individual's political duties. The decline of Muslim societies is due to the waywardness of Muslims from true Islam and to the rigid adherence to it. The renewal and transformation of Islam to cope with the modern age are, therefore, essential for advancement and progress.[13]

As the leader of the ITM, al-Ghannoushi had distinguished between religion and notions of citizenship to portray an acceptable image of his movement to the government. Thus, in 1985, he declared that the Shari'ah might not be able to provide answers for all modern problems and, therefore, needed to be restructured into a contemporary Islamic system.[14] This becomes understandable in the absence of any religious authority in Islam and if the Islamic text is, indeed, a "flexible form, [which] did not confine us to any particular shape or form, but left us with a set of values and rules." The flexibility of the text, thus, underlines the importance Islam places on the power of man's rationality, guided by revelation. The role of the *ummah* in interpreting the text is further indicated by the plethora of Islamic schools of thought over the centuries.[15]

Al-Ghannoushi, in a conference at the London School of Economics on February 29, 1992, emphasized the importance of modernity for Islam, but "only in so far as it means absolute intellectual freedom; scientific and technological progress; and promotion of democratic ideals . . . Only when we dictate the pace with which it penetrates our society and not when French, British or American interpretations impose it upon us. It is our right to adopt modernity through methods equitable to our people and their heritage."[16] He goes on to explain, "Our problem is that we had to deal with the West from a position of both psychological and material weakness. Excessively admiring it and paralyzed by our inferiority complex, we tried even harder to ape it and to take whatever it had to offer in every domain . . . To tell the truth, [however], the only way to accede to modernity is by our own path, that which has been traced for us by our religion, our history, and our civilization."[17]

From his exile in London, al-Ghannoushi denounced the use of violence and advocated a gradual process of social reform and political participation in the hope of the eventual establishment of an Islamic state. Like al-Turabi, he stressed the need for change at the grassroots level, rather than the imposition of an Islamic system by force. In an interview to a Kuwaiti magazine, he explained, "We must respect the wishes of the masses if they decided to choose a way other than ours. We are not guardians over the people. So, if our society decided one day to be an atheistic or communist one, what can we do?"[18]

Since the family is the heart of Muslim society, al-Ghannoushi, like others before him, gives the status and role of women special attention. Another reason for this interest is that women, in all societies, have tended to constitute the "weaker link" in the social fabric. Women in Arab societies, particularly in the wake of the violent transformation brought on by direct contact with the West and its civilization throughout the twentieth century, have had to pay the heaviest price. Each time the two social models —Western and Muslim—meshed, the ensuing violence more often than not affected women more than other sectors of society, due to their weakness, lack of autonomy, and submission to the dominant male sector. Thus, in 1929, Bourguiba, fighting the French, defended the veil, which had been banned by the French, as the symbol of Tunisian identity and the basis of the legitimacy of the struggle for independence. The same Bourguiba, in 1956, promulgated the Tunisian Personal Status Code liberating women and granting them their long-sought-after rights as a sign of modernity and Westernization.

Al-Ghannoushi was a prominent critic of the new Personal Status Code and the abolition of polygamy, and in 1984 he chastised the nationalists for hailing this change as a "liberating asset." However, in 1987, he reversed his stand, opining that the Qur'anic verse on polygamy is subject to several interpretations and legitimizing the new laws on the ground that the head of state is in charge of the "application of religion." This move was probably a prelude to the tacit recognition of the ITM by the government, thereby facilitating its participation in the promulgation of the National Pact and declaring Bourguiba's Personal Status Code one of the pillars of the Tunisian Republic.[19] Since 1984, the Islamic Tendency Movement had been criticizing the "modernity" of the 1956 Personal Status Code of Habib Bourguiba for distancing itself from Islamic traditions and interpretations, resulting in the disintegration of Tunisian society. Al-Ghannoushi called for a public referendum "to reexamine the situation of the Tunisian family" and to study "the effects of the law on the family." "Has the Tunisian family," asks al-Ghannoushi, "become more harmonious as a result of this law or not?"[20]

In the wake of the advent of Zein el-Abedin Ben Ali to power on November 7, 1987, al-Ghannoushi, in a move to placate the new regime and carve a niche for himself in it, renounced the use of violence, promised not to politicize the army, and declared the Personal Status Code "a body of choices and decisions which are part of different schools of Islamist thought," citing the principle of *ijtihad* as an example, which every Muslim is entitled to. This was not to be sacralized, however, as all human efforts are fallible and need periodic reevaluation without calling the actual text into question. However, the government required a more extensive commitment to include ITM in the political process. In the words of the president himself, "Nothing justifies the creation of a group as long as it has not defined the type of society it commends, clarified its position towards a certain number of civilizational issues, and committed itself to respect the equality of rights and duties of citizens, men and women, as well as the principles of tolerance and of liberty of conscience."[21]

The impact of Islamist thought, according to al-Ghannoushi, has been clearly visible in the increasing adoption of and reliance upon Islamic teachings, whose clarity, goodness, and justice far exceed those of other religions and philosophies. It has freed Muslims of old fallacies and behavior, as well as of the influence of the decadent Western culture. The spread of the Islamist message to other countries, with the exception of Iran, al-Ghannoushi argues, has unfortunately been limited, due to persistent impurities within the movement exemplified by the adherence to old ossified interpretations unfit to cope with the modern world.[22] Such shortcomings include the lack of understanding of what the working classes need to wrest them from capitalism and socialism; and the lack of utilization of women, who remain ignored and suppressed into serfdom against all Islamic teachings, rendering them easy prey to Western inducements in the hope of bettering their lot and gaining their freedom. These same inducements have led Western society to fragmentation and the enslavement of women by political and commercial institutions that exploit their sexuality for financial gains.

Thus, for Islam to be eternal and ubiquitous, it has to be able to cope with and adapt to all changes and absorb them into its realm, to provide solutions to human problems as they arise.[23] The Qur'an, though eternal, reflects a clear image of the times of its appearance; and being realistic, it has spoken to people through their existing conditions, customs, and culture but laid down rules and regulations applicable across time and place. The Qur'anic text defies definition and does not fit any world, its significance and meaning continuing to unfold with the advancement of knowledge. Al-Ghannoushi maintains that the Qur'an seeks to care for and improve the lot of man to realize his full natural potential irrespective of race, color, or sex. He quotes Ibn Abbas as saying that "the Qur'an will be solved by time only."[24]

The importance of the question of gender, according to al-Ghannoushi, lies in the significant role women play in society. He starts with the traditional argument that women make up half the population and bring up and educate the other half. This unique position of the female sector renders it imperative to raise awareness in and sensitize the young Islamist generations against the current oppression, degradation, subordination, and stifling they have endured for centuries in Muslim societies, reducing them to sex objects, suitable only for the provision of pleasure in the name of religion. This oppression, in the absence of any religious support and the silence of the clerics, who have continued to ignore their plight, has made them ready to welcome the banners of liberation hailing from the West. In fact, Muslim women, according to al-Ghannoushi, have been so oppressed and their status so instilled into their psyche that they could no longer differentiate between true Islam, on the one hand, and the veil, home segregation, and seclusion for the gratification of men's sexual desires, on the other.

Al-Ghannoushi held that women were, therefore, faced with two options: either choose the path to "freedom, knowledge, or self-determinism," achieved only through rising against Islam and its values and replace them with Western values and customs, or simply remain dehumanized and isolated. It was at this juncture, al-Ghannoushi maintains, that the Islamist movement took upon itself the task of guiding them back to true Islamic "liberation." The Islamists explained that the Western call to liberation was a sham that exposed women to nudity and eroticism, and made them leave the home and mingle with men.[25] Once their eyes were opened through regular educational meetings extolling the virtues of Islam and its liberation of women, preparing them to pray regularly, and teaching them to be faithful, virtuous housewives donning the Islamic dress, equipped with minimal education for the required role of home life, they voluntarily returned to Islam. They returned, however, with trepidation, fearing a return to the age of decline, where women were kept in the harem unable to be in charge of their own destinies. But al-Ghannoushi reassured them, claiming that what mattered was the struggle against Westernization and the "oppression and enslavement of mankind as a whole, the denial of the right to decide one's own destiny, and the transformation of mankind into an object, a thing."[26] The Muslim woman, in accepting Western values, would simply move from one form of enslavement to another, bringing to mind Simone de Beauvoir in her attempt to trace the oppression of women and their possible liberation. Al-Ghannoushi borrows her description of women's absurd condition and explains that when women are liberated from home and husband and enter the marketplace, they find themselves enslaved by capitalist institutions in a catch-22 situation—no matter what they do, they can never shed their slavery, unless they live in a harmonious society of fraternity. Al-Ghannoushi goes on to argue that what the Muslim woman needs is a liberation movement that would "restore her to herself and to her innate nature as a guardian of the heritage of mankind and a companion of man in the jihad to liberate herself and him from the forces of exploitation and oppression in the world and to liberate herself from all control and submission, except to God."[27]

Before the Islamic Reform Movement, al-Ghannoushi described women as being persecuted, robbed of their self-esteem and independence, the right to education or choice of husband, and the right of inheritance, owning property, and dispensing with it at will. Women were treated like objects to be used for sex and progeny. The Islamic Reform Movement of the nineteenth century and the first half of the twentieth century, through its *Magazine on Personal Status*, defended women, tried to enlighten public opinion to their plight, and help them regain their self-esteem. However, the liberal movement of Bourguiba led to some excesses in emulation of the West, involving women in all fields to prove gender equality: women joined the police force and the army, drove cars, and flew planes with all the attendant problems of the breakdown of social and moral values and overall deterioration. Thus, sex was liberalized, punishable only if coerced; abortion and contraception became prevalent; virginity was no longer a stipulation for the annulment of marriage; and illegitimate children were cared for and adoption permitted. The new Personal Status Code freed women in name only, while actually subjecting them to a new form of sexual slavery and commercial exploitation through subliminal control, transforming them into Janus-faced individuals being both commodity and consumer.[28]

Women, according to al-Ghannoushi, came to occupy 75 percent of job opportunities afforded by capitalism between the years 1943 and 1976, as a means of exploiting and destroying social order. They were underpaid, assigned minor jobs, and exploited to control and direct society through the destruction of Islamic values and the regulation of sexual and family relations. Control of the family, the cornerstone of intellectual and cultural development of the newer generations, would help to destroy Muslim social order and replace it with Western values like birth control and reduced marriage and birthrates. This would result in the further exploitation of women as guinea pigs in testing new contraceptives, which have since proved dangerous to women's health and that of their families. Current statistics in the West indicate that 25 percent of women have stopped using these drugs after they have been proved to be carcinogenic and the cause of fatal malformations. In addition, they help destroy morals and liberalize sex.[29]

Thus, while the *Magazine on Personal Status* professed to strive for the liberation of women, al-Ghannoushi argues, it was actually mounting a new crusade to deconstruct Tunisian society and destroy its Arab and Muslim identity. Its staunchest supporters were forced to object when, in 1982, the law was modified to allow divorced women to keep their marital home and acquire a lifelong stipend (alimony). They objected on the grounds that such a stipulation would deter marriage and would, therefore, be counterproductive for women. The magazine, therefore, offered women only nominal gains in the form of weak laws that could be amended at will. However, thanks to the Islamic movement, women are now fully aware of this, as evidenced by their return to true Islamic life and values, rejecting the false Western "civilization" that actually exploited them, destroyed their family ties, and pitted them in competition against men instead of living in a fruitful cooperation with them.[30] Al-Ghannoushi reassures Muslim women further by claiming that "women can get as many rights from Islam as they are guaranteed by man-made law, any injustice perpetrated against them being the result of cultural backwardness, not Islam . . . It is a problem of culture and education. In order to remedy injustice, we have to look for the root of the problem, for the real reason of injustice."[31]

Al-Ghannoushi argues that the image of the modern Muslim woman is a relic of the age of decadence that set in after the early glorious age of Islam. Thus, "The woman is born hated and despised . . . she has to be compassionate, pliant, an obedient being to her husband as a means to affirm his power and strength. She is raised in oppression by her father and the brother—regardless of the fact that he may be younger than she is—and then the husband. Despite the fact that Islam banned burying females, the period of decadence prepared a new burial for her personality and dignity. It instilled in her a sense of dependency, a lack of confidence and an openness to ridicule and abuse."[32] This family structure and the policy of abuse and oppression adopted in the upbringing of women, help crush the individual in the family and create a superficial woman interested only in gossip, cosmetics, and children instead of being taken up by the pressing cultural and political issues pervading the Muslim world. "This was," according to al-Ghannoushi, "a fruit of the seclusion which kept her from knowledge and made her into an instrument of reproduction and a cheap thrill to be enjoyed by the man who crushes her and casts her aside." This attitude was fomented and supported by religious leaders, who acted as tools of authoritarian governments.[33]

Women, al-Ghannoushi maintains, must not only be "liberated" according to Islamic principles but should also be recruited to help build a popular Islamic movement, for "a movement, whose aspirations do not go beyond teaching women to cover themselves and perform their religious duties, will be elitist and not populist." Women must, therefore, be encouraged to be daring and intrepid, for nothing in Islam, according to him, enjoins women to work in the house and rear children. Such voluntary works should be compensated for by the husband either financially or through the expression of gratitude for an unsolicited job well done. Moreover, a good husband must help his wife with housework in emulation of the Prophet, who always helped his wives.[34]

In his attempt to deal with the predicament of women in the contemporary world, al-Ghannoushi explains that women have traditionally been perceived as deceitful and cunning; carrying the burden of the "original sin," and branded as evil. This attitude is contrary to Islamic teachings, for nowhere in the Qur'an is Eve held responsible for tempting Adam and disobeying God, and nowhere in the Sunna or Qur'an are women singled out as deceitful or cunning; instead, all references to human attributes apply to both men and women. Hence, the problem in contemporary Islam is the confusion between Islamic truth and pre-Islamic inherited beliefs and traditions, especially with regard to women.[35] God created women and men of the same soul and not from Adam's rib as traditionally claimed. In fact, as Muhammad Abduh states, the Qur'anic text does not preclude the possibility of the first soul being Eve and not Adam as the Jews claim. This is further confirmed, al-Ghannoushi maintains, by the Shi'ite scholar Muhammad Hussain Tabtaba'i and Sayyid Qutb. Therefore, there should be no gender discrimination, but equality and brotherhood without any prejudice.[36]

The individual, al-Ghannoushi continues, has been endowed with intelligence and free will to achieve human perfection. This can only be achieved through the constant struggle to discover and understand human nature and control and develop it to fit into God's divine plan to create a free and just society, where exploitation and cruelty are nonexistent. The individual's success in accomplishing this will ensure paradise. Women are as endowed and honored as men and subject to all their duties, privileges, trials, and tribulations.[37]

Al-Ghannoushi declares that the Qur'an does not incriminate Eve alone with the "original sin," a Judean-Christian belief that insidiously infiltrated Islamic thought and contributed to the demeaning concept of women as sources of seduction and evil, who care only for their bodies, the ammunition of their trade.[38] The equality of men and women, al-Ghannoushi continues, is further confirmed by the Qur'an in calling the Virgin Mary a prophet and the Prophet himself describing her as "the mistress of the women of Paradise." However, the phrase "Males are unlike females," contrary to the common belief that it represents male superiority, actually introduces incontrovertible proof of the honorable position the Qur'an affords women.[39] The Qur'an honors Mary, and through her all women, as a prophet, who nonsexually bore 'Issa (Jesus) and was given the task of raising him, a mighty prophet, alone. Moreover, the prophet 'Issa was named after her, "'Issa ibn Maryam" [Jesus son of Mary], and not, as was the custom, after his father. The assertion of Mary as prophet further underlines the Qur'an's elevation of women, since in prophecy there is an indication that women can attain human perfection and divine honor. The potential for greatness is thus open for both sexes.[40] Furthermore, women at the time of the Prophet practiced politics, gave legal opinions (*fatwa*), and participated in warfare. Later on, Ibn Jarir al-Tabari, Imam Abi Hanifa, and the jurist Ibn Hazm allowed women to vote, join political parties, and hold government positions, including judgeships.[41]

The term "*kayd*" in the phrase "*kaydahunna la'adhim*" [their cunning and deceit is great], al-Ghannoushi maintains, is used in the Qur'an to refer to both men and women, the devil, and even God. Thus, *kayd* is not necessarily derogatory but may even be complimentary, as in situations where the term *kayd* is used to denote overcoming difficulties or attaining certain goals be they noble or not. Women, therefore, cannot be blamed for the use of their innate and natural attributes of deceit and cunning or their powers of seduction to arrive at their goals in the absence of any other means at their disposal. Moreover, even admitting that their *kayd* is greater than men's only indicates that their wiles and tactics in reaching their objectives are more efficient than men's, reflecting thereby their own viability, intelligence, and patience, qualities that are laudable in themselves but may prove to be destructive if the goals allowed them by society do not transcend their basic instinctual ones. Moreover, the verses in the Qur'an dealing with human nature do not distinguish between male and female. Hence, the quotation "Women are evil, but are indispensable" is against all Islamic values and is being propagated by the enemies of Islam.[42]

Women, al-Ghannoushi argues, possess tremendous potential that can be used for good or evil and should, therefore, be tapped to benefit from their positive qualities. Women are hardy and patient, as evidenced by the lack of any apostates among them, unlike men, even at the time of the Prophet. Thus, women are to be allowed to participate in all Islamic activities like men, and assisted in promoting their self-confidence and autonomy. They should be encouraged to assume leadership positions in the Movement, and to study the goals and achievements of Islamic and international women's movements.[43]

Since women, as mentioned earlier, represent one half of society and raise the other half, they are, according to al-Ghannoushi, invaluable and should be well educated and prepared and allowed to fully contribute to society. Improving the condition of women should, therefore, play an important role in the legal system as is evidenced by the agreement on gender equality, except in matters relating to their physical differences. Islam, according to him, not only encourages the education of women but was the first religion in history to require not only elementary but advanced education as well. All males and females are to be educated in reading, writing, mathematics, civics, and morality. Admitting the early overzealousness of the Movement on the gender issue, inspired by their hostility to Bourguiba, al-Ghannoushi retraced his steps and declared that a careful study of the Qur'an will show that women are equal to men and equally responsible to God. The Prophet said that women were the sisters of men, and God said, "I have created you of the same soul." This equality, however, does not negate physical differences and different roles in a contemporary fashion: equality in humanity and in the eyes of God, but different roles dictated by natural differences.[44]

In old rural Muslim societies, al-Ghannoushi maintains, women participated in field work and animal husbandry alongside men to help the family in an "atmosphere of innocence and spontaneity" without sexual arousal. Al-Ghannoushi questions how this mingling can be accepted, while other forms of commercial and industrial work are condemned, especially so since the religious texts do not specify the type of work to be allowed and since women may be forced to work to help their husbands, while observing proper Islamic dress and behavior. Unless wives are allowed to help their husbands support their families, the latter will refrain from marriage. This is, of course, keeping in mind that women's basic function remains the raising and preparing of new generations. However, if they combine both functions, they are bound to collapse. It is laudable, therefore, if they voluntarily assume both duties, in which case their husbands must help them with housework. The ideal solution, however, would be for the state to compensate women for their housework and spare them the exhaustion of added outside work, since their essential duties are caring for children. In addition to helping their husbands financially by working outside, women's presence in the workplace serves to spread Islamic principles and teachings, which is an activity of vital importance and should be encouraged. Moreover, women leaders, armed with Islamic virtues and aware of current problems and needs, are needed by the Islamic movement to counter the "Bourguiba women," who advocate outside work and neglect their homes.[45] Al-Ghannoushi here quotes Sheikh Abdallah Daraz of the Azhar, who states in his book, *The Ethical Constitution of the Qur'an*, "[T]he Qur'an dictates the partnership of men and women in society and government with few exceptions relative to their

sexual differences and allows women full participation in social and political activities. And the view that women are ignorant, fit only for housework and raising children, is absurd, since most Arab Muslim men are
equally ignorant and remain eligible for everything."[46]

Al-Ghannoushi explained that the Constitution of the Islamic Republic, the embodiment of the Islamic Reform Movement, allows women to
achieve high-ranking positions in keeping with the Qur'anic verse: "And
the believers, men and women, are protecting friends one of another; they
enjoin the right and forbid the wrong" (9:71). Article 21 of the Constitution stipulates that the government guarantees the full rights of women in
the context of Islamic values. However, to facilitate women's equal participation, all mental and physical barriers must be removed to enable them to
increase their knowledge and stature and be a generation well prepared for
the service of Islam. Al-Ghannoushi draws on history to demonstrate the
equal status of men and women, including in such positions as heads of
state. Among the many examples he enumerates is that of Aisha, who led
an army of three thousand soldiers or more and had the authority to
command, negotiate, make speeches, and appoint the imam; al-Hurrah
al-Sulayhiyyah, who ruled for more than forty years; Ghazalah Umm
Shuhayb, who acted as head of state after the death of her son; and Umm
Salma, who advised the Prophet and suggested a solution to the Hadibiy-
yah incident, when his followers disobeyed him, which he adopted successfully. Takieddin al-Nabhani stated that "all who hold the nationality, being
mature, and mentally normal, may become members of the Advisory
Council, be [they] male or female."[47] Furthermore, al-Ghannoushi explained the *qiwamah* verse of the Qur'an (4:34) as being restricted to the
family, in order to minimize marital conflicts, and holding no relevance
whatsoever to the public arena.[48]

Al-Ghannoushi supports the right of women to participate in all facets
of social, political, educational, and religious life, on an equal footing with
men but within the context of Islamic values, those employed being chosen
according to qualification and not to gender or skin color. Women, in fact,
may assume the most exalted positions, including that of member of the
State Council.[49] In fact, al-Ghannoushi declares his willingness to reserve
a number of positions in the council for women to encourage them and do
away with the image of the seductive woman. Thus, women must be well
educated in preparation for such positions and for the education of their
children. Appropriate laws should, therefore, be passed to ensure this and
open the way for all women to better themselves.[50] He thus disagrees with

Abu al-ʾAʿla al-Mawdudi, who restricted this position to men, quoting the Hadith to support his position. Al-Ghannoushi maintains that this hadith, dealing with the leadership of women, was in response to a specific incident in reference to the succession of a Persian king by his daughter and was not meant to be generalized as a principle.

Al-Ghannoushi defines marriage as a "solemn pact of generosity and an awesome institution" based on mutual consent and respect, as well as the unshakable human values of trust, charity, patience, love, and justice. The most important factor that determines the fate of any group, al-Ghannoushi affirms, is its method in dealing with natural desires and instincts: desires for sex, children, and wealth. If they are surrendered to freely, they lead to regression, but if they are satisfied reasonably and are well controlled, they result in creativity and achievement and, therefore, advancement of civilization. Islam regulates these desires such that body and soul are satisfied without gluttony. It regards them as natural attributes that can be used to improve performance and potential; and utilizes them as a means of worship and of realizing God's goals in protecting and improving life. As such, they are satisfied within the framework of marriage as an aspect of religion and worship like prayer and fasting, thus purifying them.[51]

The sexual instincts, al-Ghannoushi explains, differ in men and women, but in a complementary manner: sexual function is of primary importance in women, but secondary in men. In men, hormonal maturity results in sexual excitation, satiated by intercourse. In women, it remains dormant until the dream man comes along to wake it up. Thus, sex, according to him, is a biologic function in men but a spiritual one in women. For men, sex in itself is self-satisfactory, whereas the sex life of women is tied to their partners. Sex for men is just another of their relations and activities. It is, therefore, of superficial value used as a means of self-aggrandizement, while for women it forms an integral part of their being, not to be simply satiated but to fulfill their femininity and realize themselves through childbearing.[52]

Marriage, according to him, is, therefore, necessary to complete the couple's personalities, physically and spiritually. The division of duties between married couples depends upon cooperation and natural abilities and does not imply the superiority of one over another: women are primarily charged with motherhood and caring for husband and home and are rewarded by God for a job well done, since it is regarded as being equal to man's arduous work. Motherhood, a form of worship, is deemed superior to jihad, thus, making paradise under the feet of the mothers.[53] A man is responsible for his family, his home, and his leaders. As the Prophet explains, the provision by men of protection, care, and material ease demands obedience and loyalty from their wives. Thus, a wife is not to meet with strange men or accept gifts from them, just as she is not to lend or give away her husband's belongings without his permission. Moreover, a husband has the right to limit his wife's freedom and prohibit her from leaving her home without permission. The husband, on the other hand, should be lenient and kind and allow his wife visitation rights with her family in keeping with custom. A wife should not object to moving or living with her in-laws. If the husband cannot provide for his family, his wife may work, with her husband's permission and approval of the type of work to be undertaken. The wife's income, however, is not hers but belongs to the family, and the husband retains the right to terminate his wife's work at will. The wife may also stop working at any time and request that her husband be the sole provider. But al-Ghannoushi, at this point, seems oblivious to the fact that the wife would not have been working in the first place, had her husband been able to provide for the family![54] Al-Ghannoushi draws further attention to the fact that motherhood and married life do not preclude adherence to Islamic regulations. In fact, it is a wife's duty to her society and God to provide proper guidance to all those around her; such guidance needs education and knowledge of Islam. A wife's activities are to be regulated and assigned by the Movement to make the ultimate use of her abilities.[55]

Early marriage, al-Ghannoushi goes on, is a religious obligation for the proliferation of the race, and as such, any form of contraception or abortion is prohibited (17:31). He sees marriage as a universal law and a form of worship (*'ibadah*), which embodies half of the Islamic religion. Due to the importance accorded marriage, Islam has seen fit to formulate a marital law (outlining duties and privileges) based on equality and complementarity (2:228).[56] In a society where men and women are equal in numbers, every man will naturally have one wife. However, as in times of war, when women outnumber men, the social fabric has to be protected by providing supernumerary women with the chance of sex and motherhood. Thus, women may choose between celibacy and sharing a man with another woman.[57]

Men and women, al-Ghannoushi concludes, are thus different, though they complement each other. They have deep sexual desires for each other, but while men are content with transient biologic satisfaction concentrated in their private parts, for women, it is the quintessential function, all-consuming, seeking to melt into the other partner. For men, women are an extension of their personalities and one of their liaisons and activities, which may be compensated by other endeavors and successes, while sex is the fulcrum of women's lives and dreams and the source of their happiness or misery, and as such, it modifies their looks, behavior, and personality. Consequently, they are more steadfast, faithful, and self-sacrificing in their love and less likely to change partners unless they have been unsuccessful in finding their ideal man. Thus, al-Ghannoushi disagrees with the view that men love women more and maintains that the reverse is actually true, since it is women's nature to love deeply and consumingly, while men's love is only superficial.[58]

Finally, al-Ghannoushi calls on women to concentrate on God, who provides them with power to break the chains of cruelty, exploitation, and backward ideologies that have turned them into pleasurable ornaments. The problem today is the confusion among Muslims between Islamic truth and inherited beliefs, especially with regard to women. This attitude helps serve as a hindrance to progress and advancement.

In examining the discourse of al-Ghannoushi, one is struck by his moderation and idealism on matters of social justice, equality, and freedom and his belief in the right of every Muslim to interpret the Qur'an (*ijtihad*) so as to deal with changing conditions and circumstances imposed by the modern world and its technology. He denounces the use of violence and opts for a gradual process of social transformation and political participation as the means to achieve the long-range goal of establishing an Islamic state. He talks of institutional reform rather than violent revolution, Islamic reform rather than the imposition of traditional formulations of the Shari'ah, and spreading Islamic *da'wah* [message/call] through the masses rather than enforcing an Islamic system from above, by the use of force.

Al-Ghannoushi's critics question his apparent openness and moderation and wonder whether this openness is simply an attempt to gloss over his real intentions, what al-Turabi has called "*maslahah*." Indeed, this becomes quite obvious when he justifies his open policy regarding women as necessary for political and strategic purposes. He explains that women's participation is necessary for the spread of the Islamic movement, since women's role in the conversion of the Muslims themselves, and later the whole world, is essential. Not only are women crucial for the establishment of moral safeguards and the creation of a virtuous society but also as agents for the rejection of subservience to the West.

Many believe that al-Ghannoushi's supporters resorted to violence in Tunis to overthrow the government. His public disavowal of such operations was interpreted as being pragmatic to ensure his continued stay in England, but should his party come to power in Tunisia, he would instantly change into a different man.[59] Muhammad al-Hashimi Hamdi, a former ally of al- Ghannoushi, says, "As an exiled politician seeking support from Western circles . . . [al-Ghannoushi's] strategy has been to play the 'democratic card.'"[60] The Moroccan philosopher Abduh Filali Ansari further says, "For Ghannoushi, the principal question is always how to free the community from backwardness and dependence on the 'other.' However significant his concessions in favor of democracy . . . the community—not the individual—remains . . . the ultimate . . . objective. Democracy, freedom . . . are tools for raising the community of Muslims to the level of power and efficiency that Western nations currently enjoy."[61]

Another indication of al-Ghannoushi's possible radicalism rather than gradualism is section 6 of the 1986 ITM Basic Program, which addresses the issue of *takfir* [apostasy]: "We do not declare Muslims to be unbelievers . . . except for those who agree with words of unbelief or publicly reject the faith or clearly oppose the Qur'an or interpret it in a way not supported by the grammatical rules of the Arabic language or basically behave in a way that does not support anything but unbelief."[62] Thus, while explicitly denying such actions on their part, the ITM implicitly share the same views of Qutb and the Egyptian Islamist party of al-Takfir wal-Hijrah. Moreover, al-Ghannoushi's lectures and writings in the early period drew heavily upon the ideologies of such Islamic scholar-activists as Abu al-'A'la al-Mawdudi, Hasan al-Banna, Sayyid Qutb and his brother Muhammad Qutb, Malik Bennabi, and Muhammad Iqbal. While he praised Khomeini and the Iranian Revolution, his writings were only an elaboration on the favorite themes of Sayyid Qutb during the 1950s and 1960s.

Al-Ghannoushi's equivocation and ambivalence is further evidenced by his treatment of the gender issue in Islam. While he insists that women's role in the home is determined by their biology and, therefore, preordained by God, he explains that nowhere in the Qur'an is there any reference requiring women to work in the home or rear children. In fact, should they do so voluntarily, they are to be compensated financially or emotionally and spiritually. Again, while al-Ghannoushi insists on the primacy of women's role at home, he allows them to work outside the home (at the request of the husband) to provide additional support for husband and family. But, while the Qur'an specifies that they retain their earnings, al-Ghannoushi requires that wives surrender their earnings to their husbands. He also permits their participation in the political, cultural, and social activities of the ITM to help spread the *da'wah* on the one hand, and uses them to counter the female secular model created by the regime of Bourguiba on the other. Yet, while insisting that qualifications should be the only criteria for employment, with no reference to race, color, or sex, he asserts that in case of equal qualifications between male and female, preference should go to the male. "Islam," he declares, "does not allow women to work while a battalion of men are unemployed, especially since the women can take care of the home."[63] But so can men, by his own admission, when he calls on men to emulate the Prophet and help their wives with their housework. He admits the importance of education for both men and women, yet requires his wife to quit her university education upon getting pregnant, because her place is now in the home.[64] Also, in the early period of the ITM, al-Ghannoushi, before he reversed himself, required women to wear the Islamic dress and stay at home having attained the bare minimum of education.

Moreover, while he calls for the "liberation" of women, he denounces all the "reforms" of the Bourguiba government, ranging from women working outside the home, equal educational opportunities, and political participation, to the limitation of marriage to one partner, the organization of divorce, and the requirement of alimony, as un-Islamic, casting thereby serious doubts on his concept of women's "liberation." Furthermore, his recourse to *maslahah* became obvious when he publicly endorsed Bourguiba's Personal Status Code in toto in 1987, in pleading for the political recognition of the ITM, and cited the flexibility of Islam in permitting multiple interpretations of the Qur'anic verses concerned to justify his stand.

While al-Ghannoushi extols freedom and equality as the natural gifts of God to men and women, both being slaves to none but God, he asserts that a wife's activities are to be regulated by the Movement. What is not clear, however, is whether this regulation by the Movement is in keeping with God's stipulations. This, in addition to the wife's ordained duty of submission to her husband, raises serious doubts regarding al-Ghannoushi's true intentions, especially in light of his definition of the Islamic principle of *tawhid*: "This great principle in Islam which rejects a lot of dualities between the body and the spirit, between the mind and the spirit, between the individual and society, between man and woman, between contemporary life and the afterlife, between the worshipping of God and the economic system, between morals and the economy; . . . the main gift of Islam to this world is that it gives to all these dualities something of order and some harmony among them . . . and within society itself . . . and between the human being and nature itself."[65]

Finally, while al-Ghannoushi emphatically blames tradition for the subjugation of women and demonstrates the equal status Islam grants men and women, from equality in creation to participation in politics, religious teachings, the imamate, worship, and military activities, he shies away from tackling, in depth, some basic family issues like the *hijab*, divorce, and polygamy as other ideologues have before. He also qualifies his statements on the freedom of women and their equality with men by such phrases as "within Islamic values," without making any attempt at clarifying or defining them.

In conclusion, al-Ghannoushi, very much like al-Turabi, seems to address women's issues in a twofold manner: the first documents clearly and persuasively argue the equal status afforded men and women in the Qur'an and Hadith; the imposition of the veil only on the Prophet's wives; the attribution of women's subjugation to the misinterpretation of Scripture by succeeding generations; and the importance of *ijtihad* in keeping Islam modern and dynamic. The second, however, is a carefully veiled exposition of his own views on gender roles, confining women to the home under men's hegemony and support, obliged to observe strict Islamic rules of dress and behavior, and affording them a minimal education in keeping with their "ordained" role, while aborting any role of *ijtihad* in this context. This is despite the fact that he extols women as capable of prophecy and thus of attaining human perfection and asserts their right to vote, join political parties, and hold government positions, including judgeships. Finally, like al-Turabi, he cites a great number of independent, liberated women, at the time of the Prophet, who participated in all domains and endeavors. He even goes so far as to explain away all statements or verses in the Hadith and Qur'an respectively that may be understood to be derogatory or discriminatory against women. Yet, as demonstrated earlier, he remains a traditionalist in mind and heart with regard to women's issues and their place in society. Thus, he requires working women to surrender their earnings to their husband in contradistinction to the Qur'an and the teachings of all other ideologues.

Finally, all the ideologues studied here have a common salient trait: They employ very persuasive arguments to prove gender equality in Islam and are very resourceful in supporting their arguments by historical data and ingeniously explaining away what appear to be contradictory hadith and/or verses. Yet, they adopt ultraconservative interpretations of Scripture and Hadith. They also adhere to discriminatory tradition and custom in their private lives or when they assume power. They also share the propensity to manipulate women and their problems to advance their own political agendas.

Chapter 10

❋

Sheikh Hussein Fadlallah

Although the eruption of the Shiʿite factor in Lebanese politics during its civil war (1975–91) took political analysts by surprise, the Shiʿite presence in Lebanon dates back to the seventh century when the Muslim community was split into Shiʿite and Sunni camps. However, from the twelfth century onward, the Shiʿites were reduced to the status of dissenters. They eventually settled in Jabal ʿAmil, part of the Mount Lebanon range in South Lebanon, specifically, the area between the Shouf district and northern Galilee; and in the north of the Biqaʿ region, around the towns of Baalbeck and Hirmil.

The Shiʿites make up one of the eighteen religious sects in Lebanon. In 1926, France, during her mandate of Lebanon, permitted them to practice their religion freely for the first time after the Ottoman suppression and prohibition of their most sacred religious festival, ʿAshura, commemorating the death of al-Husayn. Following Lebanon's independence in 1943, the Shiʿites were given the office of speaker of parliament, while the presidency went to the Maronites and the office of prime minister to the Sunnis. Their political awakening, however, did not take place until an Iranian cleric by the name of Musa al-Sadr was invited by the prominent Sharaf ed-Din family to become the religious leader of the Shiʿite Lebanese in 1959. Within a decade of his arrival in Lebanon, he emerged as the Shiʿite champion and managed to create a sense of communal identity. He founded the Movement of the Deprived (Harakat al-Mahrumin), which won immediate success and popularity with the masses. He had also started a militia, Amal, a word that means hope in Arabic and is the acronym of Afwaj al-Muqawamah al-Lubnaniyyah [Lebanese Resistance Detachments], and was trained and armed by the Palestine Liberation Organization (PLO). As Israeli reprisals against the PLO intensified in the south of Lebanon, many of the Shi'ites migrated to safer areas in the north, and Musa al-Sadr, under the slogan "Arms are an ornament to men," set up training camps in martial arts. However, five months after the Israeli invasion of South Lebanon in 1978, Musa al-Sadr suddenly vanished during an official visit to Libya.

Thomas Lippman has suggested, "There is no single worldwide Islamic resurgence, but there has been a series of coincidental upheavals in which Islam is the common expression of political dissent."[1] This observation seems to be true of Lebanon, where a series of cataclysmic events and environmental factors were decisive in the birth of the Islamic Resistance. Such events included the war in Lebanon, Israel's invasions of 1978 and 1982, al-Sadr's disappearance, and the success of the Iranian Revolution in 1979. Musa al-Sadr had already politicized the Shi'ites of Lebanon, and the Iranian Revolution catapulted all the Shi'ites of the region to the international arena. Thus, when Israel invaded Lebanon in 1982, it was the offspring of such events that ultimately emerged to evict Israel after almost two decades of occupation. Although the Muslim revivalists in Lebanon seemed to have common goals and tactics, different groups emerged for different reasons and in four different areas: the capital city of Beirut, the city of Tripoli in the north, the eastern Biqa' Valley, and the south.

Following the Israeli invasion of 1982, Revolutionary Iran sent 1,500 Iranian Revolutionary Guards to the city of Baalbeck in the Biqa' Valley. This gave opportunity and impetus to the radical Shi'ite Lebanese clerics to widen the scope of their own movement in Lebanon. The Biqa' Valley became their main base until they moved their headquarters to Beirut. Iran provided the militant Shi'ites with both a model and a source of major funding—$10 million a month. Posters of Ayatollah Khomeini became ubiquitous, and the wearing of hijab became prevalent. A faction of Amal, headed by Abbas Musawi and Sheikh Subhi Tufayli, disillusioned by the seeming passivity of the organization, defected to the Biqa' Valley and joined forces with the Iranian Revolutionary Guards. Together, they occupied a Lebanese army barracks in the area and turned it into a formidable fortress. This base, together with smaller installations in the area, would come to constitute the nucleus of an autonomous zone governed according to the principles of Islam. This new formation adopted the name of Hizbullah [the Party of God] based on a Qur'anic verse (5:56), "Lo! The party of God, they are victorious." This term was first used by a Shi'ite group in Iran, faithful to and emulating the teachings of Khomeini. Its slogan was "Only one party, the Party of Allah, only one leader, Ruhollah."[2] It was not, however, until 1985 that the movement announced its existence in Lebanon and declared its military wing, the Islamic Resistance, which until then had been operating under the umbrella of the Lebanese National Resistance dominated by Amal.

In an interview following the publication of its manifesto, Sheikh Fadlallah, the spiritual guide of Hizbullah, declared, "We want to see Islam prevail throughout the world." The manifesto pledges the party's allegiance to Khomeini and his "divinely inspired ideas." Because no compromise is allowed with non-Muslims, the manifesto calls on Lebanese Christians to convert: "O Christians, we call on you to join Islam. In Islam, you will find your safety, your happiness, the rewards of this life, and of the Hereafter."[3] The objective of Hizbullah, hence, was the establishment of an ideal Islamic state in Lebanon, for only Islam can redeem Lebanon from the ravages of civil war and foreign interference brought on by Lebanon's attempt at Westernization.[4]

Ayatollah Sayyid Muhammad Hussein Fadlallah, unquestionably the most articulate and subtle advocate of the Islamic cause in Lebanon, is generally recognized as Hizbullah's spiritual guide (al-murshid al-ruhi), though he has vehemently denied this and has never held any position in the party itself and has declared that his allegiances transcend Lebanon to embrace a universal Islam. As soon as Iranian emissaries started coming to Lebanon, Fadlallah rushed to their embrace, declaring the indebtedness of all Muslims and the Lebanese Shi'ites, in particular, to the Iranian Revolution for awakening their Islamic consciousness. As a gesture of gratitude, Ali Akbar Hashemi Rafsanjani, Iranian ambassador to Damascus at the time, visited him at home in the wake of the 1980 assassination attempt against him. Fadlallah slowly became the oracle of Hizbullah and a fountain of infallible guidance. Thus, an alliance of mutual need crystallized between Iran's emissaries, who provided him with material support and revolutionary symbols, and Fadlallah, who had a following of his own and was eager to introduce the revolution to Lebanon.

Sayyid Muhammad Hussein Fadlallah was born in 1935 in Najaf, Iraq, to a prominent religious family with roots extending back to Imam al-Hassan, son of Imam Ali Ibn Abi Talib. His father, however, originally hailed from 'Aynata in the south of Lebanon. In Najaf, Fadlallah came under the influence of radical clerics and the moderate ayatollah Abu al-Qassim al-Kho'i, famous for his apolitical stance and devotion to religious scholarship. In 1966, the repression of the country's ulema by the Iraqi secular regime prompted Fadlallah to leave Najaf for Beirut and begin a promising career in preaching, teaching, writing, and communal work. The Shi'ite scene at the time was dominated by Musa al-Sadr. Fadlallah was appointed to Nab'ah, an impoverished, overcrowded, eastern suburb of Beirut, where he galvanized its poor residents through regular talks and teaching circles culminating in the establishment of an Islamic club, the Brotherhood. He also established cultural youth clubs and free outpatient and community centers. This was parallel to the political movement of Imam Musa al-Sadr, founder of the Shi'ite Islamic Council, which the Sayyid would not join, despite the imam's constant appeals.

While the imam succeeded in broadening his base, uniting various heterogeneous Muslim groups, the Sayyid concentrated on creating a homogeneous Islamic union through vigorous education and counseling, preparing a grassroots leadership instead of an imported one. In his sermons, he called for an Islamic government as the best solution for Lebanon's social and economic ills. In 1972, he left for his native region of Bint Jubayl, to provide support for the Shi'ites of the region against the repeated Israeli offensives on Palestinian bases in south Lebanon. In 1976, Fadlallah, along with the Palestinians stationed there, had to leave Nab'ah following its occupation by the Christian forces during the Lebanese war. He settled in Bir al-'Abd in the southern suburban area of Beirut. It was probably at this time that his mentor, Ayatollah Kho'i, appointed him as his deputy (*wakil*) in Lebanon. Consequently, Fadlallah founded a large charitable institution (*mabarrah*) in Beirut, consisting of an orphanage, mosque, and school, and succeeded in filling the vacuum left by Musa al-Sadr in 1978 and expounding the revolutionary ideas of Ayatollah Khomeini. Fadlallah recognized Khomeini publicly in 1981, dissociating himself from Kho'i, and paid Khomeini a visit in 1984, which Khomeini reciprocated in 1986, naming him *marji' al-taqlid* [source of imitation/tradition]. In 1985, Fadlallah became president of the Lebanese Council of Hizbullah, comprised of the Iranian ambassador, Lebanese ulema, and security strongmen responsible for clandestine operations; and was appointed vice president of the Central Council of the International Hizbullah in Tehran. He continued to grow in political significance in Lebanon in the 1980s with his outspoken sermons and direct influence on Hizbullah.

Following the Israeli invasion of 1982, Fadlallah criticized Western involvement in Lebanon and called for the establishment of an Islamic republic in Lebanon. However, his relationship with Hizbullah's Iranian patrons started to falter when his reading of the Lebanese situation diverged from theirs, compounded further by recognizing Ruhollah Khomeini as a political leader and not as *wali-al-faqih* [chief jurisconsultant], while adopting Sayyid al-Kho'i as his theological reference. Fadlallah believed it was premature to plan an Islamic republic in Lebanon, because of the existence of powerful opponents that could not be eliminated by intimidation or violence; rather, he thought this opposition could best be eroded through a campaign of persuasion of which he was a master. Iran, despite Fadlallah's ideological independence, continued to rely on his brilliant Arabic rhetoric to convey its revolutionary ideas.[5]

Fadlallah carefully balanced his independence between Hizbullah, with whom he avoided direct overt association, on the one hand, and the Iranian emissaries, with whom he diverged on matters of principle, on the other. Yet, it was impossible for Fadlallah to escape being identified, in Lebanon and abroad, as the mentor of Hizbullah, especially because "at times he did serve Iran's emissaries and Hizbullah's clerics as advisor, jurist, strategist, tactician, spokesman, and mediator." His fate and fortunes soon became inseparable from Hizbullah's, and "As the man and the movement embraced, they began a dizzying ascent to success."[6]

Judith Miller compares Fadlallah to Hasan al-Turabi in the influence they both exercised over millions of Arab Muslims. Both expressed absolute certainty that Islam was the panacea for all ills, and, borrowing Marxist terminology, Turabi declared, "Objectively, the future is ours." Miller describes both as charismatic leaders and orators. They are both mesmerizing and spellbinding students and intellectuals. She says, "They are 'modern' Islamic leaders in that they defend and promote Islam in terms beyond the Qur'an and are fond of incorporating Western techniques and arguments in their criticisms of the West."[7]

Fadlallah produced his best scholarship in *'Uslub al- da'wah fi al-Qur'an* [Style of the call in the Qur'an] and *al-Islam wa mantiq al-quwwah* [Islam and the logic of power] when he was still in Nab'ah. His lectures and sermons were simple, clear, and reflective, and, at times, firm and radical. He was gifted and precocious: at the age of ten, in collaboration with some friends, he published a handwritten journal. His mastery of the Arabic language drove him to defy convention, writing poetry in free verse.[8] Ibrahim M. Abu-Rabi' calls him "the foremost liberation theologian in contemporary Arab Islam."[9]

Although, intellectually, Fadlallah preaches principles similar to those of Khomeini, he owes little to him or Iran. He had taught and preached the doctrine of the Islamic state since he came to Lebanon in the sixties, long before the Iranian Revolution. He is certainly the most eloquent speaker and advocate of Islam in Lebanon and proud of his independence of thought and action. He declares, "I am not an agent for anybody's policy. I am simply trying to implement my policy which is based on Islam and which complements all the Islamic world's forces."[10] Thus, Fadlallah's views cannot always be assumed to coincide with Hizbullah's; indeed, he differs with them on a number of issues. For one thing, his views are less doctrinaire than those of the party and reflect the wariness of an older and more resourceful man, well versed in the intricacies of Lebanese, regional, and international politics. His ultimate goal is the establishment of an Islamic government in Lebanon, the destruction of Israel, and the purification of Muslim society from all forms of imperialism. However, being a "realist," he admits that this cannot be achieved in the foreseeable future. In fact, he keeps reiterating that Lebanon is not yet ready for such an Islamic government and that Islamic resistance from Lebanon alone will not be enough to liberate Palestine. He appealed for Islamic unity with the Sunnis and Druze of Lebanon and called for a dialogue with the Christians to combat secularism and its consequent evils. Fadlallah's views can thus be described as representative of Hizbullah only when the latter adopt and embellish them. Fadlallah's thought, in addition to being influenced by other Islamist ideologues such as Hasan al-Banna and Sayyid Qutb, was also influenced by such revolutionaries as Franz Fanon and Karl Marx. He describes himself as "one of those who have helped formulate the Islamic concepts of this generation over the past eighteen years. The generation has now begun to carry Islam far from the traditions which held that Islam was just a way of knowledge."[11]

His political ideology is structured upon an uncompromising and unconditional adoption of Islam as the source and basis of any political, social, and religious order toward the creation of an Islamic state by revolution from within existing systems or by external violent imposition.[12] To achieve this, certain preparations have to be completed:

1. The modernization of Islam. The Islamic world, he argues, is backward, even in the true understanding of Islamic dogma and Shari'ah, as a result of blind adherence to historical misinterpretations and misbeliefs. Heritage is not sacred, and antiquated concepts must be rethought, especially because Islam stresses intellect and knowledge as guiding principles for Qur'anic interpretation. Interpretation is never absolute and is open to modification in the light of new advances in knowledge. Such dynamic interpretation allows Islam to

remain up to date, able to cope with new developments and problems of contemporary civilization. This also requires that Islam be transferred from a purely theoretical into a pragmatic system, concentrating on applicable ideas and theories.

2. Unification of all Muslims. The various Islamic movements are diverse, lacking a common sociopolitical plan to counter any destructive movement. A common ideology and plan of action are, therefore, essential to lay the groundwork for an Islamic state. They require a steady nurturing and growth of Islamic faith, sustained by encouragement of free thinking to mesh spiritual values with the realities of life. Differences among the various Islamic movements rest upon differing interpretations of the Qur'an and Sunna and, as such, are not basic and should be easily resolved, since Islam is one homogeneous unit. Only through such a union can Islam confront and do away with all disruptive forces, and this is made possible by emulating the Islamic Republic of Iran, which successfully revolutionized Islam.

The Sayyid, however, recognizes the impossibility of creating such an Islamic state in Lebanon because of its inherent multidenominational nature and unique system that remains internationally guaranteed.[13] He explains that a Muslim is required by his faith to live in an Islamic state. "When a Muslim lives in a state that does not adopt Islam," he argues, "his life remains confused, because of the dualism [of authority] that he is living under . . . The Christian, by contrast, does not have this problem when living in an Islamic society."[14] He therefore set out to create an alternative revolutionary theoretical structure through which he could oppose the dominant ideas currently pervading society, such as the colonial tradition, which, in the words of Marx, "weighs like a nightmare on the minds of the living."[15]

Fadlallah agrees with Qutb that 'aqidah [creed] is not enough in its abstract theoretical form. To become so, it has to act as a guiding light, a beacon for all issues troubling the contemporary Muslim world. Jihad can, therefore, remain an ongoing dynamic process only if Islam is "an independent economic, political, and conceptual equation that faces the infidel and arrogant equations [of foreign powers]."[16] The relationship between man and God, Fadlallah explains, is essentially emancipatory. "It is a basic source of power that energizes man continuously, and propels him to an autonomous movement of perpetual growth and renewal, so that he can renew life around him and push it forward."[17] The Qur'an, argues Fadlallah, condemns oppression and calls on man to rebel against it. However, the oppressed in the Qur'an are of two categories: the oppressed who have the means to rebel but remain content, lulled by a false sense of safety and material profits, who therefore lack the will to change their condition; and those who are born to objective oppressive conditions and are encouraged to emigrate in an attempt to break the circle of fear and oppression that is suffocating them. Thus, man lacks "the flexible and strong thought that enables him to open up to Truth, and, consequently, he lacks the intellectual methods that enable him to possess either detailed or comprehensive knowledge as a means of discerning different views."[18] This is precisely the condition that the powerful and oppressors would like to keep the rest in, impervious to their condition and unaware of their oppression.

Fadlallah, thus, sees oppression in the world around him—socially, economically, politically, and culturally—as a "process of dehumanization" negating thereby the freedom assured man in the Qur'an. The poor are robbed of their autonomy in decision making by the wealthy, which alienates them further. Economic power, hence, "abolishes the autonomous will of man" and robs him of his essential values.[19] The oppressed, in addition to their social and economic exploitation, suffer most of all from their self-depreciation. Revolution thus becomes necessary as "the expression of a dynamic thought that reflects the deep pain, oppression, and exploitation of man. In this regard, revolution is a universal human phenomenon . . . that cannot be a commodity subject to export and import. Revolution is debate, dialogue, challenge, and movement, and once these are achieved, it becomes a natural phenomenon in the world."[20] The poor and oppressed, to be empowered, must first and foremost shed their fears and embrace the truth of their cause, the willingness to sacrifice themselves—martyrdom—in the hope of certain rewards in the hereafter. For once they are convinced of this truth, they will, in turn, instill fear in their most powerful adversaries.[21] "Legitimate and effective violence," Fadlallah further asserted, "could only proceed from belief welded to sober calculation."[22]

The religious scholar (*alim*), maintains Fadlallah, is not only the guardian of religious texts and their interpreter but also the "conscience" of the Muslim community, moved by its misery, pain, and sorrow. The individual is more important than land or nation, for "as long as a human being is humiliated and enslaved, land has no value at all. And as long as enemies invade and settle in the individual's psyche and emotions, nation has no value."[23] He therefore urges the ulema to reconstruct basic Islamic precepts in the light of contemporary conditions and immerse themselves in the lives of their people. He thus attacks traditional jurisprudence in Qutbian style and calls it the jurisprudence of ignorance, backwardness, and compromise.

Like Khomeini, Fadlallah adhered to the *'usuli* [fundamentalist] tradition in contradistinction to the *akhbari* [textual] tradition. *'Usuli* tradition valorizes *ijtihad* to meet the problems of modernity and provide authoritative advice to counter problems not covered by tradition. Existing authorities, however, are numerous and varied, and Fadlallah, therefore, advises dependence on one *marji' taqlid*, with his own particular tradition. But even then, Fadlallah also advises *taqiyyah* [to act contrary to one's principles of faith for expediency] in concrete daily behavior without necessarily having to refer back to the *marji'*. The time of *taqiyyah* is that of education, preparation, and organization in a disciplined group until such time as assurance of success propels its members to revolution. Such a time came with the success of the Iranian Revolution, which he views as universal. Failure to support such a revolution can no longer be seen as *taqiyyah* but as outright *nifaq* [duplicity]. Like Khomeini and Muhammad Baqir al-Sadr, Fadlallah reinterpreted Shi'ite faith and history and emphasized the role of social reform and political activism. Muslims were urged to shed their passivity in anticipation of the return of the twelfth Imam, and revolt against all forms of injustice.[24]

Men and women, Fadlallah argues, share the same soul—"And God created you of the same soul and from it created a spouse" (4:1), spouse denoting either male or female, making it impossible to assign precedence to one over another, and dictating absolute equality in all basic premises with differences in applicability dictated by inherent gender differences. Islamic history, however, reveals radical departures from Qur'anic teachings concerning women. This came about following the transformation of the caliphate system into a monarchical one anxious to build harmonious ties with its non-Islamic neighbors. In addition, there followed a dearth of strong religious leadership, the imams being isolated from Islamic life, and a degeneration into a chaotic Islamic society. All this led to a progressive suppression of women into a secondary backward state through unjust, backward laws.[25]

The successive Islamic movements, Fadlallah continues, were male dominated and continued to marginalize women using quotes and expressions from the Qur'an and Hadith as evidence of their "ordained" inferior status:

1. *Al-wat'* [literally meaning "trampling"]. Fadlallah explains that this word was originally used in older, backward societies, where women were vastly inferior to men. Its current use, however, denotes relationships between men and women where one is physically atop the other as in sexual intercourse and has no derogatory connotation.

2. *Al-tafdil* [favoring one over another]. This term, Fadlallah goes on, refers to the granting of favors and does not constitute a value judgment. Thus, the Qur'anic verse "Men are responsible for women" (4:34) applies only to married life where the husband is obligated to protect and provide for his family without necessarily being superior to his wife. This is ordained by the fact that in the family sphere there is room for only one manager of its affairs. The choice of the man for this position is dictated by the physical and psychological differences between the sexes and the method of spending. As to "And they [women] have rights similar to those [of men] over them in kindness, and men are a degree above them" (2:228), this "degree" refers only to man's right to divorce and his other marital rights.

3. Inheritance laws. The fact that men inherit twice as much as women (4:11), Fadlallah argues, does not constitute an indication of the superiority of men but reflects their duty to provide for their womenfolk—the *mahr* and provision for children and family—while women have no financial responsibilities. Thus, the difference here is not due to the superiority of one over the other in humanity but is relative to their duties and obligations.

4. Although the issue of blood money (*diyyah*) in case of death distinguishes between the two sexes with respect to the amount paid, Fadlallah justifies this by the economic situation: a man's death constitutes a greater financial loss to his heirs than a woman's, since he is usually the provider of the family.

5. The fact that two women are needed as witnesses, while one male suffices, is explained away by women being more emotional and, therefore, more liable to forget or distort facts. "One [woman] may be confused and is corrected by the other" (2:282). In such cases, two women are needed to correct one another. In purely feminine matters, or if the witness is known to be virtuous, just, and truthful, the testimony of one woman is sufficient.

6. The claim that women are merely decorative, a tool for man's desires and pleasure, is clearly fallacious: women's roles as wives and mothers do not preclude their involvement in other endeavors, provided these do not subvert their family duties.[26]

7. Quotations such as "No people can succeed if led by a woman" and "Let no woman be a judge," Fadlallah dismisses as either inaccurate or misinterpreted. Moreover, the latter is based on the weak hadith of Majlisi as the only reference, and the former is mentioned only once by Bukhari and does not appear in any of the Shi'ite sources. Therefore, both are undependable, and *ijtihad* may be used to clarify the issue. Thus, the Qur'an attributes to the Queen of Shiba a mental acumen far superior to men (27:32). Furthermore, jurisprudence relies on wisdom, learning, and faith. If these qualities are to be found in a woman, she may, indeed, become a judge, albeit with reservations, and interpret the Qur'an just like men. Female imams are not allowed, however, because their femininity may arouse men; but they may become imams over women. Moreover, contemporary women have proved their capabilities and astuteness in the fields of business, politics, and leadership positions and have attained high offices in various fields.

8. Fadlallah also discards the saying attributed to Imam Ali, "Women are defective in intelligence, faith, and fortune," as untrue. The fact that women are banned from prayer during menstruation does not brand them less faithful, since they are only obeying God's directives. It is true, however, that men should not obey their wives' counsel indiscriminately, lest they be led to erroneous judgments or fulfill unjust demands, thus, the sayings of Imam Ali, "Do not obey them in goodness that you may not obey them in evil" and "Be wary of their counsel." Such influence of women over men has often led the latter astray and underlies the use of women in espionage.[27]

Islam, thus, Fadlallah affirms, advocates a responsible form of freedom for both men and women, allowing full integration and self-expression. This freedom is not absolute, however, but emphasizes the provision of equal opportunities to both sexes to realize their full potential within the framework of their respective capacities and the confines of their inherent qualities and makeup. The only absolute equality lies in common humanity, but definitely not in their respective roles. Thus, it is not unjust that only women bear children and nurse them; and it is only natural that men are physically stronger, but this need not hamper women, except in matters that require physical prowess. Women, therefore, complement men and are equally responsible for the advancement of society, as evidenced in sura 9:71: "The faithful, men and women, are responsible for each other, to do good and refrain from evil."

Islam, Fadlallah argues, provides for gender equality in all things, except for the duties of motherhood and fatherhood. The wife's only obligation is the provision of sexual relief for her husband, since housework, nursing, and caring for children are not obligatory. Should the wife work outside the home, her work schedule should not interfere with the husband's sexual needs. Thus, the husband has the right to beat his wife if she refuses him sexually, since this may drive him to adultery. In this case, beating is considered a corrective measure to restore justice and peace to the home. The wife has sexual rights as well, and if her husband abstains sexually or stops providing for her, she may reciprocate but may not hit him, since he is the head of the family. If he becomes abusive, she may seek family mediation or, failing that, go to court and sue for divorce.[28] Whenever women overstep their boundaries to assume male-type roles, they relinquish their role as mothers and lose their femininity. They should, therefore, seek fulfillment in a balanced manner, preserving their roles as wives and mothers.[29]

Islam dictates that men and women are equally obligated to nurture and reinforce their faith in God and resurrection. Since this requires learning and knowledge, Fadlallah argues, women should be well educated and, in so doing, mix with men, within Islamic regulations to prevent seduction. Women are allowed to work outside the home and may even demand payment for housework and nursing as stipulated in the Qur'an: "If they nurse, pay them their due and treat them justly" (65:6). In the workplace, Islam equates men's and women's wages, while other cultures underpay women. However, while they may work, women should not be subject to feminine or sexual exploitation. If they are, the husbands have the right to prevent them from working, unless they use their wiles to assuage them. However, the husband does not own his wife and should treat her humanely, observing her full rights and privileges. Thus, while all these rights and privileges are provided by Islam, Fadlallah argues, they still have not yet managed to allow women their full roles in social leadership. However, some progress has been made in the social, political, and educational fields albeit in limited fashion. Further progress requires that women be educated and motivated to seize their rights, for "God will not improve the lot of a people, unless they cure their own ills" (13:11). This is especially important because many women refuse to fight for their due rights to safeguard extant support and privileges.[30]

Islam does not seek to suppress emotions, Fadlallah continues, since this could lead to undesirable effects. Rather, it endeavors to nurture them in a manner approved by God to prevent deprivation and deviation. Thus, un-chaperoned meetings between men and women are not condoned because they could lead to sexual liaison, for "Whenever a man and a woman meet, the devil is their companion" (Hadith). Love, however, should not be obsessive, lest it be transformed into a state of "worship" similar to that of God, which is not acceptable. "The faithful love God most . . ." (2:165) and should, therefore, love one another through their love of God. Only then does it become acceptable. Men and women may thus meet in solitude only in the marital home, where the sexual instinct has free rein and a woman's femininity is directed solely at her husband. Premarital and extramarital sex is forbidden, since it is more gratifying than marital sex and can, therefore, subvert marriage. Islam also forbids masturbation in males because it reduces potency, wastes sperm, and interferes with marital sex. Some allow it for women, Fadlallah explains, since they have no sperm to waste; it does not replace actual intercourse but is useful, especially if the husband fails to satisfy his wife.[31]

Fadlallah describes categories of love. One type is Platonic love, offered in response to attributes of the loved one, bound by mutual respect and openness. A second category is the physical, stimulated by the physical beauty of the loved one; this is instinctual and progresses to sexual desire, rendering innocent friendship between men and women almost impossible. It is also subject to adulteration into the love of one man of another and one woman of another. A third category of love is spiritual or emotional, as in the love of parents, children, friends, and relatives; this is primal and stimulates an urge to care and protect. Finally, love may be sublimated into an adoration and sacralization of the loved one, which is not acceptable. It may become distorted as in paganism or transcendental as in the love of God.

While it is an emotion, love emanates from the brain and is guided by it according to the individual's set of values. It is often involuntary and chaotic, as in the love of the opposite sex, and must therefore be controlled and bound to the marital state, since it is essential for family life.[32] Its natural progression leads to marriage and family life, and as in all other fields, Islam sets norms and regulations to cover all aspects relating to it. Engagement, Fadlallah affirms, is an agreement to marry without an actual contract. As such, it is not yet legal and the couple may not visit unchaperoned or cohabit. The prospective groom does not have to support his fiancée. However, it is the right of the prospective husband to carefully examine the woman's feminine charms (mahasin)—hair, neck, arms, legs—to make sure she is not deformed in any way, and elsewhere—he is even allowed to examine all of her body. Moreover, should the engagement period be a protracted one, the couple may decide to undergo *mut'ah* or temporary marriage for the duration.[33]

Marriage, according to Fadlallah, is advisable but not mandatory in Islam, unless the male is tempted into sinful relationships. It is contractual, with set duties and privileges, including sexual rights, binding both partners. The institution of marriage strives to protect men and women from sinful relationships and to build families. This requires maturity, responsibility, and the ability to care for and direct the family. As such, early marriage may fulfill the second, but not the first aim. Maturity, however, does not necessarily depend on age, and, in case of incomplete maturity, the partners' families will assume direction and guidance.[34]

While Islam does not specify the age of the marriage partners, explains Fadlallah, it sets the legal age of both partners at puberty. Women of legal age may marry whomever they please, without parental coercion, since Islam merely asks children to respect, protect, and care for their parents, and parental obedience is not absolute. However, they should be wise enough to make correct choices, and mature enough to make life-influencing decisions. Fadlallah does not specify who is to determine whether the children are wise enough, and he explains that maturity is not age dependent, since it may be precocious, such that a nine-year-old girl may be able to make decisions wisely and correctly. In such cases, she may forego the acquiescence of her father or guardian and seek the counsel of others to reinforce her own decisions. Furthermore, while arranging the marriage of unborn children is forbidden, parents may arrange the marriage of their prepubertal children, if this is to the children's benefit in the future.[35] If the parents refuse a child's choice of spouse, the latter should try to convince them otherwise. If the child fails, the couple should not elope, since this may endanger the stability and security of their marriage in the future. Instead, they have the choice of marrying against their parents' wishes or making a new choice. Parents' blessings are advisable only morally in keeping with their advisory rights, especially since the parents' hegemony over their children ends at the legal age.

In choosing a husband, Fadlallah argues, a woman should not seek physical beauty, wealth, or power, but, rather, morality, decency, and faith. This is further confirmed by the hadith "If a moral and decent man should ask for the hand of [your daughter or . . .] in marriage, give her to him, otherwise there will be chaos and massive corruption on earth."[36] While

Islam accepts the marriage of a Muslim male to a Christian or Jewish woman, it prohibits the reverse, since the children then would not be reared as Muslims. This is a serious issue, for while Islam recognizes and respects the religious beliefs of Jews and Christians, the latter neither respect Islam nor believe Muhammad to be a prophet, nor that the Qur'an is the word of God.[37]

The marriage contract can be drawn by the couple themselves without the assistance of a cleric. However, it should be drawn up according to accepted regulations. One such regulation is the inclusion of the *mahr* in the contract, even if it is only symbolic. Omission of the *mahr*, however, will not annul the marriage, and the amount will have to be worthy of the bride's status. Registration of the marriage contract is not mandatory, but serves to cement it.

Marriage is not intended to enslave women, Fadlallah reassures, but to allow them to live in full harmony with their husbands, in agreement with the Qur'anic implication of what a true union is in sura 2:187: "For they [women] are your garment as you are theirs." But for the marriage to be successful, both parties have to make the necessary sacrifices for the common good of the marital home, such sacrifices being divinely rewarded. Hence, Muslim women should not abuse the rights and freedom accorded to them by Islam and refuse to do the housework, raise their children and nurse them, or use that as a lever against their husbands, nor should they be concerned with material rewards. Similarly, the husband should not abuse his authority to pressure his wife. Women who fulfill such duties are considered *mujahidat* [female warriors], for they exemplify the essence of the ideal wife. Husbands should be appreciative of their wives, especially when the latter do what is not required of them.[38]

In marriage, a Muslim woman has the dual role of wife and mother, seeking God's approval through her good deeds and sacrifices in serving her husband and children, expecting nothing in return, even when her husband fails to fulfill his marital duties towards her. This is fully voluntary and may not be enforced by the husband, who has authority over his wife only in sexual matters and related details, such as leaving the home without his permission if he is present and never in his absence. Sex, being a primal hunger and hence essential in married life, must be satiated. The wife is thus obliged to satisfy her husband's sexual appetite on demand, or be considered recalcitrant and be punished: she is first admonished, then the husband follows admonishment with sexual abstinence, then, if she remains noncompliant, she is to be beaten without incurring injury. The husband should not use force to effect intercourse or use coercion to force his wife to bear children. On the other hand, the wife may not pressure her husband to impregnate her, and the husband must satisfy his wife's sexual needs even before the lapse of four months as specified by other jurisprudents, for sexual abstinence may cause the wife to go astray. Moreover, the wife may not alienate or repel her husband from having sex with her either intentionally or unintentionally, directly or indirectly. To this end, the wife can include conditions governing marital sex in the marriage contract, but only if the husband agrees.[39]

Both partners have duties toward each other and the home. Usually, the more mature and experienced should be in charge, but if they are equal, they should agree amicably on their respective roles. If the wife is more mature, she should make it a point to emphasize and compliment her husband's good qualities and share some duties with him, to bolster his self-esteem. Conversely, if the husband takes charge, he should make his wife feel valued and needed. Thus, direction of the marriage should be a cooperative effort. In any eventuality, the husband is responsible for his wife in financial and marital matters, which he provides, and in matters dictated by Islam. Otherwise, she is as free as he is. The extra male privileges in the verse "And they [women] have rights similar to those [of men] over them in kindness and men are a degree above them" (2:228) refer to the control of marital sex and divorce. However, since the husband is the actual provider, he should be in full charge of the family but may not mistreat or beat his wife, unless she does not observe his sexual rights. Beating her becomes necessary when she does not respond to chastisement by admonishment or sexual abstinence. However, the beating should be controlled so as not to cause fractures or draw blood.[40]

Extramarital sex and adultery are prohibited in Islam. However, men may be sexually frustrated because of a wife's frigidity or because of a desire for change. In that case, Islam allows multiple marriages to preempt adultery and to meet other needs: in case of wars when men are decimated, creating a surfeit of women; when a man's sexual desire, quicker to arouse than a woman's, requires multiple outlets (women, on the other hand, are by nature more faithful and prone to concentrate on one man); and, finally, when the wife's sterility or sickness dictates another marriage, if divorce is not desirable. Since sex is God-given to satisfy natural needs and ensure procreation, as evident in the hadith "I love three things in life: good food, women, and prayer," and since the sanctity of sex is further evidenced by the fact that the husband has to perform certain rituals before the sexual act, Islam repudiates celibacy in any form.[41] Since polygamy satisfies a natural need, which springs either from within the individual or is incurred by external circumstances, it is prescribed in the interest of both men and women, irrespective of its negative ramifications, since its benefits to both sexes make it imperative. This is best demonstrated by the fact that sexual abstinence causes perversion, which in turn leads to more problems than polygamy can ever incur.

However, in cases of multiple marriages, all wives must be treated equally and justly, as is evident in the Qur'an. The equality verse, "And if you fear to be unjust, then marry only one," Fadlallah explains, refers to material, not emotional matters, as evidenced in 4:129, and is not legally compulsory; in the verse "And you will not be able to treat all wives equally, even if you try," the reference is to emotional love, which is not always possible, since emotions are difficult to control. However, men are not to love one wife excessively and overtly to the neglect of others, for the Qur'an commands, "But turn not altogether away [from one], leaving her as in suspense" (4:129). While a second marriage may have negative effects on the first wife, she should adjust and continue to lead her normal life, especially because the new marriage may help the husband avoid deviant behavior that could ultimately endanger her own marital status.[42] The problem with multiple marriages, however, is that they carry a heavy financial burden and are, therefore, not affordable for many men. To circumvent this, Islam has ratified the phenomenon of temporary marriage ordained by the Prophet for special circumstances but later banned by Caliph 'Umar Ibn-al-Khattab, who reportedly said, "Two pleasures were permitted by the Prophet, and I ban them and punish those who commit them." Shi'ite sources maintain this ban was only administrative and, as such, is now null and void, rendering temporary marriage legal. The Sunnis, however, continue to consider it illegal. Nevertheless, temporary marriage, according to Fadlallah, remains a social necessity to ward off adultery and prostitution when regular marriage no longer satisfies sexual needs, as in extended travel, female frigidity, or unresponsiveness, or simply to break the monotony of routine marital sex, or in cases where regular marriage is not possible.[43]

Temporary marriage is legal with a *mahr*, *'iddah* [waiting period], duration, and full inheritance rights for legitimate offspring. However, it has a finite contract and involves no financial provisions or inheritance rights for the woman. A mature woman may enter into it without her family's consent. Some believe it demeaning for women to move from one temporary marriage to another, but sex, explains Fadlallah, is a natural instinct, and there is no shame in satisfying it legally. Moreover, women are free to refuse it or insist on such contractual conditions as protracted longevity of the marriage and reasonable financial security. Also, any resultant children may be an incentive to transform a temporary marriage into a regular one.[44]

However, Fadlallah explains, since the Sunnis, who comprise the majority of all Muslims, prohibit temporary marriages, such marriages are not publicized and are frequently frowned upon; and most men prefer the stability and security of regular marriage. Accordingly, temporary marriages are becoming less frequent. They do, however, serve other practical purposes, such as the circumvention of segregation strictures and the marrying off of a prepubertal daughter to allow her husband, who is now a *mahram,* to travel with her mother (marriage of prohibition—*ziwaj al-tahrim*); and to provide a trial period before entering into a regular marriage to test the compatibility of the partners.[45]

Fadlallah does not advise the temporary marriage of virgins, since it may be psychologically detrimental in the future if they become dependent on such marriages. It may also damage their reputation, rendering them unmarriageable afterward. He thus discourages all girls from entering into such marriages, and prefers limiting them to widows and divorcees. Also, these marriages do not produce the desired unity of the partners or the security inherent in regular marriages but remain as a means for physical and sexual release. However, Fadlallah hastens to add, they do not constitute prostitution, since they are legal marriages with advantages accruing to both parties, while prostitution is a purely animal act free of any humanity.[46]

Fadlallah finds civil marriage acceptable and legal but only if it fulfills Islamic regulations. It differs in that it does not stipulate the religious affiliation of the couple and the marriage may be annulled by civil courts. It only requires that both parties be of legal age, while Islam dictates that a Muslim male must marry a Muslim female or a woman of the People of the Book who are respected by Islam, but never an atheist. A Muslim woman, on the other hand, is not to be married except to a Muslim man. Thus, while a Muslim husband cannot abuse or be intolerant of his non-Muslim wife, a Christian husband may be intolerant of his Muslim wife's faith or of her, because Christianity and Judaism do not recognize Islam or the Prophet. Moreover, in Islam, the husband may secure his wife by endowing her with half his belongings according to Islamic law, but can will her only a third of his belongings after death in certain sects. Civil marriage, on the other hand, has no such regulations. Finally, civil divorce, according to him, is not recognized by Islam and cannot, therefore, be binding unless carried out according to Islamic rules and regulations.[47]

Divorce is abhorred by God and should not be implemented until all efforts at reconciliation have been exhausted. The right of divorce is confined to the husband unless otherwise stipulated in the marriage contract. This, according to Fadlallah, is due to the fact that the husband is the provider of the family, and women are too emotional and may seek divorce while in an irrational state, whereas men are much more careful and restrained. A wife, on the other hand, may go to court to be divorced from her husband if he maltreats her or stops providing for her; if he is impotent and remains so for one year; if he becomes insane; or if he deceives or defrauds her. She may also divorce him without recourse to court if that right is stipulated in her marriage contract. In such a case, contrary to Sunni practice, the husband will have to delegate the power of divorce to her, just as he may delegate it to any third person he may see fit. Finally, subject to his approval, she may have him divorce her by paying him a certain amount of money, which is usually her *mahr*. This form of divorce is called *khul'*. This is usually irrevocable and acceptable, since a husband has the right to delegate anyone to effect his divorce. The divorce is voided, however, if the wife was menstruating at the time it was pronounced, and the divorce then has to be repeated at a later date. Upon divorce, the wife has to observe a waiting period of three months to ascertain parenthood, if she is pregnant, and to accommodate social customs. During this mandatory waiting period following divorce, the wife is to retain the same duties and privileges as if still married. The divorced wife may keep her children until the age of two years, after which the father claims them, since he is the provider. This also makes it easier for the divorced wife to remarry. While the children are in her custody, the wife may not travel with the children, use their funds, or decide on their education without prior consultation with their father. Her duties consist merely of caring for their natural needs—nursing, feeding, bathing, and so on. Furthermore, the father may delegate anyone to care for the children. If the husband dies, the wife may choose custody of the children or relinquish it to remarry.[48]

Women, Fadlallah maintains, are provocative and can exert a seductive, subversive influence on men. Accordingly, Islam prescribes their clothing and behavior to preempt these untoward influences. Thus, a woman's beauty and femininity may be displayed only at home amid her family. When in the company of others or outside the home, she should be veiled, covering all her body, except for her hands and face. Jewelry and adornments—rings, mascara, finger dyes (hinnah), but not bracelets or decorative contact lenses—may be worn on exposed areas, provided they do not arouse. Further, since a woman's voice is provocative, she should modulate it into as neutral a tone as possible while in social circles or if she is reciting the Qur'an at a funeral or gathering. This is to enable women to appear in public as persons, not females, thus permitting them to mix with men in all innocence. And, while the husband may coerce his wife to wear the veil, it is advisable that this be done amicably to forestall any future negative reactions.

A woman may not unveil herself or undress for other men, except in specified circumstances. She may do so while undergoing a medical examination or plastic surgery, or even before male aestheticians if female ones are not available. This becomes more acceptable if it is done for her husband's benefit. She may also discard the veil if it endangers her or if it causes her husband to divorce her and, in turn, it embarrasses her. Finally, Fadlallah advises both men and women to wear a mental veil (hijab dhihni), to avoid lewd thoughts or dreams.[49]

Fadlallah, like other fundamentalist ideologues, believes strongly in the application of ijtihad, especially if it is in the interest (maslahah) of the ummah [Muslim nation]. Thus, he has gone so far as to permit birth control, in view of the ummah's suffering from overpopulation. Also, while the Lebanese criminal law still gives reduced sentences to crimes of honor, Fadlallah prohibited the practice as "pagan and tribal."[50] He has also accepted the validity of the computer in determining the dates of Ramadan and the Fitr feast rather than the ritual visualization of the moon. Yet, as the previous survey has shown, he remains as strict as ever in matters pertaining to women and their liberation from the shackles of tradition. Thus, what he grants women as a liberal with his left hand, he takes away with his right.

Based on his knowledge of the Qur'an and his awareness of the abject social, economic, political, and cultural conditions surrounding the oppressed masses of the modern Muslim world, Fadlallah formulated his own Islamic theory of oppression. Reminiscent of Marxist ideology, he describes oppression as "a process of dehumanization," which denies man the freedom guaranteed him by the Qur'an. The oppressed, exploited on all levels, including what he describes as "doctrinal oppression," suffer most of all from self-depreciation. "Doctrinal oppression," he explains, is the lack of "flexible and strong thought that enables [the human being] to open up to Truth, and, consequently, he lacks the intellectual methods that enable him to possess either detailed or comprehensive knowledge as a means of discerning different views." Fadlallah thus maintains that it is the aim of the oppressors and powerful to perpetually keep the oppressed in limbo, unaware of their condition. Moreover, Fadlallah gives Qur'anic evidence, where the two categories of the oppressed—those who can change their condition but are too lazy or unwilling to sacrifice their false sense of safety and personal gain, and those who are born into oppressive conditions—are required to free themselves or simply emigrate to escape their oppression.[51]

Reading his passionate appeals for the freedom of man and his rebellion against all kinds of oppression to regain the humanity and freedom guaranteed by the Qur'an, one cannot but be struck by the dichotomy in his thought when it comes to women's "dehumanization," "self-depreciation," and "doctrinal oppression." Although he ceaselessly reiterates the equality of men and women in the "humanity" accorded them by the Qur'an, he leaves them "dehumanized" in their domestic roles and alienated from their own means of production, since their role whether at home or in the outside world remains dependent on the needs of the husband, his children, and his commands. Fadlallah not only denies her the freedom to choose her own dress but goes further, to the point of asking her to forego what rights or privileges God has accorded her (*mahr*, abstaining from nursing and rearing her children, and performing household chores, among others) for the pleasure and happiness of her husband. The woman who emerges from his discourse, however spellbound by his art of persuasion and subtlety of expression, has false consciousness, is unaware of any "doctrinal oppression," and is "self-deprecatory" and totally "dehumanized."

Moreover, Fadlallah again denounces the economically powerful and accuses them of robbing the poor of their means of production, denying them self-sufficiency and independent decision making. Fadlallah here agrees once more with Karl Marx, who accuses the bourgeoisie (rich) of denying the proletariat (poor) of their creativity by robbing them of the fruits of their labor. This external pressure, Fadlallah argues, "paralyzes or abolishes the autonomous will of [the individual]."[52] Once again, we find Fadlallah oblivious to the fact that his description of the economically poor and their exploitation by the affluent, who "abolish the autonomous will of man" and rob him of his essential values, fits, hand in glove, the condition of women, who are robbed of any possible economic independence and exploited by their husbands, as prescribed by him. They are, hence, just like the poor, denied self-sufficiency, independent decision making, creativity, and autonomous will, and are alienated from their own means of production. This is all the more incongruous when Fadlallah simultaneously admits the equality of the sexes in their "humanity." Interestingly enough, neither he nor the other ideologues bother to define their understanding of the term "humanity" and what privileges it carries. Moreover, while he calls for a revolution as "a universal human phenomenon," a revolution of "debate, dialogue, challenge and movement," he bars women from revolting against their social and domestic condition and asks them to forego whatever rights or privileges are accorded them by the Qur'an. Fadlallah also asserts that as long as humans are debased and subjugated, land has no value. And as long as enemies invade and occupy their psyche and emotions, nation has no value. He even calls on the ulema to reconstruct basic Islamic precepts to fit contemporary conditions and accuses them of ignorance, backwardness, and compromise. However, this flurry of reform seems to be designed for the sole benefit of the male sex, while females are left to languish in "ignorance, backwardness and compromise," enslaved by the men in their lives with the blessings of those same "ignorant" and "backward" ulema.

Contradictions abound not only in his ideology and view of humanity but also within his argument regarding the role and condition of women in an Islamic society. In his discourse on Islam's requirement of two female witnesses, where only one male witness suffices, Fadlallah allows one female witness in matters concerning women's affairs and in cases where the witness is known to be "virtuous, just, and truthful." Does this imply that women are less emotional when it comes to testifying in matters pertaining to themselves, or is erring in such "feminine matters" less serious? But who is to determine these qualities, and do they in fact reduce her emotionality and enhance her rationality? Finally, in trying to explain away Imam Ali's statement that women are deficient in intelligence and religion (naqisatu 'aqlin wa din), Fadlallah reassures his readers that the requirement of two female witnesses is in no way a reflection on women's intelligence or rationality. Rather, the act of testifying heightens the witness's feelings, trust, and honesty, while rationality ('aql) deals only with thinking.[53] Could this imply that men lack any feelings to evoke and are by nature trustworthy and honest, while women tend to be blinded by their feelings and are, naturally, cunning and deceitful and, therefore, untrustworthy? If so, then the number of female witnesses becomes immaterial, since they are all untrustworthy and, therefore, unfit to testify, unless of course women are to be barred from testifying altogether, in keeping with Khomeini's ruling on the matter.

Fadlallah attributes the male's double inheritance to the financial burden the man has to bear in discharging his duties and obligations to his parents, wife, and children, duties not required of women. Such an explanation is quite reasonable in a society where women stay at home and do not work and generate income. Fadlallah, however, does not make room in his interpretation for working women, whose abilities and qualities he himself lauds and who are also responsible for their families. Moreover, while he reluctantly admits that such women do exist, he explains that their work is most often voluntary and not obligatory as is the case for men and, therefore, not worthy of compensation. In the same vein, the amount of blood money (*diyyah*) paid for the death of a man, the provider, exceeds that of a woman, although many women, by his own admission, are providers just like men.

While Fadlallah advocates full integration and self-expression for both men and women on the one hand, he explains, on the other, that this freedom is not absolute but extends only to the provision of equal opportunity to both sexes to realize their full potential within the framework of their respective natural capacities and the confines of their inherent qualities and constitution. The only absolute equality lies in their humanity, and definitely not in their respective roles. Moreover, while he would allow women to work and to earn comparable wages, he reminds them that their work schedule should not interfere with their husband's overriding sexual needs, thus simultaneously withdrawing a right he had just granted. Women, he claims, should help themselves assume the status Islam has allotted them. Yet, Fadlallah seems to forget that he robbed them of all autonomy and freedom by completely subordinating them to the will of their husbands, thus denying them any opportunity to initiate such a move without being accused of recalcitrance and rebellion.

Fadlallah goes on to explain that both partners in marriage have duties toward each other and the home, with the more mature and experienced being in charge. If they are equally mature, they should agree amicably on their respective roles. In short, the direction of marriage should be a cooperative endeavor. However, Fadlallah reminds us that the male is responsible for his wife in financial and material matters, her dress, her movements, marital sex, rearing of children, and divorce. Since man is the provider of wife and family, he should be completely in charge and can even beat his wife if she is recalcitrant. He even goes further and requires of wives who happen to be more mature than their husbands to cloak their maturity and promote the husband's self-confidence by seeking his approval for all deeds and decisions although they are actually engineered through the wife's cunning and artfulness. Needless to say, this requirement attributes to women qualities in total contradiction to their presumed emotional, unreliable, and untrustworthy nature. This becomes even more interesting in view of his opinion regarding women's emotionality vis-à-vis that of men.

While Fadlallah argues that unilateral divorce is a male prerogative because women are emotional and may resort to it while in an irrational state, he glides over the fact that a male may divorce his wife three times and reunite with her without any formalities because he is liable to be irrational himself at the time only to regret the divorce afterward. To ensure this is not repeated indefinitely, the third divorce is to be irrevocable. Should the husband regret his action again, he is not to remarry her, unless the wife is married off to another in the meantime and then divorced or widowed. Thus, the question here is what possible "rational" reasons a man could have to divorce his wife thrice and still reunite with her. Or, is it possible that emotionality and irrationality are human traits that afflict both men and women? And if so, shouldn't the right of divorce be open to both men and women?

Moreover, while he admits that marriage and the building of families require maturity, and the parents' opinion in marriage is only advisory and not obligatory, he asserts that maturity has nothing to do with age, since a precocious nine-year-old girl may be able to make wise decisions in choosing her future husband. Yet, a virgin of legal age, according to him, must consult her father or male guardian before marriage out of deference to his position and because she is still naïve and inexperienced. Are we to understand, then, that such virgins are naturally less mature and experienced than their nine-year-old sisters? Thus once again like the previous ideologues, Fadlallah refuses to use his power of *ijtihad* to ameliorate the condition of women and, instead, resorts to rhetoric to implement traditional customs and beliefs such as marrying off "precocious" nine-year-old girls while requiring grown-up virgins to have the approval of their fathers before marriage since their choice could be based on emotional reasons.

Moreover, Fadlallah reassures women that marriage is not intended to enslave them but to ensure a harmonious life with their husbands. In fact, for a marriage to work, both parties have to make necessary sacrifices for the common good of the marital home. While this is commendable, one notes that all necessary sacrifices are to be made by women. Thus, wives should not abuse the rights given them by the Qur'an, such as refusing to do the housework, raising and nursing their children, or using their children as a lever against their husbands. Nor should they demand any material rewards for this work. Husbands, on the other hand, are merely requested not to abuse their authority over their wives, nor oppress them. One may then conclude that marriage is designed solely for the comfort and well-being of the husband, with women required to make all the sacrifices. How can marital harmony exist under such oppressive conditions, especially when they are compounded by constant threats of polygamy and temporary marriage? To make matters even worse, a wife should expect nothing in return for her services and sacrifices, even when her husband fails to perform his marital duties. Finally, although Fadlallah describes sex as a "primal hunger," a wife is *obliged* to satisfy on demand or be punished, whereas the husband may abstain sexually for periods of up to four months at a time with impunity. This is surprising, since a wife may be satiated only by her husband, while the latter may have recourse to three other wives and as many temporary wives as he can afford. Finally, while women are described as too emotional to testify or to divorce their husbands, this emotionality and wealth of feelings are suddenly forgotten when it comes to their own sexual satisfaction. They are, thus, suddenly rendered emotionless and essentially, asexual, while husbands are allowed access to polygamy and temporary marriage in order to avoid adultery, prostitution, and sexual license.

Finally, while he emphasizes the importance of hijab and segregation of the sexes because of man's uncontrollable animal instinct, he calls on men to discipline themselves not to love irrationally, or be controlled or influenced by their wives. The implication here is the admission of Fadlallah that men are able to control their instincts when it is in their interest to do so, especially when this leads to the further subjugation and isolation of women. Paradoxically, he also maintains that love emanates from the brain and is controlled by it according to the individual's value system. If so, then man's animal instinct is by definition controlled and does not require a veil to keep it from irrational behavior. Moreover, if love is controlled according to one's value system, then no good Muslim would be irrationally aroused by an unveiled woman. And last but not least, a prospective husband, while examining the body of his prospective wife, can, it seems, "freeze his feelings" for the duration.[54] Thus, if Fadlallah believes men to be so adept at controlling their emotions just like women in certain situations, how then does he justify the imposition of the hijab and the segregation of the sexes, the reason for the veil having just been nullified.

In conclusion, while the general trend of his discourse is that of modernization and liberalism, like the other ideologues studied here, one finds Fadlallah straddling modernism and traditionalism in matters relating to women. His adoption of traditionalism in such matters is practiced even when Islam lends itself to more liberal interpretation (*ijtihad*), especially when it is ambivalent about certain instances and quite clear in others relating to women's rights. Thus, although Fadlallah asserts women's rights to refuse household chores or even nurse their children, he goes on to require this of them for the well-being of the family and the husband, such sacrifices being divinely rewarded and considered a form of jihad. Yet, nowhere in his discourse does he advise men to relinquish any of their rights in the interest of equality or harmony, although he does ask them to be appreciative of virtuous wives without, of course, specifying how this appreciation is to be demonstrated. He even asks women to acquiesce to a small *mahr* during periods of economic decay to enable men to marry. Thus, although sacrifice is the essence of a harmonious marriage, Fadlallah requires it only of women and protects the men's rights to beat their wives in case of recalcitrance. The question to ask, then, is whether Fadlallah himself is equivocal in these matters, or is he wary of disagreeing with and, therefore, antagonizing the traditionalists. Or, is this his subtle way of deluding Shi'ite women into believing he is on their side, while, in fact, he is brainwashing them into a false sense of freedom and security to win their support in the social domain, and placate them in the face of the Western call for the liberation of women.

It would be apropos at this point to compare Fadlallah with the previous ideologues studied here and portray the similarities in their outlook concerning the status of women despite their other ideological differences. Although they all preach and encourage *ijtihad* in the interest of modernization and liberalization, women are left constrained by the same patriarchal conservative traditions the ideologues all criticize when related to other issues. Although they all insist on the sanctity of Scripture, a novel interpretation is invariably devised to justify their ideological programs,

but the sanctity is upheld in matters pertaining to women. In contradistinction, where the Scripture is crystal clear on the rights of women, it is
invariably glossed over and often flagrantly contradicted without any attempt at justification of such unabashed disregard of Qur'anic instructions. And, finally, when a liberal interpretation of a verse is possible with
regard to women's issues, the most conservative and strict alternative is
adopted instead. The only difference between the ideologues in these matters is the style and rhetoric used to convey the same conservative and
traditional message. In this, Fadlallah supercedes all of his colleagues, even
al-Turabi, in his art of persuasion and the ability to camouflage his conservative gender discourse with an attractive garb of modern liberalism.

Chapter 11

✳

Conclusion

> Men and women live on a stage, on which they act out their assigned roles, equal in importance. The play cannot go on without both kinds of performers. Neither of them "contributes" more or less to the whole; neither is marginal or dispensable. But the stage is set, conceived, painted, defined by men. Men have written the play, have directed the show, interpreted the meanings of the action. They have assigned themselves the most interesting, most heroic parts, giving women the supporting roles.
>
> Gerda Lerner, *The Creation of Patriarchy*

All of the ideologues studied here agree on the central role the patriarchal family plays in creating the ideal integrated Islamic *ummah*. They also consider unsatisfied male sexuality to be a social danger and female seductive powers as conducive to *fitnah* or social anarchy and chaos. Due to physical and psychological gender differences, they all envision a sexually segregated society, as ordained by the Qur'an and the Shari'ah, as enhancing productivity. Men are viewed as having an insatiable sexual desire aroused by the sight, smell, or voice of a woman, thereby distracting and diverting their energy from productive endeavors to wasteful sexual activity. This is best curtailed through gender segregation. Women, on the other hand, are seen as sexual beings with no social role outside the confines of the marital home, unless, of course, it meets with the interest and approval of the husband.

While fundamentalists differ on methodology, they all agree on the pivotal role the traditional Muslim family plays in bringing the ideal Islamic state to fruition. Thus, rather than speaking of the Iranian, Egyptian, Sudanese, Tunisian, Pakistani, or Lebanese woman, each having her own specificities, they consistently speak of the ideal "Muslim woman" transcending all forms of particularism. Their ideal order of freedom, lawfulness, social equality, economic justice, affluence, unity, and victory is con-structed on the basis of patriarchy where women are veiled and excluded from the public sphere. Yet, they perceive women as the embodiment of cultural identity and the custodians of cultural values. Despite the vast differences in their religio-political and economic ideologies, they agree with conservative Muslim thinkers and ulema in emphasizing woman's natural and God-given domesticity, the special status awarded her in Islam, and the calamity that may befall Muslim society should she give up her traditional role as loving wife and nurturing mother whose jihad is the protection of Islamic values. Her conduct, domesticity, and veil are vital for the survival of the Islamic way of life without which culture, religion, and morality will crumble.

Three common elements can be identified in the fundamentalist dis-course on women: domesticity as women's primary role; gender differ-ences, where the physical, physiological, biological, and psychological dif-ferences between the sexes are viewed as universal and immutable in the social and intellectual domains, dictating parallel differences in the respec-tive roles of husband and wife, both, however, remaining spiritually equal; and the element of danger inherent in women's nature. Women, they all claim, are not inferior to men, but different, created for a special function in life. Liberation, therefore, should not entail the acquisition of masculine characteristics but should afford women the opportunity to fulfill the des-tiny for which they were created. All these ideologues share the belief that men are totally helpless and highly susceptible to female lures and se-ductive powers, such that the mere presence of a woman can undermine a man's better judgment, concentration, productivity, and rationality. Women thus encapsulate at once the qualities of the benevolent, nurturing mother and wife and the destructive sexual carnivore.

Men, they all agree, are physically stronger and, therefore, fit for the heavy work of the public sphere; they enjoy a higher mental acuity, mak-ing them more suitable for the rational judgments required in decision-making positions; and they are the providers and protectors of women. Men's lust is primordial and aggressive and, if left unchecked, will be the source of their destruction and downfall. Therefore, to maintain order and guarantee the sanctity of the family, their sex drive must be controlled by removing the source of temptation. This is most efficiently solved by veil-ing and segregating women. Women, on the other hand, are incapacitated by menstruation, childbearing, and child rearing, making it difficult for them to work in the public sphere, and they are, therefore, necessarily con-fined to the home. Moreover, due to their emotional nature and lack of rational judgment, women are best suited for housework and the support of their husbands. Due to the superior mental acuity of men, God chose them for the roles of prophecy, religious leadership, judgeship, giving evidence in court, and voting. Being the providers and protectors of women makes them eligible for larger shares of inheritance, unilateral divorce or repudiation, and the total obedience of their wives. However, when it comes to sexual behavior, even though the wife is the emotional partner, she is able to control her passion, unlike her husband, despite his superior rational powers. Women's delicate and fragile physical constitution and mental inferiority are compensated for by their emotional strength, which, although unsuitable for rational work, allows them to raise and rear children and tend to men's emotional and sexual needs.

Male sexual needs, including variety, are recognized by all the ideologues studied here and by Islamic law itself in granting men permission to marry four women simultaneously, the right of unilateral divorce, *mut'ah* marriage (Shi'ites), the ban on wives leaving home without the husband's approval, and the right of husbands to have sex on demand, even during menstruation, prayer, or fasting. While in theory women may abstain from sex while on pilgrimage, fasting, praying, nursing, or menstruating, the fundamentalist discourse specifies leeway at such times through which men may satisfy their needs—sodomy and absolution from the duties of prayer, fasting, or pilgrimage. The fundamentalist conception of women seems to identify their sexuality with their whole being, where woman, the human being, is conflated with woman the object, to be owned and jealously controlled. Thus, veiling becomes an expression of the concealment of sexuality itself, and women become Janus-faced: They are the personification of sexuality, love, desire, sexual fulfillment, procreation, and motherhood, and, simultaneously, the embodiment of shame, seductiveness, deceit, infidelity, *fitnah*, and anarchy. They are also viewed as weak in moral judgment, deficient in cognitive capacity, and economically dependent on men, yet they are in charge of the household budget and the education of children as steadfast Muslims, and they are responsible for providing their husbands with a tranquil and relaxing home atmosphere despite their emotionality and erratic behavior. They are chaste in their sexual desires, paragons of virtue, yet susceptible to corruption and the cause of man's distraction, as well as the possible destruction of the whole society.

However, sexuality, as such, has a number of positive functions in Muslim society. It serves as an instrument of procreation to swell the number of Muslim believers and maintain social order; it affords the Muslim a "foretaste of the delights secured for men in Paradise,"[1] thus inciting them to follow the commandments of God on earth in anticipation of what is to come; and, finally, sexual gratification is good in itself to sharpen man's intellect. Thus, the satisfaction of male sexual demands ensures a well-ordered, efficient, and productive society.

Family is considered by all fundamentalists to be the nucleus of civilization. It is the cradle of human society, providing a healthy and secure environment for parents and children. It is the guardian of human sexual desires, channeling them into a wholesome, socially adjusted activity. It is further the "breeding ground" for such virtues as love, kindness, and mercy and the ultimate refuge against one's troubles, be they internal or external. Men, in the fundamentalist message, seem to be provided with a divine mandate to exercise authority over the family, with little interference or restraint, and with total obedience and submission of wives and children. With the wife responsible for the happiness and well-being of all members of the family, the home becomes a private niche for men, removed from the encroachments of the external world of work, where they may relax and savor their own authority. In short, while women's lives are bound by the unilateral dimensions of the family, men's lives transcend this to extend into the social, political, economic, or any other field they may choose, in addition to being the effective guardians of women, who are reduced to total dependence on their husbands.

This preoccupation with the "Muslim woman," her sexuality, moral conduct, and seductive powers, has been translated into institutions, policies, legal practices, personal status codes, and sexual treatises to determine women's role in society. As the symbol of Islamic social order and cultural continuity, female sexuality becomes the subject of restraint and discipline, differentiating between Muslim and non-Muslim. Sunni and Shi'ite extremists, moderates or radicals, have agreed on the Islamic order that governs women and their role in society. While various authors may differ in certain infinitesimal details, such as the style or thickness of the *hijab*, educational limitations, details of inheritance, or testimony in court, they remain in total agreement on the Islamic fundamentalist vision of women and gender relations. In other words, they *all* agree on the minimum degree of constraint but differ in the excesses of imposed strictures—as in the matter of the veil that is required by all with variations in prescribed color, fabric, thickness, and the areas of the body to be covered. While some, like al-Mawdudi and al-Turabi, require the face and hands to be covered, others do not. In the matter of testimony in court, *all* limit this to certain cases in which two women are required to testify, whereas one man suffices, yet Khomeini bans women from testifying altogether unless their testimony is corroborated by that of a man. *All* agree that a woman inherits half the share of a man, but Khomeini forbids women to inherit any land, trees, or buildings. In matters of education, they again all agree that women's education be kept to a minimum and limited to subjects that enhance their domestic role unless, of course, it is in the interest of society for them to pursue higher education.

From a spiritual perspective, men and women are viewed as equal, promised identical rewards for their good deeds, and simultaneously warned against any misdeeds that will bring about similar punishments. All religious duties are required of both sexes, except for the jihad. As to material matters, the male is exclusively responsible for his family and womenfolk.

The mixing of the sexes should be controlled and limited to "necessity" and for "logical reasons." In the home, the woman must never be alone with any man who is not a *mahram*, other than her husband. She may leave the house for urgent business, but only after securing her husband's permission, modestly dressed, and veiled. Segregation of the sexes should start at puberty in school, at work, and in public life. The fundamentalists place paramount importance on the veil, which they believe to be the first and most basic criterion in guiding women onto the right path of Islam and ensuring social order and harmony. The veil serves to protect women from the stares of strange men and preserve the husband's exclusive right to see his wife unveiled and enjoy her charms. It also protects men from the wiles and seductive powers of women. Male sexual conduct is not dependent upon that of women and remains arbitrary according to arousal, sexual gratification being required on demand. Thus, female sexuality is seen as having a twofold function: the satisfaction of male sexual needs and the reproduction of the family.

Fundamentalists' emphasis on human sexuality—male and female—clarifies the importance they attribute to marriage in general: marriage is seen as the nucleus of society that assures the physical fulfillment of natural desires, provides a healthy channel for sexual and psychological needs, nurtures society through its progeny, and promotes social harmony and solidarity. Celibacy is, therefore, a deviation, contrary to the order of the universe as created by God, and endangers the goals of life on earth. Thus, a Muslim girl should be brought up and educated in preparation for the roles of wife and mother, any other education being superfluous if not harmful. Legally, "Marriage is a contract of exchange with defined terms and unified legal effects."[2] It consists of an offer made by the woman or her father, the acceptance of the man, and a *mahr* [dower] specified by the woman or her guardian and paid by the husband. This is a sum of money or other valuables the husband is to pay the bride, either at marriage, at its end, or at any time she requests. The wife may refuse any sexual relationship until her dower is paid in full. In certain cases, the absence of the dower in the contract will not void it but entitles the bride to a special type of *mahr* specified according to her social class.

Marriage is considered by all ideologues as a central institution and a duty of every Muslim, as specified in the Qur'an (51:49) and the Hadith of the Prophet ("If a person marries, he has fulfilled half the religion"). Consequently, if a man does marry, he automatically deprives another woman of marriage, making her, thereby, subject to temptation. While a Muslim male may marry a Jew or a Christian, a Muslim woman must marry only a Muslim. This is dictated by the fact that Islam is a patriarchal religion and children are named after their fathers and inherit from them. Thus, if married to a Christian, a Muslim woman will be contributing to a Christian family with Christian progeny. While this is practiced and taught by all, it is not based on Qur'anic texts but is imposed by Islamic jurisprudence. With marriage seen as a duty, any extramarital sexual activity is defined as adultery and severely punished. Again, while *all* agree that the Islamic penal code should be applied, they differ in the severity of sentencing: lashing both offenders up to one hundred lashes, as specified in the Qur'an, or stoning to death, which is nonexistent in the Scripture.

Infidelity is not permitted in Islam, but polygamy, *mut'ah* (Shi'ites), and divorce are mechanisms through which a man may satisfy his sexual needs. Polygamy is defended as a means of safeguarding the family, since it does not necessitate divorce of the first wife. Moreover, it is necessary in cases where the wife is sterile, sick, menopausal, or sexually frigid. In times of war, it helps maintain equilibrium between the abundance of women and shortage of men and ensures that orphan girls neither go unmarried nor risk the possible abuse of the management of their property. The husband, however, has to ensure fair and equal treatment of all four wives, except, of course, in matters of love, which is beyond his control and impossible to balance. While all admit that polygamy may be abused and the conditions necessitating it are often absent, they agree neither to abolish it nor to restrict it, leaving any problem or impurity to be solved spontaneously in due time. Polygamy is, thus, seen to be beneficial for women, to be exercised out of compassion for them, and out of a sense of socioeconomic duty. Moreover, motherhood is considered a natural instinct of women, the satisfaction of which provides them with a sense of fulfillment and identity, impossible outside the bounds of marriage, especially during times of need and shortage of men. The Shi'ite fundamentalists argue forcefully for the implementation of *mut'ah* marriage as well, whose uses in society are the same as those of polygamy, in addition to the role it plays in bringing the practices of prostitution and adultery to an end. It would, thus, provide a legal atmosphere or environment for teenagers' first experience with sex; satisfy those engaged to marry who cannot contain their desires; and provide a legal shelter for the sexes to mix on the "spiritual" level. The *mut'ah* marriage, however, requires no witnesses, no clergy, and no registration.

While they all agree that divorce is necessary for the happiness of the couple and the harmony of the family, the man has the sole right to repudiate his wife at any time without necessarily informing her until the end of her *'iddah*, at which time he may extend the period further by having intercourse with her. While all Sunni fundamentalists agree that an irrevocable divorce pronounced in one sitting is a *bid'ah* [innovation or heresy] and not allowed in Islam, they still condone and legalize it. A woman, on the other hand, may not repudiate her husband unless this is stipulated in the marriage contract (*'ismat*, according to the Sunnis, and *tafwid*, according to the Shi'ites). She may, however, divorce him by refunding the dower he gave her in marriage or by going to court, the latter being limited to very few and difficult conditions. Again, while they all admit the abuse of repudiation and the prevention of women from divorce, except in limited cases, they oppose any regulations and restrictions to safeguard women's rights, including the minutest obligation, such as the registration of divorce. Finally, although there are certain differences in detail among the different schools of jurisprudence, they *all* agree on the lucid Qur'anic regulations stipulated in suras 2:227–33, 236–7, 241; 4:20–4; 65:1 ff.

Fundamentalist discourse has also devoted a great deal of attention to women's education. The discussion centers mainly around the content, purpose, and utility of that education. All are in agreement that girls should be educated but segregated from boys and taught by female teachers. They also agree that girls should follow a different curriculum from that of boys, due to their natural sexual differences. While no subject of study is forbidden to women in Islam, except the study of law, which might lead to judgeship, the "welfare" of society poses limits to absolute freedom of selection. Therefore, a minimal education in general is suggested, and in case of specialization, the fields to be chosen should be those in accord with the character and role of women in society, lest they sacrifice their "femininity" and "sensitivity."

A Muslim wife has a biological need to create a home and nurture her children. Her marriage will, therefore, be more secure if she has ample time to care for her children and husband and focus on her housework rather than seek self-fulfillment and additional income from outside work. Fulfillment through her interests and talents and the pursuit of a career would lead to the emulation of men in tactics and attitudes of competitiveness and aggressiveness, and working side by side with men would lead to temptation, seduction, and moral depravity. Qutb calls working women the "third sex," and Ghazali considers competing with men for work a sin. A woman's progress is not to be measured by achievements in the public sphere but in the development of her "humanity": "the education of her mind, the elevation of her character, and the purification of her heart and nature."[3] They all claim that the West has capitalized on female sexuality, beauty, and femininity for commercial gains. "Religion does not forbid woman to work, but it does forbid her to flee from her natural place without excuse."[4] To work outside is acceptable only if there is a real, substantiated need, and then only if she is dressed properly and behaves according to Islamic rules and propriety, and if she is ready to give up her work at the earliest possibility or whenever her husband dictates. For the social anarchy generated by her work outside the home is most keenly felt at home by playing havoc with man's *qiwamah*. Moreover, the institution of the family itself may suffer, as working women would necessarily shirk their religious and social duties, postpone getting married, and avoid pregnancy. Men, in turn, would be drawn into illegitimate sexual activities, being surrounded by beautiful unveiled women.

All fundamentalists agree that Islam forbids women access to positions of public leadership. This is based on a hadith in Bukhari stating that "a people who have appointed a woman to be their ruler will not thrive." They also oppose the enfranchisement of women, since to participate in elections implies running for them as well. Therefore, "The end disqualifies the means."[5] This is again based on what may be called "ideology of domesticity" or "ideology of gender differences," where the physical, physiological, biological, and psychological differences are translated into permanent differences defining their social and intellectual capacities. One such difference that disqualifies women from public office is their actual inferiority brought on by the emotion/reason dichotomy. Moreover, their physical attractiveness to men imposes a negative influence on the latter's productivity.

Finally, *all* fundamentalists agree that ritual duties are exclusive to men. Thus, women's visits to mosques are discouraged; participation in joint Friday prayers is also discouraged, and if women do participate, they are to be positioned behind the men or separated from them in some manner, and they should leave through different exits. The special pilgrimage garment is worn exclusively by men. Due to their menstruation and childbirth, women are considered "impure" and therefore not permitted to perform any of the cultic duties. They are even relieved of daily prayers and fasting during those periods. But here again these restrictions are regarded as "privileges" bestowed upon women by Islam over men. However, these same privileges/duties may be circumvented to satisfy their husbands' sexual needs.

It is significant to note that none of the fundamentalist ideologues discussed here imposes the same strictures on rural women, who labor in the fields outside their homes, away from their children and domestic duties. In fact, they are not even required to be veiled or segregated but work side by side with "strange" men in the fields. Fundamentalist discourse is, thus, limited to the urban centers. In fact, Khomeini goes to the extreme of proclaiming that his strictures are to be imposed only on urban women and not on the "virtuous rural" women. This phenomenon may be due to a number of factors: Urban women compete with men in the public arena for the same positions, in contrast to rural women, who help and support men in the fields rather than compete with them. The economic independence of urban women would deter early marriage. Rural women, on the other hand, due to the nature of their work and their need to advance in that domain, tend to marry at an early age. Moreover, rural children are often in the field close to their mothers, helping in the work, while urban children are neglected at home. Finally, the absence of *hijab* and segregation in rural areas is due to the same socioeconomic and political factors that caused its imposition in the cities in the first place, religion having nothing to do with it.

In conclusion, it becomes evident that all the fundamentalist thinkers studied here, despite differences in sex, political ideology, nationality, school of jurisprudence, sect, and methodology (radical or moderate), agree on one single image of the "Muslim woman," albeit with minor differences in rhetoric and the severity of imposed constraints. What seems to be at stake is not the role of women per se but the validity of Islam as the final revelation of God to man and its role as the panacea for all the socioeconomic and political ills of the Muslim world. The only available and visible means to implement it other than revolution and jihad is the implementation of the Islamic family law in its strictest and most striking fashion.

· · ·

Of all Islamic sources, fundamentalists rely on the Qur'an itself as being of primary importance and the Sunna and Hadith next, but only insofar as they are in agreement with the Qur'anic text. Should there be any variation, the Qur'an is, invariably, to take precedence.[6] Consequently, while they all support the authority of the Sunna and the authenticity of the Hadith, in general, they staunchly defend the necessity of reinterpretation of this corpus. This is due to the difficulty in demonstrating its infalliblity and the need to reintroduce Islamic law in *relevant* form to modern Muslim society. By doing this, the door of *ijtihad* is thrown wide open once again in a pragmatic approach to interpret and understand Islam in the milieu of the twentieth century and its exigencies. However, this is not to take place on the grounds of social necessity alone. Such interpretation must be based on a juristic foundation and supported by such principles as can be endorsed explicitly or implicitly by the divine will.[7] The will of God, however, is never as rigid and inflexible as the traditionalist conservatives have maintained, but proclaims general principles that lend themselves to different interpretations and applications according to the circumstances of the time. This is the doctrine of *taghayyur al-ahkam bitaghayyuri al-azman* [rules change with changing times].[8] Thus, the second caliph, 'Umar Ibn al-Khattab, did not abide by the Qur'an or Sunna when he refused to give a portion of *zakat* to *mu'allafat al-qulub* [those whose hearts were to be won/reconciled] (9:60), though it is required by the Qur'an and was practiced by the Prophet himself in certain circumstances.[9] He also refused to cut off the hands of thieves who stole out of hunger, and he abolished the custom of *mut'ah* marriage.

Fundamentalists themselves have practiced *ijtihad* and introduced such revolutionary measures as legalizing the right to revolt against an existing government (Qutb, Khomeini, al-Turabi); the establishment of *wilayat al-faqih* by Khomeini; the introduction of banking and the accruing of interest as "transactions of trade" and "gain of profit"; the acceptance of the

principle of nation-states and the principle of "republic" in contradistinction to the concept of *ummah*; and permitting fathers to marry off
their daughters at birth, or while still minors, transcending thereby the
Qur'anic precept of bridal consent. They even preached and, at times, actually practiced the principles of *taqiyyah* and *maslahah* and the dictum *al-
darurat tubih al-mahzurat* [necessities render forbidden things permis-
sible] to circumvent any obstacles that might be posed by the Scripture.
Taqiyyah [to act contrary to one's principles of faith for expediency] is
practiced by all fundamentalists.[10]

Fundamentalist thinkers, as mentioned earlier, utilize all that Islam can
provide for dynamism and flexibility to meet the needs of the times, making thereby interpretation and adjustment to present conditions smooth
and fairly simple. In addition, classical jurisprudence itself categorizes
Qur'anic injunctions into imperative (*fard*), recommended (*mandub*), permissible (*mubah*), reprehensible (*makruh*), and forbidden (*haram*), giving
itself room to adapt to circumstances. When the need arises, it resorts to
the principle of gradual modification of behavior toward perfection, a practice used extensively in *tafsir* [interpretation], such as the prohibition of
alcoholic intoxication and the ritual of fasting. Yet, none of these methods
was applied to any matter relating to gender relations or women's rights,[11]
claiming such relations to be God's divine will and, therefore, not subject
to change. Thus, the enigmatic sura 4:34 enjoining men to admonish their
wives in cases of *nushuz* [recalcitrance], taken literally by the fundamentalists, is to be understood, according to Siddique, as referring only to
sexual misbehavior, and it must, therefore, be interpreted as "Your right on
them is that they not let men whom you like not come to your beds. If they
do such, beat them lightly . . . not to leave a mark."[12] This becomes even
more evident in view of the fact that this is the only reference to any violence against women, while there is an abundance of verses in the Qur'an
prohibiting any harsh treatment of women, even when the husband dis-
likes his wife intensely (4:19). Moreover, in the final verses in the Qur'an
on sexual immorality and adultery, sura 24, the husband, rather than beating his wife, as in sura 4:34, is only enjoined to swear that his wife has been
unfaithful and invoke the curse of God on himself if he is lying. Finally, the
existence of differences among the schools of jurisprudence on the matter
of marriage clearly indicates that the Qur'anic injunctions are open to
radically different interpretations, even by individuals who share the same
outlook and vision. Yet, all fundamentalists have been careful to interpret
all references to women in the Qur'an in such a manner as to impose more

social constraints and to further subordinate them to their husbands. More-over, no attempt has been made to reconcile the rights granted women in Islam, such as the management of their property and the right to work, with other Shari'ah regulations that seem in direct conflict with them, such as the right of the husband to keep his wife at home isolated from the external world.

Thus, despite the radicalism of the fundamentalist ideologues, their in-novations, the different methods of interpretation at their disposal, and the ambiguous nature of the Qur'anic verses regarding women and their re-sultant amenability to different interpretations, the ideologues have per-sisted in emulating the traditional worldview of gender relations. And de-spite their eagerness for Islam to be the panacea for all social, economic, and political ills, they categorically have refused to introduce the minutest of changes. In fact, while retaining their rigidity in removing any of the constraints imposed on women over the centuries, they have permitted more constraints to be imposed in flagrant contradiction of Qur'anic in-junctions. Thus, in their zeal to keep women out of the political arena, they rely on one hadith, narrated by Abu Bakra and reported by Bukhari, that any community ruled by a woman will never succeed. Not only is this a hadith whose fallacy has been demonstrated, but Abu Bakra himself is re-ported to have been punished in public for bearing false witness, thus go-ing against the Qur'anic injunction of such practice (24:4). Fadlallah and Ghannoushi have even tried to give this hadith a different interpretation to rid it of its significance. Yet, like the others, both continued to oppose women's political leadership, even though this hadith was discredited and all the great women of history were cited in rebuttal. They have also by-passed Ibn Jarir al-Tabari's permission to allow women the position of judgeship in all matters, since they are allowed to pronounce religious *fatwa*.[13]

This is further corroborated by the abundance of interpretations per-taining to the veil. It is clear that the injunctions in the Qur'an and the references in the Hadith concern only the Prophet's wives (23:59), while modesty is required of both men and women (24:30–1). In fact, the refer-ences in the Hadith reflect men and women conversing, working, and fighting alongside each other for Islam.[14] Moreover, only three Qur'anic verses refer specifically to the veil. Suras 33:32–3 and 33:53 refer specifi-cally to the wives of the Prophet; only sura 24:31 refers to all Muslim women. In fact, the latter implies mixed gatherings, since women are asked to lower their gaze and draw their garments over their bosoms with no mention of the veil. Furthermore, the restrictions quoted are not meant to confine women to the house in isolation, as traditionalists and fundamentalists claim, nor to impose a special type of veil. The *jilbab* and *khimar* mentioned in the text, while their etymologies are still uncertain, probably refer to the fashion of the day, rather than any habit imposed by the Qur'an. Women were asked not to exhibit their *zinah* and sexual charms. *Zinah*, another controversial term, denotes adornments or ornaments external to the body. The term also may be used metaphorically, but it never refers to any specific bodily part, nor does it define the area it adorns. Such ambiguities have generated confusion and multiple interpretations.[15]

In fact, it was not until the thirteenth century that al-Bayda, a Persian Muslim and one of the most famous commentators on the Qur'an, allowed the social customs of his time to influence the interpretation of 24:31 on the veil. It was he who arbitrarily decided that "ornaments" referred to the face and hands.[16] My guess is that women at the time of the Prophet must have worn ornaments on body parts other than limbs and face. The veracity of such an assumption may be further substantiated by the prohibition on women stamping their feet, to avoid revealing hidden jewelry that might inflame men's imagination. Also, the fashion of dress at the time is still not clear, which makes such current strictures in dress uncalled for and segregation of the sexes totally contrary to the Qur'an. Moreover, al-Jabir reports the hadith "If one of you sees a woman he desires, let him go home [that is, to his wife], for that will satisfy and control him"; and single men are to "abstain and be chaste until God's generosity satisfies them." The implication here, of course, is that veiling and segregation, to avoid *fitnah*, were neither imposed by the Prophet nor practiced at his time.[17] The discourse on the veil becomes even more complex when one realizes it is imposed only on urban women, while their rural sisters were neither segregated nor veiled. In fact, their role in the rural economy itself makes one wonder about the fundamentalist moral sanctions imposed on urban women in the name of Islam. Qur'anic injunctions never distinguish between the urban and the rural populace; they are universal, addressing all believers, males, and females alike.

Muslim ulema throughout history, as well as the fundamentalist ideologues themselves, not only have chosen the most constraining interpretations of verses concerning women and have refused to modify them to fit the times, but they go on to disregard either part or all of other verses that are quite specific in the rights they accord women. They are also in tacit agreement with Muslims who engineer such radical changes as the total deprivation of daughters of their inheritance, or the use of the institution of *waqf* for their own purposes.[18] They further refuse to exercise their right in interpreting ambiguous verses to the benefit of women. The Qur'an makes it crystal clear that men and women are equal before God (49:10) and provide protection and warmth to each other (3:195; 4:124; 9:71–2; 16:97; 23:35), just as they are equal in rewards for practicing Islamic principles (33:35; 16:97). They are also equal in creation (4:1), in seeking knowledge (96:1–4), voting (60:12), receiving and dispensing inheritance (4:7), and before God (49:10). Yet, Muslim societies, ulema, and fundamentalist ideologues withhold such equality in practice, although some do admit the "spiritual" equality of the sexes.

Men have also been given the authority to prevent women from fulfilling their religious duties to gratify their own physical pleasures, on the basis of local custom, Hadith literature, and two important Qur'anic passages (4:34 and 2:288). However, these same verses may very well be interpreted in favor of women,[19] in agreement with all other verses, which favor equality at all levels (22:41; 2:229) as well as the hadith that declares "All people are equal, as equal as the teeth of a comb. There is no claim of merit of an Arab over a non-Arab, or of a white over a black person, or of a male over a female. Only God-fearing people merit a preference with God."[20] In fact, the obedience the Qur'an teaches, as Siddique argues, is toward God and not other men, as made clear in sura 33:35, where "devoutly obedient" refers to God just as Muslim men are described as "devoutly obedient" to God. This is further evidenced by the pledge of allegiance God commanded the Prophet to extract from women. No reference in this verse, either explicitly or implicitly, is made to women's obedience to their husbands. Rather, it draws attention to the independence of women and their ability to make independent decisions and actions. Obedience in this oath, administered in 557 A.D. at the conquest of Mecca, is directed at the Prophet himself. Thus, the only three clear prescriptions of obedience in the Qur'an are to God, the Prophet, and those in authority or rulers.[21]

Moreover, while there is only one verse in the Qur'an where wife beating is mentioned, all other exhortations extol love and mercy. Thus Bukhari quotes the Prophet as having said, "Don't beat your wife as if she is a slave. Would you beat her and then at the end of the day have sex with her?" And Abu Daoud, in his *Sunan*, narrates that the Prophet replied to a question about the rights of women: "Feed and clothe them, as well as you do yourself, and do not beat them, and do not abuse them." Despite such evidence in both Qur'an and Hadith emphasizing fair treatment of women and prohibiting physical abuse, none of the ideologues prohibit the beating of women, and they *all* agree on the total submission of wives to their husbands as they would to God.

Furthermore, fundamentalists stress that the education of women be kept to a minimum, yet, all through history, wealthy women received their education at home, and the Hanbali jurist, the forerunner of contemporary fundamentalist ideologues (d. 1328), listed two women among his teachers. Also some female descendants of the Prophet, such as his granddaughter Zaynab and great great . . . granddaughter Nafisah, are recognized as women of learning and wisdom, and the Prophet himself urged all Muslims, males and females, to learn (35:28).[22]

Moreover, although divorce was denounced by the Qur'an and the Prophet, who said, "Marry and do not divorce your wives, for divorce causes God's throne to tremble," yet divorce is extremely common and fully supported by all the ideologues, who categorically refuse to impose any strictures to discourage it.[23] Besides, Hafiz Ibn Qayyim (a disciple of Ibn Taymiyyah) rejected the irrevocable triple divorce, and the Sunni jurists, including Imams Abu Hanifa and Malik Ibn Anas, described it as *talaq bid'ah* [unorthodox or heretical divorce] and considered it the "most arbitrary and non-Qur'anic (2:229–31) form of divorce." Yet, none of the Sunni ideologues attempt to discredit its practice. And finally, despite the hadith narrated by Nasa'i, according to which the Prophet, when told of such a divorce, stood up in anger and said, "You make fun of Allah's book and I am still here among you," and despite the fact that *bid'ah* is considered a deadly sin in orthodox Islam, since it is perceived not only as an error but as a crime for having strayed from the straight path of Islam (*al-tariq al-mustaqim*) and challenges the very existence of order based on consensus, none of the Sunni fundamentalist ideologues have prohibited it.

On the question of the *mahr*, the Qur'an itself is completely clear, and Shaykh Khalil, the most prominent Maliki jurist, sees the relationship of the *mahr* to marriage as a transaction: "In the market one buys merchandise, in marriage the husband buys the genital *arvum mulieris*. As in any other bargain and sale, only useful and ritually clean objects may be given in dower." Also, the most prominent Shi'ite jurist, Muhaqqiq al-Hilli, defines marriage as "a contract whose object is that of dominion over the vagina, without the right of its possession,"[24] and fundamentalists themselves allow men to dispatch their nonvirgin wives, without their *mahr*, as damaged goods. Yet, until the eighteenth and nineteenth centuries, virginity, in Syria, was irrelevant to the validity of marriage. Khayr al-Din Ibn Ahmad al-Ramli, in his *Kitab al-fatawa al-kubra li-naf' al-birriyyah* [The book of major juridical opinions for the benefit of humanity], published in 1856–57, argues against the condition of testing virginity, since the hymen had nothing to do with the legal consummation of marriage, and, therefore, the only way to dissolve it would be through divorce with all its concomitant obligations. Moreover, he questions the ability of the groom to ascertain virginity, since its loss could have been incurred by sickness, accident, or any number of means; it is, therefore, the woman's testimony that should take precedence.[25] It is thus clear from the preceding that the only requirement of a Muslim wife is sexual pleasure and happiness at home. Yet, all the ideologues studied here deemphasized the importance of *mahr*, agreed on a symbolic sum, and encouraged women to accept it,[26] in flagrant disregard of the Qur'anic injunction and interpretations of renowned jurists of earlier centuries.

Finally, although there is ample room to interpret the verse on polygamy (al-Tabari already in the ninth century gives five different interpretations) as preferring monogamy, fundamentalists and traditionalists refuse to even consider this possibility. Moreover, this verse (4:3), in the context of the verses on orphans revealed after the Battle of Uhud (4:2–3), leads one to the understanding that three or four orphans are to be married to ensure fair treatment of their property. What is also fascinating is that all the ideologues studied here, despite their staunch support of polygamy and their refusal to even make it conditional, were all monogamous with the exception of Qutb, who remained single all his life.[27]

Fundamentalists have also committed serious errors of omission in their presentation of Hadith literature, overlooking those hadith that promote gender equality and allow both sexes to pray in mosques. Thus women actually conducted prayers in mosques at the time of the Prophet, as affirmed by the hadith "Do not prevent women from the houses of God."[28] Yet, traditionalists and fundamentalists seem to have followed al-Ghazali (d. 1111) instead, who recommended that women not go to mosques, in explicit contradiction of the clear commands of the Prophet and, in so doing, institutionalizing an uncalled-for distinction between the religious duties of men and women. Hence, Friday prayer is considered an obligation for mature, sane, and free males only, confining women to the same category as the slave, child, and insane,[29] in direct contradiction of the Qur'an itself.

Further, no obstacle can be found anywhere that prevents women from leading men. Women of the first community went to war and participated in all activities including listening in on the Prophet's discourse. They were active interlocutors in matters pertaining to the faith and other matters. The Prophet granted women the right to speak on all matters and responded to all their queries and comments and went as far as to schedule extra sessions to instruct them on Qur'anic matters so they could catch up with the men. In addition, all verses, beginning with sura 33:35, were addressed to both male and female believers, after women expressed their concern that the verses were directed only at men. Both Abu Bakr and 'Umar, just before their deaths, entrusted their daughters, Aisha and Hafsah, not their sons, with the important responsibilities of distributing their property, disposing of public funds, and the keeping of the first copy of the Qur'an. 'Umar himself also appointed women to serve as officials (*muhtasib*) in the market of Medina, while Hanbali jurisprudence allows women to serve as judges. And Mernissi mentions fifteen or so queens who, though ignored by historians, did indeed rule over extensive empires, had coins minted, and Friday prayers recited in their names. Furthermore, every human being in Islam is *mukallaf* [charged with the realization of divine will], thus personalizing responsibility and denying the possibility of vicarious accountability, and emptying thereby the claims of fundamentalists that a husband may prevent his wife from fulfilling her religious duties (4:103; 39:41). Finally, if the Prophet himself is not to act as a "warder," should the husband do so over his wife (3:195)?

It thus becomes obvious that fundamentalist thinkers, like traditionalists, not only imposed tasks upon a Muslim wife over and above the call of duty, including motherhood, but opted for the strictest possible interpretation of isolated Qur'anic verses or hadiths. Thus, not only did they disregard clear commandments in favor of women, but they actually disobeyed them. Consequently, they interpreted Qur'anic texts against their actual context as in the injunctions of veiling, rules on adultery, nursing, housework, childbearing and child rearing, and inheritance; and refused to accord women their rights in such cases as compensation for domestic work and childrearing. The Qur'an seems to have been followed only to buttress men's position; any evidence for the support of women's rights and privileges has either been glossed over or flagrantly disobeyed. Thus, despite this admitted ambiguity and/or flexibility in the interpretation of Qur'anic text and Sunna, the fundamentalist thinkers under study have shown not only rigidity in their interpretation but selectivity of evidence as well to justify a strict patriarchal reading of the text.

The selectivity and arbitrariness of these ideologues is further exemplified by their engagement in a double role of coercion and co-optation of women. Thus, after having repealed the Iranian Family Protection Law in 1986 as being un-Islamic, the Majlis [parliament], in the same year, passed a twelve-article law on marriage and divorce limiting the privileges given men at the inception of the revolution. Divorced women were given the rights to alimony and a share of the property acquired during marriage. In 1992, the Council of Expediency approved a bill allowing unfairly divorced women to be compensated for services rendered during the course of the marriage. The twelfth article of the 1986 law reinstated the provision of the Family Protection Law to grant the wife the right of divorce in case of a multiple marriage.[30] Al-Mawdudi, after vehemently opposing women's participation in politics and arguing for their incompetence, promptly reversed himself and fully supported the candidacy of Fatimah al-Jinnah for the presidency. Khomeini, after decrying voting rights for women as un-Islamic in 1963, went on to solicit their votes for an Islamic republic, declaring the vote "religious, Islamic, and a divine duty." Al-Ghannoushi changed his stand on the segregation of women and their minimal education when he discovered the importance of the role they could play for the Islamic Tendency Movement in the realms of public relations and the propagation of the Islamic message. Al-Turabi frequently changed his stance on the role of women, according to what he described as *maslahah* for the Muslim community. The private life of Zaynab al-Ghazali differed drastically from her public stand on the role of women in society and at home. Qutb called working women the "third sex," yet allowed them to work in support of their husbands and families. Ali Akbar Hashemi Rafsanjani, just before his accession to the presidency in 1989, called for reform measures to improve the status of women, in the belief that economic and political exigencies required a restructuring of gender relations.[31]

Thus, we see from the preceding discussion that the ideologues felt free to withdraw the rights of women and cede them back at will to serve their own interests, demonstrating that the very strict path mapped by them for women was purely for the pleasure and convenience of men in the name of God and Islam. The ideologues seem to have a preset Weltanschauung according to which they select verses and stands that best support their intellectual universe. Thus, while all the Qur'anic normative statements clearly and unambiguously dictate equality between the sexes, and the contextual ones can easily be interpreted in favor of that, especially when compared with the mode of life at the time of the Prophet, the ideologues have opted for an Islamic society where gender relations are unequal. This selective usage of tradition and Qur'anic text, as well as religious interpretations, to create such an image of women by people presumably clamoring for dignity, freedom, and authenticity, raises serious queries concerning etiology and motivation.

.   .   .

To understand the importance fundamentalist discourse and practice attribute to the role of women in society, their dress, and duties, one has to view gender discourse as a "coded" message that reflects political and ideological choices. Depending on the political nature of their programs, modern Muslim states have either co-opted the help of the female population or assisted patriarchal groups in subordinating them. Women's organizations have either been supported or considered divisive and actively discouraged. As religious or ethnic identities become more politicized, women's rights are the first to be sacrificed, and governments struggling for legitimacy always choose to relinquish control of women to their patriarchal groups. In cases where the state itself sponsors Islamic fundamentalism, as in Iran, Pakistan, and Sudan, patriarchal authority is extended beyond the immediate family to include the clergy, the police, or any other patriarchal groups or individuals who take it upon themselves to monitor the behavior and dress of Muslim women.

Admittedly, not all of the ideologues studied here were involved in establishing an Islamic government, nor were they all radicals or males, yet they *all* agreed on their image of the ideal Muslim woman and her role in society. They all followed an interventionist policy on women's issues and family matters. Liberal, conservative, or radical interpretations are drawn upon to meet the *maslahah* of the state or the fundamentalist movement, irrespective of the needs or opinions of women themselves. A member of the Iranian National Assembly bluntly explained the enactment of the *hijab* as being political. "The *hijab*," he said, "is not being discussed as a religious issue, but as a political, social, and economic issue."[32] Hence, the veiled woman signaled a redefinition of gender roles and the transformation of society. Iranian women thus became the "public face" of the Islamic Republic, and any defiance, such as unveiling, was punishable, without a trial, by seventy-four lashes in public, since the *hijab* was "basic to Islamic ideology" in symbolizing "deliverance from the yoke of imperialism."[33]

Thus, a careful study of fundamentalist gender theory and practice has demonstrated the chasm that exists between the ideals of these movements and the rights or needs of women. Fundamentalist ideologues, whether in government or out of it, have followed the erroneous tendency of combining the needs of both and declaring them as one and the same. "Revolutionary equality," often claimed to be achieved by male and female fighters, is replaced in the postrevolutionary period by the confinement of women to a purely domestic role, leaving the public sphere and positions of power to men.[34] This in no way undermines the centrality of the status of women and the sexual differentiation of social and familial roles in the fundamentalist discourse; it only links gender identity with Islam and Muslim society.

It is a discourse within which another history can be traced, a history of Western domination and the struggle for independence and assertion of identity. The controls on women and the limitations imposed on the space they occupy and their independence are not limited to fundamentalist theory but constitute the first step taken once the fundamentalists assume power. The politico-religious discourse of fundamentalists and their constant appearance in the political arena have stimulated the interest of the government in the role it could play in expressing and implementing the discourse. The first manifestation of this has always been the status of women, being the most visible, weakest, or easiest area to target. Thus, while social, economic, and political changes are sought after, such as civil law, taxation, constitutional laws, laws of contracts and obligations, banking, trade, and other domains or branches, to keep up to date with modernization and globalization, family law and women's space remain tenaciously frozen in their traditional garb. What is it that makes patriarchal fundamentalist society hurt so badly? What is it they are so afraid to lose? What is behind this paradox? How can women be given such a central and active role in the creation of society and be so marginalized afterward? Why do women, their segregation, and subordination play such an important role in fundamentalist discourse?

The debate over the ideal society Muhammad intended to establish has not abated from the time of his death in A.D. 632, through the Abbasid period (A.D. 750–1258), and down to the present. From the beginning, controversy raged over what aspect of Islam was to be emphasized. Were the regulations to be normative and permanently binding, or only ephemeral aspects of the religion denoting a particular period of a particular society? As it evolved, it was those who viewed Islam as an androcentric religion with particular androcentric laws and institutions that held sway throughout history beginning with the Abbasid period. This again raises the question: Did the androcentric approach itself win credence over the centuries, or was it a tool of those in power to affirm their authority and consolidate their power? Based on this study, I believe that the confinement of women was the major political ploy used by political elites and governments to establish their rule and consolidate their power. Rigidity and inflexibility were in ratio and proportion to the stability and prosperity of the particular regime: the more secure and dominant the political order was, the more flexible it was with regard to women and their role in society, and the more politically unstable and economically oppressive, the more rigid and uncompromising with the female population it became. Thus, the most visible and striking feature of contemporary fundamentalist discourse in theory and practice has been the dress, mobility, and general status of women, endowing the discourse with a uniformity or universality it lacked in many other domains.

This universal pattern that propagates the "powerlessness of women within the structure of public political life," especially during periods of political unrest characterized by a higher female political profile, while men increase "their efforts to control women and try to reinforce the boundary that separates the domestic from the public sphere," and their efforts to "[appropriate] women's reproductive capacity, and [glorify] motherhood,"[35] have been attributed to diverse factors by Islamic and feminist scholars. Gender boundaries have been viewed as serving a variety of political, economic, psychological, and social functions. These have always been negotiable and never constant or permanent; their origin and everlasting presence, especially in Islamic fundamentalism, have been attributed by some to patriarchy, "a historic creation formed by men and women in a process which took" thousands of years to be completed.[36] The basic unit of this "archaic state" was the patriarchal family, which generated, expressed, and reinforced its rules and values. Thus, the ruler's power was secured when men were completely dependent on him, just as their families were dependent on the men. Consequently, female sexual control was transferred to the state and became an essential feature of its power.[37] In order to preserve patriarchal morality, which seemed to be slipping away with modernization and increasing female economic independence, fundamentalists resorted to measures stricter than those of traditional rural patriarchy, where social values still revolved around the patriarch of the family or clan. This is all the more understandable in view of the Muslim conception of women as sources of sedition and anarchy.

Several theories have been advanced to explain the subordination of

Muslim women. Deniz Kandiyoti distinguishes between Islam as an ideology and practice and what she calls "classic patriarchy," to which she attributes such uniformities in gender inequality. She argues that "distinct systems of male domination, evident in the operations of different kinship systems, exercise an influence that inflects and modifies the actual practice of Islam, as well as ideological constructions of what may be regarded as properly 'Islamic.'"[38] Haideh Moghissi maintains that women's subordination is "produced, reproduced, and upheld through entrenched sexist and misogynist cultural norms and practices that shape relations between the sexes in every sphere of social life."[39] And, Germaine Tillion argues that women's oppression has nothing to do with Islam but is to be traced back to endogamy, marrying within the family, in patrilineal society long before Islam.[40]

Feminist studies have further shown that during periods of socioeconomic transformations, sexual politics is further heightened by the aggravation of social inequalities, dislocation of local communities, massive migration, and the invasion of the labor force by women, causing serious damage to the economic and normative "underpinnings of patriarchy," making conservative and traditional Islamic ideology a haven to retreat to.[41] One commentator stated, "The stability and sanctity of family life, kinship ties, and loyalties, the fabric of religious observance and custom—all these are maintained largely through women who are looked upon as preservers and upholders of social virtues."[42] The slow adjustment of the ordinary individual to the socioeconomic changes, where the husband is dependent on his wife's wages, his daughter is attracted by advertisements of high fashion, and rich men are driving expensive flashy cars, may cause him to view urbanization and modernization as moral problems best dealt with by returning women to their confined domestic roles and distancing them from the prevailing "eroticization" of gender relations. Reverting to patriarchal traditions and their impact on welfare and security reduces the state's burden in the provision of such services. Moreover, women's explicit expression of their desires and the pursuit of their interests contradicts the interests of men and violates their entrenched sense of family honor and societal order. Thus, rapid social change and its threat to existent patriarchal structures, as well as the impact of colonialism, advanced technology, and economic dependency, have led fundamentalists to an assertion of identity best vocalized by gender restrictions. Cultural authenticity is further linked to the image of a purely Muslim woman uncontaminated by Western culture and untarnished by the modern world.[43]

Moreover, Karen Brown maintains that in groups where men's identity is built by contrasting it with the external "other," great emphasis is placed in turn on controlling the "other" within their group.[44] The "other" plays an important role in fundamentalist ideology, especially because it—the West—seems to have eluded its control. This naturally leads them to expend extensive efforts to control the "other" that is within the group, namely women, or more precisely, Westernized women. The Westernized woman becomes the embodiment of all the perceived ills of moderniza-tion—divorce, prostitution, homosexuality, women's exhibitionist dress, and pornography—all readily solved by sending her back to the home to transmit Islamic values to her children.[45] Object relations theory shifts the emphasis placed by Freud on the Oedipal stage to the "earliest and most formative period of human development." It is a highly vulnerable period during which language is unknown. This causes emotions, such as joy, fear, hunger, and longing, "to have an oceanic, engulfing quality" in the early exclusive company of women, prompting thereby overwhelming and threatening feelings associated with women in times of stress later on in life. To overcome these feelings, women have to be subdued. Dinnerstein further argues that "the crucial psychological fact is that all of us, female, as well as male, fear the will of woman." Male domination is, thus, a social construct derived from "a terror that we all feel: the terror of sinking back wholly into the helplessness of infancy."[46] Thus, women are idealized only when their sphere of activity is well contained and controlled.

In fundamentalism, women are both highly honored as mothers and loathed as causes of *fitnah*. Mernissi maintains that in societies where women are secluded and closely monitored, the implicit conception of an active female sexuality prevails, in contrast to societies where the con-cept of female sexuality is passive and such controls do not exist. Accord-ing to her, this fallback on tradition and the confinement of women is "a defense mechanism against profound changes in both sex roles and the touchy subject of sexual identity" incurred by rapid social transforma-tion. It should, therefore, be viewed as "anxiety-reducing mechanisms in a world of shifting, volatile sexual identity."[47] Mernissi thus corroborates Wilhelm Reich's theory that males do not usually externalize their sexual frustration against all manifestations of political, social, or economic re-pression, but internalize the problem at the religious and moral defense levels. And Hani Shukrallah maintains that "frustration at work or lack of social or educational achievement, accentuated by sexual anxiety and/or repression in the male, may then project itself into a kind of floating ag-

gression, to be released against all female relatives." The same may, therefore, be applied to "the national sense of humiliation suffered by Arab
males as a result of the Israeli defeat, and the social sense of humiliation
caused by the prospect of class demotion that may result from the reversal
of certain socioeconomic policies in a number of Arab countries—these
two types of humiliation, leading to a sense of lost dignity—may have
contributed to a process that turns women into an easy target for the 'restoration' of dignity."[48]

Others believe nostalgia for a forgotten past, where harmony, peace,
and tranquility existed, has prompted fundamentalists to redress women
in such a role by infusing that bygone time with a sense of perfection
related to a male-dominated society. Reassertion of traditional identity in
the face of external threats is also best demonstrated by the control of
women. "To embrace traditional sexual roles proudly, is to embrace the
ideal of independence to stand up in militant opposition to the aggressor."[49] Women thus function as symbols of cultural and religious identity.
Mernissi, therefore, argues that "the fundamentalist wave is a statement
about identity," due to the "painful, but necessary, and prodigious reshuf-
fling of identity that Muslims are going through in these often confusing,
but always fascinating times."[50] Susan E. Marshall, however, maintains
that "while females have less authority than males, they paradoxically
remain powerful objects of kinship exchanges, thus, becoming targets of
exaggerated male control during periods of social disorganization. Large-
scale social upheaval triggers the demand for a reintegration of the self
within a stable meaning system, and, consequently, thrusts the ideology
of traditional womanhood to a prominent position in the revival movement."[51]

While all these theories and considerations may have provided contributing factors in the subordination of women at various times and different
circumstances, I propose that as women symbolized *fitnah* in society, their
public dress and behavior came to attract an inordinate amount of attention, converting them into symbols subject to control. They became the
symbols of virtue if controlled, and sedition if uncontrolled. Since male
power was perceived as the only source of control, the state stepped in to
control this symbol in the interest of the whole of society. Islamic leadership, whether in the state or in sociopolitical movements, in its drive to
consolidate its power and reinforce its popularity, adopted a rapid process
of Islamization, the simplest, safest, and most graphic expression of which
being the veiling and segregation of women. Hiding women from any-

thing Western and guarding their bodies and minds from any Western influence came to symbolize protection of Islamic identity, dignity, the continuity of Islamic culture and society, and the enhancement of self-esteem and confidence. The promise and objective of the Islamic leadership was to enable Muslims to lead a good and dignified life as required of them by God. Their worth and their good and evil deeds were measured by the extent to which this objective was accomplished, for they had been ordered "to enjoin good and forbid evil."

Women's behavior and appearance, including the range and quality of their activities, came to be defined by the leadership's political, cultural, or economic objectives. Thus, in some projects, women were linked to modernization and progress, and in others they were identified with rejuvenation and religious orthodoxy, emphasizing and even fetishizing women's reproductive roles and sacralizing motherhood. Indeed, the survival of this leadership and its success in national and international economics and military competition, as well as the maintenance of internal law and order, depend on the leaders' manipulation of selective ideologies consistent with their political goals. They opportunistically draw upon existing patterns of gender inequalities in Muslim societies and strategically promote male domination. However, since gender is being manipulated for political survival, many public policies have come to reflect contradictory tendencies and practices. In their eagerness to eliminate rival sources of power and alleviate economic ills pervading society, these leaders offer an illusory bargain solution to men: in return for ceding political power and economic and social resources to the ruling class, they gain absolute control over their women and the public sphere. This is made abundantly clear by the reversal of stances of al-Mawdudi, al-Ghannoushi, and al-Turabi on women's affairs whenever their power bases needed shoring up. Further, Saneʻi describes Khomeini as being afraid to tamper with existing patriarchal norms on women lest he incur the animosity of various power centers.[52] Thus, the institutionalization of male interests and the subordination of women are not to be seen or understood as irrational fundamentalist policies but as carefully studied strategies grounded in politics and the hunger for power. The political viability of the leaders is normally tied to their successful achievements in economic development, lifestyle improvements, and prosperity. But these achievements require time, sacrifice, and Westernization, which the masses do not have much of nor desire for. The easiest and most practical road to follow to satisfy their subjects and remain in power always remains the revival of tradition, with Islam as the best vehicle.

Given the centrality of the family in Islamic institutions, the sacralization of motherhood, sexual segregation, and the principle of male domination of the public sphere, it is only natural that the traditional subordinate status of women is revived and emphasized, providing the masses with the eagerly anticipated moral safeguards and everyday security. The expedience of Islamic ideology as a strategy of political consolidation is best observed in Sudan, Tunisia, Pakistan, and Iran. Hence, it is the precarious possession of the reins of power, the factionalism that may pervade the political elite or arena, or identity reformulation, that force the elite to legitimize their power by a traditional ideology. In this case, Islamic ideology is resorted to because Islam is still the most acceptable and adhered-to basis for authority for the majority of Muslims. Moreover, since brute force as a means of political domination is short-lived and the cause of subsequent subversive activities and rebellion, the shortest, most effective, and most popular means of domination is the subordination of women legitimated by their own particular reading of Islam. Bernard Lewis describes "Islamic political language" as "full of metaphor, some of it dead, buried, and forgotten, some of it to varying extents alive and conscious." The commonest of these metaphors "are those which are called spatial, denoting position and direction in space . . . Sometimes the metaphors of power are not merely verbal, but material, and appear as symbols."[53] This is best manifested in the role assigned women. Changing these religious prescriptions or requesting their change becomes blasphemous as a brazen insult to divine authority.

Thus, Gustav Thaiss drew attention to the use of women as metaphors in the sermons of the clergy during the seventies in Iran. The Islamic community was portrayed either as a pure innocent virgin violated by the aggressive West, or impure adulterous woman "having an affair" with the West, thereby cheating and dishonoring her husband. Such sermons, Thaiss maintained, aroused male apprehensions regarding gender relations and stimulated their sense of masculinity and virility.[54] Wilhelm Reich argued further that attempts to influence the masses by correlating political and national notions with family and honor are to be found in fascism as well. Family, according to him, "is the nation in miniature . . . thus, nationalistic sentiments are the direct continuation of the family tie and are likewise rooted in the fixated tie to the mother."[55] Thus, Khomeini achieved national prominence in 1962–63 for his opposition to the shah's attempt to enfranchise women rather than to his implementation of land reforms, which had immediate consequences on the clergy's income. Khomeini, with nine other clerics, issued a communiqué denouncing women's suffrage as "trampling on the Qur'an and exigent Islamic decrees and encouraging prostitution."[56] Fundamentalist Mutahhari and modernist Shari'ati expressed their rejection of Western "socioeconomic domination" by rejecting the Westernized woman ubiquitous in the public sphere.

Mutahhari thus epitomizes Talcott Parsons' identification of ideology as "cognitive legitimation of patterns of value orientation," and Helena Deutsch's definition of legitimacy as "the effect produced by the association of experience with value-laden symbols."[57] And feminist Joan Scott explained the attention authoritarian governments in particular give to women "whether at a crucial moment for Jacobian hegemony in the French Revolution, at the point of Stalin's bid for controlling authority, during the implementation of Nazi policy in Germany, or with the triumph in Iran of the Ayatollah Khomeini, domination, strength, central authority, and ruling power have been legitimized as masculine . . . [or] that coding has been literalized in laws" by putting women in their place.[58] Finally, Maxine Molyneux argued that when revolutionary governments give attention to the status of women during the early periods of economic and social transformation, they have three objectives in mind: extension of the base of the government's political support; enhancing the size and quality of the labor force; and helping co-opt the family for the process of "social reproduction."[59]

What is, therefore, clear by now is that the concern of fundamentalist thinkers and rulers with women's issues and the incredible similarities in their arguments, despite differences in other areas, result from their sexual politics and their role in the building of an Islamic state. Hence, the transformation of women was in tandem with social, political, and economic transformations of society. Veiling proclaimed a revaluation and redefinition of gender roles and, therefore, a moral and cultural transformation of society. There is nothing specifically Islamic to be gleaned from these texts: the wrapping may be Islamic, but the content is purely political in combination with lust for power. No other interpretation can explain the differences in ideology, geography, history, sectarianism, nationalism, sex, space, and time coupled with a unanimity on the status of women and unison in rhetoric. Nothing else can explain the rampant contradictions in their arguments pertaining to women, when they are quite consistent in the rest of their ideological arguments. Nothing else would explain their resistance to any change in the position of women, even when they are in unabashed contradiction with Qur'anic texts, or their selective approach in attempting to prove the subordinate position of women in Islam while consciously ignoring numerous references to gender equality in the text and Hadith. Last, but not least, this explains why women themselves are such ardent fundamentalists: they too want a piece of the cake but can only obtain it by helping men subordinate the rest of their kin, as clearly demonstrated by the actions and prison memoirs of Zaynab al-Ghazali. This can also be motivated by women, at a loss for an alternate course of action, attempting to identify and exploit loopholes in the system that suffocates them while seeming to accept it.[60]

Thus, Susan Moller Okin, a Western feminist scholar, argues, "The existence of a distinct sphere of private, family life, separated off from the realm of public life, leads to the exaggeration of women's biological differences from men, to the perception of women as primarily suited to fulfill special 'female' functions within the home, and, consequently, to the justification of the monopoly by men of the whole outside world."[61] Michel Foucault, in *History of Sexuality*, further emphasizes the role the sexual domain, as well as its management, plays in the economic and political spheres and its underlying influence on all their strategies. Therefore, the failure, so far, of fundamentalism to reverse urbanization and restore the wealth and privilege lost to the West through colonization, or in eradicating the appeal of Western materialism and consequent consumerism, prompted fundamentalists to effect changes in the easiest and most visible domain, that of women. Women, the weakest link in the social fabric, the rivals of men in the public sphere, the objects of men's sexual fears and fantasies, the bearers of men's progenies and their teachers, yet still dependent on men, form an easy target for fundamentalists in their struggle to assume power and consolidate it. By their subordination and return to traditional Islam and customs and the further tightening of constraints, men have experienced a resurgence of power and authority they felt had been wrested from them by modernization. They reveled in the newly repossessed power and privileges, reassured that this embodies the natural environment for women as well and is conducive to their happiness. Having been given a share of power, albeit directly in the private sphere and indirectly in the public sphere, men were willing to delegate the rest to the movement or state, as the case may be, which, in turn, will help them consolidate their own power over women.

The question to be asked now is why women themselves become fundamentalists. Helen Hardcare attributes the involvement of women in fundamentalist groups to their being inspired by anticolonial and national feelings and sharing with men feelings of alienation and deprivation. They are further attracted by the fundamentalists' interpersonal networks that convey a family atmosphere and a return to tradition. Such networks help women persuade men of the importance of marriage and domesticity. Other factors may be fear of reprisals by men or divine disapproval, leading to a voluntary surrender of power in the hope of eternal salvation.[62] Leila Ahmed views women's participation in fundamentalism as having psychological and social dimensions carrying the comfort of transporting the traditional values of childhood and family to a city full of "foreign and over-whelming ways," to provide them with feelings of inner ease and resolution, in addition to a sense of community.[63] Miriam Cooke coined the concept of "multiple critique" to describe a system that enables women to remain in an oppressive society while criticizing its problems— a form of internal subversion.[64] Moreover, the Islamic dress, in addition to economic and practical advantages, defuses women's presence in the public sphere from any challenge to or violation of the Islamic sociocultural ethic and, hence, helps them "carve out a legitimate public space for themselves." Islamic dress, then, according to Ahmed, is to be seen as a "uniform of transition," a "uniform of arrival" announcing their entrance into modernity.[65]

Gustavo Benavides, following Weber's definition of power, defines the latter as "the chance to impose one's will against the resistance of others." Whether this is exercised by those already in power or as a bid for power, Benavides argues, the central characteristics of power remain the same: "Power is a tension between interests, ideologies, classes, or individuals, and is always contested, using all the weapons—physical and ideological— at the group's disposal." This tug of war, according to him, does not take place in a vacuum, but "within structures that are themselves constituted by power relations . . . in a space structured hierarchically . . . according to preexistent relations based on unequal access to goods, status, ritual purity, or anything that a group defines as desirable."[66] Talcott Parsons defines power as a "generalized means" for achieving one's goals, through dominating one's environment, accomplished either individually by mastering others, or collectively when people cooperate as a group to dominate another.[67] Finally, Michael Mann derives ideological power from "its control of concepts and categories of meaning imposed upon sense perception," and he writes that "norms, shared understandings of how people should act morally in their relations with each other are necessary for sustained social cooperation." Thus, any ideological movement, and particularly a religious one, "increases the mutual trust and collective morale of a group" by enhancing "their collective powers" to be rewarded by "more zealous adherence." The route to power is, therefore, through a monopoly of norms and meaning, the ruling elite keeping the masses acquiescent by institutionalizing their control into the laws and norms of the social group. If human beings are "restless, purposive . . . striving to increase their enjoyment of the good things of life and capable of choosing and pursuing appropriate means for doing so," they become the original source of power, as Mann maintains.[68]

If these definitions of power are correct, and I believe they are, then it is clear why the most zealous adherents of fundamentalism are women. Being human, chained and subordinated to men, they realize that the only way open for them to exercise their freedom and power, albeit in Islamic garb, lies in joining the fundamentalists and helping them subordinate the rest of their own group. By playing this role, they acquire freedom, independence, authority, and equality. Thus, fundamentalist ideology fits the "interest theory," which Geertz defined as a "mask and a weapon,"[69] and Nietzsche's identification of a universal human drive as disguised behind a variety of viable masks in his concept of "will to power." Moreover, according to Gerda Lerner, women participate in their own subordination because they have been "psychologically shaped" to internalize their own inferiority. Unawareness of their own past achievements and their "connectedness" to familial structures place obstacles in the way of their solidarity as a group, thus epitomizing M. Vovelle's "dungeons of long duration," the bars of which not only prevent people from breaking out but also from perceiving them as such—creating thereby a state of what Karl Marx called "false consciousness."[70]

The human body has been used throughout history to demonstrate and support power struggles by reflecting the dominant group's system of domination and bearing its taboos and punishments. This is best encapsulated in the treatment of the female body as symbolizing power, hierarchy, and exploitation.[71] Max Weber wrote, "Politics for us, means striving to have power or striving to influence the distribution of power."[72] Islamic ideals are, thus, appropriated by fundamentalist leaders whose overriding concern and goal is power. Foucault explained that power "must be analyzed as something that circulates . . . It is never localized here or there, never in anybody's hands, never appropriated as a commodity or piece of wealth . . . And not only do individuals circulate between its threads; they are always in the position of simultaneously undergoing and exercising this power . . . In other words, individuals are the vehicle of power."[73] Subordinates, thus, according to Foucault, along with the dominant group, partake of the locus of intersecting forces of power. In fact, they are themselves implicated in the continual recreation of power, as epitomized by fundamentalist women's active role in their own subordination.

In conclusion, fundamentalist ideologues, in their struggle to seize power, attracted women through promises of liberation and acquisition of long-lost rights to garner their assistance in propagating their message, burnishing their image, recruiting new followers, and participating in revolutionary activities. However, once in power, the need for speedy consolidation necessitated a reversal of stance to ensure the now critical support of the male sector. This involved resorting to the traditional weapon of patriarchy with its attendant subordination of women, reinvigorating males through regaining full control of women, as well as the monopoly of the public sphere, at the expense of women's rights and freedom. In doing so, fundamentalists were essentially offering the male population a bargain: in return for ceding control of political power and social resources to the movement or state, men gain power through increased control of their own families. This simultaneously augments male domination, sets clear boundaries between the public and private spheres, and subordinates the private to the public, while the state rules supreme over both sectors of society—male and female.

This reading of fundamentalist ideology of gender relations fully explains the ideologues' fixation on women and their status in society, the contradictions between theory and practice, the numerous contradictions within their arguments, their categoric refusal to use *ijtihad* for the amelioration of women's condition, their willful prejudiced interpretation of Qur'an and Hadith, emphasizing a handful of verses and hadiths that could be interpreted pejoratively while ignoring numerous other verses and hadiths that stress clearly and unambiguously gender equality. This also explains Qutb's change of heart toward women and al-Mawdudi's support of Fatimah Jinnah's candidacy, and Khomeini's vacillation between evicting women from the public sphere and inviting them back in. It further explains the apparent discrepancy in women fundamentalists who assist in the continual recreation of male power and proclaim in unison that women are "the foundation of the virtuous Islamic society." Thus, Shirley Ardener, in her book *Defining Female*, argues, "Members of muted groups, instead of ignoring the dominant group or merely tolerating its demands, may even go further and accept the burden of maintaining or 'policing' a system, which to the onlooker appears to disadvantage them."[74] Zaynab al-Ghazali, following this path, achieved the highest of positions in the Muslim Brotherhood and even took pride in having been sent to the Liman Tura male prison for a protracted period of time before she was finally sent to the women's prison where she derided the inmates and considered herself superior to them. Finally, a Tunisian fundamentalist woman declared that an Islamist woman "leaves the usual role of women in our society" for a cause. She needs to continue to work outside the home "to propagate Islam, militate, pursue the battle in the field," rather than be isolated in the home away from life.[75]

Notes

Chapter 1. Introduction

1. The term "Westoxification" is taken from Jalal Al-e Ahmad, *Gharbzadeqi* [Westoxification], rev. ed. (Tehran: Entesharat-e Ferdaws, 1993).

2. Dekmejian, "Islamic Revival," 9–10; Gerholm, "Islamization of Contemporary Egypt," 146.

3. Cited in Abu-Rabiʿ, *Islamic Resurgence,* 9 n. 18.

4. An-Naʿim, "The Dichotomy," 58; Hussain, *Political Perspectives,* 167–68; Khadduri, "From Religious to National Law," 39.

5. Donohue and Esposito, *Islam in Transition,* 3–6; Mortimer, *Faith and Power,* 86–88; Nasr, *Traditional Islam,* 14–17; Khadduri, "From Religious to National Law," 41.

6. Ahmed, *Discovering Islam,* 55–58.

7. Ibid., 57; Afshar, "Khomeini's Teachings," 60; Sachedina, "Activist Shiʿism," 403; Zubaida, "Quest for the Islamic State," 42.

8. Riesebrodt, *Pious Passion,* 101; Voll, *Islam,* 83–84.

9. Sivan, "Islamic Radicalism," 49–50; Keddie, "Iran: Change in Islam," 532–33; Ramazani, "Iran's Export of Revolution," 48.

10. Cited in Tibi, "Worldview of Sunni Arab Fundamentalists," 85.

11. Mir-Hosseini, *Islam and Gender,* 105–6.

12. Cited in Sayeed, *Western Dominance and Political Islam,* 119.

Chapter 2. Hasan al-Banna

1. Dekmejian, *Islam in Revolution,* 75–76.

2. Sullivan, "Muslim Brotherhood," 187–88; Hoveyda, *Broken Crescent,* 24; al-Abdin, "Political Thought," 220; Esposito, *Islam and Politics,* 3d ed. 131–33; Sagiv, *Fundamentalism,* 30–32; Abu-Rabiʿ, *Intellectual Origins,* 67–68; Hiro, *Islamic Fundamentalism,* 60; el-Affendi, *Turabi's Revolution,* 11; Kedourie, *Politics in the Middle East,* 329.

3. Hoveyda, *Broken Crescent,* 25–26.

4. Dekmejian, *Islam in Revolution*, 75–77; Kedourie, *Politics in the Middle East*, 329–31; Zubaida, "Quest for the Islamic State," 34; al-Abdin, *"Political Thought,"* 230–31.

5. Kepel, *Muslim Extremism*, 36–37.

6. Esposito, *Islam and Politics*, 3d ed. 132–33; Sagiv, *Fundamentalism*, 30; Davis, "Ideology," 145–48; Esposito, *Voices of Resurgent Islam*, 9–10.

7. Sullivan, "Muslim Brotherhood," 187–88; Hiro, *Islamic Fundamentalism*, 61; Mitchell, *Society of Muslim Brothers*, 14; al-Abdin, "Political Thought, 219–20; Enayat, *Modern Islamic Thought*, 85; Ismael and Tareq, *Government and Politics*, 62–64.

8. Hoveyda, *Broken Crescent*, 24–25; Ramadan, "Fundamentalist Influence," 154; Lewis, *Shaping of the Modern Middle East*, 115–16.

9. Abu-Rabi', *Intellectual Origins*, 79; Dekmejian, *Islam in Revolution*, 75–76.

10. Ramadan, "Fundamentalist Influence," 154; al-Abdin, "Political Thought," 231.

11. Commins, "Hasan al-Banna," 144; Hussain, *Political Perspectives*, 175; Abu-Rabi', *Intellectual Origins*, 67; Sonbol, "Egypt," 30; Enayat, *Modern Islamic Thought*, 84; Dekmejian, "Resurgent Islam," 205–6.

12. Dekmejian, "Multiple Faces," 6–8; Farhi, "Class Struggles," 90–113; Zubaida, "Quest for the Islamic State," 40. For further reading on militant Islamist groups, see Lawrence, *Shattering the Myth*, 67; Zubaida, "Quest for the Islamic State," 26, 40–41; Sullivan and Abed-Kotob, *Islam in Contemporary Egypt*, 21–26; Ayubi, "Political Revival," 488–94; Ansari, "Islamic Militants," 123–24, 140–41; Voll, *Islam*, 314–16; Hiro, *Islamic Fundamentalism*, 3; Baker, "Invidious Comparisons," 123–27; Gerholm, "Islamization of Contemporary Egypt," 127–30, 146.

13. For a full discussion of the causes of Muslim deterioration, see al-Abdin, "Political Thought," 221.

14. Davidson, *Islamic Fundamentalism*, 89; Bagader, "Contemporary Islamic Movements," 117; Commins, "Hasan al-Banna," 125, 134–35; Kedourie, *Politics in the Middle East*, 331; Mitchell, *Society of Muslim Brothers*, 30.

15. Hiro, *Islamic Fundamentalism*, 64.

16. Moussalli, *Moderate and Radical*, 108–9, 129–30.

17. Ibid.

18. Husaini, *The Moslem Brethren*, 72; see also al-Abdin, "Political Thought," 223.

19. Ayubi, *Political Islam*, 131–32.

20. Ramadan, "Fundamentalist Influence," 179 n.16; Enayat, *Modern Islamic Thought*, 85; Moussalli, "Hasan al-Banna," 166–69.

21. Ahmed, *Women and Gender*, 194–95.

22. Zuhur, *Revealing Reveiling*, 88–89; Hiro, *Islamic Fundamentalism*, 57.

23. Commins, "Hasan al-Banna," 138–40; Ismael and Tareq, *Government and Politics*, 64–67.

24. Commins, "Hasan al-Banna," 143–44; al-Banna, *al-Mar'ah al-muslimah*, 7–21.

25. Zubaida, "Quest for the Islamic State," 40.

Chapter 3. Abu al-'A'la al-Mawdudi

1. Marty and Appleby, *Glory and Power*, 152–53; Mortimer, *Faith and Power*, 201.

2. Marty and Appleby, *Glory and Power*, 152–53; Brohi, "Mawlana-Abu A'la-Mawdudi," 290, 381; Adams, "Mawdudi," 99; Nasr, "Mawdudi," 98, 104; Ahmad, "Islamic Fundamentalism," 464; Nasr, *Mawdudi*, 3; Nasr, "Mawdudi, Sayyid Abu al-A'la," 71; Hoveyda, *Broken Crescent*, 66–69; Binder, *Islamic Liberalism*, 171; Ahmad and Ansari, "Mawlana Sayyid Abu A'la Mawdudi," 364; Mir, "Features of Mawdudi's Tafhim," 233–34; Adams, "Ideology of Mawlana Mawdudi," 371.

3. Ibid., 372–80; Ahmad and Ansari, "Mawlana Sayyid Abu A'la Mawdudi," 360–63; Davidson, *Islamic Fundamentalism*, 97–98; Nasr, *Mawdudi*, 9, 26, 41–49, 127–33; Adams, "Mawdudi," 100–11; Nasr, "Mawdudi," 101–4; Lawrence, *Defenders of God*, 208; Lawrence, *Shattering the Myth*, 58, 60–61; Marty and Appleby, *Glory and Power*, 152–53; Sayeed, *Western Dominance*, 120–21; Nasr, "Islamic Opposition," 136–37; Nasr, *The Vanguard*, xiv; Nasr, "Jama'at-i Islami," 356.

4. Nasr, *Mawdudi*, 135–36.

5. Ibid., 136–38.

6. Jameelah, "Appraisal," 117; Adams, "Ideology," 386–87; Ahmad and Ansari, "Mawlana Sayyid Abu A'la Mawdudi," 376; Mortimer, *Faith and Power*, 203–4. For the guidelines Mawdudi gives for *ijtihad*, cf. Abbot, "Maulana-Maududi," 9.

7. Husain, *Global Islamic Politics*, 78.

8. Beckford and Luckmann, *Changing Face of Religion*, 115.

9. Ahmad, "Mawdudi and Orthodox Fundamentalism," 374; Mawdudi, *Islamic Way of Life*, 374; Jameelah, "Appraisal," 127.

10. Nasr, "Mawdudi, Sayyid Abu al-A'la," 104–5.

11. Cited in Ahmad, "Islamic Fundamentalism," 466, 487–89; Nasr, *Mawdudi*, 4–6.

12. Nasr, *Mawdudi*, 4–6, 56; Lawrence, *Shattering the Myth*, 59; Nasr, *The Vanguard*, 78.

13. Nasr, "Mawdudi, Sayyid Abu al-A'la," 105–6; Binder, *Islamic Liberalism* 175–78; Nasr, *Mawdudi*, 49–52; Ahmad and Ansari, "Mawlana Sayyid Abu A'la Mawdudi," 365–74; Doumato, "*Jahiliyyah*," 353.

14. Cited in Nasr, *Mawdudi*, 50–51.

15. Ibid., 50–52, 60.

16. Cited in Choueiri, *Islamic Fundamentalism*, 123.

17. Ahmad, "Islamic Fundamentalism," 487–89; Ayubi, *Political Islam*, 128–32; Ayubi, "Islamic State," 322; Jameelah, "Appraisal," 126; Hoveyda, *Broken Crescent*, 68–69; Binder, *Islamic Liberalism*, 175. See also Kramer, *Arab Awakening*, 148.

18. Davidson, *Islamic Fundamentalism*, 98; Ahmad, "Mawdudi and Orthodox Fundamentalism," 373; Butterworth, "Prudence versus Legitimacy," 96.

19. Nasr, *Mawdudi*, 59; Ahmad, "Mawdudi and Orthodox Fundamentalism," 375; Nasr, "Mawdudi," 106–8; Adams, "Mawdudi," 111–22.

20. Mawdudi, *The Islamic Way of Life*, 40–41.

21. Nasr, *Mawdudi*, 127–35; Ahmad, "Islamic Fundamentalism," 464; Butterworth, "Prudence versus Legitimacy," 108; Ahmad and Ansari, "Mawlana Sayyid Abu A'la Mawdudi," 362–63; Brown, *Rethinking Tradition*, 75–76; Lawrence, *Defenders of God*, 208; Adams, "Mawdudi," 101–2.

22. Haq, "Women, Islam, and the State," 162.

23. Mawdudi, *al-Hijab*, 5–10, 27–35, 45; Hasan, *Sayyid Abu A'la Mawdudi*, 213; Mayer, "Islam and Human Rights," 104–5.

24. Mawdudi, *al-Hijab*, 137–43.

25. Ibid., 61–66, 144–52, 156–57, 174–80.

26. Lemu and Heeren, *Woman in Islam*, 37.

27. Mawdudi, *Huquq al-zawjayn*, 33, 93, 111.

28. Ibid., 34, 93, 113–16.

29. Ibid., 35, 39, 41, 116–17.

30. Ibid., 43, 44. Cited in Haeri, "Obedience versus Autonomy," 186.

31. Mawdudi, *Huquq al-zawjayn*, 46, 48–49, 52, 136.

32. Ibid., 57–58, 64, 66, 70, 75, 82, 84.

33. Ibid., 118, 120–23, 126, 129–30, 132–33.

34. Ibid., 101–2, 106, 110.

35. Ibid., 97–98, 135–36.

36. Mawdudi, *al-Hijab*, 183–91.

37. Ibid.

38. Ibid., 192–93.

39. Ibid., 123–27.

40. Ibid., 197–98.

41. Ibid., 199–203, 211, 215–19.

42. Ibid., 229–32.

43. Ibid., 232–36, 239–40.

44. Ibid., 241–44.

45. Ibid., 253–54; Mawdudi, *Nidham al-hayat*, 13–16.

46. Mawdudi, *Huquq al-zawjayn*, 264–68, Mawdudi, *Tafsir surat al-nur*, 32–34.

47. Mawdudi, *al-Hijab*, 269–79, 282–85; Hasan, *Sayyid Abu A'la Mawdudi*, 218.

48. Mawdudi, *al-Hijab*, 289–300, 315–20.

49. Ibid., 315–27.

50. Ibid., 328–32; Mawdudi, *Nidham al-hayat*, 10–11, 15–16.

51. Ibid., 41–45; Mawdudi, *Tadwin al-dustur*, 45–48.

52. Ibid., 84–85.

53. Nasr, *Mawdudi*, 135–36.

54. Abbot, "Maulana Maududi," 13.

55. Brown, *Rethinking Tradition*, 76–78.

56. Cited in ibid., 86.

57. Ibid.

58. Nasr, *Mawdudi*, 136–38.

59. Cf. 'Amarah, *Abu al-A'la al-Mawdudi*, 385–94.

60. Cited in Abbot, "Maulana Maududi," 13–14.

61. Cited in Nasr, *Mawdudi*, 50–51.

62. Mawdudi, *The Islamic Way of Life*, 40–41.

63. Adams, "Ideology," 382.

64. Hasan, *Sayyid Abu A'la Maududi*, 484–85. See also Abbot, "Maulana Mau-dudi," 13–14; Rahman, "Islamic Modernism," 326; Nasr, *Mawdudi*, 133; Haq, "Women, Islam, and the State," 165–66; Saulat, *Maulana Maududi*, 59–60.

Chapter 4. Sayyid Qutb

1. Ayubi, "The Political Revival," 489.

2. Kedourie, *Politics in the Middle East*, 331.

3. Akhavi, "Qutb, Sayyid," 400–2; Sagiv, *Fundamentalism*, 36; Moussalli, *Radical Islamic Fundamentalism*, 21–38; Shepard, *Sayyid Qutb*, xvi; Sivan, *Radical Islam*, 22; Haim, "Sayyid Qutb," 147–50; Haddad, "Sayyid Qutb," 68; Gerholm, "Islamization of Contemporary Egypt," 148–49; Hoveyda, *Broken Crescent*, 27; Moussalli, *Moderate and Radical*, 97–98, 132–33.

4. Qutb, *al-Taswir al-fanni fi al-Qur'an* (Aesthetics in the Qur'an) (Cairo: N.p., 1963), 7. See also Abu-Rabi', *Intellectual Origins*, 104.

5. Sagiv, *Fundamentalism*, 36–42; Kepel, *Muslim Extremism*, 42–43, 28; Moussalli, *Moderate and Radical*, 97–98; Shepard, *Sayyid Qutb*, xvii.

6. Agbetola, "Equality of Man and Woman," 131; Akhavi, "Qutb, Sayyid," 400; Haddad, "Sayyid Qutb," 67–69; Abu-Rabi', *Intellectual Origins*, 93.

7. For an analytical list of his books, see Fadlallah, *Ma'Sayyid Qutb*, 57–59.

8. Akhavi, "Qutb, Sayyid," 400; Moussalli, *Radical Islamic Fundamentalism*, 21–24; Moussalli, *Moderate and Radical*, 132; Shepard, *Sayyid Qutb*, xv–xvi.

9. Kepel, *Muslim Extremism in Egypt*, 37; Binder, *Islamic Liberalism*, 32; Akhavi, "Qutb, Sayyid," 403; Moussalli, *Moderate and Radical*, 97–98; Hoveyda, *Broken Crescent*, 27; Shepard, *Sayyid Qutb*, xvii; Abu-Rabi', *Intellectual Origins*, 140–41.

10. Qutb, *Fi zilal al-Qur'an*, 10:117. See also Haddad, "Sayyid Qutb," 77–78.

11. Al-Nadawi, *Mudhakarat sa'is fi al-sharq al-'arabi* (Memoirs of a politician in the Arab east), 3d ed. (Beirut: N.p., 1978), 96. See also Haim, "Sayyid Qutb," 148–49.

12. Binder, *Islamic Liberalism*, 171.

13. Haim, "Sayyid Qutb," 147; Moussalli, *Radical Islamic Fundamentalism*, 244; Akhavi, "Qutb, Sayyid," 403; Shepard, *Sayyid Qutb*, ix; Haddad, "Sayyid Qutb," 67; Nettler, *Past Trials and Present Tribulations*, 25; Kepel, *Muslim Extremism*, 23; Moussalli, *Moderate and Radical*, 101; Ayubi, *Political Islam*, 142–43.

14. Cited in Moussalli, *Radical Islamic Fundamentalism*, 14.

15. Cragg, *The Pen and the Faith*, 54.

16. Akhavi, "Qutb, Sayyid," 401; Hoveyda, *Broken Crescent*, 27; Esposito, *Voices of Resurgent Islam*, 64.

17. Abu-Rabi', *Intellectual Origins*, 126.

18. Cited in Haddad, "Sayyid Qutb," 77; Moussalli, *Radical Islamic Fundamentalism*, 70–71.

19. Moussalli, *Moderate and Radical*, 133–35; Moussalli, *Radical Islamic Fundamentalism*, 80–85.

20. Moussalli, *Radical Islamic Fundamentalism*, 94–98; Moussalli, *Moderate and Radical*, 137–39; Haddad, "Sayyid Qutb," 74–75.

21. Moussalli, *Moderate and Radical*, 137–39; Haddad, "Sayyid Qutb," 76; Moussalli, *Radical Islamic Fundamentalism*, 107.

22. Moussalli, *Radical Islamic Fundamentalism*, 111–16; Haddad, "Sayyid Qutb," 76; Moussalli, *Moderate and Radical*, 137–39.

23. Moussalli, *Moderate and Radical*, 137–39; Haddad, "Sayyid Qutb," 77; Moussalli, *Radical Islamic Fundamentalism*, 117–21.

24. Moussalli, *Radical Islamic Fundamentalism*, 121–24; Haddad, "Sayyid Qutb," 77; Moussalli, *Moderate and Radical*, 139.

25. Haddad, "Sayyid Qutb," 71; Qutb, *Ma'rakat*, 66.

26. Haddad, "Qur'anic Justification," 22.

27. Mitchell, *Society of Muslim Brothers*, 243–45.

28. For a full discussion of *jahiliyyah*, see Doumato, "Jahiliyyah," 353; Zubaida, "Quest for the Islamic State," 38–39; Sivan, *Radical Islam*, 23–24; Moussalli, "Sayyid Qutb," 43 n. 1; Binder, *Islamic Liberalism*, 178–79; Gerholm, *Islamization of Contemporary Egypt*, 150; Boullata, *Trends and Issues*, 58–59.

29. Akhavi, "Qutb, Sayyid," 402; Ayubi, *Political Islam*, 141; Arjomand, "Unity and Diversity," 184–85; Ramadan, "Fundamentalist Influence," 156–57; Moussalli, *Radical Islamic Fundamentalism*, 37–42; Marty and Appleby, *Glory and Power*, 153–54; Cragg, *The Pen and the Faith*, 57–58; Haddad, "Sayyid Qutb," 79; Taylor, *The Islamic Question*, 57–59, Butterworth, "Prudence versus Legitimacy," 100; Moussalli, *Moderate and Radical*, 129.

30. Ayubi, "Islamic State," 322.

31. Kepel, *Muslim Extremism*, 45; Ayubi, "Islamic State," 322.

32. Moussalli, *Radical Islamic Fundamentalism*, 225–28; Kepel, *Muslim Extremism*, 53; el-Affendi, *Turabi's Revolution*, 14–15; Marty and Appleby, *Glory and Power*, 153–55; Kramer, *Arab Awakening*, 148–49; Haddad, "The Qur'anic Justification," 17; Moussalli, *Moderate and Radical*, 101; Zubaida, "Quest for the Islamic State," 38–39; Sivan, *Radical Islam*, 25; Binder, *Islamic Liberalism*, 176; Akhavi, "Qutb, Sayyid," 402–3.

33. Moussalli, *Radical Islamic Fundamentalism*, 162–63.

34. Ibid.

35. Cited in Haddad, "The Qur'anic Justification," 20.

36. Mitchell, *Society of Muslim Brothers*, 246.

37. Agbetola, "Equality of Man and Woman," 132; Shepard, *Sayyid Qutb*, 127;

Butterworth, "Prudence versus Legitimacy," 100–1; Moussalli, *Radical Islamic Fundamentalism,* 173–77; Abu-Rabiʿ, *Intellectual Origins,* 114, 120–21.

38. Qutb, *al-Islam,* 73.

39. Qutb, "Social Justice," 127; Shepard, *Sayyid Qutb,* 126–27; Moussalli, *Radical Islamic Fundamentalism,* 175–86.

40. Shepard, *Sayyid Qutb,* 127.

41. Ibid., 66; Haim, "Sayyid Qutb," 152; Agbetola, "Equality of Man and Woman," 134; Abu-Rabiʿ, *Intellectual Origins,* 159; Choueiri, *Islamic Fundamentalism,* 100.

42. Qutb, *al-ʿAdalah,* 32–55; Qutb, *Fi zilal al-Qurʾan,* 1:642, part 2; Qutb, *al-Islam wa mushkilat al-hadarah,* 66–68.

43. Qutb, *Fi zilal al-Qurʾan,* 1:648–52; Stowasser, "Gender Issues," 38.

44. Qutb, *al-ʿAdalah,* 32–35; *Fi zilal al-Qurʾan,* 1:335–36.

45. Ibid., 589; Qutb, *al-ʿAdalah,* 32–55.

46. Qutb, *Fi zilal al-Qurʾan,* 1:234–36, 580; 2:644.

47. Qutb, *al-Islam,* 66–68, 131–32.

48. Ibid., 135.

49. Ibid., 66–68; Qutb, *Fi zilal al-Qurʾan,* 2:646; Qutb, *al-ʿAdalah,* 57.

50. Qutb, *al-Islam,* 66–68.

51. Qutb, *Fi zilal al-Qurʾan,* 2:643, 645.

52. Choueiri, *Islamic Fundamentalism,* 127–28; Moghadam, *Modernizing Women,* 102.

53. Qutb, *Fi zilal al-Qurʾan,* 1:240–41; 2:3096, 3619.

54. Ibid., 2:650.

55. Ibid., 2:651–52.

56. Ibid., 2:653.

57. Ibid., 2:769.

58. Ibid., 1:238, 375; 4:2513–15, 2533; Qutb, *al-Islam,* 132.

59. Akhtar, *A Faith for All Seasons,* 52–55; Qutb, *Fi zilal al-Qurʾan,* 2:578, 625, 631, 927.

60. Ibid., 2:582, 578, 770; Akhtar, *A Faith for All Seasons,* 52–55.

61. Akhtar, *A Faith for All Seasons;* Qutb, *Fi zilal al-Qurʾan,* 2:771.

62. Qutb, *Fi zilal al-Qurʾan,* 1:245–47; 6:3593.

63. Ibid., 1:256; 5:2875.

64. Ibid., 6:3599.

65. Ibid., 1:248–51.

66. Ibid., 1:254.

67. Ibid., 1:255.

68. Ibid., 2:599; 4:2487.

69. Ibid., 2:599.

70. Ibid., 2:588–89; 4:2490–92.

71. Ibid., 2:600; 4:2488.

72. Qutb, *Tifl,* 155.

73. Cited in Mitchell, *Society of Muslim Brothers,* 238–39.

74. For a full discussion of this subject, see Moussalli, *Radical Islamic Fundamentalism*, 78–79, 126, 133–36, 149–50, 161–62; Haddad, "Sayyid Qutb," 71; Moussalli, *Moderate and Radical*, 135–37, 40–41; Abu-Rabi', *Intellectual Origins*, 198; Mitchell, *Society of Muslim Brothers*, 237–39; Boullata, *Trends and Issues*, 61; Moussalli, "Sayyid Qutb," 72–73.

75. Qutb, *al-'Adalah*, 55; also cited in Agbetola, "Equality of Man and Woman," 132–33.

76. Cited in Taylor, *The Islamic Question*, 58–59; and Haddad, "Sayyid Qutb," 87.

77. Shepard, *Sayyid Qutb*, 127.

78. Moussalli, *Radical Islamic Fundamentalism*, 89.

79. Ibid., 186.

80. Ibid., 179.

81. Ibid., 200.

82. Qutb, *Fi zilal al-Qur'an*, 2909.

83. Shepard, *Sayyid Qutb*, 126–27.

84. Mitchell, *Society of Muslim Brothers*, 254.

85. Moussalli, *Radical Islamic Fundamentalism*, 86–87.

86. Qutb, *al-'Adalah*, 57; Agbetola, "Equality of Man and Woman," 135.

87. Shehadeh, "Women in Discourse of Qutb," 53.

88. Ibid., 51.

Chapter 5. Ayatollah Ruhollah Khomeini

1. Cited in Hoveyda, *Broken Crescent*, 89.

2. Sanasarian, *Women's Rights*, 124; Hegland, "Islamic Revival," 196; Omid, *Islam and the Post-revolutionary State*, 1; Bakhash, *Reign of Ayatollahs*, 3–4; Dekmejian, "Multiple Faces," 10; Menashri, *Revolution*, xi, 2–3; Cottam, "Inside Revolutionary Iran," 3; Arjomand, "Shi'ite Jurisprudence," 88.

3. Afshar, "Khomeini's Teachings," in *In the Shadow of Islam*, 75–76; Hegland, "Islamic Revival," 196.

4. Omid, *Islam and the Post-revolutionary State*, 4–6.

5. Cited in Marty and Appleby, *Glory and Power*, 160–61.

6. Jansen, *Dual Nature of Islamic Fundamentalism*, 4.

7. Voll, *Islam*, 295–96; Cottam, "Inside Revolutionary Iran," 4; Moin, "Khomeini's Search for Perfection," 64. For more information on his life, see ibid., 65–69; Hoveyda, *Broken Crescent*, 72–74; Davidson, *Islamic Fundamentalism*, 95; Algar, "Introduction, 13; Algar, "Imam Khomeini," 264–68; Dabashi, *Theology of Discontent*, 410.

8. Algar, "Introduction," 14–15; Algar, "Imam Khomeini," 268–71; Dabashi, *Theology of Discontent*, 410; Davidson, *Islamic Fundamentalism*, 95; Hoveyda, *Broken Crescent*, 73; Moin, "Khomeini's Search for Perfection," 72.

9. Ibid., 78.

10. Algar, "Introduction," 14–16; Moin, "Khomeini," 427–30; Hoveyda, *Broken*

Crescent, 73–74; Davidson, *Islamic Fundamentalism*, 95–96; Moin, "Khomeini's Search for Perfection," 83–86.

11. Sachedina, "Activist Shi'ism," 403–4.

12. Algar, "Introduction," 18–21; Moin, "Khomeini," 427–30; Hoveyda, *Broken Crescent*, 73–74, 86–88; Moin, "Khomeini's Search for Perfection," 86–90; Zubaida, "Quest for the Islamic State," 44–45; Bakhash, *Reign of Ayatollahs*, 40–44; Algar, "Imam Khomeini," 273–82; Esposito, "The Iranian Revolution," 21–26.

13. Cited in Moin, "Khomeini's Search for Perfection," 78; Algar, "Imam Khomeini," 263–64.

14. Schirazi, *The Constitution of Iran*, 61, 297; Moin, "Khomeini's Search for Perfection," 90–92; Bakhash, *Reign of the Ayatollahs*, 241–42.

15. Moin, "Khomeini's Search for Perfection," 92; Ferdows, "Khomaini and Fadayan's Society," 244; Dabashi, *Theology of Discontent*, 419; Marty and Appleby, *Glory and Power*, 160–61; Khomeini, "Islamic Government," 33.

16. Sachedina, "Activist Shi'ism," 403–4; Choueiri, *Islamic Fundamentalism*, 155; Kramer, *Arab Awakening*, 149–50.

17. Khomeini, "Islamic Government," 37.

18. Kelidar, "Ayatollah Khomeini," 79–83; Dabashi, *Theology of Discontent*, 444–46; Ismael and Tareq, *Government and Politics*, 95–96; Parvin, "Islamic Rule," 87; Bakhash, *Reign of Ayatollahs*, 38–39; Khomeini, "Islamic Government," 36–37, 41–43, 53–66, 76–80; Ferdows, "Khomaini and Fadayan's Society," 242–47; Enayat, "Iran: Khumayni's Concept," 164; Hunter, "Islam in Power," 267–68; Arjomand, "The State and Khomeini," 154–56; Akhavi, *Religion and Politics*, 164–66.

19. Bakhash, *Reign of the Ayatollahs*, 63.

20. Ayubi, "Islamic State," 322–23, Ayubi, *Political Islam*, 151.

21. Rajaee, *Islamic Values*, 51–54.

22. Paidar, *Women and the Political Process*, 257–58.

23. Ibid., 185–86, 212–14, 265–66.

24. Bakhash, *Reign of the Ayatollahs*, 24; Ferdows, "Women and the Islamic Revolution," 290–91; Khomeini, *A Clarification of Questions*, 381; Khomeini, "Legal Rulings," 441–42.

25. Paidar, *Women and the Political Process*, 214.

26. Ferdows, "Khomaini and Fadayan's Society," 253–54.

27. Irfani, *Iran's Islamic Revolution*, 211.

28. Ibid., 211–12; Ferdows, "Women in Shi'i Islam," 77–78.

29. Khomeini, *Makanatu al-mar'ah*, 143–53.

30. Ibid., 78–79, 103–6, 155–59, 161–70.

31. Ibid., 20, 38–40, 42, 62–63, 67–68, 311–15.

32. Ibid., 93–100, 111–14, 122–26, 247–51, 253–55, 257–59, 274, 319–24.

33. Ibid., 81, 84, 86, 167, 287–96, 301.

34. Khomeini, *A Clarification of Questions*, 311–13, 323.

35. Ibid., 319–20.

36. Sanasarian, *Women's Rights,* 134.

37. Khomeini, *A Clarification of Questions,* 318–19.

38. Ibid.

39. Ibid., 351–55.

40. Hussain and Radwan, "The Islamic Revolution," 49–50; Afshar, "Khomeini's Teachings," 61–62, 78.

41. Khomeini, *A Clarification of Questions,* 329–36.

42. Ibid., 371–72.

43. Afshar, "Women, Marriage, and the State," 73.

44. Khomeini, *A Clarification of Questions,* 320–21.

45. Afshar, "Khomeini's Teachings," 62–63.

46. Ferdows, "Women and the Islamic Revolution," 292; Ferdows, "Shari'ati and Khomeini," 79; Omid, *Islam and the Post-revolutionary State,* 75–76.

47. Ibid., 76.

48. Kelidar, "Ayatollah Khomeini," 77; Keddie, "Is Shi'ism Revolutionary?" 94; Akhavi, "Islam, Politics, and Society," 406. For further reading, see also Pipes, "The Western Mind," 63; Kramer, *Arab Awakening,* 149–50. See also Ayubi, *Political Islam,* 150.

49. Paidar, *Women and the Political Process,* 217–19; Ferdows and Ferdows, "Women in Shi'i Fiqh," 56.

50. Omid, *Islam and the Post-revolutionary State,* 74–75.

51. Paidar, *Women and the Political Process,* 305–7.

52. Schirazi, *The Constitution of Iran,* 67.

53. Afshar, "Khomeini's Teachings," in *In the Shadow of Islam,* 70–71, 86.

54. Irfani, *Iran's Islamic Revolution,* 211–12; Ferdows, "Shari'ati and Khomeini," 78–79; Afshar, "Khomeini's Teachings," 81.

55. Moghadam, "Women, Work, and Ideology," 226.

56. Afshar, "Khomeini's Teachings," in *In the Shadow of Islam,* 69–70, 84–86; Ferdows, "Shari'ati and Khomeini," 78–81.

57. Sanasarian, *Women's Rights,* 133–34.

58. Rajaee, "Islam and Modernity," 116.

59. Cited in Omid, *Islam and the Post-revolutionary State,* 182–84.

60. Roy, "Islamists in Power," 73; Hoodfar, "Women and Personal Status," 36–37.

61. Schirazi, *The Constitution of Iran,* 175.

62. Ibid., 206.

63. Ibid., 237–43.

64. Moin, "Khomeini's Search for Perfection," 83–86; Paidar, *Women and the Political Process,* 324, 231–33; Omid, *Islam and the Post-revolutionary State,* 75–76.

65. Mir-Hosseini, *Islam and Gender,* 160.

66. Paidar, *Women and the Political Process,* 218–19; Hussain and Radwan, "The Islamic Revolution," 50; Afshar, "Khomeini's Teachings," 63.

67. Sanasarian, *Women's Rights,* 117.

68. Ibid., 119–20; Afshar, "Khomeini's Teachings," 62–64; Paidar, *Women and the Political Process*, 214–15; Tabari, "Islam and the Struggle," 11–14.

Chapter 6. Ayatollah Mortaza Mutahhari

1. Algar, "Introduction," 17; Dabashi, *Theology of Discontent*, 150–51; Darrow, "Woman's Place," 312.

2. Mutahhari, *Mas'alatu al-hijab*, 5–7, 10–11, 13–14; Mutahhari, *al-Ta'arruf 'ala al-Qur'an*, 8–14; Dabashi, *Theology of Discontent*, 148–51; Algar, "Introduction," 9–20; Algar, "Mutahhari," 213; Azari, "Islam's Appeal," 17–18.

3. Dabashi, *Theology of Discontent*, 187; Algar, "Mutahhari," 213–14.

4. Algar, "Introduction," 12–13; Mutahhari, *Huquq al-mar'ah*, 108–14.

5. Omid, *Islam and the Post-revolutionary State*, 55–57.

6. Ibid., 57–58.

7. Dabashi, *Theology of Discontent*, 200.

8. Ibid.

9. Ibid., 201. Abdullah Yusuf Ali translates sura 39:17–18: "Those who listen / To the Word, / And follow / The best [meaning] in it; / Those are the ones / Whom God has guided, and those / Are the ones embued / With understanding" in *The Holy Qur'an* (Tahrike Tarsile Qur'an: Elmhurst, N.Y., 2001), 1241.

10. Lawrence, *Shattering the Myth*, 115; Ferdows, "Status and Rights of Women," 18; Yeganeh and Keddie, "Sexuality and Shi'i Social Protest," 129; Moghissi, *Populism and Feminism*, 63.

11. Yeganeh, "Women's Struggles," 43–44.

12. Dabashi, *Theology of Discontent*, 206–18; Moghissi, *Populism and Feminism*, 65–66.

13. Mutahhari, *Huquq al-mar'ah*, 119, 121–23, 129, 153, 163, 173–75, 175–76; Mutahhari, *Mas'alatu al-hijab*, 44, 52–53. See also Ferdows, "Status and Rights of Women," 18–19; Yeganeh and Keddie, "Sexuality and Shi'i Social Protest," 126–27; Ferdows, "Women in Shi'i Islam," 73; Azari, "Islam's Appeal," 19–20; Moghissi, *Populism and Feminism*, 64; Lawrence, *Shattering the Myth*, 115–16; Dabashi, *Theology of Discontent*, 204–15.

14. Moghadam, *Modernizing Women*, 102.

15. Mutahhari, *Huquq al-mar'ah*, 191–93, 196–97, 206–17, 208, 215–16, 218–20, 225; Mutahhari, *Mas'alatu al-hijab*, 44. See also Darrow, "Woman's Place," 313; Moghissi, *Populism and Feminism*, 64; Dabashi, *Theology of Discontent*, 207–18.

16. Hussain and Radwan, "The Islamic Revolution," 47.

17. Mutahhari, *Huquq al-mar'ah*, 267–68.

18. Ibid., 208.

19. Ibid., 49–51, 226, 230, 232; Mutahhari, *Mas'alatu al-hijab*, 47.

20. Yeganeh, "Women's Struggles," 47–48; Dabashi, *Theology of Discontent*, 208–19; Mahdavi, "Position of Women," 262; Yeganeh and Keddie, "Sexuality and Shi'i Protest," 126; Mutahhari, *Huquq al-mar'ah*, 363, 315, 331–41, 348–50, 355–56, 361, 387–88.

21. Ibid., 365–67, 369.

22. Ibid., 324–25, 326–28.

23. Ibid., 66–68; Azari, "Islam's Appeal," 18; Haeri, "Temporary Marriage," 112; Haeri, "Mutʻa," 257.

24. Mutahhari, *Huquq al-marʾah*, 43–48, 53, 58, 64.

25. Ibid., 257–59, 267–70; Mutahhari, *Masʾalatu al-hijab*, 140.

26. Mutahhari, *Huquq al-marʾah*, 277–78, 289, 292–93, 294–97, 303–14.

27. Ibid., 282–84.

28. Mutahhari, *Masʾalatu al-hijab*, 21, 31–32.

29. Ibid., 54–55, 71.

30. Ibid., 63–66.

31. Ibid., 67–70.

32. Ibid., 71, 73–80.

33. Ibid., 82–87.

34. Ibid., 89–94, 105–15, 122–23.

35. Ibid., 48, 148–53, 155, 168.

36. Mutahhari, *Huquq al-marʾah*, 76–80, 240.

37. Ibid., 123–29.

38. Ibid., 180–81.

39. Ibid.

40. Nashat, "Women in the Ideology of the Islamic Republic," 204.

41. Ibid.

42. Nashat, "Women in Islamic Republic," 180–81.

43. Moghissi, *Populism and Feminism*, 65.

44. Mutahhari, *Masʾalatu al-hijab*, 82–85.

45. Ibid., 97–99.

46. Ibid., 117–20.

47. Ibid., 100–11.

48. Mutahhari, *Huquq al-marʾah*, 353–54.

49. Mahdavi, "Position of Women," 263–64.

50. Mutahhari, *Huquq al-marʾah*, 257–59.

51. Ibid., 265–67.

52. Ibid., 285–88.

53. Ibid., 223–26, 230. See also 218–20.

54. Ibid., 277–79, 282–84, 303–4.

Chapter 7. Zaynab al-Ghazali

1. Karam, *Women*, 206; Zuhur, *Revealing Reveiling*, 45.

2. Hoffman-Ladd, "Zaynab al-Ghazali," 64; Hoffman, "Islamic Activist," 237–38; al-Hashimi, *al-Daʻiyah Zaynab al-Ghazali*, 17–18.

3. Hoffman-Ladd, "Zaynab al-Ghazali," 64; Cooke, "Ayyam Min Hayati," 149; Sullivan and Abed-Kotob, *Islam in Contemporary Egypt*, 104–15.

4. It is difficult to determine the exact date, since on one occasion she specified the first encounter to have been six months after the foundation of the association, and at another, she quoted the 1939 date. Other dates quoted are 1940–41 or 1941–42. See also al-Hashimi, *al-Daʿiyah Zaynab al-Ghazali*, 19–32.

5. Hoffman, "Islamic Activist," 239.

6. Sullivan and Abed-Kotob, *Islam*, 105.

7. Hoffman, "Islamic Activist," 240. For more information on her political activities, see also Hoffman-Ladd, "Zaynab al-Ghazali," 64–65; Ahmed, *Women and Gender in Islam*, 196–98; Cooke, "Zaynab al-Ghazali," 2; Boullata, *Trends and Issues*, 123–25.

8. Hoffman, "Islamic Activist," 242–45; Sullivan and Abed-Kotob, *Islam in Contemporary Egypt*, 105–16; Ahmed, *Women and Gender in Islam*, 197–98; Roded, *Women in Islam*, 258; Boullata, *Trends and Issues*, 126. Other sources mention a twenty-five-year sentence. See also Hoffman-Ladd, "Zaynab al-Ghazali," 65–66; al-Ghazali, *Ayyam min hayati*, 8–16.

9. Boullata, *Trends and Issues*, 125; Ahmed, *Women and Gender in Islam*, 201.

10. See note 8.

11. Cooke, "Ayyam Min Hayati," 148; Hoffman-Ladd, "Zaynab al-Ghazali," 64–65; Cooke, "Zaynab al-Ghazali," 13.

12. Cooke, "Ayyam Min Hayati," 148; Hoffman-Ladd, "Zaynab al-Ghazali," 64–65.

13. Cooke, "Prisons," 151.

14. Boullata, *Trends and Issues*, 125; Hoffman, "Islamic Activist," 247–48; al-Ghazali, *Ayyam min hayati*, 34–35.

15. Karam, *Women*, 213.

16. Cooke, "Ayyam Min Hayati," 147; Cooke, "Zaynab al-Ghazali," 12–13.

17. Cited in Cooke, "Ayyam Min Hayati," 148.

18. Cf. the opposite view in ibid., 149.

19. Hoffman, "Islamic Activist," 233; Karam, *Women*, 208; al-Hashemi, *al-Daʿiyah Zaynab al-Ghazali*, 28.

20. Cited in Cooke, "Ayyam Min Hayati," 148.

21. Hoffman-Ladd, "Zaynab al-Ghazali," 65.

22. Ibid.; Hoffman, "Islamic Activist," 235–36.

23. Cited in Cooke, "Zaynab al-Ghazali," 3.

24. Al-Hashemi, *al-Daʿiyah Zaynab al-Ghazali*, 47–48.

25. Hatem, "Political Liberalization," 202–3.

26. Karam, *Women*, 210.

27. Ibid., 212.

28. Ibid., 209.

29. Ahmed, *Women and Gender in Islam*, 198. See also al-Hashimi, *al-Da'iyah Zaynab al-Ghazali*, 58–59.

30. Cooke, "Ayyam Min Hayati," 162.

31. Al-Hashimi, *al-Da'iyah Zaynab al-Ghazali*, 49–50, 58–59, 69–70; al-Ghazali, *Nadharat fi Kitab Allah*, 297–98.

32. Zuhur, *Revealing Reveiling*, 98; Boullata, *Trends and Issues*, 124; Hoffman, "Islamic Activist," 236. See also al-Hashimi, *al-Da'iyah Zaynab al-Ghazali*, 55–56.

33. Hoffman, "Muslim Fundamentalists," 215–16.

34. Karam, *Women*, 210; Hoffman-Ladd, "Polemics on Modesty and Segregation," 41; al-Hashimi, *al-Da'iyah Zaynab al-Ghazali*, 28.

35. Hatem, "Secularist and Islamist Discourses," 96–97.

36. Jansen, *Dual Nature of Islamic Fundamentalism*, 156.

37. Hatem, "Secularist and Islamist Discourses," 93–96; al-Hashimi, *al-Da'iyah Zaynab al-Ghazali*, 75–76; al-Ghazali, *Nadharat fi Kitab Allah*, 338.

38. See also ibid., 281.

39. Cooke, "Zaynab al-Ghazali," 3; al-Hashimi, *al-Da'iyah Zaynab al-Ghazali*, 87–88.

40. Hoffman, "Islamic Activist," 237.

41. Karam, *Women*, 213.

42. Al-Hashimi, *al-Da'iyah Zaynab al-Ghazali*, 97.

43. Al-Ghazali, *Nadharat fi Kitab Allah*, 298.

44. Al-Hashimi, *al-Da'iyah Zaynab al-Ghazali*, 143–44.

45. Ibid., 38, 146; Zuhur, *Revealing Reveiling*, 90–91.

46. Ahmed, *Women and Gender*, 201.

47. Ibid.

48. Ibid., 201–2.

49. Ibid., 200.

50. Cooke, "Ayyam Min Hayati," 150.

51. Ibid.; Cooke, "Zaynab al-Ghazali."

52. Ibid., 16.

Chapter 8. Hasan al-Turabi

1. Lowrie, *Islam, Democracy, the State*, 27; Nettler, *Past Trials and Present Tribulations*, 61, 87, 137, 189, 191–92; Hale, "Ideology and Identity," 119–20; Voll, "Political Crisis," 153–56; Esposito, "Sudan," 190; Dekmejian, *Islam in Revolution*, 186–87; Esposito, *Islam and Politics*, 3d ed., 231; Esposito, *Islam and Politics*, 2d ed., 286; Voll, "Fundamentalism," 390–91; Ayubi, *Political Islam*, 109; Mahmoud, "Sufism and Islamism," 185, 180; Warburg, "The Sudan," 25; Woodward, "Sudan," 95.

2. Ibid., 100–1. For more historical background, see also Hale, "Women of Sudan," 235–37; Dekmejian, *Islam in Revolution*, 187–88; Voll, "Islamization in the Sudan," 299.

3. Viorst, "Sudan's Islamic Experiment," 53.

4. Kok, "Hasan Abdallah al-Turabi," 185–86. See also Davis, *Between Jihad and Salaam*, 4.

5. Ibid.

6. Dekmejian, *Islam in Revolution*, 188. For more information, see also Esposito, *Islam and Politics*, 3d ed., 234; el-Affendi, *Turabi's Revolution*, 63–64, 74–76; Warburg, "Muslim Brotherhood," 198; Davis, *Between Jihad and Salaam*, 8–9; Lowrie, *Islam, Democracy, the State*, 11–12; Woodward, "Sudan," 98–99; Voll, "Fundamentalism," 375, 391; Dekmejian, *Islam in Revolution*, 187–88; Esposito, *Islam and Politics*, 2d ed., 284–85; Ayubi, *Political Islam*, 107–10.

7. Hale, "Women of Sudan," 236–37; Voll, "Fundamentalism," 391; Ayubi, *Political Islam*, 106–9; Dekmejian, *Islam in Revolution*, 188; Lowrie, *Islam, Democracy, the State*, 11–12; Davis, *Between Jihad and Salaam*, 9; Mitchell, *Society of Muslim Brothers*, 8–9; Mahmoud, "Sufism and Islamism," 180–86; Hale, "New Muslim Woman," 176; Warburg, "Sudan," 26–27; Voll, "Political Crisis," 155–56.

8. Hoveyda, *Broken Crescent*, 99.

9. Mayer, "Fundamentalist Impact," 141; Woodward, "Turabi," 241; Hale, "Women of Sudan," 234; Mahmoud, "Sufism and Islamism," 186–88; Hale, "Ideology and Identity," 127; Woodward, "Sudan," 101–2; Nettler, *Past Trials and Present Tribulations*, 88–89.

10. Dekmejian, *Islam in Revolution*, 188–89; Viorst, "Sudan's Islamic Experiment," 46.

11. Hale, "Women of Sudan," 245.

12. See note 9.

13. Dekmejian, *Islam and Revolution*, 189.

14. Marty and Appleby, *Glory and Power*, 170–72.

15. Warburg, "Sudan," 27–28; el-Affendi, *Turabi's Revolution*, 64; Lowrie, *Islam, Democracy, the State*, 19.

16. El-Affendi, *Turabi's Revolution*, 179.

17. Ibrahim, "Dialogue with Turabi," 4. See also Miller, "Global Islamic Awakening," 218–19.

18. El-Affendi, *Turabi's Revolution*, 162–63; Voll, "Fundamentalism," 375; Kramer, *Arab Awakening*, 153.

19. Davis, *Between Jihad and Salaam*, 14.

20. Westerlund, "Reaction and Action," 325; Turabi, "Principles of Governance," 5.

21. Warburg, "Sudan," 31.

22. Moussalli, "Modern Islamic Fundamentalist Discourses," 110.

23. Warburg, "Sudan," 31; el-Affendi, *Turabi's Revolution*, 171–72.

24. Ibrahim, "Dialogue with Turabi," 15.

25. Turabi, *Tajdid al-fikr al-Islami*, 45–46; el-Affendi, *Turabi's Revolution*, 160.

26. Ibid., 170–72.

27. Moussalli, *Moderate and Radical*, 156–62.

28. Ali, "Islamism in Practice," 192.

29. Lowrie, *Islam, Democracy, the State,* 12; Miller, "Global Islamic Awakening," 218; Miller, "Faces of Fundamentalism," 126.

30. Davis, *Between Jihad and Salaam,* 25–26.

31. Ibid., 14–15.

32. Miller, "Global Islamic Awakening," 202–3; el-Affendi, *Turabi's Revolution,* 173–74; Moussalli, *Moderate and Radical,* 91–92.

33. El-Affendi, *Turabi's Revolution,* 175.

34. Miller, "Global Islamic Awakening," 202–3; Davis, *Between Jihad and Salaam,* 16.

35. Moussalli, "Modern Islamic Fundamentalist Discourses," 110; el-Affendi, *Turabi's Revolution,* 173–74.

36. Turabi, *al-Ittijah al-Islami,* 21–22; Shehadeh, "Women in Islamic Fundamentalism," 69.

37. An-Na'im, *Toward an Islamic Reformation,* 41.

38. Shehadeh, "Women in Islamic Fundamentalism," 70; Turabi, *al-Ittijah al-Islami,* 19–21; Turabi, "The Islamic State," 244.

39. Lowrie, *Islam, Democracy, the State,* 47.

40. Davis, *Between Jihad and Salaam,* 11.

41. Lowrie, *Islam, Democracy, the State,* 36.

42. Davis, *Between Jihad and Salaam,* 17.

43. Shehadeh, "Women in Islamic Fundamentalism," 70; Turabi, *al-Ittijah al-Islami,* 42.

44. Ibid., 43.

45. Ibid., 41.

46. Hale, "New Muslim Woman," 195; Lowrie, *Islam, Democracy, the State,* 36; Hale, *Gender Politics,* 243.

47. Pipes, "The Western Mind," 59–60.

48. Gruenbaum, "The Islamist State," 29.

49. Ibid., 30.

50. Hale, *Gender Politics,* 89, reported in the *Sudan Democratic Gazette,* no. 19 (December 1991), 8.

51. Lowrie, *Islam, Democracy, the State,* 48.

52. Miller, "Global Islamic Awakening," 204.

53. Hale, "Ideology and Identity," 132–33.

54. Ibid.

55. Ibid., 131–33.

56. Hale, *Gender Politics,* 199.

57. Esposito, *Islam and Politics,* 3d ed., 142; Davis, *Between Jihad and Salaam,* 37–45.

58. Hale, "Ideology and Identity," 132–33.

59. Hale, *Gender Politics,* 185.

60. Miller, "Global Islamic Awakening," 203.

61. Davis, *Between Jihad and Salaam,* 37–41.

62. Hale, *Gender Politics*, 61–62.

63. Sidahmed, "Women under Sudan's Fundamentalist Regime," 20.

64. Lowrie, *Islam, Democracy, the State*, 46.

65. Davis, *Between Jihad and Salaam*, 16–17, 21, 35.

66. Lowrie, *Islam, Democracy, the State*, 46.

67. Davis, *Between Jihad and Salaam*, 42–45.

68. Ibid., 21.

69. Woodward, "Sudan," 100; Warburg, "Muslim Brotherhood," 200.

70. Ibid., 200–1.

71. Davis, *Between Jihad and Salaam*, 11, 25–26.

72. Miller, "Global Islamic Awakening," 202.

73. Ibrahim, "Dialogue with Turabi," 4.

74. Ibid.

75. Brumberg, "Rhetoric and Strategy," 21.

76. Miller, *God Has Ninety-Nine Names*, 162.

77. Lawyers Committee for Human Rights, 32.

78. Ibid., 40.

79. Hale, *Gender Politics*, 137–39; Davis, *Between Jihad and Salaam*, 11; Hale, "Women of Sudan," 236; Hale, "Ideology and Identity," 121, Hale, "New Muslim Woman," 188.

80. Kok, "Hasan al-Turabi," 189.

81. Hale, "Women of Sudan," 243.

82. Cf. Nazlee, *Feminism and Muslim Women*, 30–31.

83. Lindholm and Vogt, *Islamic Law Reform*, 145; Gruenbaum, "The Islamist State," 30.

84. Hatem, "Political Liberalization," 195.

85. Miller, "Global Islamic Awakening," 204–5; Mayer, *Islam and Human Rights*, 118; Moghissi, *Feminism and Islamic Fundamentalism*, 11 n. 4; *Report of the Omdrum Centre for Women's Studies* (Cairo: N.p., 1998); Woodward, "Sudan," 102; Hale, *Gender Politics*, 142 n. 27.

86. Ibid., 199–200; Hale, "Ideology and Identity," 126–27; an-Na'im, *Toward an Islamic Reformation*, 41.

87. Brumberg, "Rhetoric and Strategy," 21, 330.

88. Hale, *Gender Politics*, 215–18.

89. Miller, "Global Islamic Awakening," 205–7.

90. Ibid., 206.

91. Turabi, "Principles of Governance," 8.

92. Turabi, "The Islamic State," 247–48; Miller, *God Has Ninety-Nine Names*, 162; Moussalli, "Modern Islamic Fundamentalist Discourse," 110–11; Moussalli, *Moderate and Radical*, 93; el-Affendi, *Turabi's Revolution*, 160–62; Turabi, "Principles of Governance," 8.

93. El-Affendi, *Turabi's Revolution*, 160; Turabi, *Qadaya al-hurriyyah*, 2–3.

94. El-Affendi, *Turabi's Revolution*, 160; Turabi, "Principles of Governance," 3–5,

7–8; Viorst, "Sudan's Islamic Experiment," 53–54; Turabi, "The Islamic State," 245.

95. El-Affendi, *Turabi's Revolution*, 169–70; Moussalli, *Moderate and Radical*, 163.

96. Turabi, "Principles of Governance," 2–3.

97. Moussalli, "Hasan al-Turabi," 52–53.

98. Westerlund, "Reaction and Action," 309 n. 2; Ibrahim, "Dialogue with Turabi," 4–5.

99. Davis, *Between Jihad and Salaam*, 3.

100. Ibrahim, "Dialogue with Turabi," 5.

101. Miller, *God Has Ninety-Nine Names*, 162.

102. Ali, "Islamism in Practice," 193–94; Krämer, "Cross-Links and Double Talk," 46.

103. Lawyers Committee for Human Rights, 12.

104. Hale, "Ideology and Identity," 120–21; Hale, *Gender Politics*, 103–4; Sidahmed, "Women under Sudan's Fundamentalism," 20.

105. Cited in Hale, *Gender Politics*, 196–99; "The Women of Sudan," 235.

Chapter 9. Rashid al-Ghannoushi

1. Ayubi, *Political Islam*, 113. For more information, see also Zghal, "The New Strategy," 205; Munson, "Islamic Revivalism," 210; Grandguillaume, "Islam and Politics," 40.

2. Joffé, "Maghribi Islam," 71; Waltz, "Islamist Appeal," 652; Anderson, "Tunisia and Libya," 166; Ayubi, *Political Islam*, 113–15.

3. Cited in Waltz, "Islamist Appeal," 660–61; cf. also Joffé, "Maghribi Islam," 71; Salem, "Tunisia," 158.

4. Dunn, "al-Nahda Movement," 152; Davis, *Between Jihad and Salaam*, 83–85; Burgat and Dowell, *The Islamic Movement*, 185–88; Zghal, "The New Strategy," 213–15.

5. Jones, "Portrait of Rashid al-Ghannoushi," 20–21.

6. Davis, *Between Jihad and Salaam*, 85; Munson, "Islamic Revivalism," 211; Burgat and Dowell, *The Islamic Movement*, 185–88; Magnuson, "Islamic Reform," 170–71; Davidson, *Islamic Fundamentalism*, 92; Esposito, *Islamic Threat*, 154.

7. Burgat and Dowell, *The Islamic Movement*, 186–88; Anderson, "Tunisia and Libya," 166–68; Hermassi, "Rise and Fall," 106–21; Joffé, "Maghribi Islam," 71.

8. Esposito, *Islamic Threat*, 159–62; Burgat and Dowell, *The Islamic Movement*, 193–94; Davidson, *Islamic Fundamentalism*, 92–93; Choueiri, *Islamic Fundamentalism*, 154; Dunn, "al-Nahda Movement," 155–58; Davis, *Between Jihad and Salaam*, 86–88.

9. Munson, "Islamic Revivalism," 211.

10. Dekmejian, *Islam in Revolution*, 205.

11. Ghadbian, "Current Issues," 8–9; Lawyers Committee for Human Rights, 93.

12. Zghal, "The New Strategy," 209.

13. Magnuson, "Islamic Reform," 180.

14. Zghal, "The New Strategy," 211; Vandewalle, "From the New State," 612.

15. Lawyers Committee for Human Rights, 115–17.

16. Davis, *Between Jihad and Salaam*, 85–86.

17. Burgat and Dowell, *The Islamic Movement*, 63.

18. Shehadeh, "Women in Islamic Fundamentalism," 74; Davis, *Between Jihad and Salaam*, 88–89.

19. Burgat and Dowell, *The Islamic Movement*, 102; Salem, "Tunisia," 158; Zghal, "The New Strategy," 208–10; Jones, "Portrait of Rashid al-Ghannoushi," 21.

20. Hatem, "Political Liberalization," 197–98.

21. Ibid., 198.

22. al-Ghannoushi, *al-Mar'ah bayna al-Qur'n*, 3–5.

23. Jones, "Portrait of Rashid al-Ghannoushi," 24.

24. al-Ghannoushi, *al-Mar'ah bayna al Qur'an*, 9–11, 58.

25. Ibid., 14–16.

26. Ibid., 18–19; Jones, "Portrait of Rashid al-Ghannoushi," 23–24.

27. Ibid., 24.

28. al-Ghannoushi, *al-Mar'ah al-muslimah*, 136–40.

29. Ibid., 142–47.

30. Ibid., 147–49.

31. Lawyers Committee for Human Rights, 98.

32. Haddad, "Islam and Gender," 20.

33. Ibid.

34. Ibid., 20–21.

35. Shehadeh, "Women in Islamic Fundamentalism," 75; al-Ghannoushi, "al-Mar'ah fi al-Qur'an," 85–99.

36. al-Ghannoushi, *al-Mar'ah bayna al-Qur'an*, 59–65.

37. Ibid., 68–70.

38. Ibid., 70–72.

39. Ibid., 73–82; al-Ghannoushi, "al-Mar'ah fi al-Qur'an," 86–87.

40. Ibid., 92–94.

41. Shehadeh, "Women in Islamic Fundamentalism," 75; al-Ghannoushi, *al-Hurriyyat al-'ammah*, 129–31.

42. al-Ghannoushi, "al-Mar'ah fi al-Qur'an," 95–99; al-Ghannoushi, *al-Mar'ah bayna al-Qur'an*, 85–91.

43. Ibid., 28–32.

44. Ibid., 19–22.

45. Ibid., 23–25.

46. al-Ghannoushi, *al-Hurriyyat al-'ammah*, 62–63, 131–33, 208.

47. Ibid., 131–32.

48. Ibid., 131–33, 208; Shehadeh, "Women in Islamic Fundamentalism," 76.

49. Ibid.; al-Ghannoushi, *al-Hurriyyat al-'ammah*, 131–32.

50. al-Ghannoushi, *al-Mar'ah bayna al-Qur'an*, 92–97.

51. Ibid., 97–100.

52. Ibid., 53–54.

53. Ibid.

54. Ibid., 54–55.

55. Al-Ghannoushi, *al-Hurriyyat al-'ammah*, 62, 135.

56. Al-Ghannoushi, *al-Mar'ah bayna al-Qur'an*, 48–52.

57. Ibid., 104–5.

58. Haddad, "Islam and Gender," 20–21; Davis, *Between Jihad and Salaam*, 83, 90.

59. Brumberg, "Rhetoric and Strategy," 14.

60. Ibid.

61. Dunn, "al-Nahda Movement," 154–55.

62. Haddad, "Islam and Gender," 9.

63. Ibid., 21; Hoffman, "Muslim Fundamentalists," 214.

64. Davis, *Between Jihad and Salaam*, 99.

65. See also Shehadeh, "Women in Islamic Fundamentalism," 79.

Chapter 10. Sheikh Hussein Fadlallah

1. Cited in Wright, "Lebanon," 57.

2. Boroujerdi, "Hizbullah," 129.

3. Hoveyda, *Broken Crescent*, 96. For the structure and hierarchy of Hizbullah, see Jaber, *Hezbollah*, 62–67; Shararah, *Dawlat "Hizballah,"* 364–69; Ranstorp, *Hizb'allah*, 41.

4. For further reading, see Ranstorp, *Hizb'allah*; Cobban, "Growth of Shii Power"; Shararah, *Dawlat "Hizballah"*; Wright, "Lebanon"; Kramer, "Hizbullah in Lebanon"; Esposito, "Trailblazers"; Esposito, *Islam and Politics*, 3d ed.; Kramer, "Hizbullah: The Calculus of Jihad"; Hoveyda, *Broken Crescent*; Boroujerdi, "Hizbullah"; Ranstorp, *Hizb'allah*; Kramer, "Moral Logic of Hizballah"; Kramer, *Hezbollah's Vision*; Norton, "Lebanon"; Esposito, "The Iranian Revolution"; Kramer, "The Oracle"; Miller, "Faces of Fundamentalism."

5. For further reading on Fadlallah, see Kramer, "The Oracle"; Miller, "Faces of Fundamentalism"; Shararah, *Dawlat "Hizballah"*; Kramer, "The Moral Logic of Hizballah"; Jaber, *Hezbollah*; Kramer, "Hizbullah in Lebanon"; Carré, "Fadlallah"; Ranstorp, *Hizb'allah*; Davidson, *Islamic Fundamentalism*; Kramer, "Muhammad Husayn Fadlallah"; Esposito, *Islam and Politics*, 3d ed.; Dekmejian, *Islam in Revolution*; Abu-Rabi', *Intellectual Origins*; Marshall, "Paradoxes of Change"; Waines, "Through a Veil."

6. Kramer, "The Oracle," 107.

7. Miller, "Faces of Fundamentalism," 127–28.

8. Kramer, "Muhammad Husayn Fadlallah," 147; Carré, "Fadlallah"; 453–54; Kramer, "The Oracle," 87–88.

9. Abu-Rabi', *Intellectual Origins*, 221.

10. Kramer, *Hezbollah's Vision*, 16.

11. Wright, *Sacred Rage*, 91–94.

12. Fadlallah, *al-Khiyar al-akhar*, 88–89.

13. Fadlallah, *Ta'amullat*, 94–95, 114–16, 121–22, 125–26, 146–47; Ahmad and Ansari, *Islamic Perspectives*, 8–9, 22, 50–54; Haddad, *Contemporary Islam*, 63, 122.

14. Norton, "Shi'ism and Social Protest," 172–73.

15. Abu-Rabi', *Intellectual Origins*, 221.

16. Ibid., 231–32.

17. Ibid., 232.

18. Ibid., 230.

19. Ibid., 229.

20. Ibid., 228.

21. For further reading, see Jaber, *Hezbollah*; Kramer, *Hezbollah's Vision*; Abu-Rabi', *Intellectual Origins*; Kramer, "Muhammad Husayn Fadlallah"; Dekmejian, *Islam and Revolution*; Norton, "Shi'ism and Social Protest"; Kramer, "The Oracle"; Davidson, *Islamic Fundamentalism*; Carré, "Fadlallah."

22. Davidson, *Islamic Fundamentalism*, 90.

23. Fadlallah, *al-Harakah al-Islamiyyah*, 40. See also Abu-Rabi', *Intellectual Origins*, 228.

24. For further reading, see Abu-Rabi', *Intellectual Origins*; Carré, "Fadlallah"; Esposito, *Islam and Politics*, 3d ed.; Sivan, "The Enclave Culture."

25. Fadlallah, *Dunya al-mar'ah*, 10, 18, 19, 21–22, 35–36, 51; Fadlallah, *Qira'ah jadidah*, 21–22, 41.

26. Fadlallah, *Qira'ah jadidah*, 24–29; Fadlallah, *Dunya al-mar'ah*, 37–38, 45–47, 111–14, 116–19; Fadlallah, *Ta'ammulat Islamiyyah*, 15–16, 22–23.

27. Fadlallah, *Ta'ammulat Islamiyyah*, 13, 109–10; Fadlallah, *Qira'ah jadidah*, 32, 65, 66–68, 71; Fadlallah, *Dunya al-mar'ah*, 123.

28. Fadlallah, *Dunya al-mar'ah*, 38–39, 64–66, 67–69, 76–78, 87–90, 95–102.

29. Ibid., 50, 57, 59–60, 63–64; Fadlallah, *Ta'ammulat Islamiyyah*, 32.

30. Fadlallah, *Qira'ah jadidah*, 117–20.

31. Fadlallah, *al-Masa'il al-fiqhiyyah*, 421; Fadlallah, *Ta'ammulat Islamiyyah*, 42–47, 48–50, 55–56, 59–61, 120; Fadlallah, *Dunya al-mar'ah*, 329–30.

32. Ibid., 169–76.

33. Ibid., 201, 210–11; Fadlallah, *Ta'ammulat Islamiyyah*, 75–77; Fadlallah, *al-Masa'il al-fiqhiyyah*, 2:421.

34. Fadlallah, *Dunya al-mar'ah*, 221–27.

35. Ibid., 145–46, 185–86; Fadlallah, *Ta'ammulat Islamiyyah*, 64–65.

36. Ibid., 66; Fadlallah, *Dunya al-mar'ah*, 189–91.

37. Ibid., 253.

38. Fadlallah, *Ta'ammulat Islamiyyah*, 90–91, 94–96; Fadlallah, *Qira'ah jadidah*, 55; Fadlallah, *al-Masa'il al-fiqhiyyah*, 1:263, 2:433; Fadlallah, *Dunya al-mar'ah*, 232.

39. Fadlallah, *Ta'ammulat Islamiyyah*, 91, 103–7.

40. Ibid., 53, 116–19, 157; Fadlallah, *Ru'an wa mawaqif*, 64.

41. Fadlallah, *Ta'ammulat Islamiyyah*, 161–63; Fadlallah, *Dunya al-mar'ah*, 104–7; Fadlallah, *al-Masa'il al-fiqhiyyah*, 2:434.

42. Fadlallah, *Dunya al-mar'ah*, 306; Fadlallah, *Ta'ammulat Islamiyyah*, 26, 63–64, 127–29; Ni'meh, *al-Mut'ah*, 7, 209–11.

43. Ni'meh, *al-Mut'ah*, 213; Fadlallah, *Dunya al-mar'ah*, 289–95, 307–10; Fadlallah, *Ta'ammulat Islamiyyah*, 130.

44. Fadlallah, *Dunya al-mar'ah*, 315, 318–19.

45. Ibid., 325–27, 336, 341.

46. Fadlallah, *Ta'ammulat Islamiyyah*, 92–93.

47. Fadlallah, *Dunya al-mar'ah*, 259–60; Fadlallah, *Ta'ammulat Islamiyyah*, 136–143; Fadlallah, *al-Masa'il al-fiqhiyyah*, 2:428.

48. Ibid., 442–45; Fadlallah, *Ta'ammulat Islamiyyah*, 145–48; Fadlallah, *Dunya al-mar'ah*, 102–4.

49. Ibid., 131–33, 147–48, 161; Fadlallah, *Ta'ammulat Islamiyyah*, 31–32, 171–72; Fadlallah, *al-Masa'il al-fiqhiyyah*, 1:243–45, 250–52; Fadallah, *Qira'ah jadidah*, 81–82, 134.

50. Sivan, "The Enclave Culture," 31.

51. Abu-Rabi', *Intellectual Origins*, 230.

52. Ibid., 229.

53. Fadlallah, *Qira'ah jadidah*, 66.

54. Fadlallah, *al-Masa'il al-fiqhiyyah*, 2:421.

Chapter 11. Conclusion

1. Mernissi, *Beyond the Veil*, 44.

2. Mir-Hosseini, *Marriage on Trial*, 32.

3. Shehadeh, "Women and Sayyid Qutb," 50.

4. Ibid.

5. Stowasser, "Women's Issues," 18.

6. Dwyer, "Law and Islam"; Engineer, *Rights of Women*; Ahmed, "Early Islam"; Afshar, "Development Studies"; Hassan, "Muslim Women"; Engineer, *Justice*; Bulliet, *Islam: View from the Edge*; Mueller, "Revitalizing Old Ideas"; Fischer, "Legal Postulates"; Parvin, "Islamic Rule"; Mir-Hosseini, *Marriage on Trial*; Ayubi, *Political Islam*; Esposito, *Islam and Politics*, 3d ed.; Liebesny, "Stability and Change"; Coulson, *A History of Islamic Law*; el-Nimr, "Women in Islamic Law"; Musallam, "The Ordering of Muslim Societies"; Haddad, *Islamic Impact*; Roded, *Women in Islam*; Rahman, "Islamic Modernism"; Husain, *Global Islamic Politics*; al-Nowaihi, "Problems of Modernization"; Lewis, *Political Language*; Rahman, *Islam and Modernity*, 70.

7. Coulson, *History of Islamic Law*, 6–7.

8. Cited in Engineer, *Justice*, 28.

9. Ibid., 28. See also al-Nowaihi, "Problems of Modernization," 176–77.

10. Rahman, "Islamic Modernism," 323–24.

11. Al-Nowaihi, "Problems of Modernization," 180.

12. Siddique, *The Struggle*, 16–21. Hadith from Abu-Daoud's *Sunan* and Tirmidhi's *Jami'*, and other collections.

13. Malass, "al-Mar'ah al-muslimah," 15.

14. Ibid., 83, 93; Siddique, *The Struggle*, 139–40; Shaaban, "Muted Voices," 70–72; Rahman, "Status of Women in Islam," 290; Watson, "Women and the Veil," 145–46; el-Saadawi, "Woman and Islam," 202; Rahman, "Status of Women in the Qur'an," 40–41.

15. Same as note 14.

16. El-Solh and Mabro, *Muslim Women's Choices*, 11–12; Esposito, "Changing Role," 33.

17. Al-Ghazali, *al-Sunnah al-nabawiyyah*, 44–51.

18. Rahman, "Status of Women in Islam," 297–98; Rahman, "Survey of Modernization," 453; Esposito, "Women's Rights," 111.

19. For a liberal interpretation, cf. Hassan, "Muslim Women," 54–57; Barazangi, "Vicegerency," 87–89; and Mahmoud Taha, who explained *qiwamah* as conditional to the security and economic dependence of women; an-Na'im, *Islamic Reformation*, 99–100.

20. Cited in al-Hibri, "Study of Islamic Herstory," 218

21. Siddique, *The Struggle*, 24.

22. Hoffman-Ladd, "Women's Religious Observances," 328; Lemu and Heeren, *Woman in Islam*, 15–16.

23. Engineer, *Rights of Women*, 7–8, 124–26,; Mernissi, *Women's Rebellion*, 111; Rahman, "Survey of Modernization," 459–60; Kamali, "Divorce and Women's Rights," 85; Esposito, "Women's Rights," 112; Mernissi, "The Patriarch," 318; Madelung, "Shi'i Attitudes," 73; el-Saadawi, "Woman and Islam," 195–96; Dorphi, "Islamic Law," 172.

24. Mir-Hosseini, *Marriage on Trial*, 32.

25. Al-Ramli, *Kitab al-Fatawa*, 26; Tucker, *In the House of the Law*, 67–68.

26. Zubaida, "Quest for the Islamic State," 40.

27. Rahman, "Status of Women in the Qur'an," 45–46; el-Saadawi, "Woman and Islam," 198; al-Hibri, "Study of Islamic Herstory," 216; Engineer, *Rights of Women*, 102; Rahman, "Survey of Modernization," 451–52; Mernissi, "The Patriarch," 315–17; Rahman, "Status of Women in Islam," 298–301; Siddique, *The Struggle*, 85–88.

28. Barazangi, "Vicegerency," 80–84.

29. Ibid.; Stern, "The First Women Converts," 300–1; Stowasser, "Religious Ideology," 287–8.

30. Ramazani, "Women in Iran," 417–19.

31. For more examples, see Ramazani, "Women in Iran," 411–19. See also Tohidi, "Modernity," 135–36.

32. Sanasarian, *Women's Rights*, 138.

33. Afshar, "Women, State, and Ideology," 264–65; Haddad, "Islam, Women, and Revolution," 294–95.

34. Molyneux, "Mobilization," 280.

35. Moghissi, *Populism and Feminism*, 13–14.

36. Lerner, *Creation of Patriarchy*, 212.

37. For an excellent discussion on the development of patriarchy, see ibid., 7–10; Cooey et al., *After Patriarchy*, xi–xii.

38. Cited in Hale, "New Muslim Woman," 196.

39. Moghissi, *Populism and Feminism*, 17–18.

40. Cited in Moghadam, *Modernizing Women*, 107.

41. Kandiyoti, "Women, Islam, and the State," 9–10. See also Moghadam, "Rhetorics," 260.

42. Moghadam, "Patriarchy," 39–40.

43. Ayubi, *Political Islam*, 35, 44; Sabbah, *Woman in the Muslim Unconscious*, 16–17; Shukrallah, "Impact of Islamic Movement," 27; Moghadam, "Patriarchy," 38; Mernissi, "Feminity as Subversion," 96–97; Afshar, "Khomeini's Teachings," 75; Hale, "New Muslim Woman," 184; Mernissi, "Muslim Women and Fundamentalism," 164–65; Moghadam, *Modernizing Women*, 132; Moghisi, *Populism and Feminism*, 78–79; Kandiyoti, "Women, Islam, and the State," 185–86; Moghadam, "Islamist Movements," 273; Davis, "Concept of Revival," 50–51; Marshall, "Paradoxes of Change," 10–11; Waltz, "Islamist Appeal," 665.

44. Cited in Hawley, *Fundamentalism and Gender*, 27.

45. Ibid., 27–29.

46. Cited in Brown, "Fundamentalism," 180–81.

47. Mernissi, *Beyond the Veil*, 30. For more on the psychological theory, see Schmidt, *Veiled and Silenced*, 60; Ardener, "Ground Rules," 1–4.

48. Cited in Hoffman, "Muslim Fundamentalists," 212; Ayubi, *Political Islam*, 40–41.

49. Hawley and Proudfoot, "Introduction," 30; Awn, "Indian Islam," 76; Marshall, "Paradoxes of Change," 12.

50. Cited in Nicolaisen, "Introduction," 7–8; Schmidt, *Veiled and Silenced*, 5–11, 20–21; cf. Ahmed, *Women and Gender*, 68, 236–40.

51. Marshall, "Paradoxes of Change," 12; Moghadam, *Modernizing Women*, 94–95; Hale, "New Muslim Woman," 177.

52. Cited in Mir-Hosseini, *Islam and Gender*, 160.

53. Lewis, *Political Language*, 11–23.

54. Cited in Moghishi, *Populism and Feminism*, 62–63.

55. Cited in ibid., 63.

56. Cited in ibid., 61.

57. Merquior, *The Veil and the Mask*, 1–3.

58. Cited in Moghadam, "Women, Work, and Ideology," 226.

59. Cited in Moghadam, *Modernizing Women*, 96.

60. Cooke, *Women Claim Islam*, 109.

61. Cited in Yeganeh, "Women's Struggles," 53.

62. Hardcare, "Impact of Fundamentalisms," 141–43.

63. Ahmed, *Women and Gender*, 223–26.

64. Cooke, *Women Claim Islam*, 113.

65. Ahmed, *Women and Gender*, 223–26. See also Charrad, "Cultural Diversity," 64–65; Davis and Hessini, "Social Reform," 341.

66. Benavides, "Religious Articulations," 1.

67. Cited in Mann, *Sources of Social Power*, 1:6.

68. Ibid., 4, 6–7, 22.

69. Cited in Merquior, *The Veil and the Mask*, 7.

70. Sabbah, *Woman in the Muslim Unconscious*, 17.

71. Lerner, *The Creation of Patriarchy*, 217–18.

72. Weber, "Politics as a Vocation," 79, cited in Benavides, "Religious Articulations," 1-12.

73. Foucault, *Power/Knowledge*, 98; Gramsci, *Selections from the Prison Notebooks*; Sanasarian, "The Politics of Gender," 58.

74. For more on this, see Ardener, "Ground Rules: An Introduction," 20–29.

75. Hoffman, "Muslim Fundamentalists," 215–16.

Glossary

Ahl al-bayt: house of the Prophet, Ali and his descendants
'Alim (pl. ulema): religious scholar
Allah: God
Amir: prince or head of state
'Aqidah: religious belief, creed, or ideology
Ayyam min hayati: days of my life
Bid'ah: literally innovation, heresy. Any practice or teaching contrary to
    the Scripture
Chador: Iranian women's Islamic dress
Da'wah: Islamic call or mission
Diyyah: blood money paid to the victim's family
Al-Fa'iliyyah al-qutriyyah: regional or national activism
Faqih: a Shi'ite jurist
Fard: religious obligation
Fatwa: legal opinion to meet exigent circumstances
Fiqh: jurisprudence
Fiqh al-darurah: jurisprudence of necessity
Fitnah: chaos caused by women's charms
Fitrah: human nature, innate character
Hadith: sayings of the Prophet
Hajj: pilgrimage to Mecca
al-Hakimiyyah: the doctrine that sovereignty in the state is God's alone, to
    be exercised on his behalf by a just ruler
Hanafi: Sunni school of jurisprudence
Haram: prohibited by religion
Hijab: veil
Hizbullah: the Party of God
'Ibadah: the high regard in which marriage is held in Islam

'Iddah: waiting period after divorce or death of husband to determine paternity

Ijtihad: interpretation of Qur'anic text

Islah: reform

Islamiyyah: Islamic. The Arabic term used to identify those who wish to reestablish the ideal Islamic society of the seventh century

'Ismat: bond of marriage

'Iyha'at: religious allusions

'Iyjabiyyah: proactivity in the affirmation of one's faith

Ja'fari: Twelver Shi'i sect

Jahiliyyah: a society that does not follow the tenets of Islam and therefore in ignorance of religious truth

Jama'ah: community

Jama'at-i Islami: association founded by al-Mawdudi

Jam'iyyat-i 'Ulama'-i Hind: an organization of Indian Muslim religious scholars

Jihad: struggle

al-Jihad: holy war

al-Jihad al-Isalmi: Islamic holy war

Jilbab: loose garment worn by women at the time of the Prophet

Jinn: demons

Kasb: achievement, gain

Kayd: cunning and deceit attributed to women

Khimar: veil worn by women at the time of the Prophet

Khul': payment given by a wife to her husband to obtain a divorce

Kuttab: schools that teach religion

Li'an: sworn statement before a judge by a husband, accusing his wife of adultery, and her sworn reply

Mabarrah: Shi'ite charitable institution

Madhhab: school of jurisprudence

Madrasah: religious school

Mahr: dower

Mahram: a male to whom a woman can never be married because of a legal or family relationship

Makruh: reprehensible religious injunction

Maliki: Sunni school of jurisprudence

Mandub: recommended religious injunction

Marji' a'la: highest Shi'ite religious authority

Marji' taqlid: Shi'ite authority on tradition

Marji'iyyah: Shi'ite religious authoritative source

Maslahah: principle of utility for Islam and Muslim society

Mot'eh: Persian for concubine

Mu'allafat al-qulub: women whose hearts are to be won or reconciled to
their condition

Mubah: permissible religious injunction

Muhkamat: unambiguous Qur'anic verses and, therefore, not subject to
interpretation

Muhtasib: accounting official in the market of Medina

Mujaddid (pl. mujaddidin): renewer, reformer

Mujaddidah: female renewer, reformer

Mujahid (pl. mujahidin): male warrior

Mujahidah (pl. mujahidat): female warrior

Mujtahid: interpreter of Scriptures; authority on matters of jurisprudence

Mukallaf: charged with the duty of the realization of divine will

Mulhid: atheist

Mullah: Shi'ite religious scholar

Muqallid: imitator in matters of jurisprudence

al-Murshid al-ruhi: Shi'ite spiritual guide

Mustahab: desirable actions for the faithful as opposed to required

Mut'ah: temporary marriage

Mutashabihat: ambiguous Qur'anic verses and, therefore, subject to interpretation

al-Nafs: soul; self

Niqab: veil covering face

Nushuz: recalcitrance, specifically in women who disobey their husbands

Purdah: veil

Qiwamah: male authority over women, as dictated by Scripture

Qur'an: Koran, Islamic Scripture

al-Ra'i: individual legal opinion

Riddah: apostasy; religious desertion

Salafiyyah: that which pertains to ancestry. The Arabic term to describe
fundamentalism

Seegheh: a formula. Describes a woman taken in Mut'a marriage

Shaqa'iq al-rijal: sisters of men; women who are like men in prowess

Shari'ah: Islamic divine law

Shar'iyyat al-hukm: legitimacy of rule

Shi'a: Islamic religious sect; followers of Imam Ali

Shi'ite: member of the Shi'a sect

Shirk: association of anything or anyone with God

Shumuliyyah: comprehensiveness of religion

Shura: consultation

Shurafa: honorable people

Al-Sirat al-mustaqim: the straight or right path of Islam

Sufi: Muslim mystic

Sunni: orthodox Islamic religious sect

Sura: chapter of the Qur'an

al-Tafdil: favoring men over women in reference to a Qur'anic verse

Tafsir: interpretation of religious text

Tafwid: delegation of the power of divorce by a husband to his wife or any
    third party

Taghayyur al-ahkam bi taghayyur al-azman: Islamic principle that rules
    should change with changing times

Tajdid: periodic renewal of the faith

Takfir: apostasy

al-Takfir wal Hijrah: the Islamist group Apostasy and Emigration, also
    known as the Society of Muslims

Takhlu: devoid of

Talaq bid'ah: unorthodox or heretical divorce

Tali'ah: vanguard group of Islamists whose raison d'être is jihad

Tanfagir: explodes

Tansa: forgets

Taqiyyah: to act contrary to one's principles of faith for the sake of expedi-
    ency

Taqlid: imitation, tradition

Tawazun: equilibrium of existence

Tawhid: unicity; the oneness of God

Thabat: the constancy of the Qur'an and divine truths

Tu'azzi: consoles

Uluhiyyah: divinity

Ummah: the Muslim community

'Umra: minor pilgrimage

Usul al-fiqh: foundations of jurisprudence

Usuliyyah: Arabic translation of the Western term *fundamentalism*

Wakil: deputy

Waqf: endowment

Waqi'iyyah: feasibility and pragmatism of Islam

al-Wat': trampling of women
Wali al-faqih: chief jurisprudent
Wilayat al-faqih: guardianship of the jurist
Zakat: almsgiving
Zinah: adornments

Selected Bibliography

Abbot, Freeland K. "Maulana Maududi on Qur'anic Interpretation." *The Muslim World* 48 (1958): 6–19.

al-Abdin, A. Z. "The Political Thought of Hasan al-Banna." *Islamic Studies* 28, no. 3 (1989): 219–34.

Abrahamian, Ervand. "Khomeini: A Fundamentalist." In *Fundamentalism in Comparative Perspective,* edited by Lawrence Kaplan. Amherst: University of Massachusetts Press, 1992.

————. *Khomeinism: Essays on the Islamic Republic.* Berkeley and Los Angeles: University of California Press, 1993.

Abu-Rabi', Ibrahim M. *Intellectual Origins of Islamic Resurgence in the Modern Arab World.* Albany: State University of New York Press, 1996.

Abu-Rabi', Ibrahim M., ed. *Islamic Resurgence: Challenges, Directions, and Future Perspectives.* Tampa, Fla.: World and Islam Studies Enterprise, 1994.

Adams, Charles J. "The Ideology of Mawlana Mawdudi." In *South Asian Politics and Religion,* edited by Donald Eugene Smith. Princeton, N.J.: Princeton University Press, 1966.

————. "Mawdudi and the Islamic State." In *Voices of Resurgent Islam,* edited by John L. Esposito. New York and Oxford: Oxford University Press, 1983.

Adler, Leonore Loeb, ed. *Women in Cross-Cultural Perspective.* New York, Westport, Conn., and London: Praeger, 1991.

el-Affendi, Abdelwahab. *Turabi's Revolution: Islam and Power in Sudan.* London: Grey Seal, 1991.

Afkhami, Mahnaz, and Erika Friedl, eds. *In the Eye of the Storm: Women in Post Revolutionary Iran.* London and New York: I. B. Tauris, 1994.

————, eds. *Muslim Women and the Politics of Participation.* Syracuse, N.Y.: Syracuse University Press, 1997.

Afshar, Haleh. "Development Studies and Women in the Middle East: The Dilemmas of Research and Development." In *Women in the Middle East,* edited by Haleh Afshar. London: Macmillan, 1993.

————. "Islam and Feminism: An Analysis of Political Strategies." In *Feminism and Islam,* edited by Mai Yamani. Reading, England: Ithaca Press, 1996.

———. *Islam and Feminisms: An Iranian Case Study.* London: Macmillan, 1998.

———. "Khomeini's Teachings and Their Implications for Iranian Women." In *In the Shadow of Islam: The Women's Movement in Iran,* edited by Azar Tabari and Nahid Yeganeh. London: Zed Press, 1982.

———. "Khomeini's Teachings and Their Implications for Women." *Feminist Review* 12 (October 1982): 59–72.

———. *Women and Politics in the Third World.* London and New York: Routledge, 1996.

———. "Women and the Politics of Fundamentalism in Iran." In *Women and Politics in the Third World,* edited by Haleh Afshar. London and New York: Routledge, 1996.

———. "Women, Marriage, and the State in Iran." In *Women, State, and Ideology,* edited by Haleh Afshar. Albany: State University of New York Press, 1987.

———. "Women, State, and Ideology in Iran." *Third World Quarterly* 7, no. 2 (1985): 256–78.

———, ed. *Women in the Middle East.* London: Macmillan, 1993.

———, ed. *Women, State, and Ideology.* Albany: State University of New York Press, 1987.

Agbetola, Ade Shitu. "The Equality of Man and Woman in Islam: Sayyid Qutb's Views Examined." *Islamic Studies* 28, no. 2 (1989): 131–7.

Ahmad, Aziz. "Mawdudi and Orthodox Fundamentalism in Pakistan." *Middle East Journal* 21 (1967): 369–80.

Ahmad, Khurshid, and Zafar Ishaq Ansari. "Mawlana Sayyid Abul A'la Mawdudi: An Introduction to His Vision of Islam and Islamic Revival." In *Islamic Perspectives,* edited by Khurshid Ahmad and Zafar Ishaq Ansari. England: Islamic Foundation in association with Saudi Publishing House, Jeddah, 1979.

Ahmad, Mumtaz. "Islamic Fundamentalism in South Asia: The Jama'at-i-Islami and the Tablighi Jama'at of South Asia." In *Fundamentalisms Observed,* edited by Martin E. Marty and R. Scott Appleby. Chicago: University of Chicago Press, 1991.

Ahmed, Akbar. *Discovering Islam.* London and New York: Routledge, 1988.

Ahmed, Leila. "Early Islam and the Position of Women: The Problem of Interpretation." In *Women in Middle Eastern History,* edited by Nikki R. Keddie and Beth Baron. New Haven, Conn.: Yale University Press, 1991.

———. *Women and Gender in Islam.* New Haven, Conn.: Yale University Press, 1992.

Ahmed, Ramadan A. "Women in Egypt and Sudan." In *Women in Cross-Cultural Perspective,* edited by Leonore Loeb Adler. New York, Westport, Conn., and London: Praeger, 1991.

Akhavi, Shahrough. "Islam, Politics, and Society in the Thought of Ayatollah Khomeini, Ayatollah Taliqani, and Ali Shari'ati." *Middle Eastern Studies* 24, no. 4 (1988): 404–31.

———. "Qutb, Sayyid." In *The Oxford Encyclopedia of the Modern Islamic World,* edited by John L. Esposito. New York and Oxford: Oxford University Press, 1995.

———. "Sayyid Qutb: The Poverty of Philosophy and the Vindication of Islamic Tradition." In *Cultural Transitions in the Middle East,* edited by Serif Mardin. Leiden: E. J. Brill, 1994.

Akhtar, Shabbir. *A Faith for All Seasons.* London: Bellew Publishing, 1990.

Algar, Hamid. "Imam Khomeini, 1902–1962: The Pre-revolutionary Years." In *Islam, Politics, and Social Movements,* edited by Edmund Burke III and Ira M. Lapidus. Berkeley and Los Angeles: University of California Press, 1988.

———. Introduction to *Fundamentals of Islamic Thought,* by Murtaza Mutahhari. Translated by R. Campbell. Berkeley, Calif.: Mizan Press, 1985.

———. "Mutahhari, Murtaza." In *The Oxford Encyclopedia of the Modern Islamic World,* edited by John L. Esposito. New York and Oxford: Oxford University Press, 1995.

———. *The Roots of the Islamic Revolution.* London: Open Press, 1983.

Ali, Haydar Ibrahim. "Islamism in Practice: The Case of Sudan." In *The Islamist Dilemma.* International Politics of the Middle East Series. Reading, England: Ithaca Press, 1995.

Altorki, Soraya. "Role and Status of Women." In *The Oxford Encyclopedia of the Modern Islamic World,* edited by John L. Esposito. New York and Oxford: Oxford University Press, 1995.

'Amarah, Muhammad. *Abu al-A'la al-Mawdudi wal-sahwah al-Islamiyyah* (Abu al-A'la al-Mawdudi and the Islamic Awakening). Beirut: Dar al-Wihdah, 1986.

Anderson, Lisa. "Tunisia and Libya: Responses to the Islamic Impulse." In *The Iranian Revolution: Its Global Impact,* edited by John L. Esposito. Miami: Florida International University Press, 1990.

Ansari, Hamied N. "The Islamic Militants in Egyptian Politics." *International Journal of Middle East Studies* 16 (1984): 123–44.

Ardener, Shirley. "Ground Rules and Social Maps for Women: An Introduction." In *Women and Space: Ground Rules and Social Maps,* edited by Shirley Ardener. Rev. ed. Oxford and Providence: Berg, 1993.

———, ed. *Defining Females.* London: Croom Helm, 1978.

———, ed. *Women and Space: Ground Rules and Social Maps.* Rev. ed. Oxford and Providence: Berg, 1993.

Arjomand, Said Amir. "Shi'ite Jurisprudence and Constitution Making in the Islamic Republic." In *Fundamentalisms and the State,* edited by Martin E. Marty and R. Scott Appleby. Chicago: University of Chicago Press, 1993.

———. "The State and Khomeini's Islamic Order." *Iranian Studies* 13, nos. 1–4 (1980): 147–64.

———. "Unity and Diversity in Islamic Fundamentalism." In *Fundamentalisms Comprehended,* edited by Martin E. Marty and R. Scott Appleby. Chicago: University of Chicago Press, 1995.

Awn, Peter J. "Indian Islam: The Shah Bano Affair." In *Fundamentalism and Gender*, edited by John Stratton Hawley. New York and Oxford: Oxford University Press, 1994.

Ayubi, Nazih N. M. "Islamic State." In *The Oxford Encyclopedia of the Modern Islamic World*, edited by John L. Esposito. New York and Oxford: Oxford University Press, 1995.

———. *Political Islam: Religion and Politics in the Arab World*. London and New York: Routledge, 1994.

———. "The Political Revival of Islam: The Case of Egypt." *International Journal of Middle East Studies* 12 (1980): 481–99.

Azari, Farah. "Islam's Appeal to Women in Iran: Illusions and Reality." In *Women of Iran: The Conflict with Fundamentalist Islam*, edited by Farah Azari. London: Ithaca Press, 1983.

———. "Sexuality and Women's Oppression in Iran." In *Women of Iran: The Conflict with Fundamentalist Islam*, edited by Farah Azari. London: Ithaca Press, 1983.

———, ed. *Women of Iran: The Conflict with Fundamentalist Islam*. London: Ithaca Press, 1983.

Azzam, Maha. "Gender and the Politics of Religion in the Middle East." In *Feminism and Islam*, edited by Mai Yamani. Reading, England: Ithaca Press, 1996.

Badran, Margot. "Islam, Patriarchy, and Feminism in the Middle East." *Trends in History* 4, no. 1 (1985): 49–71.

Bagader, Abubaker A. "Contemporary Islamic Movements in the Arab World." In *Islam, Globalization, and Post-modernity*, edited by Akbar S. Ahmed and Hastings Donnan. London and New York: Routledge, 1994.

Baker, Raymond William. "Invidious Comparisons: Realism, Postmodern Globalism, and Centrist Islamic Movements in Egypt." In *Political Islam: Revolution, Radicalism, or Reform?* edited by John L. Esposito. Boulder, Colo.: Lynne Rienner, 1997.

Bakhash, Shaul. *The Reign of the Ayatollahs: Iran and the Islamic Revolution*. New York: Basic Books, 1984.

———. "Veils of Fears: Khomeini's Strange Way of Wooing Iranian Women." *New Republic* (October 28, 1985): 15–6.

al-Banna, Hasan. *Five Tracts of Hasan al-Banna (1906–1949)*. Translated and annotated by Charles Wendell. Berkeley and Los Angeles: University of California Press, 1978.

———. *al-Mar'ah al-muslimah* (The Muslim woman). Beirut: Dar al-Jile, 1988.

Barazangi, Nimat Hafez. "Vicegerency and Gender Justice." In *Islamic Identity and the Struggle for Justice*, edited by Nimat Barazangi, M. Raquibuz Zaman, and Omar Afzal. Gainesville: University Press of Florida, 1996.

Bauer, Janet L. "Sexuality and the Moral 'Construction' of Women in Islamic Society." *Anthropological Quarterly* 58, no. 3 (1985): 120–9.

Beck, Lois, and Nikki R. Keddie, eds. *Women in the Muslim World.* Cambridge: Harvard University Press, 1978.

Beckford, James A., and Thomas Luckmann, eds. *The Changing Face of Religion.* London: Sage Publications, 1989.

Benavides, Gustavo. "Religious Articulations of Power." In *Religion and Political Power.* Albany: State University of New York Press, 1989.

Benavides, Gustavo, and M. W. Daly, eds. *Religion and Political Power.* Albany: State University of New York Press, 1989.

Bernard, Cheryl. "Islam and Women: Some Reflections on the Experience of Iran." *Journal of South Asian and Middle Eastern Studies* 4, no. 2 (1980): 10–26.

Binder, Leonard. *Islamic Liberalism: A Critique of Development Ideologies.* Chicago: University of Chicago Press, 1988.

Bloom, Irene, J. Paul Martin, and Wayne L. Proudfoot, eds. *Religious Diversity and Human Rights.* New York: Columbia University Press, 1996.

Bodman, Herbert L., and Nayereh Tohidi, eds. *Women in Muslim Societies.* Boulder, Colo.: Lynne Rienner, 1998.

Boroujerdi, Mehrzad. "Hizbullah." In *The Oxford Encyclopedia of the Modern Islamic World,* edited by John L. Esposito. New York and Oxford: Oxford University Press, 1995.

Boudhiba, Abdelwahab. *Sexuality in Islam.* London: Routledge and Kegan Paul, 1985.

Boullata, Issa J. *Trends and Issues in Contemporary Arab Thought.* Albany: State University of New York Press, 1990.

Brink, Judy, and Joan Mencher, eds. *Mixed Blessings: Gender and Religious Fundamentalism Cross Culturally.* New York and London: Routledge, 1997.

Brohi, Allahbukhsh K. "Mawlana Abul A'la Mawdudi. The Man, the Scholar, the Reformer." In *Islamic Perspectives,* edited by Khurshid Ahmad and Zafar Ishaq Ansari. Jeddah: Islamic Foundation, England, in association with Saudi Publishing House, 1979.

Brown, Daniel. *Rethinking Tradition in Modern Islamic Thought.* Cambridge: Cambridge University Press, 1996.

Brown, Karen McCarthy. "Fundamentalism and the Control of Women." In *Fundamentalism and Gender,* edited by John Stratton Hawley. New York and Oxford: Oxford University Press, 1994.

Brumberg, Daniel. "Khomeini's Legacy: Islamic Rule and Islamic Justice." In *Spokesmen for the Despised,* edited by R. Scott Appleby. Chicago: University of Chicago Press, 1997.

———. "Rhetoric and Strategy: Islamic Movements and Democracy in the Middle East." In *The Islamism Debate,* edited by Martin Kramer. Tel Aviv: Moshe Dayan Center for Middle Eastern and African Studies, Tel Aviv University, 1997.

Bulliet, Richard M. *Islam: The View from the Edge.* New York: Columbia University Press, 1994.

Burgat, François, and William Dowell. *The Islamic Movement in North Africa.* Austin: Center for Middle Eastern Studies, University of Texas, 1993.

Butterworth, Charles E. "Prudence versus Legitimacy: The Persistent Theme in Islamic Political Thought." In *Islamic Resurgence in the Arab World,* edited by Ali E. Hillal Dessouki. New York: Praeger, 1982.

Carré, Olivier. "Fadlallah, Muhammad Husayn." In *The Oxford Encyclopedia of the Modern Islamic World,* edited by John L. Esposito. New York and Oxford: Oxford University Press, 1995.

Charrad, M. M. "Cultural Diversity within Islam: Veils and Laws in Tunisia." In *Women in Muslim Societies,* edited by Herbert L. Bodman and Nayereh Tohidi. Boulder, Colo.: Lynne Rienner, 1998.

Choueiri, Youssef M. *Islamic Fundamentalism.* London: Printer Publishers, 1990.

Cobban, Helena. "The Growth of Shii Power in Lebanon and Its Implications for the Future." In *Shi'ism and Social Protest,* edited by Juan R. I. Cole and Nikki R. Keddie. New Haven, Conn.: Yale University Press, 1986.

Commins, David. "Hasan al-Banna 1906–1949." In *Pioneers of Islamic Revival,* edited by Ali Rahnema. London and Atlantic Highlands, N.J.: Zed Books, 1994.

"Constitution of the Islamic Republic of Iran," with Introductory Note by K. Ramazani. *Middle East Journal* 34, no. 2 (1980): 181–204.

Conway, Jill K., Susan C. Bourque, and Joan W. Scott, eds. *Learning about Women: Gender, Politics, and Power.* Ann Arbor: University of Michigan Press, 1987.

Cooey, Paula M., William R. Eakin, and Jay B. McDaniel, eds. *After Patriarchy: Feminist Transformations of the World Religions.* Maryknoll, N.Y.: Orbis, 1991.

Cooke, Miriam. "Ayyam min Hayati: The Prison Memoirs of a Muslim Sister." *Journal of Arabic Literature* 26 (1995): 147–63.

———. "Prisons: Egyptian Women Writers on Islam." *Religion and Literature* 20, no. 1 (1988): 139–53.

———. *Women Claim Islam: Creating Islamic Feminism through Literature.* New York and London: Routledge, 2001.

———. "Zaynab Al-Ghazali: Saint or Subversive?" *Die Welt des Islams* 34, no. 1 (1994): 1–20.

Cooke, Miriam, and Bruce Lawrence. "Muslim Women between Human Rights and Islamic Norms." In *Religious Diversity and Human Rights,* edited by Irene Bloom, J. Paul Martin, and Wayne L. Proudfoot. New York: Columbia University Press, 1996.

Cottam, Richard. "Inside Revolutionary Iran." In *Shi'ism and Social Protest,* edited by Juan R. I. Cole and Nikki R. Keddie. New Haven, Conn.: Yale University Press, 1986.

———. "The Iranian Revolution." In *Shi'ism and Social Protest,* edited by Juan R. Cole and Nikki R. Keddie. New Haven, Conn.: Yale University Press, 1986.

Coulson, Noel J. *A History of Islamic Law.* 1964. Reprint, Edinburgh: University Press, 1997.

Coulson, Noel J., and Doreen Hinchcliffe. "Women and Law Reform in Contemporary Islam." In *Women in the Muslim World,* edited by Lois Beck and Nikki R. Keddie. Cambridge: Harvard University Press, 1978.

Cragg, Kenneth. *The Pen and the Faith.* London: George Allen and Unwin, 1985.

Cudsi, Alexander S. "Islam and Politics in the Sudan." In *Islam in the Political Process,* edited by James P. Piscatori. Cambridge: Cambridge University Press, 1983.

Cudsi, Alexander S., and Ali E. Hillal Dessouki, eds. *Islam and Power.* Baltimore, Md.: Johns Hopkins University Press, 1981.

Dabashi, Hamid. *Theology of Discontent.* New York: New York University Press, 1993.

Darrow, William. "Woman's Place and the Place of Women in the Iranian Revolution." In *Women, Religion, and Social Change,* edited by Yvonne Y. Haddad and Ellison B. Findly. Albany: State University of New York Press, 1985.

Davidson, Lawrence. *Islamic Fundamentalism.* Westport, Conn., and London: Greenwood Press 1998.

Davis, Eric. "The Concept of Revival and the Study of Islam and Politics." In *The Islamic Impulse,* edited by Barbara Freyer Stowasser. Washington, D.C.: Center for Contemporary Arab Studies, Georgetown University, 1989.

————. "Ideology, Social Class, and Islamic Radicalism in Egypt." In *From Nationalism to Revolutionary Islam,* edited by Said Amir Arjomand. Oxford: Macmillan, in association with St. Anthony's College, 1984.

Davis, Joyce M. *Between Jihad and Salaam: Profiles in Islam.* New York: St. Martin's Press, 1997, 1999.

Davis, Susan Schaefer, and Leila Hessini. "Social Reform in North Africa." In *The Oxford Encyclopedia of the Modern Islamic World,* edited by John L. Esposito. New York and Oxford: Oxford University Press: 1995.

Dekmejian, R. Hrair. "Islamic Revival: Catalysts, Categories, and Consequences." In *The Politics of Islamic Revivalism,* edited by Shireen T. Hunter. Bloomington and Indianapolis: Indiana University Press, 1988.

————. *Islam in Revolution: Fundamentalism in the Arab World.* 2d ed. Syracuse, N.Y.: Syracuse University Press, 1995.

————. "Multiple Faces of Islam." In *Islam in a Changing World,* edited by A. Jerichow and J. Bœk Simonsen. Richmond, Surrey: Curzon, 1997.

————. "Resurgent Islam and the Egyptian State." In *The Middle East and North Africa: Essays in Honor of J. C. Hurewitz,* edited by Reeva S. Simon. New York: Middle East Institute, Columbia University Press, 1990.

Donohue, John J., and John L. Esposito, eds. *Islam in Transition: Muslim Perspectives.* New York and Oxford: Oxford University Press, 1982.

Dorphi, Kenneth Jan. "Islamic Law in Contemporary North Africa: A Study of the Laws of Divorce in the Maghreb." In *Women and Islam,* edited by Azizah al-Hibri. Oxford and New York: Pergamon Press, 1982.

Doumato, Eleanor Abdella. "Jahiliyyah." In *The Oxford Encyclopedia of the Modern*

Islamic World, edited by John L. Esposito. New York and Oxford: Oxford University Press, 1995.

Dunn, Michael Collins. "The Al-Nahda Movement in Tunisia: From Renaissance to Revolution." In *Islamism and Secularism in North Africa,* edited by John Ruedy. New York: St. Martin's Press, 1994.

Dwyer, Daisy Hilse. "Law and Islam in the Middle East: An Introduction." In *Law and Islam in the Middle East,* edited by Daisy Hilse Dwyer. New York, Westport, Conn., and London: Bergin and Garvey, 1990.

———, ed. *Law and Islam in the Middle East.* New York, Westport, Conn., and London: Bergin and Garvey, 1990.

Enayat, Hamid. "Iran: Khumayni's Concept of the 'Guardianship of the Jurisconsult.'" In *Islam in the Political Process,* edited by James P. Piscatori. Cambridge: Cambridge University Press, 1983.

———. *Modern Islamic Thought.* Austin: University of Texas Press, 1982.

Engineer, Asghar Ali. *Justice, Women, and Communal Harmony in Islam.* New Delhi: Indian Council of Social Science Research, 1989.

———. *The Rights of Women in Islam.* New York: St. Martin's Press, 1992.

Esfandiari, Haleh. "The Majles and Women's Issues in the Islamic Republic of Iran." In *In the Eye of the Storm: Women in Post-revolutionary Iran,* edited by Mahnaz Afkhami and Erika Friedl. London and New York: I. B. Tauris, 1994.

———. *Reconstructed Lives: Women and Iran's Islamic Revolution.* Washington, D.C., Baltimore, Md., and London: Woodrow Wilson Center Press, Johns Hopkins University Press, 1997.

Esposito, John L. "The Changing Role of Muslim Women." *Islam and the Modern Age* 7, no. 1 (1976): 29–56.

———. "The Iranian Revolution: A Ten-Year Perspective." In *The Iranian Revolution: Its Global Impact,* edited by John L. Esposito. Miami: Florida International University Press, 1990.

———. *Islam and Politics.* Revised second edition. Syracuse: Syracuse University Press, 1987.

———. *Islam and Politics.* Third edition. Syracuse: Syracuse University Press, 1991.

———. *The Islamic Threat: Myth or Reality.* New York and Oxford: Oxford University Press, 1992.

———. *Islam the Straight Path.* 1988. Reprint, New York and Oxford: Oxford University Press, 1991.

———. "Law in Islam." In *The Islamic Impact,* edited by Yvonne Y. Haddad, Byron Haines, and Ellison Findly. Syracuse, N.Y.: Syracuse University Press, 1984.

———. "Sudan." In *The Politics of Islamic Revivalism,* edited by Shireen T. Hunter. Bloomington and Indianapolis: Indiana University Press, 1988.

———. "Sudan's Islamic Experiment." *The Muslim World* 76 (1986): 181–202.

———. "Trailblazers of the Islamic Resurgence." In *Political Islam: Revolution, Radicalism, or Reform?* edited by John L. Esposito. Boulder, Colo.: Lynne Rienner, 1997.

———. "Women in Islam and Muslim Societies." In *Islam, Gender, and Social Change,* edited by Yvonne Yazbik Haddad and John L. Esposito. New York and Oxford: Oxford University Press, 1998.

———. *Women in Muslim Family Law.* Syracuse, N.Y.: Syracuse University Press, 1982.

———. "Women's Rights in Islam." *Islamic Studies* 14, no. 2 (1975): 99–114.

———, ed. *The Iranian Revolution: Its Global Impact.* Miami: Florida International University Press, 1990.

———, ed. *Islam and Development.* Syracuse, N.Y.: Syracuse University Press, 1980.

———, ed. *Political Islam: Revolution, Radicalism, or Reform?* Boulder, Colo.: Lynne Rienner, 1997.

———, ed. *Voices of Resurgent Islam.* New York and London: Oxford University Press, 1983.

Fadlallah, Mahdy. *Ma'Sayyid Qutb fi fikrihi al-siyasi wal dini* (With Sayyid Qutb in his political and religious thought). Beirut: Mu'assasat al-Risalah, 1978.

Fadlallah, Muhammad Husayn. *Dunya al-mar'ah* (Woman's world). Beirut: Dar al-Malak, 1997.

———. *Fiqh al-hayat* (Life's jurisprudence). Beirut: Mu'assasat al-'arif, 1997.

———. *al-Harakah al-Islamiyyah . . . humum wa qadaya* (The Islamic movement . . . concerns and issues). Beirut: Dar al-Malak, 1990.

———. *al-Islam wa mantiq al-quwwah* (Islam and the logic of power). Beirut: Dar al-Islamiyyah, 1979.

———. *al-Khiyar al-akhar: Hizballah* (The alternate choice: Hizballah). Beirut: Dar al-Hady, 1994.

———. *al-Mar'ah bayna waqi'iha wa haqqiha fi al-ijtima' al-siyasi al-Islami* (Women between their present condition and their rights in Islamic political society). Beirut: Dar al-Thiqlayn, 1995.

———. *al-Masa'il al-fiqhiyyah* (Juridical questions). 2 vols. Beirut: Dar al-Malak, 1995.

———. *Qira'ah jadidah li fiqh al-mar'ah al-huquqi* (A new reading of women's legal rights). Beirut: Publications of the Center of Women's Affairs, 1996.

———. *Ru'an wa mawaqif* (Vision and attitudes). Beirut: Dar al-Malak, n.d.

———. *Ta'ammulat fi al-fikr al-siyasi al-Islami* (Reflections on Muslim political thought). Iran: al-Tawhid Institute for Publications, 1995.

———. *Ta'ammulat Islamiyyah hawla al-mar'ah* (Islamic reflections on women). Beirut: Dar al-Malak, n.d., 4th printing.

———. *Uslub al-da'wah fi al-Qur'an* (The style of the [Islamic] call in the Qur'an). Beirut: Dar al-Malak, 2000.

Farhi, Farideh. "Class Struggles, the State, and Revolution in Iran." In *Power and Stability in the Middle East,* edited by Berch Berberoglu. London and Atlantic Highlands, N.J.: Zed Books, 1989.

Fathi, Asghar, ed. *Women and the Family in Iran.* Leiden: E. J. Brill, 1985.

Faust, Kimberly, John Gulick, Saad Gadalla, and Hind Khattab. "Young Women Members of the Islamic Revival Movement in Egypt." *The Muslim World* 82 (1992): 55–65.

Ferdows, Adele K. "Shari'ati and Khomeini on Women." In *The Iranian Revolution and the Islamic Republic.* Washington, D.C.: Middle East Institute in cooperation with Woodrow Wilson International Center for Scholars, 1982.

———. "The Status and Rights of Women in Ithna 'Ashari Shi'i Islam." In *Women and the Family in Iran,* edited by Asghar Fathi. Leiden: E. J. Brill, 1985.

———. "Women and the Islamic Revolution." *International Journal of Middle East Studies* 15 (1983): 283–98.

———. "Women in Shi'i Islam and Iran." *Oriente moderno* 62 NS 1–12 (1982): 71–81.

Ferdows, Adele K., and Amir H. Ferdows. "Women in Shi'i Fiqh: Images through Hadith." In *Women and Revolution in Iran,* edited by Guity Nashat. Boulder, Colo.: Westview Press, 1983.

Ferdows, Amir H. "Khomaini and Fadayan's Society and Politics." *International Journal of Middle East Studies* 15 (1983): 241–57.

Fischer, Michael M. J. "Legal Postulates in Flux: Justice, Wit, and Hierarchy in Iran." In *Law and Islam in the Middle East,* edited by Daisy Hilse Dwyer. New York, Westport, Conn., and London: Bergin and Garvy, 1990.

Foucault, Michel. *Knowledge/Power: Selected Interviews and Other Writings.* Edited and translated by Colin Gordon. New York: Pantheon Books, 1980.

Friedl, Erika. "Ideal Womanhood in Postrevolutionary Iran." In *Mixed Blessings: Gender and Religious Fundamentalism Cross Culturally,* edited by Judy Brink and Joan Mencher. New York and London: Routledge, 1997.

Gerami, Shahin. "Privatization of Woman's Role in the Islamic Republic of Iran." In *Religion and Political Power,* edited by Gustavo Benavides and M. W. Daly. Albany: State University of New York Press, 1989.

———. *Women and Fundamentalism.* New York and London: Garland, 1996.

Gerholm, Tomas. "The Islamization of Contemporary Egypt." In *African Islam and Islam in Africa,* edited by Eva Evers Rosander and David Westerlund. London: Hurst, 1997.

Ghadbian, Najib. "Current Issues among Islamists in the Near East." *Middle East Affairs* 2, nos. 2–3 (1995): 4–16.

al-Ghannoushi, Rashid. "Hal 'al-ittijah al-Islami' 'adat 'amal 'am'itar lil tamyiz?" (Is political Islam a tool for work or a framework for discrimination?). *al-Ghadir* 3, nos. 19–20 (1992): 164–72.

———. *al-Hurriyyat al-ammah fi al-dawlah al-Islamiyyah* (Public freedom in the Islamic state). Beirut: Center for Arab Unity Studies, 1993.

———. *al-Mar'ah al-muslimah fi Tunis: bayna tawjihat al Qur'an wa waqi' al-mujtama' al-tunisi* (The Muslim woman in Tunisia: Between Qur'anic instructions and the present condition of Tunisian society). Kuwait: Dar al-Qalam lil Nashr wal Tawzi', 1988.

——. *al-Mar'ah bayna al-Qur'an wa waqi' al-Muslimin* (Women between the Qur'an and the present condition of Muslims). Tunis: Carthage Publishers, 1993.

——. "al-Mar'ah fi al-Qur'an" (Women in the Qur'an). *al-Ghadir* 2, nos. 12–13 (1991): 85–99.

al-Ghazali, Muhammad. *al-Sunnah al-nabawiyyah bayna 'ahl al-fiqh . . . wa 'ahl al-Hadith* (The life and practices of the Prophet between jurisprudents and traditionalists). Beirut and Cairo: Dar al-Shuruq, 1996.

al-Ghazali, Zaynab. *Ayyam min hayati* (Days of my life). Cairo: Dar al-Shuruq, 1987.

——. *Min khawatir Zaynab al-Ghazali: fi shu'un al-din wal hayat* (Of Zaynab al-Ghazali's thoughts: In matters of religion and life). Cairo: Dar al-I'tisam, 1996.

——. *Nadharat fi Kitab Allah* (Views on God's Book) . Vol. 1. Beirut and Cairo: Dar al-Shuruq, 1994.

——. *Nahwa ba'thin jadid* (For a new resurrection). Beirut: Dar al-Shuruq, 1986.

——. *Return to the Pharaoh.* Translated by Mokrane Guezzou. Leicester, England: Islamic Foundation, 1994.

Gilani, Syed As'ad. *"Mawdudi": Thought and Movement.* Lahore: Matba'at al-Maktabat el-'Ilmiyyah, 1978.

Gramsci, Antonio. *Selections from the Prison Notebooks.* New York: International Publishers, 1972.

Grandguillaume, Gilbert. "Islam and Politics in North-West Africa: The Maghreb." In *Islam and the State in the World Today,* edited by Oliver Carré. New Delhi: Manohar Publications, 1989.

Gruenbaum, Ellen. "The Islamist State and Sudanese Women." *Middle East Report* (No. 179) 22, no. 6 (1992): 29–32.

el-Guindi, Fadwa. "Is There an Islamic Alternative? The Case of Egypt's Contemporary Islamic Movement." *International Insight* 1, no. 6 (1981): 19–24.

——. "Veiled Activism: Egyptian Women in the Contemporary Islamic Movement." *Peuples Méditerranéens* 22–23 (1983): 79–89.

Haddad, Yvonne Yazbik. *Contemporary Islam and the Challenge of History.* Albany: State University of New York Press, 1982.

——. "Islam and Gender: Dilemmas in the Changing Arab World." In *Islam, Gender, and Social Change,* edited by Yvonne Yazbik Haddad and John L. Esposito. New York and Oxford: Oxford University Press, 1998.

——. "Islam, Women, and Revolution in Twentieth Century Arab Thought." In *Women, Religion, and Social Change,* edited by Yvonne Y. Haddad and Ellison B. Findly. Albany: State University of New York Press, 1985.

——. "The Qur'anic Justification for an Islamic Revolution: The View of Sayyid Qutb." *Middle East Journal* 37 (1983): 14–29.

——. "Sayyid Qutb: Ideologue of Islamic Revival." In *Voices of Resurgent Islam,* edited by John L. Esposito. New York and Oxford: Oxford University Press 1983.

Haddad, Yvonne Yazbik, and Jane I. Smith. "Women in Islam: 'The Mother of All

Battles.'" In *Arab Women: Between Defiance and Restraint*, edited by Suha Sabbagh. New York: Olive Branch Press, 1996.

Haddad, Yvonne Yazbik, and John L. Esposito, eds. *Islam, Gender, and Social Change*. New York and Oxford: Oxford University Press, 1998.

Haddad, Yvonne Yazbik, and Ellison B. Findly, eds. *Women, Religion, and Social Change*. Albany: State University of New York Press, 1985.

Haddad, Yvonne Yazbik, Byron Haines, and Ellison Findly, eds. *The Islamic Impact*. Syracuse, N.Y.: Syracuse University Press, 1984.

Haddad, Yvonne Yazbik, J. O. Voll, and John L. Esposito, eds. *The Contemporary Islamic Revival: A Critical Survey and Bibliography*. New York, Westport, Conn., and London: Greenwood Press, 1991.

Haeri. "Ambivalence toward Women in Islamic Law and Ideology." *Middle East Annual* 5 (1985): 45–67.

———. "The Institution of Mutʿa Marriage in Iran: A Formal and Historical Perspective." In *Women and Revolution in Iran*, edited by Guity Nashat. Boulder, Colo.: Westview Press, 1983.

———. "Mutʿah." In *The Oxford Encyclopedia of the Modern Islamic World*, edited by John L. Esposito. New York and Oxford: Oxford University Press, 1995.

———. "Mutʿa: Regulating Sexuality and Gender Relations in Postrevolutionary Iran." In *Islamic Legal Interpretation*, edited by Muhammad Khalid Masud, Brinkley Messick, and David S. Powers. Cambridge: Harvard University Press, 1996.

———. "Obedience versus Autonomy: Women and Fundamentalism in Iran and Pakistan." In *Fundamentalisms and Society*, edited by Martin E. Marty and R. Scott Appleby. Chicago: University of Chicago Press, 1993.

———. "Of Feminism and Fundamentalism in Iran and Pakistan." *Contention: Debates in Society, Culture, and Science* 4, no. 3 (1995): 129–49.

———. "Temporary Marriage and the State in Iran: An Islamic Discourse on Female Sexuality." *Social Research* 59, no. 1 (1992): 201–23.

———. "Temporary Marriage: An Islamic Discourse on Female Sexuality." In *In the Eye of the Storm: Women in Post-revolutionary Iran*, edited by Mahnaz Afkhami and Erika Friedl. London and New York: I. B. Tauris, 1994.

———. "Women, Law, and Social Change in Iran." In *Women in Contemporary Muslim Societies*, edited by Jane I. Smith. Lewisburg, Pa.: Bucknell University Press; London: Associated University Press, 1980.

Haim, Sylvia G. "Sayyid Qutb." *Asian and African Studies* 16 (1982): 146–56.

Hale, Sondra. *Gender Politics in Sudan*. Boulder, Colo.: Westview Press, 1996.

———. "Gender Politics and Islamization in Sudan." *South Asia Bulletin* 14, no. 2 (1994): 51–66.

———. "Ideology and Identity: Islamism, Gender, and the State in Sudan." In *Mixed Blessings: Gender and Religious Fundamentalism Cross Culturally*, edited by Judy Brink and Joan Mencher. New York and London: Routledge, 1997.

———. "'The New Muslim Woman': Sudan's National Islamic Front and the Invention of Identity." In *Women in the Islamic Maelstrom*, edited by Ghada Talhami. Special issue of *The Muslim World* 86, no. 2 (1996).

———. "The Wing of the Patriarch: Sudanese Women and Revolutionary Parties." *Middle East Report* (No. 138) 16, no. 1 (1986): 25–30.

———. "The Women of Sudan's National Islamic Front." In *Political Islam*, edited by Joel Beinin and Joe Stork. Berkeley and Los Angeles: University of California Press, 1997.

Halliday, Fred. "The Politics of Islamic Fundamentalism: Iran, Tunisia, and the Challenge to the Secular State." In *Islam, Globalization, and Postmodernity*, edited by Akbar S. Ahmed and Hastings Donnan. London and New York: Routledge, 1994.

Hambly, Gavin R. G., ed. *Women in the Medieval Islamic World*. New York: St. Martin's Press, 1998.

Haq, Farhat. "Women, Islam, and the State in Pakistan." *The Muslim World* 86, no. 2 (1996): 158–75.

Hardcare, Helen. "The Impact of Fundamentalisms on Women, the Family, and Interpersonal Relations." In *Fundamentalisms and Society*, edited by Martin E. Marty and R. Scott Appleby. Chicago: University of Chicago Press, 1993.

Harris, Jay M. "'Fundamentalisms': Objections from a Modern Jewish Historian." In *Fundamentalism and Gender*, edited by John Stratton Hawley. New York and Oxford: Oxford University Press, 1994.

Hasan, Masdul. *Sayyid Abul A'la Mawdudi and His Thought*. Lahore: Islamic Publications, 1984.

al-Hashimi, Ibn. *al-Da'iyah Zaynab al-Ghazali: masirat jihad wa hadith min al-dhikrayat min khilal kitabatiha* (Zaynab al-Ghazali: A journey of struggle and reminiscences through her writings). Cairo: Dar al-I'tisam, 1988.

Hassan, Riffat. "Equality before Allah? Woman-Man Equality in the Islamic Tradition." *Harvard Divinity Bulletin* 17 (1987): 2–4.

———. "Muslim Women and Post-patriarchal Islam." In *After Patriarchy*, edited by Paula M. Cooey, William R. Eakin, and Jay B. McDaniel. Maryknoll, N.Y.: Orbis, 1991.

Hatem, Mervat F. "Egyptian Discourses on Gender and Political Liberalization: Do Secularist and Islamist Views Really Differ?" *Middle East Journal* 48 (1994): 661–76.

———. "Political Liberalization, Gender, and the State." In *Political Liberalization and Democratization in the Arab World*. Vol. 1, edited by Rex Brynen, Baghat Korany, and Paul Noble. Boulder, Colo.: Lynne Rienner, 1995.

———. "Secularist and Islamist Discourses on Modernity in Egypt and the Evolution of the Postcolonial Nation-State." In *Islam, Gender, and Social Change*, edited by Yvonne Yazbik Haddad and John L. Esposito. New York and Oxford: Oxford University Press, 1998.

Hawley, John Statton, ed. *Fundamentalism and Gender*. New York and Oxford: Oxford University Press, 1994.

Heer, Nicholas, ed. *Islamic Law and Jurisprudence.* Seattle: University of Washington Press, 1990.

Hegland, Mary Elaine. "Islamic Revival or Political and Cultural Revolution?" In *Religious Resurgence,* edited by Richard T. Antoun and Mary Elaine Hegland. Syracuse, N.Y.: Syracuse University Press, 1987.

Hélie-Lucas, Marie-Aimée. "Women's Struggles and Strategies in the Rise of Fundamentalism in the Muslim World: From Entryism to Internationalism." In *Women in the Middle East,* edited by Haleh Afshar. London: Macmillan, 1993.

Hermansen, Marcia K. "The Female Hero in the Islamic Religious Tradition." *Annual Review of Women in World Religions* 2 (1992): 111–43.

Hermassi, Elbaki. "The Rise and Fall of the Islamist Movement in Tunisia." In *The Islamist Dilemma,* edited by Laura Guazzone. International Politics of the Middle East Series. Reading, England: Ithaca Press, 1995.

al-Hibri, Azizah. "A Study of Islamic Herstory: Or How Did We Ever Get into this Mess?" In *Women and Islam,* edited by Azizah al-Hibri. Oxford and New York: Pergamon Press, 1982.

———, ed. *Women and Islam.* Oxford and New York: Pergamon Press, 1982.

Higgins, Patricia J. "Women in the Islamic Republic of Iran: Legal, Social, and Ideological Changes." *Signs* 10, no. 31 (1985): 477–94.

Hiro, Dilip. *Islamic Fundamentalism.* 2d ed. London: Paladin Grafton Books, 1989.

Hjärpe, Jan. "The Attitude of Islamic Fundamentalism Towards the Question of Women in Islam." In *Women in Islamic Societies: Social Attitudes and Historical Perspectives,* edited by Bo Utas. London and Malmö: Curzon Press, 1983.

Hoffman, Valerie J. "An Islamic Activist: Zaynab al-Ghazali." In *Women and the Family in the Middle East,* edited by Elizabeth Warnock Fernea. Austin: University of Texas Press, 1985.

———. "Muslim Fundamentalists: Psychosocial Profiles." In *Fundamentalisms Comprehended,* edited by Martin E. Marty and R. Scott Appleby. Chicago: University of Chicago Press, 1995.

Hoffman-Ladd, Valerie J. "Polemics on the Modesty and Segregation of Women in Contemporary Egypt." *International Journal of Middle East Studies* 19 (1987): 23–50.

———. "Women's Religious Observances." In *The Oxford Encyclopedia of the Modern Islamic World,* edited by John L. Esposito. New York and Oxford: Oxford University Press, 1995.

———. "Zaynab al-Ghazali." In *The Oxford Encyclopedia of the Modern Islamic World,* edited by John L. Esposito. New York and Oxford: Oxford University Press, 1995.

Holt, Maria. "Lebanese Shiʿi Women and Islamism: A Response to War." In *Women and War in Lebanon,* edited by Lamia Rustum Shehadeh. Gainesville: University Press of Florida, 1999.

Hoodfar, Homa. "Devices and Desires: Population Policy and Gender Roles in the

Islamic Republic." In *Political Islam*, edited by Joel Beinin and Joe Stork. Berkeley and Los Angeles: University of California Press, 1997.

———. "Women and Personal Status Law in Iran." *Middle East Report* (No. 198) 26, no. 1 (1996): 36–8.

Hoveyda, Fereydoun. *The Broken Crescent: The "Threat" of Militant Islamic Fundamentalism*. A National Committee on American Foreign Policy Study. Westport, Conn., and London: Praeger, 1998.

Hunter, Shireen T. "Islam in Power: The Case of Iran." In *The Politics of Islamic Revivalism*, edited by Shireen T. Hunter. Bloomington and Indianapolis: Indiana University Press, 1988.

Husain, Mir Zohair. *Global Islamic Politics*. New York: HarperCollins College Publishers, 1995.

Husaini, Ishak Musa. *The Moslem Brethren*. Beirut: Khayat's College Book Cooperative, 1956.

Hussain, Assaf. *Political Perspectives on the Muslim World*. London and Basingstoke: Macmillan, 1984.

Hussain, Freda, ed. *Muslim Women*. London and Sydney: Croom Helm, 1984.

Hussain, Freda, and Kamelia Radwan. "The Islamic Revolution and Women: Quest for the Qur'anic Model." In *Muslim Women*, edited by Freda Hussain. London and Sydney: Croom Helm, 1984.

Ibrahim, Mahmoud. "Dialogue with Hasan al-Turabi Reveals Enigmatic Complex Islamist Intellectual." *al-Jadid* 4, no. 25 (fall 1998): 4–5, 15.

Irfani, Suroosh. *Iran's Islamic Revolution: Popular Liberation or Religious Dictatorship?* London: Zed Books, 1983.

Ismael, Tareq Y., and Jacqueline S. Tareq. *Government and Politics in Islam*. London: Frances Printer, 1985.

Jaber, Hala. *Hezbollah: Born with a Vengeance*. New York: Columbia University Press, 1997.

Jameelah, Maryam. "An Appraisal of Some Aspects of Maulana Sayyid Ala Maudoodi's Life and Thought." *Islamic Quarterly* 31 (1987): 116–30.

Jansen, Johannes J. G. *The Dual Nature of Islamic Fundamentalism*. Ithaca, N.Y.: Cornell University Press, 1997.

Joffé, George. "Maghribi Islam and Islam in the Maghrib." In *African Islam and Islam in Africa*, edited by Eva Evers Rosander and David Westerlund. London: Hurst, 1997.

Jones, Linda G. "Portrait of Rashid al-Ghannoushi." *Middle East Report* 18, no. 4 (1988): 19–24.

Joseph, Suad. "Gender and Civil Society." In *Political Islam*, edited by Joel Beinin and Joe Stork. Berkeley and Los Angeles: University of California Press, 1997.

Kamali, Hisham. "Divorce and Women's Rights: Some Muslim Interpretations of S. 2:228." *The Muslim World* 74 (1984): 85–99.

Kandiyoti, Deniz. "Islam and Patriarchy: A Comparative Perspective." In *Women in*

Middle Eastern History, edited by Nikki R. Keddie and Beth Baron. New Haven, Conn.: Yale University Press, 1991.

————. "Women, Islam, and the State." In *Political Islam,* edited by Joel Beinin and Joe Stark. Berkeley and Los Angeles: University of California Press, 1997.

————, ed. *Women, Islam and the State.* Philadelphia: Temple University Press, 1991.

Karam, Azza. *Women, Islamisms, and the State.* London and New York: Macmillan and St. Martin's, 1998.

Karmi, Ghada. "Women, Islam and Patriarchalism." In *Feminism and Islam,* edited by Mai Yamani. Reading, England: Ithaca Press, 1996.

Keddie, Nikki R. "Ideology, Society, and the State in Post-Colonial Muslim Societies." In *State and Ideology in the Middle East and Pakistan,* edited by Fred Halliday and Hamza Alavi. New York: Monthly Review Press, 1988.

————. "Iran: Change in Islam; Islam and Change." *International Journal of Middle East Studies* 11 (1980): 527–42.

————. "Is Shi'ism Revolutionary?" In *The Iranian Revolution and the Islamic Republic,* edited by Nikki R. Keddie and Eric Hooglund. Washington, D.C.: Middle East Institute in cooperation with Woodrow Wilson International Center for Scholars, 1982.

————. "Religion, Society, and Revolution in Modern Iran." In *Continuity and Change in Modern Iran,* edited by Michael E. Bonine and Nikki R. Keddie. Albany: State University of New York Press, 1981.

————. *Roots of Revolution.* With a section by Yann Richard. New Haven, Conn.: Yale University Press, 1981.

————, ed. *Debating Gender, Debating Sexuality.* New York and London: New York University Press, 1996.

————, ed. *Religion and Politics in Iran.* New Haven, Conn.: Yale University Press, 1983.

Keddie, Nikki R., and Farah Monian. "Militancy and Religion in Contemporary Iran." In *Fundamentalisms and the State,* edited by Martin E. Marty and R. Scott Appleby. Chicago: University of Chicago Press, 1993.

Keddie, Nikki R., and Beth Baron, eds. *Women in Middle Eastern History.* New Haven, Conn.: Yale University Press, 1991.

Keddie, Nikki R., and Eric Hooglund, eds. *The Iranian Revolution and the Islamic Republic.* Washington, D.C.: Middle East Institute in cooperation with Woodrow Wilson International Center for Scholars, 1982.

Kedourie, Elie. *Politics in the Middle East.* Oxford and New York: Oxford University Press, 1992.

Kelidar, Abbas. "Ayatollah Khomeini's Concept of Islamic Government." In *Islam and Power,* edited by Alexander S. Cudsi. Baltimore, Md.: Johns Hopkins University Press, 1981.

Kelly, Joan. "The Doubled Vision of Feminist Theory: A Postscript to the 'Women and Power' Conference." *Feminist Studies* 5, no. 1 (1979): 216–27.

Kepel, Gilles. *Muslim Extremism in Egypt: The Prophet and Pharaoh*. Berkeley and Los Angeles: University of California Press, 1986.

Khadduri, Majid. "From Religious to National Law." In *Modernization of the Arab World*, edited by Jack H. Thompson and Robert D. Reischauer. Princeton, N.J.: D. Van Nostrand Company, 1966.

Khomeini, Ruhollah. *Ahkam al-Islam bayna al-sa'il wal Imam* (Rulings of Islam between the Imam and the inquirer). Beirut: Dar al-Wasilah, 1993.

———. *A Clarification of Questions*. Translated by J. Borujerdi, with a foreword by Michael M. J. Fischer and Mehdi Abedi. Boulder, Colo.: Westview Press, 1984.

———. *Islam and Revolution*. Translated and annotated by Hamid Algar. Berkeley, Calif.: Mizan Press, 1981.

———. "Islamic Government." In *Islam and Revolution*, by Ruhollah Khomeini. Translated and annotated by Hamid Algar. Berkeley, Calif.: Mizan Press, 1981.

———. "Legal Rulings." In *Islam and Revolution*, by Ruhollah Khomeini. Translated and annotated by Hamid Algar. Berkeley, Calif.: Mizan Press, 1981.

———. *Makanatu al-mar'ah fi fikr al-Imam al-Khomeini* (Women's status in Imam Khomeini's thought). Tehran: Mu'assasat Tandhim wa Nashr Turath al-Imam al-Khomeini, 1996.

———. "Speeches and Declarations." In *Islam and Revolution*, by Ruhollah Khomeini. Translated and annotated by Hamid Algar. Berkeley, Calif.: Mizan Press, 1981.

Khuri, Fuad I. *Imams and Emirs: State, Religion, and Sects in Islam*. London: Saqi Books, 1990.

Kian, Azadeh. "Gendered Occupation and Women's Status in Post-revolutionary Iran." *Middle Eastern Studies* 31 (1995): 407–21.

King, Ursula, ed. *Religion and Gender*. Oxford and Cambridge, Mass.: Blackwell, 1995.

Kok, Peter Nyot. "Hasan Abdallah al-Turabi (Hasan 'Abdallah al-Turabi)." *Orient* 33 (1992): 185–92.

Krämer, Gudrun. "Cross-Links and Double Talk? Islamist Movements in the Political Process." In *The Islamist Dilemma*, edited by Laura Guazzone. International Politics of the Middle East Series. Reading, England: Ithaca Press, 1995.

Kramer, Martin. *Arab Awakening and Islamic Revival*. New Brunswick, N.J., and London: Transaction Publishers, 1996.

———. *Hezbollah's Vision of the West*. Policy Papers No. 16. Washington, D.C.: Washington Institute for Near East Policy, 1989.

———. "Hizbullah in Lebanon." In *The Oxford Encyclopedia of the Modern Islamic World*, edited by John L. Esposito. New York and Oxford: Oxford University Press, 1995.

———. "Hizbullah: The Calculus of Jihad." In *Fundamentalisms and the State*, edited by Martin E. Marty and R. Scott Appleby. Chicago: University of Chicago Press, 1993.

———. *The Moral Logic of Hizbullah.* Dayan Center for Middle Eastern and African Studies. Shiloah Institute. Occasional Papers, No. 101. Tel Aviv University, 1987.

———. "The Moral Logic of Hizballah." In *Origins of Terrorism,* edited by Walter Reich. Washington, D.C.: Woodrow Wilson Center Press, 1990, 1998.

———. "Muhammad Husayn Fadlallah." *Orient* 26, no. 2 (1985): 147–49.

———. "The Oracle of Hizbullah: Sayyid Muhammad Husayn Fadlallah." In *Spokesmen for the Despised,* edited by R. Scott Appleby. Chicago: University of Chicago Press, 1997.

Lawrence, Bruce B. *Defenders of God.* San Francisco: Harper and Row, 1989.

———. "Muslim Fundamentalist Movements: Reflections toward a New Approach." In *The Islamic Impulse,* edited by Barbara Freyer Stowasser. 1987. Washington, D.C.: Center for Contemporary Arab Studies, Georgetown University, 1989, 2d paperback printing.

———. *Shattering the Myth.* Princeton, N.J.: Princeton University Press, 1998.

———. "Woman as Subject/Woman as Symbol: Islamic Fundamentalism and the Status of Women." *Journal of Religious Ethics* 22, no. 1 (1994): 163–85.

Lawyers Committee for Human Rights. *Islam and Justice.* New York, 1997.

Lemu, B. Aisha, and Fatima Heeren. *Woman in Islam.* London: Islamic Council of Europe. Chesterfield, England: Derby Shire Print, 1976.

Lerner, Gerda. *The Creation of Patriarchy.* New York and Oxford: Oxford University Press, 1986.

Lewis, Bernard. *The Political Language of Islam.* Chicago: University of Chicago Press, 1988.

———. *The Shaping of the Modern Middle East.* New York and Oxford: Oxford University Press, 1994.

Liebesny, Herbert J. "Stability and Change in Islamic Law." *Middle East Journal* 21 (1967): 16–34.

Lindholm, Tore, and Kari Vogt, eds. *Islamic Law Reform and Human Rights: Challenges and Rejoinders.* Copenhagen: Nordic Human Rights Publications, 1993.

Lowrie, Arther L., ed. *Islam, Democracy, the State, and the West: A Round Table with Dr. Hasan Turabi, May 10, 1992.* Clearwater, Fla.: The World and Islam Studies Enterprise, 1993.

Mabro, Judy. *Veiled Half-Truths.* London and New York: I. B. Tauris, 1996.

Madelung, Wilfred. "Shiʿi Attitudes toward Women as Reflected in Fiqh." In *Society and the Sexes in Medieval Islam,* edited by Afaf Lutfi al-Sayyid-Marsot. Malibu, Calif.: Undena Publications, 1979.

Magnuson, Douglas K. "Islamic Reform in Contemporary Tunisia: Unity and Diversity." In *Tunisia: The Political Economy of Reform,* edited by I. William Zartman. Boulder, Colo.: Lynne Rienner, 1991.

Mahdavi, Shireen. "The Position of Women in Shiʿa Iran: Views of the ʿUlama." In *Women and the Family in the Middle East,* edited by Elizabeth Warnock Fernea. Austin: University of Texas Press, 1985.

————. "Women and the Shii Ulama in Iran." *Middle Eastern Studies* 19, no. 1 (1983): 17–27.

Mahmoud, Muhammad. "Sufism and Islamism in the Sudan." In *African Islam and Islam in Africa,* edited by Eva Evers Rosander and David Westerlund. London: Hurst, 1997.

Majid, Anouar. "The Politics of Feminism in Islam." *Signs* 23, no. 2 (1998): 321–61.

Malass, Mustafa. "*al-Mar'ah al-muslimah wal qada': ru'ya mu'asirah*" (The Muslim woman and the judiciary: Contemporary vision). *al-Nahar Daily,* August 8, 1998, 15.

Mann, Michael. *The Sources of Social Power.* Vol. 1. Cambridge, London, and New York: Cambridge University Press, 1986.

Marshall, Susan E. "Paradoxes of Change: Culture Crisis, Islamic Revival, and the Reactivation of Patriarchy." *Journal of Asian and African Studies* 19, nos. 1–2 (1984): 1–17.

————. "Tradition and the Veil: Female Status in Tunisia and Algeria." *Journal of Modern African Studies* 19, no. 4 (1981): 625–46.

Marty, Martin E. "Fundamentals of Fundamentalism." In *Fundamentalism in Comparative Perspective,* edited by Lawrence Kaplan. Amherst: University of Massachusetts Press, 1992.

Marty, Martin E., and R. Scott Appleby, eds. *Accounting for Fundamentalisms.* Chicago: University of Chicago Press, 1994.

————, eds. *Fundamentalism Comprehended.* Chicago: University of Chicago Press, 1995.

————, eds. *Fundamentalisms and Society.* Chicago: University of Chicago Press, 1993.

————. *Fundamentalisms and the State.* Chicago: University of Chicago Press, 1993.

————, eds. *Fundamentalisms Observed.* Chicago: University of Chicago Press, 1991.

————. *The Glory and the Power: The Fundamentalist Challenge to the Modern World.* Boston: Beacon Press, 1992.

Masud, Muhammad Khalid, Brinkley Messick, and David S. Powers, eds. *Islamic Legal Interpretation.* Cambridge: Harvard University Press, 1996.

Maudoodee, Abul Ala. *The Islamic Way of Life.* Lahore, Pakistan: Markazi Maktaba Jama'at-e-Eslami, 1955.

Mawdudi, Abu al-A'la. *al-Hijab.* Beirut: Dar al-Fikr, n.d.

————. *Huquq al-zawjayn* (Marital rights). Cairo: al-Mukhtar al-Islami, 1979.

————. *Nidham al-hayat fi al-Islam* (Way of life in Islam). Beirut: Dar al-Fikr, n.d.

————. "Political Theory of Islam." In *Islam: Its Meaning and Message,* edited by Khurshid Ahmad. Qum, Iran: Center of Islamic Studies, 1978.

————. *Tadwin al-dustur al-Islami* (Recording the Islamic constitution). Damascus: Dar al-Fikr, 1953.

———. *Tafsir Surat al-Nur* (Interpretation of the Sura of Light). Beirut: Dar al-Fikr, 1959.

Mayer, Ann Elizabeth. "The Fundamentalist Impact on Law, Politics, and Constitutions in Iran." In *Fundamentalisms and the State,* edited by Martin E. Marty and R. Scott Appleby. Chicago: University of Chicago Press, 1993.

———. "Islam and Human Rights: Different Issues, Different Contexts. Lessons from Comparisons." In *Islamic Law Reform and Human Rights: Challenges and Rejoinders,* edited by Tore Lindholm and Kari Vogt. Copenhagen: Nordic Human Rights Publications, 1993.

———. "The Shariʿah: A Methodology or a Body of Substantive Rules?" In *Islamic Law and Jurisprudence,* edited by Nicholas Heer. Seattle: University of Washington Press, 1990.

Menashri, David. *Revolution at a Crossroads.* Washington, D.C.: Washington Institute for Near East Policy, Policy Paper No. 43, 1997.

Mernissi, Fatima. *Beyond the Veil.* Rev. ed. Bloomington and Indianapolis: Indiana University Press, 1987.

———. "Femininity as Subversion: Reflections on the Muslim Concept of Nu-shuz." In *Speaking of Faith: Global Perspectives on Women, Religion, and Social Change,* edited by Diana L. Eck and Devaki Jain. Philadephia: New Society Publishers, 1987.

———. "Muslim Women and Fundamentalism." In *Arab Women: Between Defiance and Restraint,* edited by Suha Sabbagh. New York: Olive Branch Press, 1996.

———. "The Patriarch in Moroccan Family: Myth or Reality?" In *Women's Status and Fertility in the Muslim World,* edited by James Allman. New York and London: Praeger, 1978.

———. *Women's Rebellion and Islamic Memory.* London and Atlantic Highlands, N.J.: Zed Books, 1996.

Merquior, J.G. *The Veil and the Mask.* London, Boston, and Henley: Routledge and Kegan Paul, 1979.

Miller, Judith. "Faces of Fundamentalism: Hasan al-Turabi and Muhammed Fadlallah." *Foreign Affairs* 73, no. 6 (1994): 123–42.

———. "Global Islamic Awakening or Sudanese Nightmare? The Curious Case of Hasan Turabi." In *Spokesmen for the Despised,* edited by R. Scott Appleby. Chicago: University of Chicago Press, 1997.

———. *God Has Ninety-Nine Names.* New York: Simon and Schuster, 1996.

Mir, Mustansir. "Some Features of Mawdudi's Tafhim al-Qurʾan." *American Journal of Islamic Social Sciences* 2, no. 2 (1985): 233–44.

Mir-Hosseini, Ziba. "Divorce in Islamic Law and Practice: The Case of Iran." *Cambridge Anthropology* 11, no. 1 (1986): 41–69.

———. *Islam and Gender: The Religious Debate in Contemporary Iran.* Princeton, N.J.: Princeton University Press, 1999.

———. *Marriage on Trial: A Study of Islamic Family Law.* London and New York: I. B. Tauris, 1993.

———. "Stretching the Limits: A Feminist Reading of the Shari'a in Post-Khomeini Iran." In *Feminism and Islam,* edited by Mai Yamani. Reading, England: Ithaca Press, 1996.

———. "Women and Politics in Post-Khomeini Iran: Divorce, Veiling and Emerging Feminist Voices." In *Women and Politics in the Third World,* edited by Haleh Afshar. London and New York: Routledge, 1996.

———. "Women, Marriage, and the Law in Post-Revolutionary Iran." In *Women in the Middle East,* edited by Haleh Afshar. London: Macmillan, 1993.

Mitchell, Richard. *The Society of the Muslim Brothers.* London: Oxford University Press, 1969.

Moghadam, Valentine. "Islamist Movements and Women's Responses in the Middle East." *Gender and History* 3, no. 3 (1991): 268–84.

———. *Modernizing Women: Gender and Social Change in the Middle East.* Boulder, Colo.: Lynne Rienner, 1993.

———. "Patriarchy and the Politics of Gender in Modernising Societies: Iran, Pakistan and Afghanistan." *International Sociology* 7, no. 1 (1992): 35–53.

———. "Revolution, Islam, and Women: Sexual Politics in Iran and Afghanistan." In *Nationalisms and Sexualities,* edited by Andrew Parker, Mary Russo, Doris Sommer, and Patricia Yaeger. New York and London: Routledge, 1992.

———. "Rhetorics and Rights of Identity in Islamist Movements." *Journal of World History* 4, no. 2 (1993): 243–64.

———. "Women, Work, and Ideology in the Islamic Republic." *International Journal of Middle East Studies* 20 (1988): 221–43.

Moghissi, Haideh. *Feminism and Islamic Fundamentalism.* London and New York: Zed Books, 1999.

———. *Populism and Feminism in Iran.* London: St. Martin's Press, 1994.

Moin, Baqer. "Khomeini, Ruhollah al-Musavi." In *The Oxford Encyclopedia of the Modern Islamic World,* edited by John L. Esposito. New York and Oxford: Oxford University Press, 1995.

———. "Khomeini's Search for Perfection: Theory and Reality." In *Pioneers of Islamic Revival,* edited by Ali Rahnema. London and Atlantic Highlands, N.J.: Zed Books, 1994.

Molyneux, Maxine. "Mobilization without Emancipation? Women's Interests, State, and Revolution." In *Transition and Development,* edited by Richard R. Fagen, Carmen Diana Deere, and José Luis Coraggio. New York: Monthly Review Press, 1986.

Monshipouri, Mahmood. *Islamism, Secularism, and Human Rights in the Middle East.* Boulder, Colo.: Lynne Rienner, 1998.

Mortimer, Edward. *Faith and Power.* London: Faber and Faber, 1982.

Moussalli, Ahmad. "Hasan al-Banna's Islamist Discourse on Constitutional Rule and Islamic State." *Journal of Islamic Studies* 4, no. 2 (1993): 161–74.

———. "Hasan al-Turabi's Islamist Discourse on Democracy and Shura." *Middle Eastern Studies* 30 (1994): 52–63.

———. *Moderate and Radical Islamic Fundamentalism.* Gainesville: University Press of Florida, 1999.

———. "Modern Islamic Fundamentalist Discourses on Civil Society, Pluralism and Democracy." In *Civil Society in the Middle East,* edited by Augustus Richard Norton. Leiden, New York, and Cologne: E. J. Brill, 1995.

———. *Radical Islamic Fundamentalism: The Ideological and Political Discourse of Sayyid Qutb.* Beirut: American University of Beirut, 1992.

———. "Sayyid Qutb: The Ideologist of Islamic Fundamentalism." *al-Abhath* 38 (1990): 42–73.

Mueller, Eric. "Revitalizing Old Ideas: Developments in Middle Eastern Family Law." In *Women and the Family in the Middle East,* edited by Elizabeth Warnock Fernea. Austin: University of Texas Press, 1985.

Munson, Henry Jr. "Islamic Revivalism in Morocco and Tunisia." *The Muslim World* 76 (1986): 203–18.

Murata, Sachiko. *The Tao of Islam.* Albany: State University of New York Press, 1992.

Musallam, Basim. "The Ordering of Muslim Societies." In *The Cambridge Illustrated History of the Islamic World,* edited by Francis Robinson. New York: Cambridge University Press, 1996.

Mutahhari, Murtaza. *al-Dawabit al-khuluqiyyah lil-suluk al-jinsi: min khilal nadhratay al-Islam wal-gharb* (Behavioral regulators for sexual behavior: From the points of view of Islam and the West). Beirut: Dar al-Rasul al-Akbar Lil-tiba'a wal-Nashr, 1988.

———. *Fundamentals of Islamic Thought.* Translated by R. Campbell. Berkeley, Calif.: Mizan Press, 1985.

———. *Mas'alatu al-hijab* (The question of the veil). Beirut: Dar al-Islamiyyah, 1987.

———. *al-Mujtama' wal ta'rikh* (Society and history writing). Beirut: Mu'assasat al-Wafa', 1983.

———. *Nidham huquq al-mar'ah fi al-Islam* (Women's rights in Islam). Beirut: Dar al-Ta'aruf Lilmatbu'at, 1992.

———. *al-Ta'arruf 'ala al-Qur'an* (Introduction to the Qur'an). Beirut: Dar al-kitab al-Islami, 1983.

an-Na'im, Abdullahi Ahmed. "The Application of Shari'ah [Islamic Law] and Human Rights Violations in the Sudan." In *Islamic Law Reform and Human Rights: Challenges and Rejoinders,* edited by Tore Lindholm and Kari Vogt. Copenhagen: Nordic Human Rights Publications, 1993.

———. "The Dichotomy between Religious and Secular Discourse in Islamic Societies." In *Faith and Freedom: Women's Human Rights in Islam,* edited by Mahnaz Afkhami. London and New York: I. B. Tauris, 1995.

———. *Toward an Islamic Reformation.* Syracuse: Syracuse University Press, 1990.

———. "Toward an Islamic Reformation: Responses and Reflections." In *Islamic Law Reform and Human Rights: Challenges and Rejoinders,* edited by Tore Lindholm and Kari Vogt. Copenhagen: Nordic Human Rights Publications, 1993.

Najmabadi, Afsaneh. "Feminism in an Islamic Republic." In *Islam, Gender, and Social Change,* edited by Yvonne Yazbik Haddad and John L. Esposito. New York and Oxford: Oxford University Press, 1998.

Nakanishi, Hisae. "Power, Ideology, and Women's Consciousness in Postrevolutionary Iran." In *Women in Muslim Societies,* edited by Herbert L. Bodman and Nayereh Tohidi. Boulder, Colo.: Lynne Rienner, 1998.

Nashat, Guity. "Women in the Ideology of the Islamic Republic." In *Women and Revolution in Iran,* edited by Guity Nashat. Boulder, Colo.: Westview Press, 1983.

———. "Women in the Islamic Republic of Iran." *Iranian Studies* 13, nos. 1–4 (1980): 165–94.

———, ed. *Women and Revolution in Iran.* Boulder, Colo.: Westview Press, 1983.

Nasr, Seyyed Vali Reza. "Islamic Opposition in the Political Process: Lessons from Pakistan." In *Political Islam: Revolution, Radicalism, or Reform?* edited by John L. Esposito. Boulder, Colo.: Lynne Rienner, 1987.

———. "Jama'at-i Islami." In *The Oxford Encyclopedia of the Modern Islamic World,* edited by John L. Esposito. New York and Oxford: Oxford University Press, 1995.

———. "Mawdudi and the Jama'at-i Islami: The Origins, Theory and Practice of Islamic Revivalism." In *Pioneers of Islamic Revival,* edited by Ali Rahnema. London and Atlantic Highlands, N.J.: Zed Books, 1994.

———. *Mawdudi and the Making of Islamic Revivalism.* New York and Oxford: Oxford University Press, 1996.

———. "Mawdudi, Sayyid Abu al-A'la." In *The Oxford Encyclopedia of the Modern Islamic World,* edited by John L. Esposito. New York and Oxford: Oxford University Press, 1995.

———. *Traditional Islam in the Modern World.* London and New York: Routledge and Kegan Paul, 1987.

———. *The Vanguard of the Islamic Revolution.* London and New York: I. B. Tauris, 1994.

Nazlee, Sajda. *Feminism and Muslim Women.* Edited by Huda Khattab. London: Ta-Ha Publishers, 1996.

Nettler, Ronald L. *Past Trials and Present Tribulations.* Oxford: Pergamon Press, 1987.

Nicolaisen, Ida. "Introduction." In *Women in Islamic Societies: Social Attitudes and*

Historical Perspectives, edited by Bo Utas. London and Malmö: Curzon Press, 1983.

Ni'meh, Abdallah, ed. *al-Mut'ah wa mashru'iyyataha fi al-Islam* (Temporary marriage and its legitimacy in Islam)—Dialogue with Sayyid Muhammad Husayn Fadlallah. Beirut: Dar al-Zahra', 1982.

el-Nimr, Raga'. "Women in Islamic Law." In *Feminism and Islam,* edited by Mai Yamani. Reading, England: Ithaca Press, 1996.

Norton, Augustus Richard. "Lebanon: The Internal Conflict and the Iranian Connection." In *The Iranian Revolution: Its Global Impact,* edited by John L. Esposito. Miami: Florida International University Press, 1990.

———. "Religious Resurgence and Political Mobilization of the Shi'a in Lebanon." In *Religious Resurgence and Politics in the Contemporary World,* edited by Emile Sahliyeh. Albany: State University of New York Press, 1990.

———. "Shi'ism and Social Protest in Lebanon." In *Shi'ism and Social Protest,* edited by Juan R. I. Cole and Nikki R. Keddie. New Haven, Conn.: Yale University Press, 1986.

al-Nowaihi, Mohamed. "Problems of Modernization in Islam." *The Muslim World* 65 (1975): 174–85.

Omid, Homa. *Islam and the Post-Revolutionary State in Iran.* New York: St. Martin's Press, 1994.

Osman, Dina Sheikh el-Din. "The Legal Status of Muslim Women in the Sudan." *Journal of Eastern African Research and Development* 15 (1985): 124–42.

Paidar, Parvin. *Women and the Political Process in Twentieth-Century Iran.* Cambridge and New York: Cambridge University Press, 1995.

Papanek, Hanna. "Purdah: Separate Worlds and Symbolic Shelter." In *Separate Worlds,* edited by Hanna Papanek and Gail Minault. Delhi: Chanakya Publications, 1982.

Papanek, Hanna, and Gail Minault, eds. *Separate Worlds.* Delhi: Chanakya Publications, 1982.

Parvin, Manoucher. "Islamic Rule, Economics, Woman and Man: An Overview of Ideology and Reality." *Comparative Economic Studies* 31, no. 3 (1989): 85–102.

Pateman, Carole, and Nancy J. Hirschmann. "Political Obligation, Freedom, and Feminism." *American Political Science Review* 86, no. 1 (1992): 179–89.

Peteet, Julie. "Women and National Politics in the Middle East." In *Power and Stability in the Middle East,* edited by Berch Berberoglu. London and Atlantic Highlands, N.J.: Zed Books, 1989.

Peteet, Julie, and Barbara Harlow. "Gender and Political Change." *Middle East Report* 21, no. 173 (1991): 4–8.

Pickthall, Marmaduke, trans. *The Holy Qur'an.* Beirut: al-Kitab al-Lubnani, 1970.

Pipes, Daniel. "The Western Mind of Radical Islam." In *The Islamism Debate,* edited by Martin Kramer. Dayan Center Papers 120. Tel Aviv University, 1997.

Piscatori, James P. "The Shia of Lebanon and Hizbullah, the Party of God." In *Politics of the Future,* edited by Christine Jennett and Randal G. Stewart. South Melbourne, Australia: Macmillan, 1989.

Qutb, Sayyid. *al-ʿAdalah al-ijtimaʿiyyah fi al-Islam* (Social justice in Islam). Cairo: Maktabat Misr wa Matbaʿatha, 1954.

———. *Fi zila al-Qurʾan* (In the shade of the Qurʾan). 6 vols. Cairo: Dar al-Shuruq, 1998.

———. "Islamic Approach to Social Justice." In *Islam: Its Meaning and Message,* edited by Khursid Ahmad. Qum, Iran: Center of Islamic Studies, 1978.

———. *al-Islam wa mushkilat al-hadarah* (Islam and the problems of civilization). N.p.: Dar Ihyaʾ al-Kutub al-ʿArabiyyah, 1962.

———. *Maʿrakatu al-Islam wal-raʾsmaliyyah* (The battle of Islam and capitalism). Cairo: Matbaʿat Dar al-Kitab al-ʿArabi, 1952.

———. *al-Salam al-ʿalami wal-Islam* (World peace and Islam). Cairo: Maktabat Wehbeh, 1951.

———. "Social Justice in Islam." In *Islam in Transition: Muslim Perspectives,* edited by John Donohue and John L. Esposito. New York and Oxford: Oxford University Press, 1982.

———. *Tiflun min al-qaryah* (A child from the village). Köln, Germany: Al-Kamel Verlag, 1999.

Rahman, Fazlur. *Islam and Modernity.* Chicago: University of Chicago Press, 1982.

———. "Islamic Modernism: Its Scope, Method, and Alternatives." *International Journal of Middle East Studies* 1 (1970): 317–33.

———. *Role of Muslim Women in Society.* London: Seerah Foundation, 1986.

———. "The Status of Women in Islam: A Modernist Interpretation." In *Separate Worlds,* edited by Hanna Papanek and Gail Minault. Delhi: Chanakya Publications, 1982.

———. "Status of Women in the Qurʾan." In *Women and Revolution in Iran,* edited by Guity Nashat. Boulder, Colo.: Westview Press, 1983.

———. "A Survey of Modernization of Muslim Family Law." *International Journal of Middle East Studies* 11 (1980): 451–65.

Rajaee, Farhang. "Islam and Modernity: The Reconstruction of an Alternative Shiʿite Islamic Worldview in Iran." In *Fundamentalisms and Society,* edited by Martin E. Marty and R. Scott Appleby. Chicago: University of Chicago Press, 1993.

———. *Islamic Values and World View.* Lanham, Md., New York, and London: University Press of America, 1983.

Ramadan, Aziz. "Fundamentalist Influence in Egypt: The Strategies of the Muslim Brotherhood and the Takfir Groups." In *Fundamentalisms and the State,* edited by Martin E. Marty and R. Scott Appleby. Chicago: University of Chicago Press, 1993.

Ramazani, K. "Constitution of the Islamic Republic of Iran." *Middle East Journal* 34 (1980): 181–204.

Ramazani, Nesta. "Behind the Veil: Status of Women in Revolutionary Iran." *Journal of South Asian and Middle Eastern Studies* 4, no. 2 (1980): 27–36.

————. "The Veil—Piety or Protest?" *Journal of South Asian and Middle Eastern Studies* 7, no. 2 (1983): 20–36.

————. "Women in Iran: The Revolutionary Ebb and Flow." *Middle East Journal* 47 (1993): 409–28.

Ramazani, R. K. "Iran's Export of the Revolution: Politics, Ends, and Means." In *The Iranian Revolution: Its Global Impact,* edited by John L. Esposito. Miami: Florida International University Press, 1990.

————, ed. *Iran's Revolution: The Search for Consensus.* Bloomington and Indianapolis: Indiana University Press, in association with the Middle East Institute, Washington, D.C., 1990.

al-Ramli, Khayr al-Din Ibn Ahmad. *Kitab al-fatawa al-Kubra li naf' al-birriya* (Book of the great fatwas for the benefit of mankind). 2 vols. Cairo: Bulaq: 1856.

Ranstorp, Magnus. *Hizb'allah in Lebanon.* London: Macmillan, 1997.

Riesebrodt, Martin. *Pious Passion: The Emergence of Modern Fundamentalism in the United States and Iran.* Berkeley, Los Angeles, and London: University of California Press, 1993.

Roded, Ruth, ed. *Women in Islam and the Middle East: A Reader.* London and New York: I. B. Tauris, 1999.

Rose, Gregory. "Velayet-e Faqih and the Recovery of Islamic Identity in Thought of Ayatollah Khomeini." In *Religion and Politics in Iran,* edited by Nikki R. Keddie. New Haven, Conn.: Yale University Press, 1983.

Roy, Olivier. *The Failure of Political Islam.* Translated by Carol Volk. London: I. B. Tauris, 1994.

————. "Islamists in Power." In *The Islamist Debate,* edited by Martin Kramer. The Moshe Dayan Center for Middle Eastern and African Studies, Tel Aviv University, 1997.

el-Saadawi, Nawal. "Woman and Islam." *Women's Studies International Forum* 5, no. 2 (1982): 193–206.

Sabbagh, Suha, ed. *Arab Women: Between Defiance and Restraint.* New York: Olive Branch Press, 1996.

Sabbah, Fatna. *Woman in the Muslim Unconscious.* Translated by Jo Lakeland. Oxford and New York: Pergamon Press, 1984.

Sachedina, Abdulaziz A. "Activist Shi'ism in Iran, Iraq, and Lebanon." In *Fundamentalisms Observed,* edited by Martin E. Marty and R. Scott Appleby. Chicago: University of Chicago Press, 1991.

Sagiv, David. *Fundamentalism and Intellectuals in Egypt, 1973–1993.* London: Frank Cass, 1995.

Sahliyeh, Emile, ed. *Religious Resurgence and Politics in the Contemporary World.* Albany: State University of New York Press, 1990.

Salem, Norma. "Islam and the Status of Women in Tunisia." In *Muslim Woman,* edited by Freda Hussain. London and Sydney: Croom Helm, 1984.

———. "Tunisia." In *The Politics of Islamic Revivalism,* edited by Shireen T. Hunter. Bloomington and Indianapolis: Indiana University Press, 1988.

Sanasarian, Eliz. "The Politics of Gender and Development in the Islamic Republic of Iran." *Journal of Developing Societies* 8 (1992): 56–68.

———. *The Women's Rights Movement in Iran: Mutiny, Appeasement, and Repression from 1900 to Khomeini.* New York: Praeger, 1982.

Sapiro, Virginia. "Engendering Cultural Differences." In *The Rising Tide of Cultural Pluralism,* edited by Crawford Young. Madison: University of Wisconsin Press, 1993.

Saulat, Sarwat. *Maulana Maududi.* Karachi, Pakistan: International Islamic Publishers, 1979.

Sayeed, Khalid Bin. *Western Dominance and Political Islam: Challenge and Response.* Albany: State University of New York Press, 1995.

Schacht, Joseph. "Law and Justice." In *The Cambridge History of Islam.* Vol. 2, edited by P. M. Holt, A.K.S. Lambton, and Bernard Lewis. Cambridge: Cambridge University Press, 1970.

Schirazi, Asghar. *The Constitution of Iran.* Translated by John O'Kane. New York and London: I. B. Tauris, 1997. Paperback edition, 1998.

Schmidt, Alvin John. *Veiled and Silenced: How Culture Shaped Sexist Theology.* Macon, Ga.: Mercer University Press, 1989.

Seif-Amirhosseini, Zahra. "Underlying Reasons for Women's Oppression." *Islam* 21, no. 22 (2000): 12–3.

Shaaban, Bouthaina. "The Muted Voices of Women Interpreters." In *Faith and Freedom: Women's Human Rights in Islam,* edited by Mahnaz Afkhami. London and New York: I. B. Tauris, 1995.

Shapira, Shimon. "The Origins of Hizballah." *Jerusalem Quarterly* 46 (1988): 115–30.

Shararah, Waddah. *Dawlat "hizballah": Lubnan mujtama'an Islamiyyan* (The state of "Hizballah": Lebanon, an Islamic society). Beirut: Dar al-Nahar lil-Nashr, 1996.

Sharoni, Simona. "Women and Gender in Middle East Studies: Trends, Prospects, and Challenges." *Middle East Report* (No. 205) 27, no. 4 (1997): 27–9.

Shehadeh, Lamia Rustum. "An Exploration of the Role Assigned to Women in Islamic Fundamentalism: The Discourse of Abu al-'A'la al-Mawdudi." Forthcoming in *Journal of South Asian and Middle Eastern Studies.*

———. "Women in Islamic Fundamentalism: The Discourses of Turabi and Ghannoushi." *Journal of South Asian and Middle Eastern Studies* 22, no. 2 (1999): 61–79.

———. "Women in the Discourse of Sayyid Qutb." *Arab Studies Quarterly* 22, no. 3 (2000): 45–60.

———, ed. *Women and War in Lebanon.* Gainesville: University Press of Florida, 1999.

Shepard, William E. *Sayyid Qutb and Islamic Activism.* London, New York, and Cologne: E. J. Brill, 1996.

Shoaee, Rokhsareh S. "The Mujahid Women of Iran: Reconciling 'Culture' and 'Gender.'" *Middle East Journal* 41, no. 4 (1987): 519–37.

Shukrallah, Hala. "The Impact of the Islamic Movement in Egypt." *Feminist Review* 47 (1994): 15–32.

Sidahmed, Awatef. "Women under Sudan's Fundamentalist Regime." *Middle East International*, no. 381 (3 August 1990): 20.

Siddique, Kaukab. *The Struggle of Muslim Women.* American Society for Education and Religion, 1983.

Sivan, Emmanuel. "The Enclave Culture." In *Fundamentalisms Comprehended*, edited by Martin E. Marty and R. Scott Appleby. Chicago: University of Chicago Press, 1993.

———. "Islamic Radicalism: Sunni and Shi'ite." In *Religious Radicalism and Politics in the Middle East*, edited by Emmanuel Sivan and Menachem Friedman. Albany: State University of New York Press, 1990.

———. "The Islamic Resurgence: Civil Society Strikes Back." In *Fundamentalism in Comparative Perspective*, edited by Lawrence Kaplan. Amherst: University of Massachusetts Press, 1992.

———. *Radical Islam, Medieval Theology, and Modern Politics.* New Haven, Conn.: Yale University Press, 1985.

———. "Sunni Radicalism in the Middle East and the Iranian Revolution." *International Journal of Middle East Studies* 21 (1989): 1–30.

Sivan, Emmanuel, and Menachem Friedman, eds. *Religious Radicalism and Politics in the Middle East.* Albany: State University of New York Press, 1990.

Smith, Jane I. "Women, Religion, and Social Change in Early Islam." In *Women, Religion, and Social Change*, edited by Yvonne Y. Haddad and Ellison B. Findly. Albany: State University of New York Press, 1985.

el-Solh, Camillia Fawzi, and Judy Mabro, eds. *Muslim Women's Choices.* Providence and Oxford: Berg Publishers, 1994.

Sonbol, Amira el-Azhary. "Egypt." In *The Politics of Islamic Revivalism*, edited by Shireen T. Hunter. Bloomington and Indianapolis: Indiana University Press, 1988.

Stern, G. H. "The First Women Converts in Early Islam." *Islamic Culture* 13 (1939): 290–305.

Stowasser, Barbara F. "Gender Issues and Contemporary Qur'an Interpretation." In *Islam, Gender, and Social Change*, edited by Yvonne Yazbik Haddad and John L. Esposito. New York and Oxford: Oxford University Press, 1998.

———. "Liberated, Equal, or Protected Dependent? Contemporary Religious Paradigms on Women's Status in Islam." *Arab Studies Quarterly* 9 (1987): 260–83.

———. "The Mothers of the Believers in the Hadith." *The Muslim World* 82 (1992): 1–36.

———. "Religious Ideology, Women, And the Family: The Islamic Paradigm." In *The Islamic Impulse*, edited by Barbara Freyer Stowasser. Washington, D.C.:

Center for Contemporary Arab Studies, Georgetown University, 1987. Second paperback printing, 1989.

———. "The Status of Women in Early Islam." In *Muslim Women,* edited by Freda Hussain. London and Sydney: Croom Helm, 1984.

———. "Women's Issues in Modern Islamic Thought." In *Arab Women: Old Boundaries, New Frontiers,* edited by Judith E. Tucker. Bloomington and Indianapolis: Indiana University Press, 1993.

———, ed. *The Islamic Impulse.* Washington, D.C.: Center for Contemporary Arab Studies, Georgetown University, 1987. Second paperback printing, 1989.

Sullivan, Denis J. "Muslim Brotherhood in Egypt." In *The Oxford Encyclopedia of the Modern Islamic World,* edited by John L. Esposito. New York and Oxford: Oxford University Press, 1995.

Sullivan, Denis J., and Sana Abed-Kotob. *Islam in Contemporary Egypt: Civil Society vs. the State.* Boulder, Colo.: Lynne Rienner, 1999.

Tabari, Azar. "The Enigma of Veiled Iranian Women." *Feminist Review,* no. 5 (1980): 19–31.

———. "Islam and the Struggle for Emancipation of Iranian Women." In *In the Shadow of Islam: The Women's Movement in Iran,* edited by Azar Tabari and Nahid Yeganeh. London: Zed Press, 1982.

Tabari, Azar, and Nahid Yeganeh, eds. *In the Shadow of Islam: The Women's Movement in Iran.* London: Zed Press, 1982.

Taha, Daa'iyah Muhammad. *Women in al-Qur'an: A Reference Guide with Glossary, Indices, and Appendices.* Oakland, Calif.: American Islamic Life Institute, 1993.

Talhami, Ghada, ed. *Women in the Islamic Maelstrom.* Special Issue of *The Muslim World* 86, no. 2 (1996).

Taylor, Alan R. *The Islamic Question in Middle East Politics.* Boulder, Colo.: Westview Press, 1988.

Taylor, Ann Elizabeth. "The Fundamentalist Impact on Law, Politics, and Constitutions in Iran, Pakistan, and the Sudan." In *Fundamentalisms and the State,* edited by Martin E. Marty and R. Scott Appleby. Chicago: University of Chicago Press, 1993.

Tessler, Mark, and Jolene Jesse. "Gender and Support for Islamist Movements: Evidence from Egypt, Kuwait and Palestine." *The Muslim World* 86, no. 2 (1996): 200–28.

Tibi, Bassam. "The Worldview of Sunni Arab Fundamentalists: Attitude toward Modern Science and Technology." In *Fundamentalisms and Society,* edited by Martin E. Marty and R. Scott Appleby. Chicago: University of Chicago Press, 1993.

Tohidi, Nayereh. "Gender and Islamic Fundamentalism: Feminist Politics in Iran." In *Third World Women and the Politics of Feminism,* edited by Chandra Talpade Mohauty, Ann Russo, and Lourdes Torres. Bloomington and Indianapolis: Indiana University Press, 1991.

———. "The Issues at Hand." In *Women in Muslim Societies: Diversity within Unity,* edited by Herbert Bodman and Nayereh Tohidi. Boulder, Colo.: Lynne Rienner, 1998.

———. "Modernity, Islamization, and Women in Iran." In *Gender and National Identity,* edited by Valentine M. Moghadam. London and Atlantic Highlands, N.J.: Zed Books, 1994.

Toubia, Nahid, ed. *Women of the Arab World.* London and Atlantic Highlands, N.J.: Zed Books, 1988.

Tripp, Charles. "Sayyid Qutb: The Political Vision." In *Pioneers of Islamic Revival,* edited by Ali Rahnema. London and Atlantic Highlands, N.J.: Zed Books, 1994.

Tucker, Judith E. *In the House of the Law.* Berkeley, Los Angeles, and London: University of California Press, 1998.

———, ed. *Arab Women: Old Boundaries, New Frontiers.* Bloomington and Indianapolis: Indiana University Press, 1993.

al-Turabi, Hasan. "*Fi nidham al-hayat: Ta'sis al-jama'ah al-mu'minah*" (In the organic structure of life: The foundation of the faithful society). *al-Ghadir* 3, nos. 19–20 (1992): 173–90.

———. *al-Harakah al-Islamiyyah fi al-Sudan* (The Islamic movement in the Sudan). Khartoum, Sudan: N.p., 1989.

———. *al-Iman: 'Atharuhu fi hayat al-'insan* (Faith: Its impact on man's life). Kuwait: Dar al-Qalam, 1974.

———. "The Islamic State." In *Voices of Resurgent Islam,* edited by John L. Esposito. New York and Oxford: Oxford University Press, 1983.

———. *al-Ittijah al-Islami yuqaddim al-mar'ah bayna ta'alim al din wa taqalid al-mujtama'* (The Islamic trend presents women between religious instructions and societal traditions). Jeddah: Dar al-Sa'udiyyah lil-Nashr wal-Tawzi', 1984.

———. "Principles of Governance, Freedom, and Responsibility in Islam." *American Journal of Islamic Social Sciences* 4, no. 1 (1987): 1–11.

———. *Qadaya al-hurriyah wal-wihdah; al-shura wal-dimocratiyyah; al-din wal-fan* (Issues of freedom and unity; consultation and democracy; religion and art). Jeddah: Dar al-Sa'udiyyah lil-Nashr wal-Tawzi', 1987.

———. *Tajdid al-fikr al-Islami* (Revival of Islamic thought). Jeddah: Dar al-Sa'udiyyah lil-Nashr wal-Tawzi', 1987.

———. "The West and Islamic Revivalism." *Middle East Affairs* 2, nos. 2–3 (1995): 17–25.

Vandewalle, Dirk. "From the New State to the New Era: Toward a Second Republic in Tunisia." *Middle East Journal* 42 (1988): 602–20.

Viorst, Milton. "Sudan's Islamic Experiment." *Foreign Affairs* 74, no. 3 (May/June 1995): 45–58.

Voll, John Obert. "The Evolution of Islamic Fundamentalism in Twentieth Century Sudan." In *Islam, Nationalism, and Radicalism in Egypt and the Sudan,* edited by Gabriel R. Warburg. New York: Praeger Special Studies, Praeger, 1983.

———. "Fundamentalism." In *The Oxford Encyclopedia of the Modern Islamic World,* edited by John L. Esposito. New York and Oxford: Oxford University Press, 1995.

———. "Fundamentalism in the Sunni Arab World: Egypt and the Sudan." In *Fundamentalisms Observed,* edited by Martin E. Marty and R. Scott Appleby. Chicago: University of Chicago Press, 1991.

———. *Islam: Continuity and Change in the Modern World.* 2d ed. Syracuse, N.Y.: Syracuse University Press, 1994.

———. "Islamization in the Sudan and the Iranian Revolution." In *The Iranian Revolution: Its Global Impact,* edited by John L. Esposito. Miami: Florida International University Press, 1990.

———. "Islam's Democratic Essence." *Middle East Quarterly* 1, no. 3 (1994): 3–11.

———. "Political Crisis in Sudan." *Current History* 89 (1990): 153–6, 178–80.

———. "Relations among Islamist Groups." In *Political Islam: Revolution, Radicalism, or Reform?* Boulder, Colo.: Lynne Rienner, 1997.

———. "Renewal and Reform in Islamic History: Tajdid and Islah." In *Voices of Resurgent Islam,* edited by John L. Esposito. New York and Oxford: Oxford University Press, 1983.

———. "Revivalism and Social Transformations in Islamic History." *The Muslim World* 76 (1986): 168–80.

———. "Sudan: State and Society in Crisis." *Middle East Journal* 44 (1990): 575–8.

Waal, Alex de. "Turabi's Muslim Brothers: Theocracy in Sudan." *Covert Action Quarterly* 49 (1994): 13-19, 60-61.

Wadud, Amina. *Qur'an and Woman.* New York and Oxford: Oxford University Press, 1999.

Waines, David. "Through a Veil Darkly: The Study of Women in Muslim Societies." *Comparative Studies in Society and History* 24 (1982): 642–59.

Walther, Wiebke. *Women in Islam.* Princeton, N.J.: Markus Wiener, 1995.

Waltz, Susan. "Islamist Appeal in Tunisia." *Middle East Journal* 40 (1986): 651–70.

Warburg, Gabriel R. "Muslim Brotherhood in the Sudan." In *The Oxford Encyclopedia of the Modern Islamic World,* edited by John L. Esposito. New York and Oxford: Oxford University Press, 1995.

———. "The Sudan under Islamist Rule." In *Religious Radicalism in the Greater Middle East,* edited by Bruce Maddy-Weitzmann and Efraim Inbar. London and Portland, Ore.: Frank Cass, 1997.

Warburg, Gabriel R., and Uri M. Kupferschmidt, eds. *Islam, Nationalism, and Radicalism in Egypt and the Sudan.* New York: Praeger Special Series, Praeger, 1983.

Watson, Helen. "Women and the Veil: Personal Responses to Global Process." In *Islam, Globalization, and Post-modernity,* edited by Akbar S. Ahmed and Hastings Donnan. London and New York: Routledge, 1994.

Weeramantry, C.G. *Islamic Jurisprudence: An International Perspective.* London: Macmillan, 1988.

Weiss, Anita. "Challenges for Muslim Women in a Post-modern World." In *Islam, Globalization, and Post-modernity,* edited by Akbar S. Ahmed and Hastings Donnan. London and New York: Routledge, 1994.

Westerlund, David. "Reaction and Action: Accounting for the Rise of Islamism." In *African Islam and Islam in Africa,* edited by Eva Evers Rosander and David Westerlund. London: Hurst and Company, 1997.

Wild, Stefan, ed. *The Qur'an as Text.* Leiden, New York, and Cologne: E. J. Brill, 1996.

Williams, John Alden. "Veiling in Egypt as a Political and Social Phenomenon." In *Islam and Development,* edited by John L. Esposito. Syracuse, N.Y.: Syracuse University Press, 1980.

Woodward, Peter. "Sudan: Islamic Radicals in Power." In *Political Islam: Revolution, Radicalism, or Reform?* edited by John L. Esposito. Boulder, Colo.: Lynne Rienner, 1997.

Wright, Robin. "Lebanon." In *The Politics of Islamic Revivalism,* edited by Shireen T. Hunter. Bloomington and Indianapolis: Indiana University Press, 1988.

———. *Sacred Rage: The Wrath of Militant Islam.* New York: Simon and Schuster, 1986.

Yamani, Mai, ed. *Feminism and Islam.* Reading, England.: Ithaca Press, 1996.

Yeganeh, Nahid. "Women's Struggles in the Islamic Republic of Iran." In *In the Shadow of Islam: The Women's Movement in Iran,* edited by Azar Tabari and Nahid Yeganeh. London: Zed Press, 1982.

Yeganeh, Nahid, and Nikki R. Keddie. "Sexuality and Shi'i Social Protest." In *Shi'ism and Social Protest,* edited by Juan R. J. Cole and Nikki R. Keddie. New Haven, Conn.: Yale University Press, 1986.

Zakaria, Fouad. "The Standpoint of Contemporary Muslim Fundamentalists." In *Women of the Arab World,* edited by Nahid Toubia. London and Atlantic Highlands, N.J.: Zed Books, 1988.

Zghal, Abdelkader. "The New Strategy of the Movement of the Islamic Way: Manipulation or Expression of Political Culture?" In *Tunisia: The Political Economy of Reform,* edited by I. William Zartman. Boulder, Colo.: Lynne Rienner, 1991.

Zisser, Eyal. "Hizballah in Lebanon—At the Crossroads." In *Religious Radicalism in the Greater Middle East,* edited by Bruce Maddy-Weitzman and Efraim Iubar. London and Portland, Ore.: Frank Cass, 1997.

Zubaida, Sami. "Is Iran an Islamic State?" In *Political Islam,* edited by Joel Beinin and Joe Stork. Berkeley and Los Angeles: University of California Press, 1997.

———. "The Quest for the Islamic State: Islamic Fundamentalism in Egypt and Iran." In *Studies in Religious Fundamentalism,* edited by Lionel Caplan. Albany: State University of New York Press, 1987.

Zuhur Sherifa. *Revealing Reveiling.* Albany: State University of New York Press, 1992.

Index

Lamia Rustum Shehadeh is associate professor of cultural studies at the American University in Beirut. Her most recent book is *Women and War in Lebanon* (1999).